Los Angeles

BIOGRAPHY OF A CITY

Los Angeles :

BIOGRAPHY OF A CITY

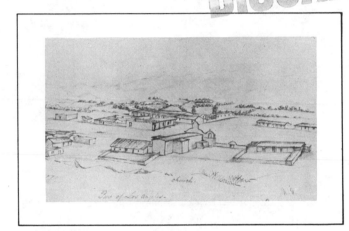

JOHN & LAREE CAUGHEY,

UNIVERSITY OF CALIFORNIA PRESS,

Berkeley : Los Angeles   London

UNIVERSITY OF CALIFORNIA PRESS
BERKELEY AND LOS ANGELES, CALIFORNIA
UNIVERSITY OF CALIFORNIA PRESS, LTD.
LONDON, ENGLAND

SECOND CLOTH-BOUND PRINTING 1977
FIRST PAPERBACK EDITION 1977
ISBN: 0-520-03079-6 CLOTH-BOUND
0-520-03410-4 PAPER-BOUND
LIBRARY OF CONGRESS CATALOG CARD NUMBER: 75-17300
COPYRIGHT © 1976, BY THE REGENTS OF THE UNIVERSITY OF CALIFORNIA
DESIGNED BY WARD RITCHIE
PRINTED IN THE UNITED STATES OF AMERICA

Contents

*

THE GABRIELINO AND THEIR HOME / 1

THE SPANIARDS STEAL THE SCENE / 39

Contents

PASTORAL INTERLUDE / 79

AMERICAN TAKEOVER / 113

AN AMERICAN CITY EMERGES / 159

Contents

✻

SPECTER OF NO GROWTH / 207

✻

AUTOS AND MOVIES AND OIL / 245

Contents

Contents

✳

CITY LIMITS OR NEW HORIZONS / 447

✳

PROSPECTS OF NEW HORIZONS / 489

✳

ix

Illustrations

✳

Illustrations

xi

Preface

*

Los Angeles is a remarkable city. Its setting is distinctive—a mountain-embraced coastal plain surrounded by chaparral and deserts. Its history, complex and varied, is backed by a prehistory giving evidence of Indians on the scene for at least 12,000 years and accented by tar-pit fossils of dinosaurs, dire wolves, and saber-toothed tigers. Within a mere two hundred years, evolving step by step from an unlettered and preagricultural community to the most sophisticated attainments in theoretical and applied science, Los Angeles has recapitulated world history—the experience of mankind thus far.

Incubation of the city began at a slow pace in a small Spanish town dedicated to subsistence farming and stockraising. A shorter Mexican pastoral period and another as a tough western cowtown covered a hundred years. In the 1870s Los Angeles was called the Queen of the Cow Counties; in other words it was a hick town. The next hundred years saw a spectacular growth that made it by 1920 the chief city in western America and in another half century the queen of the second largest metropolitan complex in the hemisphere.

Many famous writers who either lived in or wrote about California—Bret Harte, Mark Twain, Josiah Royce, Robert Louis Stevenson, Frank Norris, John Muir, Ambrose Bierce, Jack London, and John Steinbeck—never lifted a pen for Los Angeles. Nevertheless, there is an impressive literature. Several selections for this book are from commentators who were merely passing through.

Early in the American period the town acquired a resident pundit in Horace Bell, who set a trend. From the time of Harris Newmark on, there have been Angelenos who looked back and recorded their reminiscences with delight. Jack Lemmon, for instance, recalls, "One of the first mornings here, as long as I live I'll never forget it, I had a little second-hand MG and a little apartment in Westwood and, driving into town on Sunset, I looked up and there were the mountains on a clear morning with snow on top and I was sitting in a T-shirt and the ocean was behind me." The affection of others for the city is laced with concern and in some instances with outrage. There are attempts to dissect and analyze the Los Angeles style as a curiosity or as a foretaste of the national pattern of the future.

In 1942 Will Robinson drew on his wide reading for a light-hearted collation of quotable characterizations, but to the best of our knowledge *Los Angeles: Biography of a City* is the pioneer in its field. It is an anthology in which the flow of selected writings threaded on historical guidelines tells the city's kaleidoscopic story.

Many friends, often at considerable inconvenience, assisted greatly in the formulation of this anthology. Ward Ritchie came out of retirement to design the book and Robert Zachary guided its production. We are greatly obliged to those who permitted inclusion of chosen passages and illustrations. We are indebted also to the hundred authors drawn upon in this book. Their cumulative writings are a rich legacy to our city.

J. & L. C.

The Gabrielino and Their Home

"The earth grew ever to the southward and the people followed."

—Gabrielino creation legend

Gabrielino rock painting

1

The Gabrielino and Their Home

The California Indians, as Theodora Kroeber has observed, were true provincials. They shared abundance and sometimes hunger with family, friends, and tribe. Contemplative and philosophical, they were at ease with the supernatural and the mystical as well as the material. Progress and change meant little to them. They accepted as proper the customs and the way of life into which they and all their tribe were born. To them life was as it had always been.

Until as recently as 1771 the Gabrielino were the unchallenged occupants of the Los Angeles area. They lived in several score rancherías (villages) of fifty to more than one hundred persons. Expert in fishing and in hunting and snaring game, they were industrious gatherers of acorns and seeds of all sorts. The women made beautiful baskets and soapstone vessels; the men fashioned sewed-plank boats seaworthy for trips to the offshore islands. They were an affable people, willingly exchanging gifts with visitors. For several generations they continued to be the most numerous residents of the area, and, though taken advantage of, they learned to perform much useful work at the missions, in town, and on the ranchos.

Our knowledge of them is astonishingly fragmentary. By the time that anthropological curiosity blossomed, the Gabrielino were almost extinct and their culture displaced. Many archaeological sites were reached first by bulldozers and builders. There are bits and pieces of recorded testimony about the Gabrielino, but the main written sources are Gerónimo Boscana's observations as missionary from 1811 to 1826 at San Juan Capistrano among Indians marginal to the Gabrielino; Hugo Reid's retrospective letters written in 1851; and the B. D. Wilson report as Indian agent in 1852.

What anthropologists and archaelogists have been able to reconstruct is represented here in the brief comment by A. L. Kroeber; in

3

Arthur Woodward's analysis of evidence from caves on San Clemente and fieldwork elsewhere; and in the principal monograph on the Gabrielino by Bernice Eastman Johnston. George Nidever's account of removal of Indians from San Nicolas Island and, eighteen years later, the "rescue" of the lone woman left behind symbolizes the decimation and disappearance of these first residents.

Eliminating all the buildings and pavements and exotic plants, one can imagine what the domain of the Gabrielino was like—the Los Angeles Plain and the connecting valleys from San Fernando to San Gabriel to San Pedro, the circling mountains, and the offshore islands. By traditional standards this is a poorly watered land; indeed, Los Angeles is the only big city set down in a desert or even a semidesert. The Gabrielino, without irrigating and without even planting, comfortably supported more persons to the square mile than lived in any Indian region elsewhere in the United States except the small Pueblo acreage and along the Northwest Coast fisheries. The climate was favorable. The fish and game and particularly the seeds, nuts, and berries of the chaparral forest and the brush and grasslands provided reliable food supply. For the Angelenos in that prehistoric time the indications are it was a good life.

The Gabrielino

A. L. KROEBER

A. L. Kroeber, a luminary among anthropologists was the leader in the development of the distinguished center of anthropological studies at Berkeley. His handbook of the Indians of California, here quoted, is cyclopedic.

The Gabrielino held the great bulk of the most fertile lowland portion of Southern California. They occupied also a stretch of pleasant and

4

sheltered coast and the most favored one of the Santa Barbara Islands. They seem to have been the most advanced group south of Tehachapi, except perhaps the Chumash. They certainly were the wealthiest and most thoughtful of all the Shoshoneans of the State, and dominated these civilizationally wherever contacts occurred. Their influence spread even to alien peoples. They have melted away so completely that we know more of the fine facts of the culture of ruder tribes; but everything points to these very efflorescences having had their origin with the Gabrielino.

A. L. Kroeber, *Handbook of the Indians of California* (Washington, 1925), 631.

People of the Chaparral
BERNICE EASTMAN JOHNSTON

Charles F. Lummis built the Southwest Museum near the center of the Gabrielino homeland. Although richer in non-Gabrielino data, the museum was an excellent base for Bernice Eastman Johnston's appreciative study of these first Angelenos. It was published serially in the museum's Masterkey *and subsequently reshaped as a book.*

Gaspar de Portolá, the Spanish Pathfinder, found the Gabrielino in happy possession of the coastal plain from Aliso Creek in Orange County to a point somewhere between Topanga and Malibu. Kroeber estimates that in 1770 the population was about 5,000. Today only an anonymous handful remains, and these few have little first-hand information as to the language or customs of their ancestors.

The time has long gone by when it would have been possible to make an exact map showing the locations of these villages, and our sources of information are now largely crystallized. In all writing on the American Indians, even of those groups living in historic time, a great deal must be labeled as unknown or uncertain, but in the case of

5

the vanished Gabrielinos even the tribal name by which they are designated comes from a time, late in their history, when they were attached to the Mission San Gabriel Arcangel as satellites of a culture and a religion literally as remote to them as west is to east.

No one knows how long it took the Asiatics who became the American Indians to fan out across the new continents into the patterns of occupancy which existed when the first Europeans appeared. The Uto-Aztecan linguistic stock spread so far in its age-long migrations that between some divisions there remains only the whisper of a relationship, and in the Shoshonean branches of it, to which the Gabrielinos belonged, are included such distant cousins as the buffalo-hunting Comanche of the Great Plains and the peace-loving Hopi farmers of the mesa pueblos in Arizona.

These Shoshoneans were not the first Indians to find a homeland on Southern California's coastal plains. Their arrival seems to have been comparatively late and to have driven a great wedge between tribes of another language stock, the Hokan. There is nothing to show exactly when this change of occupancy took place or that the newcomers displaced the Hokan-speaking tribes by force or even found them in possession. Yet Shoshoneans occupied, at last, an immense wedge of land tapering from an expanse of 600 miles on the Nevada border to a mere 100 miles of seacoast, where they stood between the Yuman tribes of the southern border counties and an immense patchwork of diversified groups to the north of the Tehachapi, the Tejon and the Santa Susana watershed.

Legends are not safe substitutes for history, but it is interesting to note that, as if in memory of the vast empty lands once traversed, a feeling of awe colors a portion of the creation legend in which it is said that the earth grew ever to the southward and the people followed. It is quite certain that these Shoshoneans drifted across from the Great Basin by way of the mountain passes. Legend assigns a camp of the "first people" to a place in the Cajon Pass, at a time when "the earth was still soft." No warfare is mentioned, only naked, cold and lonely people, led by a wise "captain" southward into an ever-expanding land.

Somewhere in their former wanderings these primitive folk had been in touch with the earliest and as yet underdeveloped Pueblo cultures. What little they brought into California with them contained but faint vestiges of the cultural seeds which were later to flower in the Southwest. They, themselves, were never to attain the artistic eminence of their fellow Shoshoneans, the Hopi, yet they were not without a special gift of their own which would develop along the lines of its own genius.

In Arizona and New Mexico archaeologists have been able to satisfy a thirst for specific dates through pottery and tree-ring studies, among other methods, but these are of no use here. The Gabrielinos, in particular, made no pottery before Mission times, preferring the fine cooking pots of steatite, or soapstone, from Santa Catalina Island. The willow frameworks that formed the skeletons of their tule-thatched huts, which the Spanish were to call "jacales," long ago were burned or withered to dust.

Estimating the time necessary for languages to split off from the common tongue and to become obviously separate dialects, Kroeber postulated four periods, during the first of which the Hokan-speaking tribes lived almost undisturbed. After that, possibly about 500 B.C., other tribes began filtering in, gradually forming the great northern "patchwork" and the Shoshonean "wedge" so noticeable on Kroeber's map of the California Indians. By about 500 A.D. the cultures of all these tribes had begun to differentiate, to take on special characteristics in social and political structure and in religious formations. In the fourth period, which is placed in this tentative scheme as that following 1200 A.D., these cultures crystallized into the forms noted by the Spanish during their explorations.

Long before the coming of the Hokan-speaking tribes, back in still deeper and more shadowy reaches of time, yet other peoples had explored or settled here, leaving faint traces which form exceedingly dusty clues with which the archaeologists must work in an effort further to clarify the story of early man in California. Even the comparatively recent Gabrielinos must be studied in this way. For example, in an excavation by the Southwest Museum of a known Fernandeno site at Big Tujunga Wash, pottery fragments were found that were indentified as those of one vessel of Hohokam ware of the

7th, 8th, or 9th century, A.D. Such an item from southern Arizona indicates contact, possibly through the Mohave Indians who were enterprising traders, and provides a date to show that by the time this item reached them the coastal Shoshoneans were well established, with a definite culture based on long occupancy.

In our own time, when steam-shovel, bulldozer and paving machines are busily changing the face of the once Gabrielino earth, the old landmarks of these early Shoshoneans are rapidly being destroyed; indeed, even the fact of the existence of these Indians is almost forgotten. Yet occasionally a broken metate, a mortar, an arrowhead, or even a rare skeleton, disturbed in its rest by a mechanical ditch-digger, serve as reminders. Sometimes also an imaginative home-owner allows his thoughts to dwell for a moment on what his land looked like in Spanish times or when it was occupied by the quiet brown folk of the chaparral, long before the white man came.

Bernice Eastman Johnston, *California's Gabrielino Indians* (Los Angeles: Southwest Museum, 1962), 1–5.

A Way of Life

HUGO REID

Hugo Reid, Susanna Bryant Dakin's Scotch Paisano, *is the principal informant on the Gabrielino. To the* Los Angeles Star *in 1851 he contributed a series of letters on them. A clerk and then a ranchero, Reid wrote on the basis of twenty years on the scene and marriage to a Gabrielino woman, Doña Victoria Bartolomea Comicrabit.*

Before the Indians belonging to the greater part of this county were known to the Whites, they comprised as it were one great Family under distinct Chiefs. They spoke nearly the same language, with the exception of a few words; and were more to be distinguished by a local intonation of the voice than anything else. . . .

Their language is simple, rich, and abounding in compound expressive terms. Although they have words denoting *to desire, to like, to possess, to regard, to have an affection for*, and *to esteem;* yet, they have no word to express *Love*. At the same time they have many phrases to which we have no equivalent. . . .

The government of the people was invested in the hands of their Chiefs: each Captain commanding his own lodge. The command was hereditary in a family. If the right line of descent ran out, they elected one of the same kin, nearest in blood. Laws in general were made as required, with some few standing ones. Robbery was never known among them. Murder was of rare occurrence, and punished with death. Incest was likewise punished with death: being held in such abhorrence, that marriages between kinsfolk were not allowed. The manner of putting to death was by shooting the delinquent with arrows. . . .

If a quarrel ensued between two parties, the chief of the Lodge took cognizance in the case, and decided according to the testimony produced. But, if a quarrel occurred between parties of distinct Lodges, each chief heard the witnesses produced by his own people; and then, associated with the chief of the opposite side, they passed sentence. In case they could not agree, an impartial chief was called in, who heard the statements made by both, and he alone decided. There was no appeal from his decision.

Whipping was never resorted to as a punishment; therefore all fines and sentences consisted in delivering money, food and skins. . . .

They believed in one God, the maker and creator of all things, whose name was (and is) held so sacred among them, as hardly ever to be used; and when used only in a low voice. That name is *Qua-o-ar*. When they have to use the name of the Supreme Being on any ordinary occasion, they substitute in its stead, the word *Y-yo-ha-rivg-nain*, or "The Giver of Life."

The world was at one time in a state of chaos, until God gave it its present formation; fixing it on the shoulders of *Seven Giants*, made expressly for this end. They have their names, and when they move themselves, an earthquake is the consequence. Animals were then

9

formed; and lastly man and woman were formed separately from earth, and ordered to live together. The man's name was TOBOHAR, the woman's PABAVIT. God ascended to Heaven immediately afterwards, where he receives the soul of all who die. They had no bad spirit connected with their creed; and never heard of a "Devil" or a "Hell" until the coming of the Spaniards. . . .

The animal food in use among them was deer meat, young coyotes, squirrels, badgers, rats, gophers, snakes, racoons, skunks, wildcats, the small crow, the blackbirds, hawks, ground owls, and snakes, with the exception of the rattle snake. A few eat the bear, but in general it is rejected, on superstitious grounds hereafter to be mentioned. The large locust or grasshopper was a favorite morsel, roasted on a stick at the fire. Fish, whales, seals, sea-otters, and shellfish, formed the principal subsistence of the immediate coast-range of Lodges and Islands.

Oak Grove, a favorite Indian habitat   John Palmer

Acorns, after being divested of their shell, were dried, and pounded in stone mortars, put into filterns of willow twigs worked into a concave form, and raised on little mounds of sand, which were lined inside with a coating of two inches of sand; water added and mixed up

—then filled up again and again with more water, at first hot, then cold, until all the tannin and bitter principle was extracted. The residue was then collected and washed free of any sandy particles it might contain. On settling, the water was poured off. After being well boiled, it became a sort of mush, and was eaten when cold. The next favorite food was the kernel of a species of plum which grows in the mountains and islands, called by them, *Islay* (pronounced eeslie). Some Americans call it the *Mountain Cherry*, although it partakes little either of the plum or cherry. It has a large stone, to which numerous fibres are attached, pervading the pulp, of which there is very little. Its color, when perfectly ripe, inclines to black, and very much like what in Mexico is called the *Ciruela*. This, cooked, formed a very nutritious, rich, saccharine aliment; and looked much like dry boiled frijoles. *Chia*, which is a small, gray, oblong seed, was procured from a plant apparently of the thistle kind, having a number of seed vessels on a straight stalk, one above the other, like wild sage. This, roasted and ground into meal, was eaten with cold water, being of a glutinous consistency, and very cooling. Pepper grass seed was also much used, the tender stalks of wild sage, several kinds of berries and a number of roots. All their food was taken either cold or nearly so, which, of course, tended to preserve the teeth. Salt was used very sparingly in their food, from an idea that it had a tendency to turn their hair *grey*.

The men wore no clothing, but the women in the interior had a deer-skin wrapped round the middle, while those on the coast had sea-otter skins put to the same purpose. Their covering at night consisted of rabbit skins, cut square and sewed together in the form of a bedspread. Rings or ornaments of any kind were never attached to the nose, although all the Indians of Buenaventura and Santa Barbara used them. The men inserted a reed or a piece of cane through each ear; while the women wore regular earrings; each of which was composed of four long pieces of a whale's tooth, ground down smooth to a cylindrical form of eight inches in length, and half an inch in diameter. These were hung with the feathers of the hawk and turkey-buzzard, from a ring made of the oblong shell. Their necklaces were very heavy and large consisting of innumerable strings of various lengths, of their money beads, of beads made of black stones, and pieces of whale's teeth, ground round and perforated. They used bracelets on both wrists, of very small shell beads.

During the season of flowers, the females and children decked themselves in splendor; not only entwining them in the hair, but stringing them with the stalks and leaves, making boas of them.

Chiefs had one, two or three wives, as their inclinations dictated. The subjects only one. When a person wished to marry, and had selected a suitable partner, he advertised the same to all his relations, even to the nineteenth cousin. On a day appointed, the male portion of the lodge, and male relations living at other lodges brought in a collection of money beads. The amount of each one's contribution was about twenty-five cents. All the relations having come in with their share, they (the males) proceeded in a body to the residence of the bride, to whom timely notice had been given. All of the bride's female relations had been assembled, and the money was equally divided among them; the bride receiving nothing, as it was a sort of purchase. After a few days the bride's female relations returned the compliment by taking to the bridegroom's dwelling baskets of meal made of *Chia*, which was distributed among his male relations.

These preliminaries over, a day was fixed for the ceremony, which consisted in decking out the bride in innumerable strings of beads, paint, feathers and skins. On being ready, she was taken up in the arms of one of her strongest connections, who carried her dancing toward her sweetheart's habitation. All of her family, friends and neighbors accompanied, dancing around, and throwing food and edible seeds at her feet every step, which were collected in a scrabble as they best could by the spectators. The relations of the man met them half way, and taking the bride, carried her themselves, joining in the ceremonious walking dance. On arriving at the bridegroom's (who was sitting within his hut) she was inducted into her new residence by being placed along side of her husband: while baskets of seeds were liberally emptied on their heads, to denote blessing and plenty. This was likewise scrambled for by the spectators; who on gathering up all of the bride's seed cake, departed, leaving them to enjoy their "Honey Moon," according to usage.

A grand dance was of course given on the occasion, where might be seen warriors and hunters in full costume, making their various gestures in character, indicative of their respective callings. The old women took a part in the dance either as if carrying off game, or of dispatching their wounded enemies, as the avocation of their husbands called for. The younger portion of the women and old men sat around as singers.

The wife never visited her relations from that day forth, although they had undebarred leave to visit her.

In case her "Lord" ill used her, and continued to beat her in a cruel manner, she gave advice of it to her kin, who in consequence collected together all the money which had been paid in at the marriage, and taking it in deputation to the husband's hut, left it with him, leading off the wife. They immediately married her to another. . . .

When a person died, all the kin collected to lament and mourn his or her loss. Each one had his own peculiar mode of crying or howling, as easily distinguished, the one from another, as one song is from another. After lamenting awhile, a mourning dirge was sung, in a low whining tone, accompanied by a shrill whistle, produced by blowing into the tube of a deer's leg bone. Dancing can hardly be said to have formed a part of the rites, as it was merely a monotonous action of the foot on the ground. This was continued alternately until the body showed signs of decay, when it was wrapt up in the covering used in life. The hands were crooked upon the breast, and the body tied from head to foot. A place having been dug in their burial place, the body was deposited, with seeds, etc., according to the means of the family. . . .

A great number of their young men being hunters, they of course had their peculiar superstitions. During a hunt they never tasted food; nor on their return did they partake of what they themselves killed, from an idea that whoever ate of his own game hurt his hunting abilities. Before going on a hunting expedition they stung themselves all over with nettles, more particularly the eyes, the lids of which were opened to introduce the leaves. This was done to make them watchful, vigilant and clear sighted. The skin of a deer's head and neck was put on their own, and on seeing game they would feign to be grazing—lifting up the head occasionally to stare about. By such means they approached near to make the first arrow tell.

13

To make them hardy and endure pain without wincing (for cowardice as to corporeal suffering was considered, even among the women, as disgraceful) they would lie down on the hill of the large red ant, having handfuls of them placed in the region of the stomach and about the eyes. Lastly, to insure a full dose, they swallowed them in large quantities, alive!

A small string of buckskin was tied around the neck of those who were swift of foot.

When a girl came to the edge of puberty, it was a joyful occasion for her relations. She underwent a purification in the same manner as women did at child birth, accompanied by singing, and all were informed of her being marriageable.

The children were not without some education, for if an adult asked a boy or girl for a drink of water, they were not allowed to put it to their lips until the other had satisfied his thirst. If two persons were in conversation, a child was not permitted to pass between them, but made to go round them on either side. No male from childhood upward was allowed to call his sister *liar* even in jest. The word for liar being *yayare*. . . .

The principal (game) was *churchurki* or *peon* as it is called by the Spaniards. It consists of guessing in which hand a small piece of stick was held concealed by another. Four persons on a side composed a set, who sat opposite each other. They had their singers, who were paid so much a game, and an umpire who kept count, held the stakes, settled disputes and prevented cheating. He was paid so much a night, and had to provide the firewood. He was provided with fifteen counters, which were of reed and eight or ten inches long. The guessers never spoke, but giving the palm of the left hand a sharp slap with the right pointed with the finger to the side they guessed contained the peon. Those who guessed right, won the peon, and the others took a counter each, and so on, until they possessed all the counters or lost all the peons, when the opposite side took the counter part.

The peon was white, of an inch or two in length; but they had also a black one, which to prevent fraud, they had to remove to the other hand on changing, so as always to retain one in each hand, to show when called upon.

This was their favorite game, and they at times bet their all on it. It still continues to be their ruling passion to bet at this game in preference to any other; for the by-standers take as much interest and wager as heavily as those principally concerned. . . .

The Indians were sadly afraid when they saw the Spaniards coming on horseback. Thinking them gods, the women ran to the brush, and hid themselves, while the men put out the fires in their huts. They remained still more impressed with this idea, when they saw one of their guests take a flint, strike a fire and commence smoking, having never seen it produced in this simple manner before. An occurrence however soon convinced them that their strange visitors were, like themselves, mortals, for one of the Spaniards leveled his musket at a bird and killed it. Although greatly terrified at the report of the piece, yet the effect it produced of taking life, led them to reason, and deduce the impossibility of the "Giver of Life" to murder animals, as they themselves did with bows and arrows. They consequently put them down as human beings, of a *nasty white color, and having ugly blue eyes!*

Hugo Reid, "The Indians of Los Angeles County," *Los Angeles Star,* 1851; reprinted with foreword by Arthur M. Ellis (Los Angeles, 1926), 1–2, 6–9, 11–17, 20–22, 27–28, 44.

Channel Island Artifacts

ARTHUR WOODWARD

For many years Arthur Woodward was curator of anthropology in the Los Angeles County Museum. The springboard for his commentary on the material culture of the Indians of San Clemente and Santa Catalina was his discovery of the diary of one of the Franciscans, Juan Vizcaino, who came to California on the San Antonio *in 1769.*

At the time when the *San Antonio* cruised along the eastern coast of San Clemente there were many small Indian rancherías scattered along the beaches between Pyramid Head and China Point. It was here that Fr. Vizcaíno noted the smoke arising from the campfires and it was from these beaches that the tar-caulked plank canoes shoved off to greet the alien visitors.

In 1939–1940 the members of the Los Angeles Channel Island Survey party camped at the beaches of Pyramid Cove and at the smaller beach known locally as Horse Beach, just southwest of the larger strand. As archaeologist of the survey I visited all of the small village sites at the eastern end of San Clemente Island and excavated a large cave in the face of the rocky cliff a short distance north of China Point, near Horse Beach. From this cave in December 1939 we took many artifacts which gave us some insight into the life of the natives, some of whom Fr. Vizcaíno probably saw from the decks of the *San Antonio*. Included among the objects in the cave was the desiccated body of a large dog with tawny yellow hair. The animal had been lovingly wrapped in a sea otter fur robe. Because of this discovery we dubbed the place Big Dog Cave.

It was through these excavations and others, on San Clemente Island as well as on the islands of San Nicolas, Santa Rosa, Santa Cruz and to a lesser extent on San Miguel that I was able to corroborate in detail the keen observations made by the ethnologically inclined Fr. Vizcaíno one hundred and seventy years earlier.

The good father's notations on the laced plank canoes, the double-bladed paddles and the method of handling the leaky craft were correct in every detail.

These canoes were composed of small planks, some only nine or ten inches in length and four or five inches in width. They were ingeniously fitted together with the edges of the boards scored with indentations made by a stone knife and then daubed with boiling hot bitumen. Holes were bored about one inch from the edges with chert drills and shallow channels gouged out in which heavy cords made from the inner bast of the red milkweed or wild hemp were laid. These holes and channels were arranged in pairs opposite each other in two opposing planks and after the cords had been knotted tightly, more tar was poured in to make the joints waterproof. Since there were no stone axes used on the California coast, these planks had to be wedged from tree trunks with elk antler or whalebone wedges, and smoothed with wet sand on the beach. One account noted that for the longer planks a hole was bored in one end, to which a heavy seal sinew rope was attached. This was taken to the beach and after two or three small Indian children had climbed on the board, the plank was hauled up and down the smooth beach at water level, during which process it was beautifully sanded.

When completed the canoes were covered with tar and painted an oxide or iron red and at times bits of nacreous shell were mosaicked in the tar along the upper edge of the gunwales and at the prow. In shape these canoes were double-ended, much like the fishing dories of the eastern Atlantic coast. The plank canoes had no ribs but were fitted at intervals with solid, truncated, triangular bulkheads. The paddlers knelt and used double-bladed paddles with circular ends in a very dexterous fashion.

But, as Fr. Vizcaíno observed, in spite of all the caulking, these cranky little boats leaked and the services of a bailer, using either a large abalone shell with the gill holes caulked with tar or plugged with small sticks, or a small wooden utensil with a short handle, were needed when the craft put out to sea. In such canoes these Indians ventured as far out as San Nicolas Island, some sixty miles off shore from San Pedro, and made regular crossings between their homes on the Channel Islands and the villages of their kinfolk on the mainland.

Aside from the canoes, Vizcaíno's descriptions of the stone-bladed knives with short wide wooden hafts which the Indians carried thrust through the topknots of hair on their heads, were also accurate. The knives were of two general types. One had a short wide handle and a correspondingly wide blade, generally leaf-shaped or semi-triangular in form. The other type had a smaller blade with the rounded base set in a slot at the end of a haft which was about seven to nine inches long (or even shorter) and which tapered somewhat toward the proximal end. All of the blades were cemented firmly in place with the ever useful bitumen, the only natural mineral cement used by the tribesmen. We found examples of these hafted knives, intact in Big Dog Cave. Likewise we found two small planks of a canoe in pristine condition with fragments of the reddish fiber cords still imbedded in the tar caulking, in the cave.

When Fr. Vizcaíno drank from the tar-covered, grass water bottles

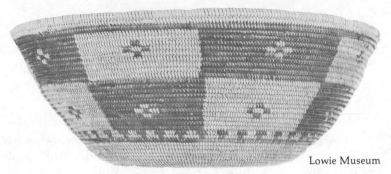

Lowie Museum

Gabrielino basket

he unknowingly corroborated other archaeological finds which we made on the Islands.

Apparently the basketry materials on the islands were confined mainly to a species of eel-grass which grows abundantly on the rocks close to shore. This tough, pliable grass was the element from which the flexible water containers were made. These bottles, for such they were in shape, had rounded bulbous bodies and slender short necks with small mouths. To render them waterproof the woman basketmaker gathered small lumps of water-worn bitumen washed on shore from submarine wells of the viscous material and dropped these pieces of hardened tar into the newly woven basket. Then she gathered a supply of small round, water-worn pebbles ranging in size from a pigeon's egg to an English walnut. These were heated in a small fire and fished out with two sticks or flattened pieces of animal bone. One by one they were popped into the basket and rolled around until the tar was melted and the pebbles cooled. Then the tar-coated stones were flipped out and new lumps of tar and fresh hot pebbles were put in and this process continued until the tar oozed through the basketry and formed a coating on the outside as well. Baskets with large openings could not be made because of the flexibility of the grass filaments. On the mainland baskets were made of stouter materials such as splints from the three-leaf sumac, deer-grass stems and the tough juncus. When baskets from these materials were woven, the orifices of the containers were wider and larger heated stones were used. I have found small piles of tarred pebbles on San Nicolas Is-

18

land which were not larger than walnuts, as many as one hundred and sixty in one heap, while the tarred stones on the mainland sites were sometimes about the size of tennis balls.

Padre Vizcaíno's description of the sea otter fur robes worn by the Indians who came off to visit the ship adds a new side light on the garb of these people. The system of making these fur garments is well known, i.e., the cutting of the skin into long strips and winding them around a central cord and then weaving or tying these cords into a semblance of soft furry textile, warm on the inside as well as out. Our discoveries of portions of these robes in Big Dog Cave corroborated Vizcaíno's observations in that these fragments showed that a reddish fiber cord (long since disintegrated) had been used. Likewise although the hide itself had decayed, the fur remained in long twisted masses. . . .

Even the fishing gear was not overlooked by the studious Franciscan. . . . What he probably saw were the circular shell fishhooks which were made by the thousands by the insular tribesmen.

These hooks were manufactured out of the abalone mussel and turban shells. Fragments of the shell were shaped by grinding on sandstone to ovoid blanks. These were then drilled with squatty chert drills and the holes later enlarged with reamers made of gritty sandstone. In the last stages the shanks, to which the sea-grass lines were attached by tar, were fashioned and the incurving points ground down to needle-like sharpness. . . . The circular shell hooks were used mainly to catch bottom-feeding fish. Modern experiments by Mr. Eugene Robinson with circular hooks made from fresh shells and fresh bone indicated that bottom-feeders were easily caught with these hooks. . . .

All of the other ethnological observations made by Fr. Vizcaíno are equally valid. Archaeologists have found the rock crystals (used as primitive "X-ray" devices by the medicine men and also as ornaments) the oxide of iron paint and even the feather "flags" on the ends of the poles. The latter were in the form of tufts of raven feathers and tasseled, red milkweed fiber cords.

Fragments of long streamers of flicker and raven feathers with fiber cords threaded through the barrels of the feathers have been found in caves in Ventura County. Such feather ornaments were used in several parts of California as bandoliers and as headgear. In the land explorations of 1769 other writers noted these feather wands set up in cleared spaces near the villages. Cabrillo saw one on Santa Catalina Island in 1542. The Spanish referred to these as "gods" worshipped by the Indians.

Arthur Woodward, *The Sea Diary of Fr. Juan Vizcaino to Alta California, 1769* (Los Angeles: Glen Dawson, 1959), xvi–xxx.

Instructing the Children
GERÓNIMO BOSCANA

Among the Franciscans in California, Gerónimo Boscana is the most informative on the culture of the Indians. At Mission San Juan Capistrano, where he served from 1811 to 1826, he was with the Luiseno, but many of their beliefs and customs derived from the Gabrielino. The extract that follows is from the translation by Alfred Robinson, long-time agent in the hide trade. Boscana minimizes the skills that boys and girls needed to learn, those of hunting and fishing and of basket-making and the acorn process. J. P. Harrington's researches suggest "Chee-ngich-ngich" or "twi-nits-nits" as the pronunciation of the name of their deity, Chinigchinich. The latter is the Gabrielino equivalent for "sabio" or wise man.

One of the difficulties most perplexing to the Indians was the rearing and educating of their children. They were unacquainted with the arts, excepting those most necessary for their maintenance, and ignorant of all useful knowledge to keep them from idleness; so that their only education consisted in the construction of the bow and arrow, with their peculiar uses, in procuring game and defending themselves from their enemies.

Although ignorant as they were of the knowledge of the true God, the moral instruction given by parents to their children was contained

20

in the precepts of Chinigchinich, which were strongly impressed upon their minds, that they might become good, and avoid the fate of the evil. The perverse child, invariably, was destroyed, and the parents of such remained dishonored.

At the age of six or seven years, they gave them a kind of god, as protector; an animal, in whom they were to place their entire confidence, who would defend them from all dangers, particularly those in war against their enemies. They, however, were not to consider this animal as the *real* God, for he was invisible, and inhabited the mountains and bowels of the earth; and if he did appear to them at any time, it was in the shape of an animal of the most terrific description. This was not Chinigchinich, but another called *Touch*, signifying a *Devil*.

That they might know the class of animal, which the God, Chinigchinich, had selected for their particular veneration, a kind of drink was administered to them, made from a plant called *Pibat* (jimson weed), which was reduced to a powder, and mixed with other intoxicating ingredients. Soon after taking this preparation they became insensible, and for three days were deprived of any sustenance whatever. During this period they were attended by some old men or women, who were continually exhorting them to be on the alert, not to sleep for fear the coyote, the bear, the crow, or the rattlesnake might come; to observe if it were furious or gentle, and to inquire of the first that should come, what were its desires.

The poor Indian thus intoxicated, without food or drink, suffering under delirium, beheld all kinds of visions; and when he made known that he had seen any particular being, who explained the observances required of him, then they gave him to eat and drink, and made a grand feast; at the same time advising him to be particular in obeying the commands of the mysterious apparition. . . .

Having undergone the ceremonies described, they placed upon the poor Indians a brand, which was done in this manner. A kind of herb was pounded until it became sponge-like; this they placed, according to the figure required, upon the spot intended to be burnt, which was generally upon the right arm, and sometimes upon the thick part of the leg also. They then set fire to it, and let it remain until all that was combustible, was consumed. Consequently, a large blister immediately formed, and although painful, they used no remedy to cure it, but left it to heal itself; and thus, a large and perpetual scar remained.

The reason alleged for this ceremony was that it added greater strength to the nerves, and gave a better pulse for the management of the bow. Besides, Chinigchinich required it of them, that they might be more formidable in war, and be enabled to conquer their enemies. Those who were not marked in this way, which was called *"potense,"* were ever unfortunate, easily conquered, and men of feeble capacities. . . .

Thus far I have explained the education given to the boys. Now I will proceed to that instilled into the minds of the females. Besides the general instructions given to the males, to observe the commandments of Chinigchinich, the girls were taught to remain at home, and not to roam about in idleness; to be always employed in some domestic duty, so that, when they were older, they might know how to work, and attend to their household duties; such as procuring seeds, and cleaning them,—making *"atole"* and *"pinole,"* which are kinds of gruel, and their daily food. When quite young, they have a small, shallow basket, called by the natives *"tucmel,"* with which they learn the way to clean the seeds, and they are also instructed in grinding and preparing the same for consumption. Those who are industrious in their youth, are flattered with promises of many admirers when they grow up to be women—that they will be generally beloved, and receive many presents.

In this neighborhood, and as I have been informed, as far south as Cape St. Lucas, the girls were tat-tooed in their infancy, from their eyebrows, down to their breasts; and some from the chin only—covering the arms entirely, in both cases—but the execution of this was not generally complied with until they reached their tenth year; and varied in the application and style. The usual method of effecting the same was by pricking the parts with the thorn of the cactus plant, until they bled, and then they were rubbed with a kind of charcoal produced from *mescal,* so that a permanent blue color remained.

The particular reason for thus tat-tooing their females was that it added to their beauty, and when well executed, would insure them many admirers—but I think, besides this motive, it signified something more, and was a necessary kind of distinction. As the devil invented the branding of the males, so he may have ordered the painting of the females, and *Chinigchinich* required its performance; so that both might have their particular mark. . . .

On arriving at the state of womanhood, a grand feast was made, and conducted with much ceremony and witchcraft. They made a large hole in the ground, in shape resembling a grave, about two feet deep: this they filled with stones and burning coals, and when sufficiently heated, the latter were taken out, and upon the former they laid branches of the *estafiarte* (a kind of perennial plant), so as to form a bed, which the natives called *"Pacsil."* Upon this they placed the young girls, and for two or three days she was permitted to eat but very little; thus continuing until the accustomed term for purification had expired. In the meantime the outside of the hole was adorned with feathers of different birds, beads, and many other baubles. Several old women with their faces painted like devils, were employed in singing songs in a tone so disagreeable that one could hardly tell whether they were crying or laughing; and the young women danced around her, at intervals, every day.

Gerónimo Boscana, *Chinigchinich*, in Alfred Robinson, *Life in California* (New York, 1846), 270–277.

Louis Choris, Voyage (1822)

First published drawing of a California grizzly

Talking to Grizzlies

BY TRACY I. STORER AND LLOYD P. TEVIS, JR.

Zoologists Storer and Tevis joined forces to produce the definitive volume in tribute to the California state animal once much in evidence in the environs of Los Angeles.

Throughout California the Indians entertained a strongly developed feeling of kinship with wild animals and particularly with the grizzly. Whether they had the cold nerve to hunt the beast or whether because of timidity they tried to stay out of its way, they felt the bear was more closely one of them than any other animal. This was true despite the fact that by nature it was the most evil and odious being of which they could conceive. A reason for this sense of relationship doubtless lay in the manlike attitudes of the bears; they have many gestures, movements, and tricks that make them appear almost human. Furthermore, an enraged grizzly stands on its hind legs and fights with its fists like a man. Such a terrifying phenomenon was cause enough to make an Indian believe that he was looking at close kin, though a monster; and many tribes insisted that at least some of their people could commune with bears. According to Joaquin Miller, the Shasta had the notion that a grizzly would talk to a human being if the person would only sit still long enough to listen to what the bear had to say instead of running away in great fright. One wrinkled old woman in particular was held in great respect because daily she hobbled over a long trail to a heap of rocks at the edge of a thicket, where, so she said, she talked with a grizzly.

The Cahuilla relied for safety on an ability to converse with the big bears. A person who met one in the mountains called it *piwil* (great-grandfather) and said in a soothing tone, "I am only looking for my food, you are human and understand me, take my word and go away." The bear would rise, brandishing its great paws in the air; then, if it intended peace, it would drop to all fours and scratch dirt to one side.

24

Talking to Grizzlies

One story of the Cahuilla is about an Indian who attended a bear-and-bull fight at the pueblo of Los Angeles. The grizzly, a cowardly individual, was getting the worst of the battle, being repeatedly knocked down. Then the Cahuilla man whispered to him, "You must fight and defend yourself, they are going to kill you." Whereupon the bear charged the bull and broke its neck.

Even a female and cubs, the most dangerous and unpredictable of ursine groups, could be influenced by the proper words spoken in a diplomatic manner. Once when a party of Cahuilla encountered a she-bear with young near the modern town of Beaumont, the oldest and most respected man stepped forward and told her that they meant her no harm and that since she was a relative of theirs she should not bother them. The grizzly looked at them, understood, and went peacefully on her way.

When a man met a bear in the mountains, the object of conversation by the Indian obviously was to assuage the beast. A Spanish-Indian half-breed, who accompanied the famous Bandini brothers on a grizzly bear hunt with rifles near Cobblestone Mountain, Ventura County, in 1873, had a different objective—but only because he was under the protection of the guns. Thus, in a sense, he perverted and degraded the ancient power that had come to him from his mother. When the bear was sighted, he demanded to be allowed to hold brief intercourse with it before the shooting began. Confronting the beast, who stopped eating berries to look at him, he called out, "Que hay vale que estas haciendo aqui? Eso mirame bien; soy tu tata" ("Well old pard what are you doing here? Look at me well; I am your daddy"). The bear seemed to resent this last insinuation, for he rubbed his claws on the ground angrily. The half-breed then launched forth on a long tirade reflecting on the bravery of all bears from time immemorial, and then, indulging in personalities, he made the most unkind and unwarranted allusions to the grizzly's own pedigree. At last, picking up a stone, he threw it at the bear with the remark, "Tu no eres hombre y me retiro" ("You are no man and I retire"). At this last insult the bear charged, and thirteen bullets were required to kill him.

Tracy I. Storer and Lloyd P. Tevis, Jr., *California Grizzly* (Berkeley and Los Angeles: University of California Press, 1955), 90–91.

Coyote and the Water

AS TOLD BY THE GABRIELINO

Although few Gabrielino examples have been preserved, the oral literature of the California Indians is rich, much of it centered on animal-named characters. Theodora Kroeber, The Inland Whale; Jaime d'Angulo, Indian Tale; and E. W. Gifford and G. H. Block, Californian Indian Nights Entertainments are convenient collections. The stream here immortalized may be identified as the Los Angeles River.

A Coyote, which, like all the rest of his kin, considered himself as the most austere animal on the face of the earth, not even excepting man himself, came one day to the margin of a small river. Looking over the bank, on seeing the water run so slow, he addressed it in a cunning manner, "What say you to a race?" "Agreed to," answered the water very calmly. The coyote ran at full speed along the bank until he could hardly stand from fatigue and on looking over the bank saw the water running smoothly on.

He walked off with his tail between his legs and had something to reflect upon for many a day afterwards.

Hugo Reid, *Los Angeles Star*, 1851, reprinted in *The Indians of Los Angeles County* (Los Angeles, 1926), 33.

Laborers and Servants

B. D. WILSON

In 1852 Don Benito Wilson, pioneer settler and well-known friend of the Indians, was asked to submit a detailed report on

*those for whom he was the designated agent. Superintendent
Edward F. Beale picked up Wilson's proposal to revive the
best of the mission system in a reservation at Tejon.*

In Santa Barbara, Los Angeles, and San Diego counties, there are
nearly 7,000 Indians, excluding the Yumas and Mojaves, and a few
petty tribes. Not half as many as the neophytes alone left by the
Mission! Still, more than half of those we have are the survivors of
the Missions.

That they are corrupt, and becoming more so every day, no candid
man can dispute. They do not always find better examples to imitate
now than they saw in the past generation of whites; for the latter have
not improved in the social virtues as fast as the Indians have declined.
What marvel that eighteen years of neglect, misrule, oppression, slavery, and injustice, and every opportunity and temptation to gratify
their natural vices withal, should have given them a fatal tendency
downward to the very lowest degradation! . . .

The Indian laborers and servants are "domesticated"; mix with us
daily and hourly; and, with all their faults, appear to be a necessary
part of the domestic economy. They are almost the only house or
farm servants we have. The San Luiseño is the most sprightly, skill-
ful, and handy; the Cahuilla plodding, but strong, and very useful
with instruction and watching.

When at work, they will do without ardent spirits, but *must* have it
on Saturday night and Sunday. Very little of the money earned during the week goes for meat and bread—their chief want with it is for
drink and cards. They are universal gamblers, and inveterately addicted to the vice; consequently their clothing continually changes
hands. Yet, I have met with some who do not drink, and have an
aspiration to decency. Some, again, are idle and vagabonds; but I have
rarely found them unwilling to work, when well paid.

If it be true that they cannot do half the work a white man can, 'tis
equally true that custom at best never allows them more than half the
wages of the latter, and, generally, much less than half. The common

pay of Indian farm hands is from eight to ten dollars per month; and one dollar per day the highest in the towns—but few pay so much. No white man here, whether American, Sonoranian, or Californian, will work for such wages, nor anything like it.

That better wages merely would make the Indian here a better man, is doubtful. With more money, he would only pursue his evil tastes to greater excess. When their weekly *juegos* (plays) were restrained by the magistrates, and only allowed at distant intervals they were much better off; and then, too, liquor shops were not so common. In some streets of this little city, almost every other house is a grog-shop for Indians. They have, indeed, become sadly deteriorated, within the last two years; and it may be long, very long, before a sound public opinion will speak like the potent voice of the Mission Fathers.

But, let us remember, these same Indians built all the houses in the country, and planted all the fields and vineyards. There is hardly any sort of ordinary work for which they do not show a good-will.

Under the Missions, they were masons, carpenters, plasterers, soapmakers, tanners, shoemakers, blacksmiths, millers, bakers, cooks, shepherds, agriculturists, horticulturists, vineros, vaqueros—in a word, filled all the laborious occupations known to civilized society. Their work must have been rudely executed sometimes, it may be well supposed; and they have forgotten much they once knew. But they acquired the rudiments of a practical knowledge which has outlived their good teachers, and contributed much to the little improvement this section of country has reached in eighteen years.

They are inferior only to the American in bodily strength, and might soon rank with the best Californian and Sonoranian in all the arts necessary to their physical comfort. They teach the American, even, how to make an adobe (sun-dried brick), mix the *lodo* (mud mortar), put on the *brea* (pitch) for roof—all these, recondite arts to the new beginner, yet very important to be known, when there are no other building materials. They understand the mysteries of irrigation, the planting season, and the harvest. Poor unfortunates! they seldom have farms of their own to till, or a dwelling to shelter them from the rain!

John W. Caughey, *The Indians of Southern California in 1852: The B. D. Wilson Report* (San Marino: Huntington Library, 1952), 21–23.

The Lone Woman of San Nicolas Island

GEORGE NIDEVER

George Nidever came to California as a fur trapper in the 1830s and gained additional fame for his adventures as a hunter. At Santa Barbara in 1878 he was interviewed by a field-worker for historian Hubert Howe Bancroft and thus is our chief source on the Gabrielino woman who was left for eighteen years in solitary on the outermost of the Channel Islands.

In the following Oct. after the return from the Leeward, as Lower Cal. was called, Isaac Sparks went over to San Nicolas Island. Others accompanied Sparks and among them Williams, of the Chino ranch in Los Angeles Co., and who was with me in the Mts.; he, with Col. Bean, having shown the white feather in our first engagement with the Indians, on the Ark. River. They removed the Indians, some 17 or 18 men, women and children, from this Island to San Pedro, and thence to Los Angeles and San Gabriel. I have heard from Sparks an account of the affair but do not remember the details distinctly. . . . Having got the Indians together on the Island, they took them to the beach and put them on board the schooner. They then took them direct to San Pedro having, however, left one Indian woman on the Island. Of the exact manner in which she was left I do not now remember, but am under the impression that Sparks told me that it happened in this way. Having got all of the Indians down on the beach, one of the women wanted to go back to their *rancheria* for her child that had been left behind, which she was allowed to do. While she was absent, a strong wind sprang up and, fearing for the safety of the schooner should they wait longer, they put off from shore and ran before the wind. Arriving safely at San Pedro, the Indians were landed, from whence they proceeded to Los Angeles, where a portion of them remained. . . .

Throughout the entire length of the coast it was known that an Indian woman had been left on the Island of San Nicolas, but no attempt was ever made to rescue her or to learn her fate, and as years passed on, all agreed that she must have perished. . . .

In April of 1852 I went over to the Islands with my sch(oone)r, accompanied by a foreigner by name Tom Jefferies, who is still living here, and 2 Indians, for sea gull's eggs. These eggs were in great demand at that time. We went direct to the San Nicolas and having arrived early in the day, Jefferies, one of the Indians, and I landed and travelled along the beach towards the upper end of the Island some 6 or 7 miles. At a short distance from the beach, about 200 yds., we discovered the footprints of a human being, probably of a woman as they were quite small. They had evidently been made during the previous rainy season as they were well defined and sunk quite deep into the soil then soft, but now dry and hard. At a distance of a few hundred yds. back from the beach and about 2 miles apart, we found 3 small circular enclosures, made of sage brush. Their thin walls (were) perhaps 5 feet high, and the whole enclosure 6 feet in diameter, and with a small narrow opening on one side. We examined them carefully, but found nothing that would indicate their having been occupied for a long time as the grass was growing within them. They all occupied slight rises of ground. Outside of the huts, however, we found signs of the place having been visited not many months before. Around each hut and a short distance from it were several stakes or poles, usually from 4 to 6, some 7 or 8 feet high, which were standing upright in the ground, and pieces of seal blubber stuck on the top of each. The blubber was already dry, but I do not think it could have been there more than 3 or 4 mos. We had come on shore early in the morning and having found these signs of the existence of some person on the Island, we intended searching further, but a N. Wester sprang up about 10 A.M. so that we were obliged to hasten back to the vessel.

We had seen enough to convince us of the existence of some human being on this Island who in all probability must be the Indian woman of whom Sparks had so often spoken. . . .

30

The Lone Woman of San Nicolas Island

Later I again fitted out for a thorough hunt among the Islands, and principally around the San Nicolas. Charley Brown accompanied me as hunter, and an Irishman whom we called Colorado from his florid complexion, with three Mission Indians manned our boats, while a fourth Mission Indian acted as cook. We reached the San Nicholas early in the day and at once went ashore for the purpose of selecting a camping place as we intended to make a stay of at least two or three months. We landed about the middle of the Island on the N.W. side, and went up towards the head of the Island. A high rocky bank ran along the edge of the water, its base for the most part being washed by the sea. A few short stretches of sandy beach occurred here and there but they were not always accessible from the bank. About ½ mile from the head of the Island we found a good spring of water just above the edge of the beach, and in the wet soil surrounding it more footprints that must have been made but a short time before. As it was already late and we were some 6 or 7 miles from the sch(oone)r, we were obliged to return without further search, determining however to make a thorough exploration of the Island on the following day.

Accordingly, the next morning early, as soon as we had breakfast, all hands but the cook went on shore, at the same place where we had landed the day before. Having on our previous visits seen most of the latest signs near the head of the Island, and, besides, there being but few springs in the middle and lower portion of the Island, we decided to search first from about the middle up towards the head. . . . Having become tired, I sat down to rest and Charley continued around the head of the Island. Reaching the place where he had seen the footprints the day before, he followed up the ridge. Near its top he found several huts made of whale's ribs and covered with brush, although it was so long since they had been occupied that they were open on all sides and grass was quite high within. Looking about in all directions from this point, he discovered at a distance, along the ridge, a small black object about the size of a crow which appeared to be in motion. Advancing cautiously towards it, he soon discovered it to be the Indian woman, her head and shoulders, only, visible above one of the small inclosures resembling those we had before discovered. He approached as near as he dared and then, raising his hat on his ramrod,

31

signalled to the men who were then re-crossing the low sandy stretch, and were plainly visible from this point.

They saw the signals, and came towards him. In the mean time, the old woman was busily employed in stripping the blubber from a piece of seal skin which she held across one knee, using in the operation a rude knife made from a piece of iron hoop stuck into a piece of rough wood for a handle. She kept up a continual jabbering to herself and every few moments would stop and look in the direction of our men, whom she had evidently been watching, her hand placed over her eyes to shade them from the sun.

Upon his first approach there were some dogs near, which began to growl. These the old woman sent away with a yell but without looking in the direction of Charley. The men having come up, they quietly surrounded her to prevent any attempt at escape.

This being done, Charley stepped around in front of her when, instead of showing any alarm, she smiled and bowed, chattering away to them in a language wholly unintelligible to all of them, even to the Indians. They seated themselves around her, after having made signs to me to come up. I at first did not care to go to where they were as I supposed that they had simply discovered something that excited their curiosity and I would hear about it when they should come down. They continued to make signs to me to come there, however, so I went up and found them seated around the old woman. She smiled and bowed to me also, and having taken a seat she took some roots of two different kinds, one called *corcomites* and the name of the other I do not know, and placed them in the fire which was burning within the inclosure. As soon as they were roasted she invited us all to eat some. The site of the inclosure or hut where we found her was on the N.W. side and near the top of the ridge that forms the upper end of the Island. It was not far from the best springs of water, near to the best point for fish and seal, and it commanded a good view of the greater portion of the Island. Just outside the inclosure or wind break, as I should call it, was a large pile of ashes and another of bones, showing that this had been her abode for a long time. Nearby were several stakes with blubber on them, as we had seen around the others (inclosures). There was blubber also hanging on a sinew rope, similar to the one already described, which was stretched between two stakes.

Near the inclosure were several baskets, some in process of construction, also two bottle-shaped vessels for holding water; these, as well as the baskets, being woven, and of some species of grass very common on the Island. There were also several other articles, as fishhooks made of bone, and needles of the same material, lines or cords of sinews for fishing and the larger rope of sinews she no doubt used for snaring seals on the rocks where they came to sleep. The old woman was of medium height, but rather thick. She must have been about 50 yrs. old, but she was still strong and active. Her face was pleasing, as she was continually smiling. Her teeth were entire but worn to the gums, the effect, no doubt, of eating the dried seal blubber. Her head, which had evidently been for years without any protection, was covered with thick matted hair, that was once black, no doubt, but now it had become of a dull brown color. Her clothing consisted of but a single garment of the skins of the shag, made in the form of a gown. It fitted close at the neck, had no sleeves, was girded at the waist with a sinew cord, and reached nearly to the feet. She had another dress of the same material and make in one of the baskets. These were sewed with sinews, the needles used being of bone. This place was undoubtedly where she usually lived, but in the rainy season she lived in a cave nearby. Having been requested by the Fathers at the Mission of Santa Barbara, to bring her off in case we found her, I asked the Indians if they thought she could be taken by force if necessary. They thought she could. Charley Brown was of the opinion that no force would be necessary in taking her. I thereupon made signs to her to go with us but she stared at me seemingly without comprehending what was wanted. Charley then placed his hand on her shoulder to call her attention and then went through the motions of putting her things in baskets and then these on his back, at the conclusion of which he said *vamoose*. This she understood without any difficulty, for she at once began putting her things into her baskets. Her basket filled, she put it on her back and followed the Indians toward the beach while we walked behind; each of us carrying some of her things. Seal meat, some of it stinking, and a seal's head from which putrefied brains was running, was all carefully put into the basket. We soon arrived at a spring of water where we stopped and on some stakes which we found standing near we hung

33

the things we were carrying, fixing them on the stakes in such a manner as to lead her to believe we took very great care of them. Near this spring there were several rocks, in the cracks of which were large numbers of fish and other bones, carefully placed. We then proceeded to the beach, where a spring issues from a shelving rock, just below the bank. The old woman stopped here to wash, the men having gone on ahead, and Charley and I remained on the bank above. This being finished, we proceeded to the boat and went on board the sch(oone)r. When we put her into the boat, she crept forward to the bow where she knelt, holding firmly on to either side of the boat. As soon as we got on board, she crept along side of the stove which was on deck. Dinner was ready and was at once served. The cook gave the old woman some pork and hard tack, which she seemed to relish, and in fact she took readily to all of our food, it always agreeing with her. Charley Brown at once set to work and made her a petticoat of ticking, (with) which, with (and) a man's cotton shirt and a black neck tie, he completed her dress, and she seemed to be very proud of it. Seeing Charley at work on her petticoat, she made signs that she wanted to sew. Accordingly, she was given a needle and thread, but Charley was obliged to thread it for her as her eyes seemed weak.

I had given her an old cloak or cape that was almost in ribbons and she sewed up all the rents and holes. Her manner of sewing was peculiar. Placing her work across her knee she thrust the needle through the cloth with the right hand and pulled the thread tought (taut) with the left. The next day we went ashore and camped, about the middle of the Island, close to the beach. We made a temporary shelter by spreading a sail over two oars driven into the side of the bank. A similar shelter was made for her of brush.

We remained here hunting about a month, when we brought her on shore with us. While on the Island with us, she busied herself in going for wood and water, about a quarter of a mile distance, and (in) working on her baskets. She brought water and wood of her own accord, the water in the vessels before mentioned.

Of the several baskets she was working (on), not one of them was completed, although she would work first on one, then on the other. One day Charley shot a she otter off shore. It was brought to land for the purpose of skinning (it). Inside of her was a young otter, within a few days of being born. The carcass was being hauled down to the water, as was customary after taking off the skin, when the old woman vigorously protested against such a waste of meat. Seizing one of the flippers she drew it back on land, where it lay until the stench obliged us to throw it in the water. By this time, however, she had come to the conclusion that our food was better than this, and she so expressed herself in her own rude way by signs. She was very fond of sugar, and in fact anything sweet, and showed her fondness for it by smacking her lips. She had evidently known hunger as she sedulously saved every scrap of food and bones, and the latter she would take out from time to time, suck them over and over, and then put them away again.

When we took her from her hut, she was very careful to place the seal's head in the basket although it was almost rotten. The young otter was skinned and stuffed, making a plaything for the old woman. She hung it by a string from the roof of her shelter and for hours at a time would amuse herself like a child in making it swing back and forth, striking it with her hand to keep it in motion. . . .

When we left the Island for Santa Barbara, we were caught in such a violent gale that we were several times on the point of turning back, but we finally got under the lee of Sta. Cruz Island, which afforded us some shelter until late in the day when the wind went down. As soon as it began to blow, the old woman conveyed to us by signs her intention to stop the wind. She then knelt and prayed, facing the quarter from which the wind blowed (sic), and continued to pray at intervals during the day until the gale was over. Then she looked at us and smiled as much as to say, "You see how I have succeeded in stopping the wind." From Santa Cruz we ran over to Santa Barbara, arriving there early the next day. Upon nearing the shore an ox-cart came in sight when the old woman's delight was unbounded. She clapped her hands and danced, pointing the while at the cart and oxen. On landing I found my sons at the beach awaiting my arrival, one of them being on horseback.

Her delight at the sight of the horse was even greater than that manifested at the sight of the ox-cart. As soon as she got out of the boat, she went up to it and began examining it, pointing at this part, then that, and talking and laughing to herself. Finally she pointed at

35

the horse and placing two fingers of her right hand astride the fore finger of her left, she imitated the motion of a horse. The news was not long in spreading, of the arrival of the old woman, and we had barely reached my house with her when half of the town came down to see her.

For months after, she and her things, as her dress, baskets, needle, &c., were visited by every body in the town and for miles around outside of it.

The old woman was always in good humor and sang and danced, to the great delight of the children and even older ones. She often visited the town and seldom returned without some present. The vessels that touched here usually brought passengers who, hearing of her, came to my house. The Capt. of the "Fremont," one of these vessels, offered to take her to San Francisco and exhibit her, giving me one half of what he could make. Capt. Trussel of this place offered me $1000 for her for the same purpose. We had all become somewhat attached to her, however, and consequently refused to listen to these proposals.

The same day (that) we arrived here, the Fathers from the Mission came down to see her. They continued to visit her, and also sent for Indians from different parts of this section, and speaking different Indian tongues, in hopes of finding some one who could converse with her. Several came, each representing a different dialect, but none of them could understand her or make themselves understood. She was continually talking and frequently made use of the *pickininy*, in referring to her child. She also used *manana*. She expressed a great many ideas by signs, so plainly that we readily understood them. By signs she told us that she did not find her child, that she wandered about for days without tasting hardly any food or drink, sometimes sleeping but little, until her clothes were torn, and her feet and legs bleeding.

After a time she forgot her child and sang and danced. She also told that she was very sick at one time; that she had seen vessels passing two (to) and fro but none came to take her off; that she saw us on the Island before we found her.

Her dresses, bone needles and other curiosities were taken possession of by Father González, with my consent, and sent to Rome.

36

The Lone Woman of San Nicolas Island

About 5 weeks after she was brought over, she was taken sick from eating too much fruit and 7 weeks from the day of her arrival died. The Fathers of the Mission baptised her *sub conditione* and named her Juana María. I left here for San Francisco just before she died, having first made her a rough coffin.

The Bancroft dictation of George Nidever, here quoted from W. H. Ellison, *The Life and Adventures of George Nidever* (Berkeley: University of California Press, 1937), 37–39, 77–89.

The Spaniards Steal the Scene

"A very advantageous settlement is established on a fertile spot somewhere in this neighborhood . . . called Pueblo de los Angeles, 'the country town of the Angels.'"

—George Vancouver

Mission San Gabriel

2

The Spaniards Steal the Scene

Spanish exploration penetrated to the California coast, Los Angeles included, as early as 1542. Not until 1769, two and a quarter centuries later, did Spain move to occupy this most remote and last of its frontier provinces.

American frontier advance all across the continent came as pioneer settlers on their own volition moved into new areas—the Piedmont in the latter half of the colonial period, Tennessee and Kentucky during and just after the Revolution and, correspondingly, into practically all the states subsequently admitted. On occasion the migration was managed, as in the Mormon move to the Great Basin, but never did the government take charge.

A special agent of the king of Spain, in the course of conducting an inspection of the viceroyalty of New Spain (Mexico), determined that California should be occupied. With the cooperation of the viceroy, he made all the implementing decisions. The officers, soldiers, sailors, and missionaries who comprised the original task force were equipped and sent by the government as were the settlers who in 1781 founded the pueblo of Los Angeles. The role of government was comparable to that in the American development of Wake Island or Guam.

As good Catholics, the king and his ministers appreciated the bringing of the Gabrielino and their neighbors into Christendom. But the prime reason for occupying California was for defense in depth to insulate New Spain against foreign encroachments, Russian or British appearing the most threatening. Spain used the standard frontier institutions of its late colonial practice: the presidio (a garrisoned fort), the mission (a predominantly Indian community intended to be self-supporting and inductive to Spanish ways), and the pueblo (a civilian town). Spain eventually would have in California four presidios, twenty missions, and three pueblos, one of which was only temporary.

In the first years the missions and presidios were dependent on supplies shipped up from Mexico. The cost drew criticism. Through the fifty-two years that California was Spanish the royal treasury was drawn on for the stipends of the missionaries and the presidial payrolls. In time mission and pueblo agriculture produced sufficient food. But Spain did not really try to make California grow; it was enough that the occupation should endure.

A realistic map of Spanish California would stretch from San Diego Bay past San Francisco Bay but cover only a narrow belt along the coast. The personnel involved was minimal. At the outset only a couple of hundred men arrived. Another three or four hundred men, women, and children came in the next dozen years. Most were clustered near the San Diego, Monterey, San Francisco, and Santa Barbara presidios, and substantial stretches along the 600-mile length had few or no Spanish-sent residents. Even in 1821 they and their descendants, the *gente de razón* (the Spanish culture bearers) were only a very few thousand, far outnumbered by the missionized Indians then approaching 20,000.

The Los Angeles district was not of top-level priority in Spanish plans. In 1771 it was chosen as site for the fourth mission, San Gabriel, and in 1797 for the seventeenth, San Fernando. Each drew two missionaries and a corporal's guard of soldiers. In 1781 the recruited pueblo founders, eleven families numbering forty-four persons, were brought up from Sinaloa. All told, that meant that the complement on which imperial Spain relied to render Spanish the entire area from the Santa Ana River through the San Fernando Valley was by modern reckoning no more than one busload.

The selections here relied on for description of the Los Angeles area in the Spanish period begin with the two earliest reportings in 1542 and 1602 and one much richer in detail on Gaspar de Portolá's ride through in 1769. Following are three reports on Mission San Gabriel, two on the origin of the pueblo, and the first application for grant of a rancho. On the next forty years, for reasons suggested, there is a great dearth of written record. Censuses and later evidence make clear that the Gabrielino were drawn in from most of their rancherías to live at

42

the missions or the pueblo or the ranchos. In dress, diet, and work they shifted markedly toward Spanish ways. Buildings of adobe, irrigated fields, gardens, orchards, and vineyards, horses to ride and mule trains for transport, and thousands of head of cattle, horses, sheep, and goats modified much of the landscape. Few though the agents of empire were, Los Angeles and its environs bore the unmistakable rubric of Spain.

First Glimpses of the Coast
JUAN RODRÍGUEZ CABRILLO

In 1542 as part of the climax of Spanish exploration which saw De Soto reaching the Mississippi, Coronado the Great Plains, and Villalobos the Philippine Islands, Juan Rodriguez Cabrillo made his voyage of discovery to the coast of California, from the Bay of San Miguel (later renamed San Diego) to Bay of Pines (later Monterey) and beyond. His San Salvador is San Clemente Island; his Vitoria is Santa Catalina; his Baia de los Fumos o Fuegos (Bay of Smoke or Fires) is identified as San Pedro; his large ensenada, Santa Monica Bay. By the time he reached Pueblo de las Canoas he was beyond Point Mugu and the county line. The one place in Los Angeles County where he came ashore was at Catalina.

On the Tuesday following, October 3, they, Cabrillo and his men, left San Miguel [San Diego], and Wednesday, Thursday, and Friday sailed on their course some eighteen leagues along the coast, where they saw many valleys and plains and many smokes and sierras inland. At nightfall they were close to some islands which are about seven leagues from the mainland, and as the wind died out they could not reach them that night. Saturday, the 7th, at daybreak, they reached them, and named them "San Salvador" and "Vitoria" [Santa Catalina]. They anchored at one and went ashore with the ship's boat to see if there were any people there. As the boat was nearing land a great number of Indians came out of the bushes and grass, shouting, dancing, and making signs to come ashore. As from the boats they saw the women fleeing, they made signs to them not to fear; so shortly they became assured and put their bows and arrows on the ground. Launching into the water a fine canoe containing eight or ten Indians, they came out to the ships. These were given some beads and presents with which they were well pleased, and shortly went back. The Spaniards afterwards went ashore and both the Indian men and women and everybody felt very secure. Here an old Indian made signs to them that men like the Spaniards, wearing clothes and having beards, were going around on the mainland. They remained at this island only until midday.

The Sunday following, the 8th, they came to the mainland in a large bay, which they named "Baia de los Fumos" [San Pedro] on account of the many smokes they saw there. Here they engaged in interchange with some Indians they captured in a canoe, who made signs to them that towards the north there were Spaniards like them. The bay is in 35°; it is an excellent harbor and the country is good, with many valleys, plains, and groves of trees. On the following Monday, the 9th, they sailed from the Baia de los Fuegos and that day went about six leagues, anchoring in a large *ensenada* [Santa Monica Bay]. From there they proceeded on the following day, Tuesday, some eight leagues along a northwest-southeast coast. They saw on land an Indian town close to the sea with large houses like those of New Spain, and they anchored in front of a large valley on the coast. Here many fine canoes holding twelve or thirteen Indians each came to the ships, and gave news of Christians who were going about inland. The coast runs northwest-southeast. Some presents were given them with which they were much pleased. They made signs that in seven days one could go to where the Spaniards were, so Juan Rodríguez decided to send on a chance two Spaniards inland with these Indians with a letter to the Christians. These explained besides that there was a large river. They named the town "Pueblo de las Canoas." The people wear some animal skins, are fisherman, and eat raw fish as well as maguey. The town is in 35° 20'. The country within is a very beautiful valley, and the Indians explained that inland in that valley there was much maize and food. Beyond this valley some high, very broken sierras were visible. They call the Christians *Taquimine*.

Summary Journal of the Cabrillo Expedition, in Henry R. Wagner, *Juan Rodríguez Cabrillo, Discoverer of the Coast of California* (San Francisco: California Historical Society, 1941), 46–47.

Along the Coast in 1602
ANTONIO DE LA ASCENSIÓN

In the sixty-year interval between the Cabrillo discovery and the inspection by Sebastián Vizcaíno, there were three recorded visits to California. In 1579 Francis Drake tarried for thirty-six days in Marin County, almost certainly on the ocean side because no mention is made of San Francisco Bay. In 1587 a commander of a Manila galleon en route to Mexico made a brief landing at Morro Bay and in 1595 another galleon hove to and was wrecked at Drake's Bay. Fray Antonio de la Ascensión was diarist for the Vizcaino expedition, outfitted in Mexico, and sent in 1602 to make a much more careful search for a California port with potential for usefulness to the annual Manila galleons. Vizcaíno's choice was Monterey.

A few leagues farther, they [the men of the Vizcaíno expedition] saw a large island, almost twelve leagues away from the mainland, and went to inspect it. This was the day of the martyr Santa Catalina, and for this reason it was named "Santa Catalina." They anchored near it

The Spaniards Steal the Scene

November 28 [November 25], but before reaching it another very much larger island southwest of it was seen, but as this was somewhat distant, they left it to be explored on the return. As the ships were approaching the Isla de Santa Catalina to cast anchor, the Indian inhabitants began to raise smokes on the beach, and when they saw they had anchored, the women, children, and old men began to shout and make demonstrations of joy in proof of their happiness. They came running to the beach to receive the guests who were arriving.

As soon as the ships anchored and the sails were furled, the *General* ordered the *Almirante* to go ashore and take with him Father Antonio, Captain Peguero with some soldiers from the *Capitana*, and Captain Alarcon with twenty-four soldiers, all armed with harquebuses and with their matches lit, to see what the Indians wanted, what there was in the island, and to bring back the information at once. When those who were with the *Almirante* landed, many old men, women, and children came up with much familiarity, friendship and affability, just as if they had seen Spaniards before. Our people asked them by signs for water. They at once brought a rush barrel full of water, which was good, and said that the spring from which they took it was somewhat distant. With this news they returned to the ships to pass the night. The following day the *General* ordered a tent to be set up on land in which Fathers Andrés and Antonio should say mass, Father Tomás being now sick. Then all went to hear mass. On this occasion a great number of young Indians had assembled, well built and robust, all naked. The day before these had been fishing in some small well-built canoes of boards fastened together, with their poops and bows like barks. Some of these canoes were so large that they would hold more than twenty people. In the small ones there are ordinarily three when they go fishing, two men with their paddles and two-bladed oars, seated or on their knees, one in the stern and the other in the bow, and a boy between to throw out such water as the canoe might make. They paddle on one side and the other in such unison and concert that they go flying. . . .

The boys and girls are white and blond, and all are affable and smiling. These Indians and those of the islands make use for their living quarters of some houses made like cabins. They cover these with a mat of rushes very closely woven, something like Moorish mats,

46

which they set up on some great upright forked poles. They are so spacious that each will hold fifty people. I think that a family lives in each one. As the houses are portable, they remove them to other places whenever it seems advisable. Neither rain nor the sun penetrates them. The vessels and pitchers in which they keep water are made of reeds. In the island there is a great quantity of something like potatoes, and small *xicamas*, which the Indians carry to the mainland to sell. They live by buying, selling and bartering. They showed us some pieces of the blue metal with which they paint themselves like the one I spoke of before. In this island and in those near by there are many Indians and many settlements and houses like those described.

The soldiers ran all over the island and in one part of it fell in with a place of worship or temple where the natives perform their sacrifices and adoration. This was a large flat patio and in one part of it, where they had what we would call an altar, there was a great circle all surrounded with feathers of various colors and shapes, which must come from the birds they sacrifice. Inside the circle there was a figure like a devil painted in various colors, in the way the Indians of New Spain are accustomed to paint them. At the sides of this were the sun and the moon. When the soldiers reached this place, inside the circle there were two large crows larger than ordinary ones, which flew away when they saw strangers, and alighted on some near-by rocks. One of the soldiers, seeing their size, aimed at them with his harquebus, and discharging it, killed them both. When the Indians saw this they began to weep and display great emotion. In my opinion, the Devil talked to them through these crows, because all the men and women hold them in great respect and fear. I saw with my own eyes some Indian women cleaning some fish on the beach for food for themselves and their husbands and children. Some crows came up to them and took this out of their hands with their bills, while they remained quiet without speaking a word or frightening them away, and were astonished to see the Spaniards throw stones at them. . . .

These Indians are very light-fingered and clever, and in stealing anything and in putting it in safety are ingenious. If it were not for being prolix in this chapter, I would relate here some of their transactions with us; I believe that they beat the gypsies in cunning and dexterity. Many of them wished to go with us, but this did not seem advisable, and so they were made to leave the ships and remain in their country. . . .

When the fleet was in sight of the mainland, and near one of the islands, which was named "Santa Barbara," the first of the channel, a canoe came flying out from the mainland with four men propelling it. Aboard was an Indian with his son and other Indians who accompanied him, who gave us to understand that he was the king or lord of that country. This canoe came up to the *Capitana*, and with great assiduity and swiftness made three turns around it, all those on board singing in their language in the manner and the tone in which the Indians of New Spain sing in their *mitotes*, or dances. They then came up to the ship and the principal Indian or petty king, grasping the end of the rope which was passed to them, came aboard without any suspicion or fear whatever, and the first thing he did on entering the ship was to make another three turns around the waist, singing in the same tone. This ceremony being concluded, standing before the *General* and the rest, he commenced a long harangue in his language, of which we could understand not a word. Having finished this, he explained by intelligible signs that the people of the Isla de Santa Catalina had notified him by four posts in canoes that the ships had arrived there and that the people on board wore clothes and beards and were kind-hearted and of good demeanor, having entertained them and given them many things, and that he should come to see us. By reason of this news he had come there to offer his country and what entertainment he could supply if we wished to receive it. He begged and prayed us to come to the shore with the ship, saying that he would provide us with everything necessary. As he did not see any women on the ship, he asked by signs if we had any, pointing to his private parts and giving us clearly to understand what he wished to say. The *General* told him he did not have any, nor were they necessary. The Indian then importuned the *General* with more energy for all to go ashore, promising to give each one ten women to serve them and entertain them. At this all of us laughed very much and the chief, thinking that we were deriding him, and that we thought he would not do what he promised, renewed his offers, and asked the *General* to send ashore a soldier in the canoe in which he had come to see with his own eyes if it was true that he could comply with what he had promised, saying that he would remain as a hostage with his son

48

while the soldier went and returned to inform himself about the truth of it. The *General* held a council about this, and it was decided that as it was already night nothing should be done until the following day, but that when it was dawn, some should go ashore to see if there was a safe and commodious port where the ships could remain at anchor, and if there was one, they would go there, and that the Indian should go back to his country that night to make the necessary arrangements. With this they dismissed him, the *General* having given him some things. He went away well paid and contented with the good behaviour and kindness which he saw in those whom he expected to have as guests on the following day, and to get something ready with which to entertain them.

Within an hour after the chief had gone back to his country a southeast wind came up, one they had not enjoyed before in all the time they had been sailing. As it was a stern wind it seemed to the *General* and the others that they should take advantage of the opportunity which Our Lord had provided, and that on the return voyage they could come back to see what the Indian chief wanted and had promised.

Translated in Henry R. Wagner, *Spanish Voyages to the Northwest Coast of America* (San Francisco: California Historical Society, 1929), 234–242.

First Travelers through the Land

Juan Crespi

Along with engineer Miguel Costansó, Fray Juan Crespi was principal diarist of the Portolá expedition of 1769 en route from San Diego to Monterey where it had been determined that the principal Spanish station in Alta California should be established. Cabrillo and Vizcaino had viewed the Los Angeles plain from shipboard. Portolá and his men were the first visitors to pass through it. Almost all the information they recorded was new: the earthquakes, the arable land readily irrigable where the Los Angeles River emerged from the pass from San Fernando Valley, the tar pits, the friendly and numerous Gabrielino.

49

The Spaniards Steal the Scene

Tuesday, August 1.—This day was one of rest, for the purpose of exploring, and especially to celebrate the jubilee of Our Lady of Los Angeles de Porciúncula. We [Crespi and the other missionary] both said Mass and the men took communion, performing the obligations to gain the great indulgence. At ten in the morning the earth trembled. The shock was repeated with violence at one in the afternoon, and one hour afterwards we experienced another. The soldiers went out this afternoon to hunt, and brought an antelope, with which animals this country abounds; they are like wild goats, but have horns rather larger than goats. I tasted the roasted meat, and it was not bad. Today I observed the latitude and it came out for us thirty-four degrees and ten minutes north latitude.

Wednesday, August 2.—We set out from the valley in the morning and followed the same plain in a westerly direction. After traveling about a league and a half through a pass between low hills, we entered a very spacious valley, well grown with cottonwoods and alders, among which ran a beautiful river [the Los Angeles] from the north-northwest, and then, doubling the point of a steep hill, it went on afterwards to the south. Toward the north-northeast there is another river bed [the Arroyo Seco] which forms a spacious water-course, but we found it dry. This bed unites with that of the river, giving a clear indication of great floods in the rainy season, for we saw that it had many trunks of trees on the banks. We halted not very far from the river, which we named Porciúncula. Here we felt three consecutive earthquakes in the afternoon and night. We must have traveled about three leagues today. This plain where the river runs is very extensive. It has good land for planting all kinds of grain and seeds, and is the most suitable site of all that we have seen for a mission, for it has all the requisites for a large settlement.

As soon as we arrived about eight heathen from a good village came to visit us; they live in this delightful place among the trees on the river. They presented us with some baskets of pinole made from seeds of sage and other grasses. Their chief brought some strings of beads made of shells, and they threw us three handfuls of them. Some of the old men were smoking pipes well made of baked clay and they puffed at us three mouthfuls of smoke. We gave them a little tobacco and glass beads, and they went away well pleased.

Thursday, August 3.—At half-past six we left the camp and forded

50

the Porciúncula River, which runs down from the valley, flowing through it from the mountains into the plain. After crossing the river we entered a large vineyard of wild grapes and an infinity of rose-bushes in full bloom. All the soil is black and loamy, and is capable of producing every kind of grain and fruit which may be planted. We went west, continually over good land well covered with grass. After traveling about half a league we came to the village of this region, the people of which, on seeing us, came out into the road. As they drew near us they began to howl like wolves; they greeted us and wished to give us seeds, but as we had nothing at hand in which to carry them we did not accept them. Seeing this, they threw some handfuls of them on the ground and the rest in the air.

We traveled over another plain for three hours, during which we must have gone as many leagues. In the same plain we came across a grove of very large alders, high and thick, from which flows a stream of water about a buey in depth. The banks were grassy and covered with fragrant herbs and watercress. The water flowed afterwards in a deep channel towards the southwest. All the land that we saw this morning seemed admirable to us. We pitched camp near the water. This afternoon we felt new earthquakes, the continuation of which astonishes us. We judge that in the mountains that run to the west in front of us there are some volcanoes, for there are many signs on the road which stretches between the Porciúncula River and the Spring of the Alders, for the explorers saw some large marshes of a certain substance like pitch; they were boiling and bubbling, and the pitch came out mixed with an abundance of water. They noticed that the water runs to one side and the pitch to the other, and that there is such an abundance of it that it would serve to caulk many ships. This place where we stopped is called the Spring of the Alders of San Estevan [Ballona Creek, west of Cienega].

Friday, August 4.—At half-past six in the morning we set out from the camp, following the plain to the northwest. At a quarter of a league we came to a little valley between small hills, and continued over plains of level land, very black and with much pasturage. After two hours travel, during which we must have covered about two leagues, we stopped at the watering place, which consists of two little springs that rise at the foot of a higher mesa. From each of the two springs runs a small stream of water which is soon absorbed; they are

51

both full of watercress and innumerable bushes of Castilian roses. We made camp near the springs, where we found a good village of very friendly and docile Indians, who, as soon as we arrived, came to visit us, bringing their present of baskets of sage and other seeds, small, round nuts with a hard shell, and large and very sweet acorns. They made me a present of some strings of beads of white and red shells which resemble coral, though not very fine; we reciprocated with glass beads. I understood that they were asking us if we were going to stay, and I said "No," that we were going farther on. I called this place San Gregorio, but to the soldiers the spot is known as the Springs of El Berrendo because they caught a deer alive there, it having had a leg broken the preceding afternoon by a shot fired by one of the volunteer soldiers, who could not overtake it. The water is in a hollow surrounded by low hills not far from the sea.

Saturday, August 5.—This day we set out about two in the afternoon, going north, as the explorers said that at the beach the mountains were steep and did not permit passage, so we veered somewhat to the northwest, where we saw that there was a pass in the mountains. We entered it by a canyon [Sepulveda] formed by steep hills on both sides, but at the end of it they were more accessible and permitted us to take the slope and ascend, though with difficulty, to the top, whence we saw a very pleasant and spacious valley. We descended to it and stopped close to the watering place, which is a very large pool. Near it we found a large village of heathen, very friendly and docile; they offered us their seeds in baskets and other things made of rushes. There were so many that if more of them had come with arms it would have caused us some suspicion, for we counted more than two hundred, men, women, and children. Each of them brought some food with which to regale us, and we reciprocated with beads and ribbons. The journey covered three leagues, and we gave to this plain the name of Valley of Santa Catalina de Bononia de los Encinos [now San Fernando Valley]. It is nearly three leagues wide and more than eight long. It has on its hills and in its valleys many live oaks and walnuts, though small. I took the latitude and it was thirty-four degrees and thirty-seven minutes.

Sunday, August 6.—This day we both said Mass, which was attended by everybody, and then we rested, receiving innumerable visits from heathen who came to see us from different parts. They had heard of the sailing of the packets to the coast and channel of Santa Barbara; they drew on the ground the shape of the channel with its islands, marking the route of the ships. They told us also that in other times bearded people, clothed and armed as they saw the soldiers, had come into their country, motioning that they had come from the east. One of them said he had been to their countries and had seen their towns formed of large houses, and that each family occupied its own. He added, besides, that in a few days march, about seven or eight leagues to the north, we would come to a great river which ran between rough mountains and could not be forded, and that farther on we would see the ocean, which would prevent us from going on in this direction. The information gave us some anxiety, but we put it off to be settled by our own eyes; therefore we are going to continue our journey with our most holy patron San José.

Monday, August 7.—A little before three in the afternoon we set out to the north and crossed the plain, which is about three leagues wide, and went to camp at the foot of the mountains in a very green valley grown with large live oaks and alders. The water was sufficient for the animals though not over abundant; it runs among rushes and reeds.

Tuesday, August 8.—About half-past six in the morning we left the place and traveled through the same valley, approaching the mountains. Following their course about half a league, we ascended by a sharp ridge to a high pass [San Fernando], the ascent and descent of which was painful, the descent being made on foot because of the steepness. Once down we entered a small valley in which there was a village of heathen, who had already sent messengers to us at the valley of Santa Catalina de Bononia to guide us and show us the best road and pass through the mountains. These poor Indians had many provisions ready to receive us. Seeing that it was our intention to go on in order not to lose the march, they urgently insisted that we should go to their village, which was some distance off the road; and we were obliged to consent in order not to displease them. We enjoyed their good will and their presents, which consisted of some baskets of pinole, made of sage and other kinds of grasses, and at the side of these baskets they had others for us to drink from. They gave us also nuts and acorns, and were presented with beads in return. They furnished some other guides to accompany us; and we went on by the same valley, arriving late at the watering place, after a march of about four leagues.

The country from the village to the watering place is delightful and beautiful in the plain, although the mountains that surround it are bare and rough. In the plain we saw many tall and thick cottonwoods and oaks; the watering place consists of an arroyo with a great deal of water which runs in a moderately wide valley, well grown with willows and cottonwoods. We stopped on the bank of the arroyo, where we found a populous village in which the people lived without any cover, for they had no more than a light shelter fenced in like a corral. For this reason the soldiers called it Ranchería del Corral, and I called it Santa Rosa de Viterbo, that this saint might be protector for the conversion of these Indians. As soon as we arrived they gave us many baskets of different kinds of seeds, and a sort of sweet preserve like raisins, and another resembling honeycomb, very sweet and purging, and made of the dew which sticks to the reed grass. It is a very suitable site for a mission, with much good land, many palisades, two very large arroyos of water, and five large villages close together.

Diary of Juan Crespi, in Herbert E. Bolton, *Fray Juan Crespi, Missionary Explorer* (Berkeley: University of California Press, 1927), 146–154.

Founding Mission San Gabriel
FRANCISCO PALOU

Appropriately enough, the first California biography was the life of the first head of the missions, Fr. Junipero Serra, by his closest associate, Fr. Francisco Palou. The eighteenth century was a time of miracles and of human frailties. Early on, San Gabriel witnessed examples of each.

On the 6th of August, 1771, the Fathers, Fr. Pedro Cambón and Fr. Angel Somera, guarded by ten soldiers, left San Diego, accompanied also by the muleteers carrying the equipment. They traveled northward along the trail marked out by the [Portolá] Expedition. After going about forty leagues they arrived at the Rio de los Temblores (River of the Earthquakes) as it had been named, and just as they were in the act of deciding as to the location of the Mission, a great multitude of gentiles came up, all armed and under the direction of two captains who, with blood-curdling yells, tried to hinder the proceedings.

As the Fathers feared that a battle was imminent which would surely result in the death of not a few, one of them produced a canvas on which was painted the image of Our Lady of Sorrows and held it up in view of the barbarians. He had scarcely done this when they all, subdued by the vision of this beautiful image, threw down their bows and arrows and came running hastily forward. The two captains threw down at the feet of the Sovereign Queen the beads and trinkets which they wore about their necks, as a sign of their greatest respect and also to indicate that they wished to make peace with out company. They invited all the people from the surrounding villages who, in great numbers, men, women and children, kept coming in to see the Most Holy Virgin, bringing with them loads of various grains which they left at the feet of Our Most Holy Lady, supposing that she needed them for food the same as the rest.

Similar demonstrations had been made by the gentile women of the port of San Diego after the inhabitants of that region had been pacified. When the Fathers exhibited there another image of our Lady, the Virgin Mary with the Holy Child Jesus in her arms, as soon as it was made known in the surrounding ranches, they all came in to see it, and as they were not allowed to enter, being excluded by the stockade, they called to the Fathers and thrusting their full breasts between the poles sought to express in this vivid way their desire to give suck to that beautiful little child of which they had heard from the Fathers.

The sight of the image of Our Lady produced a wonderful change upon the gentiles surrounding the Mission of San Gabriel, and they came very often to visit the friars, seemingly not able to sufficiently express their joy that they should have come to live among them, and the desire to show their gratitude by their good will and their presents.

The Fathers proceeded to explore the whole wide plain and began the Mission in the place which they considered most suitable, using the same ceremonies which have been referred to in the founding of the other Missions. The first Mass was celebrated under a little shelter made of branches on the day of the Nativity of Our Lady, the 8th of September, and on the next day work was begun on the chapel which was to serve as a provisional church, and also a house for the Fathers and another for the troops, all made of poles and surrounded by a stockade as a precaution against possible attack. The greater part of the wood for the building was cut down and dragged in by the pagans themselves, who also helped in the construction of the houses, and for this reason the Fathers were encouraged to hope for a great success in the work, seeing that from the very beginning there was no opposition to the gentle yoke of our Evangelical Law.

At the time when the natives seemed to be most content their good disposition toward us was seriously upset by an outrage committed by one of the soldiers upon one of the head chiefs of the village, and what was worse, by committing a sin against God Our Lord. As the gentile chief naturally thought of taking vengeance for the outrage committed against himself and his wife, he gathered together all his neighbors from the near-by villages and inviting all of the warriors to arm themselves, he led them down to the place in the field where two of the soldiers of the Mission were pasturing and taking care of the horses, one of them being the evil-doer.

As soon as the soldiers saw the armed band approaching they put on their leather jackets as a defence against the arrows and prepared themselves for battle, as there was no way by which they could advise the captain of the guard, who, by the way, was ignorant of the deed committed by the soldier. The gentiles had no sooner come within bow-shot, when they began to let fly their arrows, aiming all of them against the offending soldier. The latter immediately aimed his gun at the Indian who seemed to him to be the boldest, presuming that he was the captain, and discharging his piece, killed him on the spot. As soon as the others saw the deadly force of this new weapon, whose effect they had never before experienced, and when they also saw that their arrows did no harm, they turned and fled, leaving the unhappy captain dead upon the ground. From this deed the Indians became very much frightened. . . .

The pagans, little by little, came to forget the deed of the soldier and the death of their chief, and to bring in some of their children to be baptized. One of the first of these children was the son of the unfortunate chieftain whom the widow gladly gave to the Fathers for this purpose, and her example was followed by many others, so that the number of Christians began to increase. Two years after the founding of the Mission, on the occasion of my visit to it, they had baptized seventy-three, and at the time of the death of our Venerable Father (Junípero Serra, in 1784) the number was 1,019 neophytes.

Francisco Palou, *Relación Histórico de la Vida y Apostólicas Tareas de . . . Junípero Serra* (1787), translated by C. Scott Williams (Pasadena, 1913), 126–129.

Three Tortillas a Day
JUAN BAUTISTA DE ANZA

Juan Bautista de Anza is a California hero honored for braving the desert crossing in 1774, opening a land route from Sonora to the new province of Alta California, and returning the next winter with a large reinforcement. On his first arrival at San Gabriel he and his twenty men were an embarrassing guest list for a mission community on short supply.

Having with some difficulty effected the crossing of the river of the mission of San Gabriel, which is established in Northern California, I reached the mission just at sunset, and immediately made my arrival known to the corporal and the eight soldiers who constitute its guard.

In the mission there were four friars *de propaganda fide* of the College of San Fernando de Mexico. They welcomed us with great jubilation and demonstrations of joy, with solemn peal of the bells and the chanting of the *Te Deum*, as an act of thanksgiving for our successful arrival in this country. This was all the more pleasing to them because it was unexpected, since they had no more than a vague rumor of this expedition, which they even considered to be impracticable. Even after these friars and soldiers saw us they could not quite persuade themselves that we were from the province of Sonora, nor that so few men would undertake such a journey, nor that Sonora, and especially the Colorado River, could be so near by. . . .

March 23.— . . . With a view to continuing my route I asked various questions of the missionary fathers here.

I asked the minister himself if he could aid me with some provisions and mounts with which to make the journey, since I lacked both. Although he was generous in the matter, he made plain to me his inability, for with respect to provisions he was so hard up that he himself, his three companions, and the guard, had no other ration than three tortillas of maize and some herbs from the fields; and as for mounts, he needed the few animals which the mission possesses to send to the port of San Diego for some provisions for all these friars and their reduced Indians who are in such straightened circumstances, because the frigate mentioned is anchored there. And since the establishments from here forward, as far as the presidio of Monte Rey, which this frigate has not been able to reach, although it has attempted it, are in worse circumstances, I was not disposed to demand more than what this friar offered me, and this meant that for fifteen days I must maintain myself with all my men on the rations mentioned, which I accepted with thanks until I might find recourse elsewhere. . . .

March 25.—I sent four soldiers with seven pack mules to seek provisions at the port of San Diego. . . .

April 5.—At twelve o'clock today the men sent to the port of San Diego returned with replies from the commanders hereinbefore named, who tell me that, try as hard as they may, they can not provide more supplies than those which they are sending, these consisting of six fanegas of maize half spoiled, a tierce of jerked beef almost unfit to eat, a tierce of flour, and two fanegas of beans.

Having made a calculation from the foregoing of the time that the men of my expedition can be maintained, it is found to be scarcely sixteen days, even making use of all the beans. But these can be used here only on condition that they lend the soldiers ollas in which to cook them, for after setting out on the march, for lack of these ollas this grain can not serve as food. And the same is true of the maize, since it is not of the kind that can be reduced to pinole, which is the regular ration of the soldiers.

In view of the foregoing, the provisions are not sufficient for making our journey to Monte Rey, for we shall not be able to accomplish it in two weeks, not having reserved any extra riding animals, and ours being in such a bad condition as has been stated before. And this would be worse if we should go on to that presidio, for those experienced in the road consider it very difficult because of the many mires, and because of the continuance of the heavy rains which are being experienced the same as here, where they do not cease.

I have therefore decided, in conference with one of the fathers . . . that the present father shall return to the Colorado River with most of the troops, to await me there till I return from the presidio of Monte Rey. And to Monte Rey I shall go with six soldiers in light order of marching, to examine its situation, and in the light of this information to form a more exact opinion regarding the road which may be opened to it from Sonora, since the plan which I desired to follow and was set down on the 23rd of last month is now impossible. And I shall set out for that presidio on the 10th of this present month.

Diary of Juan Bautista de Anza, in Herbert Eugene Bolton, *Anza's California Expeditions* (Berkeley: University of California Press, 1930), II, 205–209.

The Mission Flourishes
PEDRO FONT

Having opened an overland route to California in 1774, Juan Bautista de Anza was instructed to return over that route in

The Spaniards Steal the Scene

1775–76 with soldiers, settlers, and their families, and with a herd of cattle. Early in 1776 this much larger caravan of 240 persons arrived at Mission San Gabriel, now on its new site. This excerpt is from the book-length diary of the second expedition.

Thursday, January 4, [1776].—I said Mass. We set out from the Arroyo de San Gabriel at nine oclock in the morning, and at eleven arrived at the mission of San Gabriel, having traveled some two leagues to the west-southwest, inclining somewhat to the west.—Two leagues.

The mission of San Gabriel is situated about eight leagues from the sea in a site of most beautiful qualities, with plentiful water and very fine lands. The site is level and open, and is about two leagues from the Sierra to the north, which from the pass of San Carlos we had on our right as we came along. It appears that here ends the snow but not the sierra, which is the same Sierra Madre de California; for it continues far into the interior, and according to all the signs is the same continuous sierra which Father Garcés crossed in his journey hither and called the Sierra de San Marcos. On setting out from camp we crossed the bed of a large river which was without water and has a thick grove of small cottonwoods. This is the river which runs to the old site of the mission, where there is always plentiful water.

At the mission we found the captain commander of Monterey, Don Fernando Ribera y Moncada, who, on account of the uprising of the Indians of the mission of San Diego, who destroyed it and killed their father minister, Father Fray Luis Jaume, had come from Monterey to go to the presidio, arriving at this mission on the night of the 2d. Shortly before we arrived Commander Ribera and the father minister of the mission, Fray Antonio Paterna, came out on the road to welcome us. Our coming was a matter for great rejoicing by everybody, the guard of the mission welcoming us with a volley, and the two other fathers who were here, Father Fray Antonio Cruzado and Father Fray Miguel Sánchez, with many peals of bells and with special demonstrations of joy.

The Mission Flourishes

Friday, January 5.—We remained here to rest, and the commanders conferred concerning the matter of the rebellion of the Indians of San Diego. After dinner I went with Father Sánchez to see the creek from which they made the acequia for this mission of San Gabriel, and with which it has the best of conveniences. For, besides the fact that the acequia is adequate, and passes in front of the house of the fathers and of the little huts of the Christian Indians who compose this new mission (who must be some five hundred souls recently converted, counting large and small), it is above all the plains of the immediate vicinity, which are suitable for planting or for crops, and for this reason the fields are near the pueblo. This mission has such fine advantages for crops and such good pastures for cattle and horses that nothing better could be desired. The cows which they have are very fat and they give much and rich milk, with which they make cheese and very good butter. They raise hogs and have a small flock of sheep, of which on our arrival they killed three or four wethers which they had. Their flesh was especially good, and I do not remember having eaten fatter or finer mutton. They also have a few hens.

This mission has plentiful live oaks and other trees for building timber, and consequently there is abundant firewood. It lacks only lime, which up to the present has not been found; but perhaps by careful search it will be found and will make possible the improvement of the buildings, which at present are partly adobe, but chiefly of logs and tule, and which for this reason are very insecure and exposed to fire. At present the buildings consist of a very long shed, all of one room with three divisions, which serves as a habitation for the fathers and for a granary and everything. Somewhat apart from this building there is a rectangular shed which serves as a church, and near this another which is the guardhouse, as they call it, or the quarters of the soldiers, eight in number, who serve the mission as guard; and finally some little huts of tule which are the houses of the Indians, between which and the house of the fathers the acequia runs.

In the creek celery and other plants which look like lettuce, and some roots like parsnips, grow naturally; and nearby there are many turnips, which from a little seed which was scattered took possession of the land. And near the site of the old mission, which is distant from

61

this new one about a league to the south, there is grown a great abundance of watercress, of which I ate liberally. In short, this is a country which, as Father Paterna says, looks like the Promised Land, although the fathers have suffered in it many hardships and toils, because beginnings are always difficult, especially in lands where formerly there was nothing; and besides, they suffered want because for two years the supplies failed them.

The converted Indians of this mission ... appear to be gentle, friendly and of good hearts. The men are of medium stature, the women being somewhat smaller, round-faced, flat-faced, and rather ugly. The costume of the men in heathendom is total nakedness, while the women wear a bit of deer skin with which they cover themselves, and likewise an occasional cloak of beaver or rabbit skin, although the fathers endeavor to clothe the converted Indians with something as best they can.

The method which the fathers observe in the conversion is not to oblige anyone to become a Christian, admitting only those who voluntarily offer themselves, and this they do in the following manner: Since these Indians are accustomed to live in the fields and the hills like beasts, the fathers require that if they wish to be Christians they shall no longer go to the forest, but must live in the mission; and if they leave the ranchería, as they call the little village of huts and houses of the Indians, they will go to seek them and will punish them. With this they begin to catechize the heathen who voluntarily come, teaching them to make the sign of the cross and other things necessary, and if they persevere in the catechism for two or three months and in the same frame of mind, when they are instructed they proceed to baptise them.

If any Indian wishes to go to the mountain to see his relatives or to hunt acorns, they give him permission for a specified number of days. As a rule they do not fail to return, and sometimes they come bringing some heathen relative, who remains for the catechism, either through the example of the others or attracted by the *pozole* (porridge), which they like better than their herbs and the foods of the mountain; and so these Indians are usually caught by the mouth.

Diary of Pedro Font, in Herbert E. Bolton, *Anza's California Expeditions* (Berkeley: University of California Press, 1930), IV, 174–182.

Recommending a Pueblo on the Porciúncula

PHELIPE DE NEVE

In 1777 the governor of the Californias was ordered to transfer the seat of government to Monterey. Rather than taking ship, he chose to ride up the trail from Loreto, inspecting the province as he went. In a report to the viceroy, dated June 7, 1777, he comments discerningly on the state of the province, the hazards of relying on the irregular rains, the obstacles to successful farming at the presidios, and the logic of establishing pueblos at sites where irrigation could readily be applied. Later in the year he drew enough people from the presidial communities of San Francisco and Monterey to establish the Pueblo of San José on the Guadalupe, hard by Mission Santa Clara. He asked authorization and support for another pueblo on the Porciúncula. In 1779, in his Reglamento, or Fundamental Laws for California, he spelled out in detail the procedures for recruiting settlers in Mexico, outfitting and conducting them to this remote province, and subsidizing them over a period of years until the town became self-sufficient and supportive of the presidios. This second pueblo would be Los Angeles.

Sir:

From the superior instructions which Your Excellency deigned to issue me at the time you notified me of the decision of His Majesty that I transfer my residence from Loreto to this place, I gained the idea that no other service could have so much importance as to encourage sowing, planting, and raising of cattle of all sorts at the three presidios, as well as to aid settlers, giving them all possible assistance applicable to agriculture and the raising of cattle, so that a few sites may produce the necessities to make these new establishments self-supporting, thereby avoiding the growing costs occasioned the Royal Treasury for the forwarding of grain, fruits, and cattle and the obvious risk to which they must be exposed by being dependent for all subsistence on the risks, losses, and other incidents which befall the ships which transport them.

To this end and that of reporting to Your Excellency what may be harvested at each place, I applied myself diligently to examine the lands, arroyos (intermittent streams), and watering places encountered in my march to this presidio, as well as in the one that I later made to that of San Francisco, and particularly the immediate environs of the presidios or those which it was supposed in common opinion would meet my desire, which remained frustrated at the presidios, afflicted as they are by the irregularity of the rains in this country, the scarcity of arroyos, springs of water, and running streams that are abundant and permanent, and the difficulties that offer at many of the places to make use of the waters on lands appropriately situated for this purpose. . . .

All the plains, valleys, and hills of this Northern California, with the exception of some very sharp rocky outcrops and sierras, are covered with herbage according to the quality, abundance, and fruitfulness of its pasture, which the rains fertilize, and for the duration of the rainy season their verdure is most rich and abundant with grass seed, the common foodstuff of these natives.

The rains regularly begin with small showers in the month of November; they become heavier in December, and in years of abundance the rains of January and February follow; they decline in March and in April or May only a few showers are experienced. In this sequence and abundance the rains were observed in 70 and 71, the years following the occupation of this port, a circumstance which led them to believe that these lands were suitable for all sorts of grain along the rivers, arroyos, and watering places, which later they came to know by experience was not so, and that only in such years would the lands have enough moisture to produce wheat or maize without irrigation.

The following years of 72 and 73 and 74 none of them had this benefit (with the exception of Carmel, whose lands bordered the arroyo and various lakes and had more moisture because of being close to these waters. In 75 the rains were abundant only at the mission of San Diego; that of Carmel and Monterey gathered a harvest of wheat without irrigation, but the former mission and the presidio lost their crops in 76 and 77, and in part others, but Carmel produced maize which was not irrigated (nevertheless it produced in certain fields and even that which volunteered from the preceding year). At this mission, noting the bad production, they were obliged this year to begin work on a diversion of water, in which operation they are now engaged, notwithstanding that there is not a permanent flow of water in the arroyo or in the lakes, one or the other of which was dry last year. . . .

From the foregoing I deduce that in the years which follow the rains, there will be yields in the valleys and humid lands of some crops of wheat but not of maize, for the waters at hand being most abundant in April, the time in which they are regularly sustained in this country, it cannot be produced by the said blessed mission of San Diego or that of San Antonio which have not enjoyed a harvest of this crop since their foundation.

The presidio of San Diego has various plots of land by the arroyo (which regularly is dry in May). In years of average rainfall they can make a crop of wheat, with the methods tried at the mission, which is situated on the same arroyo, and about two leagues from the presidio, with better land. In order to reap the one harvest above-mentioned, by giving it the benefit of some irrigation—and according to report it does not have a place with water running from the sierra with lands suitable for a short harvest of maize—they had to protect the clearing maintained there with an escort because there was there a large number of villages of Indians.

The unoccupied places along the main trail from San Diego to Monterey with the amount of waters to benefit cultivation are: the Santa Ana River some 28 leagues from San Diego, having abundant water and not difficult to divert as observed; at 7 leagues the San Gabriel River with much water and lands for increasing crops and with evidence of not much difficulty in diverting water about a league from the mission of the same name, which is not served by these waters because water comes very abundant and conveniently to its lands from various springs at the foot of the mountains.

Three leagues from that mission is found the Porciúncula River with much water easy to take on either bank and beautiful lands in which it all could be made use of. . . .

Farther on is the Guadalupe River, on whose banks is situated the mission of Santa Clara. It is more abundant in water and the taking of the water is not difficult by taking it in a canyon eight or ten yards wide, it can and does benefit much land on both banks, on one of which is established the mission. . . .

[Considering the deficiencies of the presidial and other sites,] I have no better advice to submit but that Your Excellency in your wisdom order the recruiting of 50 or 60 field workers or laborers to people the said localities, or rather dividing them into two groups to go to the Santa Clara and the Porciúncula.

[There follows a detailed description of subsidy in money, rations, colonizing equipment, seed and stock that should be provided for these settlers individually and collectively.]

(s) Phelipe de Neve (rubric)

Most Excellent Sir, Knight Commander
don Antonio Bucareli y Ursúa

Neve to Bucareli, Monterey, June 7, 1777. Archivo General de la Nación, Mexico, Provincias Internas, 121.

Instructions for the Recruitment of the Original Settlers of the Pueblo of Los Angeles

TEODORO DE CROIX

At Arispe in Sonora, on December 27, 1779, the commandant of the Interior Provinces of New Spain issued instructions in forty-two numbered paragraphs on the recruiting of soldiers and settlers for the reinforcement of California. Croix was implementing the proposal made by Governor Neve.

Instruction to be observed by Captain Don Fernando de Rivera y Moncada in the recruiting and equipment of families of settlers and of troops, assembling of mounts, and transportation of these and further auxiliaries solicited by and granted to Colonel Don Phelipe Neve, Governor of California, for the defense, benefit and conservation of the new and old establishments of that Peninsula (Upper as well as Lower California). . . .

6. For the recruital and gathering of the mounts, I do not limit the territory, but assign to the Comisionado the provinces of Ostimuri, Sinaloa and the rest which extend to Guadalajara. . . .

7. Twenty-four families and 59 men are at present needed in California to erect a new Presidio and Town, but if this number is taken from the territories under my charge (the Provincias Internas), there will be a scarcity what with the number which already has been taken out, and with the numbers which in future may be withdrawn for the necessary repopulation of Sonora; which is equally to the interest of California, since the two Provinces should be united and have communication one with the other through the establishments on the Rivers Colorado and Gila. And while it is expedient for them and for those of the Peninsula to secure recruits in these interior territories, it is also certain that . . . it will be necessary to apply to the neighboring provinces, commonly called *tierra afuera*, (south of Sonora). . . .

10. The head or father of each family must be a man of the soil, *Labrador de exercicio*, healthy, robust, and without known vice or defect that would make him prejudicial to the Pueblos. For these will be situated in the midst of a numerous population of Gentiles, docile and without malice, but susceptible, like all Indians, to the first impressions of good or bad example set by the Spanish who settle among them aiming to civilize them with good treatment and to win them happily through the practice of true justice and good deeds to a knowledge of our Sacred Religion, and the Sweet Dominion of our Catholic Monarch.

11. Among the said families must be included a mason, a carpenter who knows how to make yokes, ploughs, solid wooden wheels, and *carretas*, and a blacksmith, who will do if he knows how to make ploughshares, pick-axes, and crowbars.

12. The soldier recruits for California must be married, and of the same qualities and conditions as must be the settlers, adding those of greater strength and endurance for the hardships of the frontier service.

15. From the day on which enlisted, the recruits must receive: those who are destined for California and Sonora, the goods allotted to them respectively according to the Reglamentos of that province and of these frontier provinces; and the *vecino poblador* (the settler) his salary of 10 pesos a month and the customary rations. . . .

18. The *vecinos pobladores* shall enlist in the proper mode and for the same period of ten years, for either the Pueblo of San Joseph de Guadalupe or of La Reyna de los Angeles de la Porciúncula, adding after their own declarations those of their wives, sons, daughters and sisters or unmarried female relatives who of their own will desire to accompany them, for to these latter there offers the possibility that they may marry members of the troops who remain single in California for lack of Spanish women, according to the notices communicated to this Superior Government. . . .

Teodoro de Croix to Fernando de Rivera y Moncada, Arispe, December 27, 1779, Archivo General de la Nacion, Provincias Internas, 122. Translated by Marion Parks in Historical Society of Southern California, *Publication*, 1931.

The Pueblo of Los Angeles Is Founded

EDWIN A. BEILHARZ

In 1777 when Phelipe de Neve came to govern California 146 soldiers and a score of Franciscans were spread thin at eight stations from San Diego to San Francisco. Even for food the soldiers depended on shipments from Mexico. Neve regularized the government, procured reinforcements, and, among other improvements, established two pueblos which in time

68

The Pueblo of Los Angeles Is Founded

could be expected to provide food and horses for the presidial soldiers and recruits for military service. Here quoted is a passage from a succinct scholarly biography of this extraordinarily capable governor.

[Governor Phelipe de Neve] left Monterey in the early part of May [1781], and set out for the south to meet the expected parties [of settlers] and carry out the projects he had planned. He arrived at Mission San Gabriel and set up headquarters there, close to the site of the proposed town. On May 16 he wrote to Croix from the mission that he had received a report that the Los Angeles settlers had set out from Loreto in the wake of the party of soldiers. They were under the custody of Lieutenant José Zúñiga.

These settlers, their families and military escort crossed into Upper California and arrived at Mission San Gabriel on August 18. Some of the children in the party had just got over the smallpox, so, to keep the contagion from spreading, the whole group was held in quarantine some two and a half miles from the mission till all danger was passed.

While they waited, Neve busied himself making plans and drawing up instruction for the laying out of the town. He had the task finished by August 26. The town, he ordered, should be placed in the area he specified, so that the boundary of its pueblo lands included all the irrigable area. The dam and the irrigated land must be located in relation to each other so as to get the maximum volume of water. The plaza and residences were to be placed as close to the river or irrigation ditch as possible, for the sake of convenience, but they must be on ground high enough to be safe from floods, and to make it possible for the people to see their fields and get the benefit of the winds.

The plaza was to be 200 feet wide by 300 feet long, placed so as to present its corners to the cardinal points of the compass and thus be shielded somewhat from the direct north wind. Around the plaza, building lots of twenty by forty *varas* (55 by 110 feet) should be parcelled out, leaving one of the sides on the east free for public buildings and a town church. A vacant space, 200 *varas* (about 550

69

feet) wide, should be left between the town and planting fields, to be parcelled out as the population grew. Connecting streets were to be let into the plaza at right angles, four to a side if the corner streets were counted.

The planting fields should be squares, 200 *varas* each way. Each settler should receive two which could be irrigated and two which could not, the rest being reserved for partitioning to future settlers. The plots should be numbered and then drawn by lot (whence the name, *suertes*). The man drawing number one should be given number two also, and so on, so each man's land would be in one parcel.

Neve ordered Corporal José Vicente Feliz to conduct the settlers to the selected site, and there, on September 4, 1781, Feliz made the distribution of *solares*, or house lots, and *suertes*, or planting fields. With that, the town was born. It was called El Pueblo de la Reina de los Angeles, the Town of the Queen of the Angels. Neve reported the founding on November 19, 1781, and Croix sent the news on to Spain, February 28, 1782:

"The Governor of the Peninsula of the Californias, Don Phelipe de Neve, informed me last November 19 that he completed on September 4 the establishment of the new town of the Queen of the Angels on the bank of the Porciúncula River, with the settlers recruited by the late Captain Fernando de Rivera, who made their journey by sea [across to Baja California].

"The new town in question is forty-five leagues from the Presidio of San Diego, twenty-seven leagues from the designated Presidio of Santa Bárbara, and about one and a half leagues from Mission San Gabriel.

"To the twelve settlers [only eleven arrived] who compose it, and who [with their families] come to forty-six [forty-four] persons of both sexes and all ages, there have been distributed the mules, mares, cows, calves, sheep and goats, the planting fields and farming tools, on the basis of a loan from the royal treasury for the tools and animals.

"I pass this report on to you so that you may inform His Majesty, and send me his sovereign views.

"[Minister] José de Gálvez replied on October 29, 1782, from the Escorial, that he had given the news to the King.

Twelve settlers had set out for the settlement at Los Angeles, but one of them, Antonio Miranda, did not arrive for the actual founding. The ones who did were José Navarro, Basilio and Alejandro Rosas, Antonio Villavicensio, José Vanegas, Pablo Rodrígues, Manuel Camero, José Moreno, José Lara, Luis Quintero, and Antonio Mesa. Three were of Spanish blood, at least in part, two were negroes, two mulattoes, and four were Indians. Three of them, Lara, Mesa, and Quintero, were dropped from the list by March 21, 1782. The remaining eight are Los Angeles' founding fathers. With their families, they gave Los Angeles a starting population of thirty-two.

As in the case of San José (founded by Neve in 1777), the town took firm root in the new soil, bringing into the life of California a new element, neither ecclesiastical nor military. The King's officers and soldiers would disappear with their presidios in the turmoil of the colonial revolt against Spain. The missions would collapse in the secularizations of 1834 through 1836. The civilian population alone would survive and flourish. Los Angeles today is second only to Mexico City in the number of inhabitants who carry the blood and speak the beautiful tongue of the old viceroyalty of New Spain. San José is second only to Los Angeles of California cities in its population of Spanish speech. It also, with its burgeoning growth, bids fair to fill the Santa Clara Valley and become the Los Angeles of the north. The two cities have much in common—not least, that they occupy the most extensive plains in the coastal area of California. That is why Neve chose them.

Edwin A. Beilharz, *Felipe de Neve: First Governor of California* (San Francisco: California Historical Society, 1971), 107–109.

Petition for a Land Grant
MANUEL PÉREZ NIETO

Along with presidio, mission, and pueblo, another Spanish institution took root in California, the rancho. Under Spain the Los Angeles area came to have a dozen ranchos; under Mexico, a couple of hundred. The concept persists today, as wit-

*ness a station wagon with name plate, No Tengo Rancho, (I
Dont Have a Rancho). The pedigree of every real rancho
began with an application to the authorities, such as Manuel
Pérez Nietos in 1784, which at its ultimate yielded him some
167,000 acres of grazing land.*

Sir:

Manuel Pérez Nieto, soldier of the Royal Presidio of San Diego,
before Your Worship with the greatest and due honour, appears and
says: That in attention to the fact that I have my herd of horses as
well as of bovine stock at the Royal Presidio of San Diego, and because they are increasing and because I have no place to graze them,
and likewise because I have no designated place, I request Your Worship's charity that you be pleased to assign me a place situated at three
leagues distance from the Mission of San Gabriel along the road to the
Royal Presidio of San Carlos de Monterey named La Zanja, contem-

Land Claim 376 SD, Bancroft Library

*Rancho Paso de la Tijera was granted to Vicente Sánchez in 1843.
The orientation of this diseño is southward toward the Baldwin Hills.*

72

plating Sir, not to harm a living soul, principally the Mission of San Gabriel, or even less the Pueblo of the Queen of the Angels. I humbly request of Your Worship's superior government that it see fit to decide as I have requested, for if it is so, I shall receive a gift, and shall consider myself most favored, and therefore:

To Your Worship I humbly beg and request that you be pleased to decide along the tenor of my petition or as it may be to your superior pleasure, and I swear to all the necessary and that this my petition is not done in malice, nor least of all to injure any one, and not knowing how to sign I made the sign of the Cross.

(Signed) †

Attached to this petition as a marginal note:

I grant the petitioner the permission of having the bovine stock and horses at the place of La Zanja, or its environs; provided no harm is done to the Mission San Gabriel nor to the Pagan Indians of its environs in any manner whatsoever; and that he must have some one to watch it, and to go and sleep at the aforementioned Pueblo.

(signed) Pedro Fages

San Gabriel, October 21, 1784

Petition in the National Archives, Washington, D.C., Expediente No. 103, Santa Gertrudis.

The Country Town of the Angels

JOHN CAUGHEY

In 1975 the California Supreme Court settled a dispute between the City of Los Angeles and two hundred of its upstream neighbors (Burbank, Glendale, Forest Lawn, Lockheed, et al.) by upholding its pueblo right to the waters of the Los Angeles River and drainage basin. This decision took into

73

account the hydrology of the San Fernando Valley as a col-
lecting basin for natural underground storage, return flow of
spread and applied waters, and other technical matters. Ul-
timately the decision rested on the origin of Los Angeles as a
Spanish frontier pueblo intended for permanence and for
growth and with water for its irrigation and domestic needs as
its prime asset. This essay is drawn from one of the working
papers in that twenty-year litigation.

For forty years, 1781 to 1821, Los Angeles was a Spanish Pueblo. The
archives in Mexico and Spain contain the official correspondence on
the decision to establish the Pueblo and on Rivera's recruiting. Two
entire volumes detail the outlay for rations, equipment, and escort of
the founding settlers to Baja California, and on to the selected site.
Thereafter the documentation is very scanty. No description was
written of the actual founding of the pueblo on September 4, 1781.
The Los Angeles City Archives have nothing on the Spanish period.
The Provincial Archives were dissipated in mid-nineteenth century,
and most that remained was lost in the San Francisco Fire. A few
transcripts survive in the records of certain land title cases and others
in abstract or copy made for historian Hubert Howe Bancroft in the
1880s. The deeper trouble is that most of the residents were not
literate and, although insisting on regular reporting by governors and
missionaries, imperial Spain asked much less of pueblos.

For California and particularly Monterey and San Francisco, foreign visitors provided some of the most illuminating descriptions in
this period. Spanish Los Angeles was seldom visited. Father Serra
came in 1782. The total report on his visit reads: "On March 18, very
late in the day, he arrived at the new town of Nuestra Señora de los
Angeles, where he stayed overnight. Very early the next morning he
set out for Mission San Gabriel." José Longinos Martínez passed
through in 1792 but commented on little other than the tar pits to the
west of the settlement. George Vancouver, sailing by in 1793, knew of
the pueblo and looked for it, but could see nothing from shipboard.
He wrote: "A very advantageous settlement is established on a fertile

spot somewhere in this neighborhood ... called Pueblo de los Angeles, 'the country town of the Angeles.'" William Shaler, who wrote circumstantially about many places along the coast prior to 1808, never saw Los Angeles.

It is recorded that three of the eleven original heads of families were recognized as "useless" and eliminated. Subtracting them and their families cut the total to 32 persons, though as W. W. Robinson has pointed out, the pueblo guards, José Vicente Felix, Roque and Antonio de Cota, and Francisco Salvador Lugo, deserve to be included. Bancroft notes other early additions, among them Francisco Sinova, Juan José Domínguez, and the two Rosas brothers.

For 1786 there is the official report by José Arguello of the Santa Barbara presidio of his visit to the pueblo to confirm possession of house lots and farming lots and to record brands for the original settlers, eight in number plus one represented by a son. This marked the fifth anniversary of the founding and termination of subsidies and tax exemptions. For certain years, but not all, the Provincial Archives list the persons elected alcalde.

In 1790, the year of the first federal census in the United States, by coincidence there was a census in Los Angeles which found 28 men and 141 persons all told. According to Bancroft's reading there were 80 under 16, and 61 over 16, of whom 9 were over 90. That detail has been the most publicized part of the information. More careful scrutiny of the manuscript from which he was working shows that in actuality there were 9 persons over 50.

By 1790 the racial and ethnic countdown had changed considerably from those recorded in 1781. The listing was: Europeans, 1; Spaniards, 72; Indians, 7; Mulattos, 22; and Mestizos, 30. Names recorded included Alvarez, Alvitre, Arellano, Armenta, Aruz, Cruz, Domínguez, Figueroa, García, Higuera, Lobo, Ontiveros, Pico, Reyes, Romero, Ruiz, Verdugo, and Villa, plus mention a year earlier of Silvas, Soto, Sepúlveda, and Valdés.

The census also credited the pueblo with 2,980 head of large stock, 438 of small (sheep and goats), and a harvest of 4,500 fanegas (hundred-weight). It had 29 adobe houses, and granary, barracks, and house for the guard. By that date five ranchos had been granted in the vicinity: Juan José Domínquez' Rancho San Pedro of at least 75,000 acres; José María Verdugo's San Rafael of 36,000; Manuel Nieto's La Zanja of 167,000, later divided into five ranchos; Mariano de la Luz Verdugo's Portezuelo, abandoned in 1810; and Francisco Reyes' Encino, relinquished in 1797. As of the close of the Spanish period, Robinson counts twelve more ranchos granted and occupied in Los Angeles County, making 15 of the 25 in the entire province. Each of these grants contained a proviso that the grant was not to be used in such a way as to prejudice the inhabitants of the Pueblo of Los Angeles.

In 1795 Fray Vicente Santa María of Mission Buenaventura traveled from Buenaventura to San Gabriel looking for a likely site for a mission. He remarked:

"On this expedition I observed that the whole pagandom, between this mission and that of San Gabriel, along the beach, along the camino real, and along the border to the north, is fond of the Pueblo of Los Angeles, of the rancho of Mariano Verdugo, of the rancho of Reyes, and of the (rancho of the) Zanja. Here we see nothing but pagans passing, clad in shoes, with sombreros and blankets, and serving as muleteers to the settlers and rancheros, so that if it were not for the gentiles there would be neither pueblo nor rancho; and if this be not accepted as true let them bring proof. Finally, these pagan Indians care neither for the mission nor for the missionaries."

Shoes, sombreros, and blankets were not Gabrielino dress, nor was muleteer a Gabrielino occupation. These were Spanish ways that the Indians had learned since 1769 and more particularly since 1781 and 1784 with the founding of Los Angeles and the granting of the first ranchos. Fray Vicente's comment indicates considerable progress in changing the habits of the Indians without the intervention of missions or presidios.

Another of the few documents of the period is a "Diary of Occurrences" at the pueblo in the month of January, 1797. Entries include: election of alcaldes and regidores; coming and going of residents of the pueblo; payment of the tithe to the presidio of Santa Barbara; passage of pack trains belonging to the presidio and the mission of San Buenaventura; passing of the monthly courier; large numbers going to mass at San Gabriel; arrival of retired soldiers; soldiers passing through singly, in twos, and in a group of five to fifteen; an inventory of small stock and distribution of a hundred lambs to the residents.

The picture is of a safe countryside; seemingly no concern about traveling alone or in small parties with valuable pack trains. There was an abundance of corn and beans for packing to the presidios of San Diego and Santa Barbara. New residents of their own volition came to Los Angeles to live. More church-going is recorded than has been assumed.

Also in 1797 a tally of young unmarried men who might be available as presidial recruits showed sixteen, of whom six were willing to go. Others were needed at home to help a widowed mother, or an aged and infirm father, or a father who had no one else to assist him; another, besides having four brothers and sisters to support, had a physical disability. Two others were not reported on because there had not been a chance to ask their wishes.

By 1800 Los Angeles had 70 families and 315 persons. Horses and cattle numbered 12,500 and the harvest was 4,600 fanegas. By 1810 the population was 365 and, according to Bancroft would have been more had not some fifty men, over the years, enlisted as presidial soldiers. Experimental plantings of hemp and flax proved successful, but the grain harvest had been interfered with by locusts.

In 1810 a water dispute arose with the padres of San Fernando. The dossier on this complaint and its settlement once spread over twenty pages. All that survives is a summary and a quotation by Bancroft's copyist. Alcalde Francisco Avila complained on behalf of the pueblo that a diversion of water made by the padres at Cahuenga cut the flow of "the river of the pueblo." The padres were conciliatory. They represented that their intention was merely to irrigate a small field for planting, and they promised "that whenever it proves to inflict the least damage on the people of Los Angeles by diminishing the water, the mission will cease cultivating the site."

In 1815 José de la Guerra y Noriega listed 135 men in the district from Mission La Purísima to the Pueblo who were capable of bearing arms, 90 of them at Los Angeles.

As of 1820 Bancroft estimated the population of Los Angeles and its region at 650, of whom the great majority belonged to the pueblo. Monterey, with more than a hundred men in the presidio, had a total population of 700. Only one more year remained in the Spanish dispensation. Then or very shortly afterwards Los Angeles became the most populous center in California, testimony to Phelipe de Neve's wisdom forty years earlier in establishing a pueblo where the Los Angeles River emerged from the narrows and its water could be applied to the land.

Adapted from John Caughey, *The Pueblo Water Right of Los Angeles, Historically Considered* (Los Angeles, 1969), 87–98.

Pastoral Interlude

"A common bullock-driver, on horseback, delivering a message, seemed to
speak like an ambassador at an audience."

Richard Henry Dana

A. F. Harmer, Los Angeles County Museum of History

Fiesta

3

Pastoral Interlude

California's Mexican period, which lasted only half as long as the Spanish era, is habitually played down. The Mexican nation, beset by many problems, was a much less effective overlord than Spain, and this distant province was left almost entirely to its own devices. In 1846 to 1848, as if by destiny, it slipped into the American orbit.

In the Mexican quarter century, however, the hide trade with ships from Boston brought economic annexation to the United States. Rocky Mountain fur hunters came overland, followed by pioneer settlers in covered wagon trains. The missions were phased out, rancho grants multiplied, and life on the ranchos attained a legendary pastoral perfection. The Los Angeles district shared, indeed led, in much of this development. The pueblo, as E. Gould Buffum sets forth, became the most populous community and, with its surrounding ranchos, the agricultural showplace of the entire province.

Under Spain acculturation of the Indians was programmed and to a considerable degree achieved. The process continued in the 1820s and early thirties and then, with secularization, was grossly modified. Meanwhile, another cross-cultural relationship of a different sort arose with the entrance of American hide traders and trappers and, in time, shopkeepers and rancheros.

The people of Los Angeles took on some American ways, particularly in developing a taste for American wares. Father Sánchez asked Jedediah Smith's men to make him a bear trap to catch Indians in. Governor José María Echeandía set James Ohio Pattie to vaccinating. The Vigilance Committee of 1836 was not in the Spanish tradition. But the accommodations ran mostly in the other direction as suggested in Hugo Reid's permit to marry. In language, dress, table, salutations, house styles, cultivating the soil, and work and life on the

81

ranchos, the newcomers became more and more Spanish. The Carrillo anecdotes recited by Horace Bell reinforce this point, corroborated by the overall tone of pastoral California.

A Mission at Climax
HARRISON G. ROGERS

The first Americans who came overland to California were a party of beaver trappers led by Jedediah Smith, who also made the first crossing of the Sierra Nevada and the first trek from California to the Columbia River. The California port of entry for these men coming in from Great Salt Lake was Mission San Gabriel. In 1826 this mission was near the peak of its prosperity. The journal of one of Smith's men, Harrison G. Rogers, graphically describes this Spanish, now Mexican, frontier institution. Rogers also reveals much about the rough trappers who were the cutting edge of the American frontier.

[Monday, November] 27th.—We got ready as early as possible and started a W. course, and traveled 14 m. and enc[amped] for the day, we passed innumerable herds of cattle, horses and some hundred of sheep; we passed 4 or 5 Ind. lodges, that their Inds. acts as herdsmen. There came an old Ind. to us that speaks good Spanish, and took us with him to his mansion [mission], which consisted of 2 rows of large and lengthy buildings, after the Spanish mode, they remind me of the British barracks. So soon as we enc. there was plenty prepared to eat, a fine young cow killed, and a plenty of corn meal given us; pretty soon after the 2 commandants of the missionary establishment come to us and had the appearance of gentlemen. Mr. S[mith] went with them to the mansion and I stay with the company, there was great feasting among the men as they were pretty hungry not having any good meat for some time.

28th.—Mr. S. wrote me a note in the morning, stating that he was received as a gentleman and treated as such, and that he wished me to go back and look for a pistol that was lost, and send the company on to the missionary establishment. I complied with his request, went back, and found the pistol, and arrived late in the evening, was received very politely, and showed into a room and my arms taken from me. About 10 oclock at night supper was served, and Mr. S. and myself sent for. I was introduced to the 2 priests over a glass of good old whiskey and found them to be very joval friendly gentlemen, the supper consisted of a number of different dishes, served different from any table I ever was at. Plenty of good wine during supper, before the cloth was removed sigars was introduced. Mr. S. has wrote to the governor, and I expect we shall remain here some days.

29th.—Still at the mansion. We was sent for about sunrise to drink a cup of tea, and eat some bread and cheese. They all appear friendly and treat us well, although they are Catholicks by profession, they allow us the liberty of conscience, and treat us as they do their own countrymen, or brethren.

About 11 oclock, dinner was ready, and the priest come after us to go and dine; we were invited into the office, and invited to take a glass of gin and water and eat some bread and cheese; directly after we were seated at dinner, and every thing went on in style, both the priests being pretty merry, the clerk and one other gentleman, who speaks some English. They all appear to be gentlemen of the first class, both in manners and habbits. The mansion, or mission, consist of 4 rows of houses forming a complete square, where there is all kinds of macanicks at work; the church faces the east and the guard house the west; the N. and S. line comprises the work shops. They have large vineyards, apple and peach orchards, and some orrange and some fig trees. They manufacture blankets, and sundry other articles; they distill whiskey and grind their own grain, having a water mill, of a tolerable quality; they have upwards of 1,000 persons employed, men, women, and children, Inds. of different nations. The situation is very handsome, pretty streams of water running through from all quarters, some thousands of acres of rich and fertile land as level as a die in view, and a part under cultivation, surrounded on the N. with a high and lofty mou., handsomely timbered with pine, and cedar, and this mission has upwards of 30,000 head of cattle, and horses, sheep, hogs, etc. in proportion. I intend visiting the iner apartments to-morrow if life is spared. I am quite unwell to-day but have been engaged in writing letters for the men and drawing a map of my travels for the priests. Mr. Smith, as well as myself, have been engaged in the same business. They slaughter at this place from 2 to 3,000 head of cattle at a time; the mission lives on the profits. Saint Gabriel is in north latitude 34 degrees and 30 minutes. It still continues warm; the thermometer stands at 65 and 70 degrees.

30th.—Still at Saint Gabriel; everything goes on well; only the men is on a scanty allowance, as yet. There was a wedding in this place to-day, and Mr. S. and myself invited; the bell was rang a little before sun rise, and the morning service performed; then the musick commenced serranading, the soldiers firing, etc., about 7 o'clock tea and bread served, and about 11, dinner and musick. The ceremony and dinner was held at the priests; they had an ellegant dinner, consisting of a number of dishes, boiled roast meat and fowl, wine and brandy or ogadent, grapes brought as a dessert after dinner. Mr. S. and myself acted quite independent, knot understanding there language, nor they ours; we endeavored to appoligise, being very dirty and not in a situation to shift our clothing, but no excuse would be taken, we must be present, as we have been served at there table ever since we arrived at this place; they treat (us) as gentlemen in every sense of the word, although our apparel is so indifferent, and we not being in circumstances at this time to help ourselves, being about 800 m. on a direct line from the place of our deposit. Mr. S. spoke to the commandant this evening respecting the rations of his men; they were immediately removed into another apartment, and furnished with cooking utensils and plenty of provisions, they say, for 3 or 4 days. Our 2 Ind. guides were imprisoned in the guard house the 2nd. day after we arrived at the missionary establishment and remain confined as yet. Mr. S. has wrote to the commandant of the province, and we do not know the result as yet, or where we shall go from this place, but I expect to the

N.W. I intended visiting the iner apartments to-day, but have been engaged in assisting Mr. S. in making a map for the priest and attending the ceremonies of the wedding. . . .

[December] 10th.—Sunday. There was five Inds. brought to the mission by two other Inds, who act as constables, or overseers, and sentenced to be whiped for not going to work when ordered.

Each received from 12 to 14 lashes on their bare posteriors; they were all old men, say from 50 to 60 years of age, the commandant standing by with his sword to see that the Ind. who flogged them done his duty. Things in other respects similar to the last sabbath.

11th.—Nothing of consequence has taken place today more than usual, only the band of musick consisting of two small violins, one bass violin, a trumpet and triangle was played for 2 hours in the evening before the priests door by Inds. They made tolerable good music, the most in imitation to whites that (I) ever heard. Directly after the musick would cease, there was several rounds of cannon fired by the soldiers in commemoration of some great saints day or feast day. They keep at this place 4 small field pieces, 2 6-pounders and 2 2-pounders to protect them from the Inds. in case they should rebel, and, from the best information I can get from the soldiers, they appear at times some what alarmed, for fear the Inds. will rise and destroy the mission. . . .

13th.—I walked through the work shops; I saw some Inds. blacksmithing, some carpentering, others making the wood work of ploughs, others employed in making spining wheels for the squaws to spin on. There is upwards 60 women employed in spining yarn and others weaving. Things much the same, cloudy and some rain today. Our black smith[s] have been employed for several days making horse[shoes] and nails for our own use when we leave here.

14th.—I was asked by the priest to let our black smiths make a large trap for him to set in his orrange garden, to catch the Inds. in when they come up at night to rob his orchard. The weather clear and warm. Things in other respects much the same as they have been heretofore; friendship and peace prevail with us and the Spanyards. Our own men are contentious and quarrelsome amongst themselves and have been ever since we started the expedition. Last night at supper for the first time the priest questioned me as respected my religion. I very frankly informed him that I was brought up under the Calvinist doctrine, and did not believe that it was in the power of man to forgive sins. God only had that power, and when I was under the necessity of confessing my sins, I confessed them unto God in prayer and supplication, not to man; I further informed him that it was my opinion, that men ought to possess as well as profess religion to constitute the christian; he said that when he was in his church and his robe on, he then believed he was equal unto God, and had the power to forgive any sin, that man was guilty of, and openly confessed unto him, but when he was out of church and his common waring apparel on he was as other men, divested of all power of forgiving sins.

Harrison C. Dale, ed., *The Ashley-Smith Explorations* (Cleveland: Arthur H. Clark Co., 1918), 194–200, 204–206.

A Paramedic on Tour
JAMES OHIO PATTIE

Of all the fur trappers who entered California, James Ohio Pattie spun the most fascinating narrative of his adventures. Forced to cache their beaver pelts near the Colorado, he and his companions struggled in to San Diego where they were promptly jailed. Many months later, thanks to a smallpox epidemic, he was released and allowed to tour the settlements of Alta California, the entire chain of missions, the presidios, and the pueblos, vaccinating citizens, soldiers, missionaries, and Indians, by his count 22,000. Because the promised pay was made contingent on his becoming a Mexican citizen, Pattie angrily departed for Mexico to protest to the head of the republic.

On the 18th of January, 1828, I began to vaccinate; and by the 16th of February had vaccinated all the people belonging to the fort, and the Indian inhabitants of the mission of San Diego. . . . Having completed my vaccinations in this quarter, and procured a sufficient quantity of the vaccine matter to answer my purpose, I declared myself in readiness to proceed further. . . .

February 28 the General [Governor Echeandía] gave us each a legal form, granting us liberty on parole for one year, at the expiration of which period it was in his power to remand us to prison, if he did not incline to grant us our freedom. He likewise gave me a letter to the priests along the coast, containing the information that I was to vaccinate all the inhabitants upon the coast, and an order providing for me all necessary supplies of food and horses for my journey. These were to be furnished me by the people, among whom I found myself cast. They were also directed to treat me with respect, and indemnify me for my services, as far as they thought proper. The latter charge did not strike me agreeably; for I foresaw, that upon such conditions my services would not be worth one cent to me. However, the prospect of one whole year's liberty was so delightful, that I concluded to trust in Providence, and the generosity of the stranger, and think no more of the matter. With these feelings I set forth to the next mission, at which I had already been. It was called San Luis [Rey]. . . .

In the morning I entered on the performance of my duty. My subjects were Indians, the missions being entirely composed of them, with the exception of the priests, who are the rulers. The number of natives in this mission was three thousand, nine hundred and four. I took the old priest's certificate, as had been recommended by him, when I had completed my task. This is said to be the largest, most flourishing, and every way the most important mission on the coast. For its consumption fifty beeves are killed weekly. The hides and tallow are sold to ships for goods, and other articles for the use of the Indians, who are better dressed in general, than the Spaniards. All the income of the mission is placed in the hands of the priests, who give out clothing and food, according as it is required. They are also self constituted guardians of the female part of the mission, shutting up under lock and key, one hour after supper, all those, whose husbands are absent, and all young women and girls above nine years of age. During the day, they are entrusted to the care of the matrons. Notwithstanding this, all the precautions taken by the vigilant fathers of the church are found insufficient. I saw women in irons for misconduct, and men in the stocks. The former are expected to remain a widow six months after the death of a husband, after which period they may marry again. The priests appoint officers to superintend the natives, while they are at work, from among themselves. They are *alcaldes*, and are very rigid in exacting the performance of the allotted tasks, applying the rod to those who fall short of the portion of labor assigned them. They are taught in the different trades; some of them being blacksmiths, others carpenters and shoe-makers. Those trained to the knowledge of music, both vocal and instrumental, are intended for the service of the church. The women and girls sew, knit, and spin wool upon a large wheel, which is woven into blankets by the men. The alcaldes, after finishing the business of the day, give an account of it to the priest, and then kiss his hand, before they withdraw to their wigwams, to pass the night. This mission is composed of parts of five different tribes, who speak different languages.

The greater part of these Indians were brought from their native mountains against their own inclinations, and by compulsion; and then baptised; which act was as little voluntary on their part, as the former had been. After these preliminaries, they had been put to work, as converted Indians.

The next mission on my way was that called St. John the Baptist [San Juan Capistrano]. The mountains here approach so near the ocean, as to leave only room enough for the location of the mission. The waves dash upon the shore immediately in front of it. The priest, who presides over this mission, was in the habit of indulging his love of wine and stronger liquors to such a degree, as to be often intoxicated. The church had been shattered by an earthquake. Between twenty and thirty of the Indians, men, women and children, had been suddenly destroyed by the falling of the church bells upon them. After communicating the vaccine matter to 600 natives, I left this place, where mountains rose behind to shelter it; and the sea stretched out its boundless expanse before it.

Continuing my route I reached my next point of destination. This establishment was called the mission of St. Gabriel. Here I vaccinated 960 individuals. The course from the mission of St. John the Baptist to this place led me from the sea-shore, a distance of from eighteen to twenty miles. Those, who selected the position of this mission, followed the receding mountains. It extends from their foot, having in front a large tract of country showing small barren hills, and yet affording pasturage for herds of cattle so numerous, that their number is unknown even to the all surveying and systematic priests. In this species of riches St. Gabriel exceeds all the other establishments on the coast. The sides of the mountains here are covered with a growth of live oak and pine. The chain to which these mountains belong, extends along the whole length of the coast. The fort St. Peter [the port of San Pedro] stands on the sea coast, parallel to this mission.

My next advance was to a small town, inhabited by Spaniards, called the town of The Angels. The houses have flat roofs, covered with bituminous pitch, brought from a place within four miles of the town, where this article boils up from the earth. As the liquid rises, hollow bubbles like a shell of a large size, are formed. When they burst, the noise is heard distinctly in the town. The material is obtained by breaking off portions, that have become hard, with an axe, or something of the kind. The large pieces thus separated, are laid on the roof, previously covered with earth, through which the pitch cannot penetrate, when rendered liquid again by the heat of the sun. In this place I vaccinated 2500 persons.

From this place I went to the mission of St. Ferdinand, where I communicated the matter to 967 subjects. St. Ferdinand is thirty miles east of the coast, and a fine place in point of position.

James Ohio Pattie, *Personal Narrative* (Cincinnati, 1831), 211–215.

California's First Vigilance Committee

HUBERT HOWE BANCROFT

Hubert Howe Bancroft, businessman turned collector and then historian and publisher, produced what will be for all time the basic reference on California history, thirty-nine volumes filling a seven-foot shelf which he issued as his Works. They are a stupendously detailed history of the Pacific side of North America and particularly California up to their publication date in the 1880s.

By a national decree of May 23, 1835, Los Angeles was made a city and capital of California. I have noticed this fact elsewhere, and also the burst of indignation with which the news was received at Monterey. Two days after his accession, Nicolas Gutiérrez gave official publication to the decree, thus honoring the city of the Angels, and in February some efforts were made to secure proper buildings for temporary public use in the new capital; but the Angelinos were so lacking in public spirit that no citizen would furnish a building rent free, as the governor required, and the matter dropped out of sight for more than a year.

All the same, Los Angeles soon distinguished itself by producing the first California vigilance committee. Domingo Felix, who lived on the rancho bearing his name, near the town, was married to María del Rosario Villa, who had abandoned her husband to become the mistress of a Sonoran vaquero, named Gervasio Alipas. After two years of frequent efforts to reclaim the erring woman met with insults from her paramour whom he once wounded in a personal encounter, Felix invoked the aid of the authorities, and the wife was arrested at San Gabriel, and brought to town on March 24, 1836. Through the efforts of the alcalde and of friends, it was hoped that a reconciliation had been effected, though Alipas and his brother threatened vengeance. Two days later the couple started, both on one horse, for their rancho; but on the way the husband was stabbed by the paramour, and his body was dragged by the man and woman with a reata to a ravine, where it was partly covered with earth and leaves.

By March 29th the body had been found and both murderers arrested. There was great excitement in the city and on April 1st the ayuntamiento, summoned in extra session to take precautions, resolved to organize a force of citizens in aid of the authorities to preserve the peace. The danger was real, but no good citizens could be induced to aid the officers of the law, for they had resolved on a summary infliction of the penalties which justice demanded, but which, as they well knew, were not to be expected from the ordinary course of law in California, where there was no tribunal authorized to inflict the death penalty on a civilian.

At dawn on April 7th about fifty of the most prominent citizens met at the house of John Temple and organized a "junta defensora de la seguridad pública," of which Victor Prudon was chosen president, making an eloquent address, the original draft of which is in my possession. Manuel Arzaga was made secretary, and Francisco Araujo was put in command of the armed force. During the forenoon, while the organization was being perfected, two messengers were sent in succession to Padre Cabot at San Fernando, whose presence was required on the pretext that a dying Indian needed his spiritual care; but the weather was bad and the padre refused to come.

About two o'clock P.M. a copy of the popular *acta*, with a demand for the prisoners to be delivered up for execution within an hour, was sent to the alcalde, Manuel Requena. This document is preserved in the Los Angeles Archives, I, 81–91, with other records bearing on the same affair. I quote as follows:

"*Salus populi suprema lex est.* The subscribing citizens, at the invitation of the rest, justly indignant at the horrible crime committed against Domingo Felix, bearing in mind the frequency of similar crimes in this city, and deeming the principal cause thereof to be the delay in criminal cases through having to await the confirmation of sentences from Mexico, fearing for this unhappy country a state of anarchy where the right of the strongest shall be the only law, and finally believing that immorality has reached such an extreme that public security is menaced and will be lost if the dike of solemn example is not opposed to the torrent of atrocious perfidy—demand the execution or the delivery to us for immediate execution of the assassin Gervasio Alipas and the faithless María del R. Villa, that abominable monster who cruelly immolated her importunate husband in order to give herself up without fear to her frantic passions, and to pluck by homicide from the slime of turpitude the filthy laurel of her execreable treason(!) . . . Let the infernal couple perish. Such is the vow of the people, and we protest in the face of heaven that we will not lay down the arms with which we support the justice of our demand until the assassins have expiated their foul crimes. . . . Public vengeance demands a prompt example, and it must be given. Still reeks the blood of the Alvarez, of the Potiñón, of the Jenkins, and of other unhappy victims of the fury and passion of their impious murderers. . . . The world shall know that if in the city of Los Angeles judges tolerate assassination, there are virtuous citizens who know how to sacrifice their lives in order to save that of their compatriots. . . . Death to the homicide!"

There follow 55 signatures, including 14 foreigners. Four other communications are given respecting the giving up of the keys and return of the bodies.

Half an hour [after delivery of the demand] the junta marched out to the parsonage near the court and jail, and at three P.M. the alcalde was notified that the hour had expired. The ayuntamiento in session had received and considered the demand, which it was decided to refuse after two committees had been sent out to reason with the crowd. Narciso Botello, the secretary, having refused to give up the keys, they were taken, the guard was arrested, and the criminals were taken from the jail to be shot—the man at 4:30 P.M. and the woman half an hour later. It was discovered that Alipas had his shackles nearly filed off. The bodies were exposed at the jail door for two hours, and then placed at the disposal of the authorities. The alcalde fearing further disturbances, the junta volunteered to serve for a few days as a guard to aid the authorities in preserving order, and was then disbanded.

Hubert Howe Bancroft, *History of California*, III (1885), 416–419.

A Floating General Store
RICHARD HENRY DANA

With the Mexican period the retail as well as the export-import trade of California was taken over by the hide ships from Boston. The classic account is the narrative by a sailor on one of these ships, Richard Henry Dana, on leave from his studies at Harvard. His Two Years Before the Mast is one of California's best known books. The passage selected is on the trade and the Californians as witnessed early in 1835 at Santa Barbara, but most of the details apply also to the trading with the people of Los Angeles.

92

We returned by sundown, and found the *Loriotte* at anchor within a cable's length of the *Pilgrim*. The next day we were "turned-to" early, and began taking off the hatches, overhauling the cargo, and getting everything ready for inspection. At eight, the officers of the customs, five in number, came on board, and began overhauling the cargo, manifest, etc. The Mexican revenue laws are very strict, and require the whole cargo to be landed, examined, and taken on board again; but our agent, Mr. [Alfred] R[obinson], had succeeded in compounding with them for the last two vessels, and saving the trouble of taking the cargo ashore. The officers were dressed in the costume which we found prevailed through the country—a broad-brimmed hat, usually of a black or dark brown color, with a gilt or figured band round the crown, and lined inside with silk; a short jacket of silk or figured calico (the European skirted body-coat is never worn); the shirt open in the neck; rich waistcoat, if any; pantaloons wide, straight, and long, usually of velvet, velveteen or broadcloth; or else

Edward Borein, Los Angeles County Museum of History

Caballero

short breeches and wide stockings. They wear the deer-skin shoe, which is of a dark brown color, and (being made by Indians) usually a good deal ornamented. They have no suspenders, but always wear a sash round the waist, which is generally red, and varying in quality with the means of the wearer. Add to this the never-failing cloak, and you have the dress of the Californian. This last garment, the cloak, is always a mark of the rank and wealth of the owner. The "gente de razon," or aristocracy, wear cloaks of black or dark blue broadcloth, with as much velvet and trimmings as may be; and from this they go down to the blanket of the Indian, the middle classes wearing something like a large table-cloth, with a hole in the middle for the head to go through. This is often as coarse as a blanket, but being beautifully woven with various colors, is quite showy at a distance. Among the Spaniards there is no working class (the Indians being slaves and doing all the hard work); and every rich man looks like a grandee, and every poor scamp like a broken-down gentleman. I have often seen a man with a fine figure and courteous manners, dressed in broadcloth and velvet, with a noble horse completely covered with trappings; without a *real* in his pockets, and absolutely suffering for something to eat.

The next day, the cargo having been entered in due form, we began trading. The trade-room was fitted up in the steerage, and furnished out with the lighter goods, and with specimens of the rest of the cargo, and [Henry] M[ellus], a young man who came out from Boston with us, before the mast, was taken out of the forecastle, and made supercargo's clerk. He was well qualified for the business, having been clerk in a counting-house in Boston. He had been troubled for some time with rheumatism, which unfitted him for the wet and exposed duty of a sailor on the coast. For a week or ten days all was life on board. The people came off to look and to buy—men, women, and children; and we were continually going in the boats, carrying goods and passengers—for they have no boats of their own. Everything must dress itself and come aboard and see the new vessel, if it were only to buy a paper of pins. The agent and his clerk managed the sales, while we were busy in the hold or in the boats. Our cargo was an assorted one; that is, it consisted of everything under the sun. We had spirits of all kinds (sold by the cask), teas, coffee, sugar, spices, raisins, molasses, hardware, crockery-ware, tin-ware, cutlery, clothing of all kinds, boots and shoes from Lynn, calicoes and cottons from Lowell, crapes, silks; also, shawls, scarfs, necklaces, jewelry, and combs for the ladies; furniture; and in fact, everything that can be imagined, from Chinese fire-works to English cart-wheels—of which we had a dozen pairs with their iron rims on.

The Californians are an idle, thriftless people, and can make nothing for themselves. The country abounds in grapes, yet they buy bad wine made in Boston and brought round by us, at an immense price, and retail it among themselves at a *real* (12½ cents) by the small wineglass. Their hides too, which they value at two dollars in money, they give for something which costs seventy-five cents in Boston; and buy shoes (as like as not, made of their own hides, which have been carried twice round Cape Horn) at three and four dollars, and "chicken-skin boots" at fifteen dollars apiece. Things sell, on an average at an advance of nearly three hundred per cent upon the Boston prices. . . .

This kind of business was new to us, and we liked it very well for a few days, though we were hard at work every minute from daylight to dark, and sometimes even later.

By being thus continually engaged in transporting passengers with their goods, to and fro, we gained considerable knowledge of the character, dress, and language of the people. The dress of the men was as I have before described it. The women wore gowns of various texture—silks, crape, calicoes, etc.—made after the European style, except that the sleeves were short, leaving the arm bare, and that they were loose about the waist, having no corsets. They wore shoes of kid, or satin, sashes or belts of bright colors, and almost always a necklace and ear-rings. Bonnets they had none. I only saw one on the coast, and that belonged to the wife of an American sea-captain who had settled in San Diego and had imported the chaotic mass of straw and ribbon as a choice present to his new wife. They wear their hair (which is almost invariably black, or a very dark brown) long in their necks, sometimes loose, and sometimes in long braids; although the married women often do it up on a high comb. Their only protection against the sun and weather is a large mantle, which they put over their heads, drawing it close round their faces, when they go out of doors, which is generally only in pleasant weather. When in the house or sitting out in front of it, which they often do in fine weather, they usually wear a small scarf or neckerchief of a rich pattern. A band, also, about the top of the head, with a cross, star, or other ornament in front, is common. Their complexions are various, depending—as well as their dress and manner—upon their rank; or, in other words, upon the amount of Spanish blood they can lay claim to. Those who are of pure Spanish blood, having never intermarried with the aborigines, have clear brunette complexions, and sometimes even as fair as those of English women. There are but few of these families in California, being mostly those in official stations, or who, on the expiration of their offices, have settled here upon property which they have acquired; and others who have been banished for state offences. These form the aristocracy; intermarrying, and keeping up an exclusive system in every respect. They can be told by their complexions, dress, manner, and also by their speech; for, calling themselves Castilians, they are very ambitious of speaking the pure Castilian language, which is spoken in a somewhat corrupted dialect by the lower classes. From this upper class they go down by regular shades, growing more and more dark and muddy, until you come to the pure Indian, who runs about with nothing upon him but a small piece of cloth, kept up by a wide leather strap drawn round his waist. Generally speaking, each person's caste is decided by the quality of the blood, which shows itself, too plainly to be concealed, at first sight. Yet the least drop of Spanish blood, if it be only of quatroon or octoon, is sufficient to raise them from the rank of slaves, and entitle them to wear a suit of clothes—boots, hat, cloak, spurs, long knife, and all complete, though coarse and dirty as may be—and to call themselves Españolos, and to hold property, if they can get any.

The fondness for dress among the women is excessive, and is often the ruin of many of them. A present of a fine mantle, or of a necklace or pair of ear-rings gains the favor of the greater part of them. Nothing is more common than to see a woman living in a house of only two rooms, and the ground for a floor, dressed in spangled satin shoes, silk gown, high comb, and gilt, if not gold, ear-rings and necklace. If their husbands do not dress them well enough, they will soon receive presents from others. They used to spend whole days on board our vessel, examining the fine clothes and ornaments, and frequently made purchases at a rate which would have made a seamstress or waiting-maid in Boston open her eyes.

Next to the love of dress, I was most struck with the fineness of the voices and beauty of the intonations of both sexes. Every common ruffian-looking fellow, with a slouched hat, blanket cloak, dirty underdress, and soiled leather leggings, appeared to me to be speaking elegant Spanish. It was a pleasure simply to listen to the sound of the language, before I could attach any meaning to it. They have a good deal of the Creole drawl, but it is varied with an occasional extreme rapidity of utterance in which they seem to skip from consonant to consonant, until, lighting upon a broad, open vowel, they rest upon that to restore the balance of sound. The women carry this peculiarity of speaking to a much greater extreme than the men, who have more evenness and stateliness of utterance. A common bullock-driver, on horseback, delivering a message, seemed to speak like an ambassador at an audience. In fact, they sometimes appeared to me to be people on whom a curse had fallen, and stripped them of everything but their pride, their manners, and their voices.

Another thing that surprised me was the quantity of silver that was in circulation. I certainly never saw so much silver at one time in my life, as during the week that we were in Monterey. The truth is, they have no credit system, no banks, and no way of investing money but in cattle. They have no circulating medium but silver and hides —which the sailors call "California bank notes." Everything that they buy they must pay for in one of the other of these things. The hides they bring down dried and doubled, in clumsy ox-carts, or upon mules' backs, and the money they carry tied up in a handkerchief—fifty, eighty, or an hundred dollars and half dollars.

Richard Henry Dana, *Two Years before the Mast* (New York, 1840), 92–98.

A Rascally Set

FAXON DEAN ATHERTON

With the hide trade Los Angeles drew many foreign visitors and, in many instances, a barbed comment. Faxon Dean Ath-

Pastoral Interlude

*erton dropped by in 1836 as a clerk in the hide trade. Opening
a firm of his own in Valparaiso, he retained an interest in
California, visited it again in 1849, and became a Californian
in 1859.*

Monday, [July] 11, [1836]. Sailed from Sta Barbara for San Pedro 9
p.m. Arrived off the point [Fermin] at 8 next morning; came to anchor
at 11. Started for a Rancho about 3 miles off to obtain horses for the
Pueblo. At 12 arrived hot as damnation. Got a poor miserable horse
and started for the corral to get a better [one]. After about an hour's
ride through fields of mustard bushes, briars, and across gulches and
quagmires, arrived. Got a noble horse and started again going like
lightning and coming very near getting my head broke by branches of
trees which I found confounded annoying while going 10 knots and
turning short corners. Good eyesight and limber back bone were in
frequent request. At last we came on to a good and tolerably hard
road and at 2 p.m. arrived [at] the Pueblo, a distance of 30 miles from
San Pedro.

The Pueblo is situated . . . on a dry sandy soil which, notwithstanding, is said to be pretty productive especially for the grape: it is
said to be superior. There is, however, but one vineyard of consequence [Louis Vignes'], although there are a number that are now being planted. It possesses one great advantage over any other place
southward of Monterrey in having a considerable stream of water
that is never dry and which can be led over a large extent of ground in
any direction, the bed of the river back of the town being higher than
the plain on which it is situated.

The place is said to contain about 1500 inhabitants among which
are 40 or 50 foreigners. The native inhabitants are a rascally set of
vicious cut throat villains among whom, however, are some very
good men though of small abilities. The best stores are with exception the property of foreigners, principally American hunters. The
business done by them for sometime past has been very profitable,
although now it has fallen off a good deal on account of the cattle of
the mission San Gabrielle being mostly killed off in 1834, there being
25,000 hides taken from here by the Ship *Lagoda*, Capt. Bradshaw.

Doyce B. Nunis, Jr., ed., *The California Diary of Faxon Dean Atherton* (San Francisco:
California Historical Society, 1964), 24.

License To Marry

Susanna Bryant Dakin

A feature of the Mexican period, especially in the Los Angeles area, was the assimilated Californians—Don Benito Wilson, Don Abel Stearns, Don Juan Temple, and many others. Hugo Reid was representative, and Susanna Bryant Dakin's Scotch Paisano is as good a biography as we have of any of them. As this selection indicates, the formalities of acculturation sometimes were formidable.

Custom required that Hugo Reid should not marry Doña Victoria without becoming a Catholic. It was also necessary for him to produce four character witnesses who had known him for a long time; and to aid in the composition of an exhaustive "marriage investigation." First, he presented to the "superior political chief," Governor Juan Alvarado, the following, which is translated and in which he used the Spanish name "Perfecto" acquired in addition to his own "Hugo" at the time of his recent baptism:

"Perfecto Hugo Reid, native of Great Britain, Roman Catholic, resident of the City of Our Lady of the Angels, appears before your Lordship in the best legal manner to state: that during the term of three years he has lived in the above-mentioned city, engaged in business, *et cetera*, has benefited society in every way possible, and finding himself ready to enter into the state of matrimony with a native daughter of this country, respectfully requests and entreats your permission to contract this marriage.

"Wherefore, I appeal to your justice to grant me this privilege. I assure you I intend no slight to your Lordship's dignity in submitting this petition on common paper, there not being any with the corresponding seal available in this city.

PERFECTO HUGO REID

City of Los Angeles, August 6, 1837."

99

Then he advised "the Reverend Father Fray Tomás Eleuterio de Estenaga, Clergyman in the former Mission of San Gabriel Archangel," that:

"Perfecto Hugo Reid, native of Great Britain, legitimate son of Charles Reid and Essex Milchin, natives of Scotland in the County of Renfrew, resident of Our Lady of the Angels, before your Reverence, hereby makes known his intention to marry [Victoria] Bartolomea Comicrabit, a neophyte of this mission.

"I entreat your Reverence to order that the customary steps be taken to carry this out. I swear and promise, *et cetera.*

PERFECTO HUGO REID

Mission of San Gabriel, July 30, 1837."

Fray Tomás produced two witnesses: Santiago Suñer, native of Mallorca, and Nicolás Díaz, native of the city of Durango. Hugo's taking of the oath was recorded by the priest and incorporated in the "investigation":

"Immediately after, there appeared at my request the above-mentioned Perfecto Hugo Reid, who took the oath, in the name of Our Lord and the Holy Cross, to answer truthfully all questions put to him, in the presence of assisting witnesses.

"1. Question: What is your name, your parents' names, your age, and present condition. He answered that his name was Perfecto Hugo Reid, legitimate son of Charles Reid and Essex Milchin, natives of Scotland, Renfrew County, resident of Our Lady of the Angels; his age, 27 years old, single.

"2. Question: If he is pledged to marry any other women than the above-mentioned Bartolomea. He answered, no.

"3. Question: Whether any force is being exerted on him to marry. He answered, no.

"4. Question: If he is a blood relation of the above[-mentioned Bartolomea] or connected with her by affinity or some other spiritual bond. He answered, no.

"5. Question: If he has taken a vow of chastity, or a religious or any other nature, and if there exist any other obstacles. He answered, no.

"The foregoing having been read by him and confirmed by him, he signed together with me, that it be recorded, as well as of the assisting

witnesses, the second placing his mark, not knowing how to write.
PERFECTO HUGO REID
SANTIAGO SUÑER
FR[AY] TOMÁS ESTENAGA
NICOLÁS DÍAZ

"Immediately afterward, there appeared as first witness, to attest the freedom and condition of singleness of the above mentioned, Santiago Dove, native of London and resident of the City of Los Angeles, who took oath in the name of Our Lord and the Holy Cross to answer truthfully, *et cetera.*

"Question: If he knows Perfecto Hugo Reid and for how long. He answered that he has known him since 1831."

Dove was required to answer five more questions, substantiating the information that Reid had already given under oath. The three other character witnesses, all chosen by Don Perfecto himself, were Julian Pope, Joaquín Bowman, and Diego (James) Scott, former supercargo on the *Ayacucho.* Pope had known him longest—seven years.

Victoria's age was given as twenty-nine, and her parents' names as Bartolomé and Petra, of the Comicrabit *ranchería*, adjacent to the Pueblo. She was described as the widow of the Indian, Pablo María "de Yutucubit, Partida 512," by whom she had had four children.

The entire deposition was sent first to the highest secular authority in California, the governor; then to the "ecclesiastical judge of Alta California," Padre Narciso Durán. Their necessary permissions for the marriage to take place were appended to the manuscript.

"1. Santa Barbara, August 12, 1837. The author of this petition is hereby permitted to marry a native daughter of this country, as he wishes, to which end this decree will serve as a license for so doing.

ALVARADO

"2. Mission of San Fernando, August 20, 1837. Having examined the preceding marriage investigation and in spite of the fact that the attestation by the witnesses, of the bachelorhood of Perfecto Hugo Reid, is a guarantee covering only a few years, I grant the permission for the marriage *servatis servandis.*

FR(AY) NARCISO DURÁN
Ecclesiastical Judge of Alta California"

101

After Durán's permission for the alliance had been obtained, the banns had to be published on three successive feast days. During this period, Victoria and Doña Eulalia busied themselves with preparations for the wedding: fashioning the dress, trousseau, and household linen, and planning the customary *fiesta*. The date was set for the week of *la luna de la cosecha*, the harvest moon of September. A morning service in the mission would start a round of gaiety to which all San Gabriel and many out-of-town guests would be invited.

Few invitations were refused. Everyone loved and respected Doña Victoria, no one wanted to miss a *fiesta* at the Pérez place, or the pageant of a *paisano's* wedding.

Susanna Bryant Dakin, *A Scotch Paisano* (Berkeley: University of California Press, 1939), 41–44.

The Decay of the Mission
HUGO REID

The goal of the missions was to bring the neophytes to the point where they could be released from constant supervision by the padres. In California secularization came on political grounds and before the padres were ready to graduate them.

The Mission [of San Gabriel], as received by the Padre Tomás [Estenaga] was in a flourishing condition, but in 1834 (I think it was) the Mexican Congress passed a law secularizing all of the Missions, by which each Indian was to receive his share of land, gardens and stock; but immediately on the top of it a change was effected in the general government, and instead of carrying out the law, they abolished it.

102

They, however, secularized them and ordered Administrators to have charge instead of the clergy. These facts being known to the Padre Tomás, he (in all probability by order of his superior) commenced the work of destruction. The back buildings were unroofed and the timber converted into firewood. Cattle were killed on halves with people who took a lion's share. Utensils were disposed of, and goods and other articles distributed in profusion among the Neophites. The vineyards were ordered to be cut down, which, however, the Indians refused to do.

It did not require long to destroy what years took to establish. Destruction came as a thief in the night. The whites rejoiced at it. They required no encouragement, and seemed to think it would last forever. Even the mere spectators were gladdened at the sight, and many of them helped themselves to a sufficiency of calves to stock farms. . . .

General Figueroa, having been appointed political Chief and Commandant General of the territory, arrived, and his adjutant, Col. Nicholas Gutiérrez, received the Mission from the Padre Tomás, who remained as minister of the church with a stipend of $1500 per annum from the establishment, independent of his synod from the Pious Fund in Mexico. . . .

Reduced in circumstances, annoyed on many occasions by the petulancy of Administrators, he fulfilled his duties according to his conscience, with benevolence and good-humor. The nuns [the unmarried Indian women], who when the secular movement came into operation, had been set free, were again gathered together under his supervision and maintained at his expense, as were also a number of the old men and women. Everything he got was spent in charity upon those of the ranchería whom he considered as worthy of it and they remember him with gratitude and affection.

The Indians were made happy at this time in being permitted to enjoy once more the luxury of a tule dwelling, from which the greater part had been debarred for so long; they could now breathe freely again.

Administrator followed Administrator, until the Mission could support no more, when the system was broken up. I shall make no remarks here on their administration; it is to be presumed they complied either with their instructions or their own ideas.

The Indians during this period were continuously running off. Scantily clothed and still more scantily supplied with food, it was not to be wondered at. Nearly all of the Gabrielinos went north while those of San Diego, San Luis and San Juan overran this county, filling the Angeles and surrounding ranchos with more servants than were required. Labor in consequence was very cheap. The different Missions, however, had Alcaldes continually on the move, hunting them up and carrying them back, but to no purpose; it was labor in vain.

This was a period of demoralization. People from Sonora came flocking in to assist in the general destruction, lending a hand to kill off cattle on shares, which practice, when at last prohibited by government orders, they continued on their private account.

These Sonoreños overran this country. They invaded the rancherias, gambled with the men and taught them to steal; they taught the women to be worse than they were, and the men and women both to drink. Now we do not mean or pretend to say that the Neophites were not previous to this addicted both to drinking and gaming, with an inclination to steal, while under the dominion of the church; but the Sonoreños most certainly brought them to a pitch of licentiousness before unparalleled in their history.

Reprinted from the *Los Angeles Star*, 1851, in Hugo Reid, *The Indians of Los Angeles County* (Los Angeles, 1926), 64–67.

Life on the Ranchos
ROBERT GLASS CLELAND

For many years Robert Glass Cleland headed the Huntington Library research staff in southwestern history. The following selection is from his most cited book, a social and economic history of southern California's transition to American ways. The idyllic description applies to the middle and latter part of

Life on the Ranchos

The carefree life of the California rancheros a hundred years ago has been the theme of so many colorful descriptions that one hesitates to dwell upon the subject further; but the chapter would not be complete without some reference to it. From an economic and social point of view the great ranchos of the period had much in common with the medieval English manor. Except for a few luxuries obtained from trading vessels on the coast, each ranch was virtually a self-sustaining economic unit. Large numbers of Indians, recruited chiefly from the fast-decaying mission communities, served as *vaqueros*, artisans, farm laborers, and domestic servants in return for simple but abundant food, primitive shelter, and a scant supply of clothing. Some of the native families lived in the *indiada*, a cluster of primitive huts built near the main adobe *casa*, while others dwelt in small villages, called rancherias, widely scattered over the state.

The homage paid a California don, both by members of his family and by his retainers, was not unlike that once accorded a feudal lord. The members of his household were often numbered by the score. He provided a home for a host of poor relations, entertained strangers, as well as friends, with unwearying hospitality, and begat as many sons and daughters as the Hebrew patriarchs of old.

On large estates an army of Indian women were required for domestic service. "Each child (of whom there were sixteen) has a personal attendant," said Señora Vallejo of her household staff, "while I have two for my own needs; four or five are occupied in grinding corn for tortillas, for so many visitors come here that three grinders do not suffice; six or seven serve in the kitchen, and five or six are always washing clothes for the children and other servants; and, finally, nearly a dozen are employed at sewing and spinning."

The chronic dearth of money, characteristic of the entire Spanish-Mexican period, forced the Californians to resort to barter in virtually all their business dealings. Trade between the ranchers and foreign vessels, as portrayed so vividly by Richard Henry Dana in his *Two Years Before the Mast*, depended almost exclusively on this method of exchange. But the system applied with equal universality to

105

domestic transactions as well. Contracts and promissory notes were often made payable in terms of cattle, hides or tallow; judges levied fines and judgments in the same commodities; and even the smallest amount of merchandise—a few yards of cloth, a pound of sugar, a box of raisins, a handful of cigars—was purchased with the standard of currency of the province, the ubiquitous cattle hide, known, from Alaska to Peru, as the "California bank note."

Free from the pressure of economic competition, ignorant of the wretchedness and poverty indigenous to other lands, amply supplied with the means of satisfying their simple wants, devoted to "the grand and primary business of the enjoyment of life," the Californians enjoyed a pastoral, patriarchal, almost Arcadian existence until a more complicated and efficient civilization invaded their "demiparadise." One who knew by experience the simplicity and contentment of California ranch life a hundred years ago [W. A. Hawley] drew, for less fortunate generations, the following picture of its quiet charm:

"The *rancho* lay beyond the mountain range and extended over rolling hills and little valleys. A creek flowed through it, and on the banks were many sycamores. Shaded by oaks was the long, low adobe house, with its red tiled roof and wide veranda. Behind the fence of chaparral was the orchard and the melon patch, and beyond the orchard was the meadow, golden with buttercups in the early spring. In the open fields, dotted with oaks, the rich alfilerilla grew, and on the hillsides were the wild grasses which waved like billows as the breezes from the distant ocean blew across them. The sameness of recurring events of each succeeding year never seemed monotonous, but brought repose, contentment and peace. When the dew was still on the grass, we would mount our horses and herd the cattle if any had strayed beyond the pasture. In the wooded cañons where the cool brooks flowed, and where the wild blackberries grew, we ate our noon day meal and rested. And as the hills began to glow with the light of the setting sun we journeyed homeward. When the long days of summer came, we ate our evening meal beneath the oaks, and in the twilight we listened to the guitar and the songs of our people. In the autumn we harvested the corn and gathered the olives and the grapes."

Robert Glass Cleland, *The Cattle on a Thousand Hills* (San Marino, Huntington Library, 1941), 42–45.

Gold! Gold! Gold! from San Francisquito!

J. M. GUINN

An early president and long-time secretary of the Historical Society of Southern California, J. M. Guinn was one of the most prolific writers on the early history of Los Angeles. Here he deals with a matter in which southern California had a small priority over the northern part of the state.

Abel Stearns says gold was first discovered by Francisco López, a native of California, in the month of March, 1842, at a place called San Francisquito, about thirty-five miles northwest from Los Angeles. The circumstances of the discovery by López, as related by himself, are as follows:

"López, with a companion, was out in search of some stray horses, and about midday they stopped under some trees and tied their horses out to feed, they resting under the shade, when López, with his sheath-knife, dug up some wild onions, and in the dirt discovered a piece of gold, and, searching further, found some more. He brought these to town, and showed them to his friends, who at once declared there must be a placer of gold. This news being circulated, numbers of the citizens went to the place, and commenced prospecting in the neighborhood, and found it to be a fact that there was a placer of gold. . . ."

J. J. Warner visited the mines a few weeks after their discovery. He says: "From these mines was obtained the first parcel of California gold dust received at the United States mint in Philadelphia, and which was sent with Alfred Robinson, and went in a merchant ship around Cape Horn." This shipment of gold was 18.34 ounces before and 18.1 ounces after melting; fineness, .925; value, $344.75, or over $19 to the ounce, a very superior quality of gold dust. It was deposited in the mint July 8, 1843. . . .

107

A petition to the governor [Alvarado] asking permission to work the placers, signed by Francisco López, Manuel Cota and Domingo Bermúdez is on file in the California archives. It recites: "Divine Providence was pleased to give us a placer of gold on the 9th of last March in the locality of San Francisco Rancho, that belongs to the late Don Antonio del Valle." This petition fixes the day of the month this discovery was made. . . .

William Heath Davis . . . states that from $80,000 to $100,000 was taken out for the first two years after their discovery. He says that Mellus at one time shipped $5,000 of dust on the ship Alert. Bancroft says that "by December, 1843, two thousand ounces of gold had been taken from the San Fernando mines." Don Antonio Coronel informed the author that he, with the assistance of three Indian laborers, in 1842, took out $600 worth of dust in two months. De Mofras, in his book, states that Carlos Baric, a Frenchman, in 1842, was obtaining an ounce a day of pure gold from his placer.

These mines were worked continuously from the time of their discovery until the American conquest, principally by Sonorians. The discovery of gold at Coloma, January 24, 1848, drew away the miners, and no work was done on these mines between 1848 and 1854. After the latter date work was resumed, and in 1855, Francisco García, working a gang of Indians, is reported to have taken out $65,000 in one season. The mines are not exhausted, but the scarcity of water prevents working them profitably.

J. M. Guinn, *A History of California and an Extended History of Los Angeles* (Los Angeles, 1915), I, 155–156.

Carrillo Family Anecdotes
HORACE BELL

In his day Horace Bell was the most spritely and acerbic writer in Los Angeles—its Ambrose Bierce. Editor of the Porcupine *and author of the first locally published book,* Reminiscences of a Ranger *(1881), he left enough stories and commentaries to*

Carrillo Family Anecdotes

fill a sequel, in which this selection appeared. In his writings
fact is sometimes embellished but seldom misrepresented.

A great family were these Carrillos. Some of them were mighty men
and the women were all beautiful to look upon. The most noted of the
men was General José Antonio. He commanded the Californians at
the battle of Los Cuerbos, commonly called the Battle of Domínguez,
when the American marines under Captain Mervine of the frigate
Savannah were marching on Los Angeles from San Pedro during the
Mexican War. It occurred near where Compton now stands. He had
previously represented California in the Mexican Congress. A remarkable fellow he was, standing six feet four inches tall, weighing
about two hundred and forty pounds and bearing a perfect resemblance to the statues of some of the old Roman senators.

General Carrillo was full of humor and boiling over with sarcasm.
He came very near getting into a duel with a captain in the Mormon
Batallion in Los Angeles in 1847. Doña Luisa Avila was married to a
Mexican officer, Lieut. Col. Manuel Garfías, who was a nephew of
Porfirio Díaz, later ruler of Mexico for so many years. Garfías had
been a member of the famous Micheltorena Battalion which had been
expelled by the revolting Californians. He had resigned his commis-
sion in the army and returned to Los Angeles to marry the daughter of
Doña Concepción de Avila. Doña Concepción was owner of the San
Pascual grant where Pasadena now stands and which later passed into
the possession of Colonel Garfías.

A great fiesta followed the nuptials and the party developed into an
occasion of reconciliation between the American army officers and
those of the late Californian army. The generals were all there and the
captains and lieutenants. General Carrillo was there, grim and sar-
castic. He was far from being reconciled. There was a certain Mormon
captain there, too, who thought himself a great dancer. Carrillo stared
with pointed disapproval at his awkward performances and finally
remarked to some dignitary of the American faction: "That officer of
yours dances like a bear."

The Mormon captain was informed of the remark and on the
following day sent a challenge to General Carrillo to meet him in mor-
tal combat. The Californian at once accepted the challenge and ap-

109

pointed his seconds and excitement ran high on both sides. General Kearny, the commander-in-chief of the American forces of occupation, decided there must be no bloodshed and offered his services as mediator.

In the course of these peace negotiations the whole crowd, principals and all, brought up at the hospitable home of Nathaniel Pryor. The Pryor house was famous for good cheer; it was a fine house backed up by a fine vineyard that supplied a fine cellar with fine wines. The vineyard was bounded on the east by Alameda Street and extended from Aliso Street to Wolfskill's line. The place had a high whitewashed adobe wall around it and was altogether quite grand.

Going into conference again here, in the midst of these congenial surroundings, General Kearny, aided by Major Emory, brought such diplomacy to bear on General Carrillo as to persuade him that he owed an apology to the Mormon. But the friends of the Mormon stubbornly insisted that the apology must be in writing. To the pleased surprise of the sticklers for the written word Carrillo immediately agreed; whereupon it is to be presumed that the cheery stock in Nathaniel Pryor's famed cellar suffered further depletion. General Carrillo's only stipulation was that he was to be given until the next day to write and deliver the apology, delivery to be made here at this same pleasant gathering place.

At the appointed time the principals, mediators, seconds and friends were present; indeed, the crowd was considerably larger than it had been the day before. The Americans were on tip-toe to see what sort of an apology a haughty Californian ex-general and high dignitary would make to an American volunteer captain.

After the wine had circulated a translator was selected to read aloud the apology, which was as follows:

"I am a native of California; I love my country and stick up for it, the bear is my countryman so I love the bear. I now apologize to the bear for suggesting that the red-headed captain danced like a bear. The injury is to the bear, because the captain could not dance half so well.

JOSÉ ANTONIO CARRILLO"

The Mormon captain was more wroth than ever and insisted on a fight then and there. But the droll apology had struck everybody's funnybone. Both factions turned on the aggrieved redhead with so much ridicule that he was laughed off the place and the crisis was averted for good and all.

There was another Carrillo—we will call him the Judge. The Judge was a highly educated gentleman, in fact he was educated in Boston. A hide drogher carried him from Santa Bárbara around the Horn to Boston to college when he was about twelve years old, and brought him home again some four years later. That was, of course, when California was a province of Mexico.

The home coming was somewhat startling. The young graduate presented himself at the parental mansion, a delightful old adobe in the town that was the seat of old Spanish aristocracy in California, dressed in high Boston style and feeling himself to be a very important Yankee-wise cosmopolitan. The Señora, his mother, was overjoyed to see her boy and after laughter and caresses she sat him down in the *sala* to have a talk with him in dignified Castilian. But the boy seemed to have forgotten his mother tongue; his replies were couched in the Yankee idiom.

With amazement which grew to indignation the Señora de Carrillo rebuked her son, but he continued to show off his superior education. Whereupon the Señora stalked out of doors, armed herself with a length of rawhide rope, swept into the *sala* again like an avenging goddess and sailed into the embryo judge with such expletives as: "Thou canst no longer speak Spanish, hey? Well, *I'll* teach thee Spanish!" Rap! Whack! Slap!

"*Por Dios, mama—mamacita—por Dios, no, no!*" yelled the previously arrogant cosmopolite. Swish! Snap! continued the rawhide until the youth poured forth a torrent of Spanish, imploring and promising without the least trace of Boston accent. At that moment he reverted to his racial heritage and remained thenceforth quite typical, as some of the incidents of his distinguished career may suggest; although the fact that he had enjoyed a Boston education he stressed with great success in advancing himself under the American régime. He was a member of the first State Constitutional Convention that framed the Constitution of the State of California in 1849, became a state senator and a member of the judiciary.

Horace Bell, *On the Old West Coast* (New York: William Morrow, 1930), 116–119.

American Takeover

"The inhabitants of the Pueblo . . . have now become reconciled to the institutions of our country, and will, I doubt not, in a few years make as good a set of democrats as can be found in Missouri or Arkansas."

E. Gould Buffum

Jim Tetro

Chaparral-covered hills

4

American Takeover

American takeover signaled as drastic a change for Los Angeles as had occurred to the Gabrielino with the coming of the Spaniards. Important groundwork had been laid by the hide traders who had carried out economic annexation to New England and by pioneer settlers from the States who had opted to live in southern California. On the other side of the continent, war broke out between the United States and Mexico. The U.S. Navy, in the predetermined order of priority, took possession at Monterey and San Francisco Bay on July 7 and 9, 1846. At Los Angeles, forty days later, Commodore R. F. Stockton could proclaim that the conquest of California had been completed. Clearly he envisioned little change under the new caretaker and an idyllic prosperity such as Buffum etched.

Following the great gold discovery, San Francisco and the Mother Lode belt experienced instant Americanization. Los Angeles, 400 miles to the south, was stimulated but only to the point of a rapid transformation. Over the twenty-four years to 1870 Los Angeles grew but not spectacularly.

One feature of Los Angeles, especially in the fifties, was that it was a tough cowtown, prefiguring such places as Abilene and Dodge City. It was long on saloons and gambling, gun-toting and violence, vigilantism and lynchings. Leonard Pitt and Horace Bell deal with this lawlessness directly. Harris Newmark mentions revolver fire as the way of sounding a fire alarm, and William Brewer inventories the firearms that he and his fellow surveyors packed. Popular writing emphasizes this roughness.

The episode of the Washington Birthday Ball reveals tension between oldtimers and newcomers and, in other instances, between Hispanos and Anglos. A time or two in the fifties incidents came close to erupting into race war. As a carryover from earlier days, Indians

115

All persons, of whatever religion or nation, who faithfully adhere to the new government, will be considered as citizens of the Territory, and will be zealously and thoroughly protected in their liberty of conscience, their persons, and property.

No persons will be permitted to remain in the Teritory who do not agree to support the existing government, and all military men who desire to remain are required to take an oath that they will not take up arms against it, or do or say any thing to disturb the peace.

Nor will any person, come from where they may, be permitted to settle in the Territory who do not pledge themselves to be, in all respects, obedient to the laws which may be from time to time enacted by the proper authorities of the Territory.

All persons who, without special permission, are found with arms outside of their own houses, will be considered as enemies and will be shipped out of the country.

All thieves will be put to hard labor on the public works, and there kept until compensation is made for the property stolen.

The California battalion of mounted riflemen will be kept in the service of the Territory, and constantly on duty, to prevent and punish any aggressions by the Indians, or any other persons, upon the property of individuals, or the peace of the Territory; and California shall hereafter be so governed and defended as to give security to the inhabitants, and to defy the power of Mexico.

All persons are required, as long as the Territory is under martial law, to be within their houses from 10 o'clock at night until sunrise in the morning.

R. F. Stockton
Commander in chief and Governor
of the Territory of California

Ciudad de los Angeles, August 17, 1846

29 Cong., 2 sess., House Executive Document 4, 669–670.

By Far the Most Favourable Portion

E. GOULD BUFFUM

E. Gould Buffum saw Los Angeles when it had been touched by American military occupation, an occupation proclaimed, thrown off, and then reestablished. Involved were a few officers and men from the Navy, Fremont's battalion of volunteers, Kearny's Army of the West, and the Mormon Battalion that followed over the Santa Fe Trail. Buffum was with the round-the-Horn detachment and had drawn assignment to garrison duty in Baja California. Although he went on to become a prime informant on the first season of prospecting along the Mother Lode, he observed Los Angeles before it felt any effects of that northern California discovery and rush.

One hundred and ten miles south of Santa Barbara is the *Pueblo de los Angeles* (City of the Angels), the garden spot of California. It is situated at the end of an immense plain, which extends from San Pedro, the port of the *Pueblo*, twenty-five miles distant, to this point. As in all California towns, the houses are built of *adobe* and are covered with an asphaltum, which is found in great quantities, issuing from the ground near the town. The northern portion of the town is laid out in streets, and appropriated as the residence of the trading citizens, while the southern part is made up of gardens, vineyards, and orchards. Through all these a large stream runs, which is used to irrigate the soil. The vineyards are lovely spots; trimmed every year, and thus kept about six feet in height, and in the fall of the year are hanging thick with clusters of grapes. In addition to these, apples, pears, peaches, plums, and figs are raised in great abundance. An

119

American, named Wolfskill, has here a vineyard containing thirty thousand bearing grape-vines, from which he makes annually a thousand barrels of wine, and two or three hundred of *aguardiente*, the brandy of the country. Some of this wine is a very superior article, resembling in its flavour the best Madeira, while another kind, the *vino tinto*, is execrable stuff. With proper care and apparatus, however, the grape of the *Pueblo* could be made to yield as good wine as any in the world; and the whole plain, twenty-five miles in extent, reaching to the beach at San Pedro, is susceptible of the cultivation of the vine.

Until the late astonishing growth of San Francisco, the Pueblo was the largest town in California, containing about two thousand inhabitants, who are principally wealthy rancheros, and those who reside there to cultivate the grape. Game of many kinds abounds in the vicinity of the Pueblo. During the rainy season, the plains in the direction of San Pedro are covered with millions of geese and ducks, which are shot by the dozen, while the surrounding hills afford an abundance of quails, deer, elk, and antelope.

The inhabitants of the Pueblo are of the better and wealthier class of Californians, and have always been strongly disposed towards the institutions of Mexico, and at the time of the conquest of California, they fought with a determined resistance against the naval forces of Commodore Stockton. They have now, however, become reconciled to the institutions of our country, and will, I doubt not, in a few years make as good a set of democrats as can be found in Missouri or Arkansas. They are very strongly attached to the Roman Catholic Church, and are probably the most "religious," in their acceptation of the term, of any people in California. Every morning the solemn toll of the church-bell calls them to mass; at noon it is rung again, and every Poblano at the sound doffs his sombrero, and remains reverently uncovered in the hot sun, while the bell reminds him that he is to mutter over a short prayer. In whatever avocation they may be engaged, whether fiddling, dancing, singing, slaughtering cattle, or playing billards or montè, the custom is invariably followed. I have seen a party in a tavern in the Pueblo, busily engaged in betting against a montè bank, when the noonday bell tolled; a fellow, with his last dollar in the world placed upon a card, immediately doffed his hat and muttered his prayer; the dealer laid down his cards and did the same, and they continued in their humble positions till the bell ceased tolling, when the game and the swearing went on as busily as usual.

About ten miles from Los Angeles, is the mission of San Gabriel, located upon the river of that name, whose banks for miles are girdled with grape-vines. This is one of the prettiest spots in California, and affords a fine opportunity for the raising of fruit. The country around the Pueblo is by far the most favourable portion of southern California for the settlement of foreigners. Possessing a climate of unequalled mildness, and a soil of great fertility, it must inevitably, ere long, be surrounded by a large population.

E. Gould Buffum, *Six Months in the Gold Mines* (Philadelphia, 1850), 144–146 (reprinted by the Ward Ritchie Press, 1959).

A Forty-Niner Welcomed
JACOB Y. STOVER

The natural preference of the forty-niners was to go directly to the diggings. Most who entered by way of Yuma passed through Los Angeles as did a few others who left the main overland trail and struck off southwestward from Salt Lake. Of that contingent, Jacob Y. Stover was one of the more fortunate.

We went in the evening on the desert and travelled all night. Next day it rained on us, it gave us water to drink but made it slippery to walk. The second night I shall never forget. We were sleepy, tired and hungry. We went five to ten miles and stopped to rest; we burned grease wood and then lay or stood around to get warm. This was in December.

We at last got to the Mojave River. The third night, which was dry, we found a deep hole that had water in it; we drank and what horses we had left drank. We lay down on the sand and gravel and slept good. Next morning we got up and ate a bite and started up the river. It had been a little cloudy and misty down where we were; we hadn't gone more than a mile or so when all at once we saw the water coming three or four feet high abreast, carrying with it sticks, brush and logs, and on top six inches of foam. We ran to the nearest bank and just made it. Part of our men were way down below. We hallooed to them so they got out on the same side that we did.

We travelled up the stream all day but did not make very good headway, there being so much brush on the mountain side. Hunt's trail we could see now and then on the other side. Night came on we were on the wrong side of the river. The river was getting down. We went to the water edge, stripped off our clothes, waded over, got some wood, made a fire, warmed ourselves, and slept there for the night. We came to the conclusion that a cloud had bursted. We could see the mountain covered white with snow.

Next morning we started on Hunt's trail, got two or three miles when Jim and I (ahead as usual) came on two fine fat steers, drove them a few rods, were thinking of having some fine beef when we met a man hunting them. He said he was sent out with provision for us. He took us up to his wagon. We saw some tallow where he had been frying his fat beef. I think it was half an inch thick and as big as the bottom of the frying pan. We got hold of it about the same time, broke it about the middle I guess—we didn't measure it, but ate it down and looked for more. That tasted as good as pie did at home.

But we did not stop at that; we took our butcher knives, cut off chunks and put them on the coals and broiled them, wet up corn meal, put on flat rocks, and were in the business by the time the rest got there. They followed suit as quick as they saw what was going on. The man sat and looked on. We filled ourselves, then we commenced to ask him how far it was to California. He said, "Oh, you can get there tomorrow."

You better believe we felt good to think that only one more day and we would see that long-looked for place. He told us to take what meal we wanted and meat, so we did. The man went on out to meet more hungry people.

We started down the creek, crossing the creek every few rods, then wading in water, till we began to get hungry again. We stopped and baked on stones and cooked the meat on sticks and ate everything he had given us, then started on.

About sun down we got out of the canon to the loveliest place I ever saw; everything looked so nice and warm; the frogs were singing and the birds too; it seemed like we had passed into a new world. We went about one hundred and sixty rods and came to an oak grove; the wind had blown the leaves up against a log and made us a bed; we thought we would not reject the offer. We spread our blankets and turned in for the night. We were up at daylight on the road, the birds were singing; I can't describe the joy and happiness we all felt. Everything seemed so lovely.

In the afternoon we got to the first ranch, it was called Pokamongo Ranch in Spanish; in English, Negro Ranch. The owner was a negro. We came to the house, stacked our blankets in a pile, and went up where he was making wine of grapes and in rather a novel way to us. He had a beef hide with a hole in the center of the hide, four forks planted in the ground and four poles run through holes cut in the edge of the hide, which bagged down so it would hold two or three bushels of grapes. He had two forks, one on each side of the skin, and a pole tied from one fork to the other. Two buck Indians, stripped off naked, took hold of this pole with their hands and tramped the grapes. The wine would run. We ate grapes then went at the wine, caught it in our tin cups, as we all had one apiece. The old negro after awhile said, "Gentlemen, you have had a hard time of it, I know, but de first ting you know you will know noting. You are welcome to it."

The old negro was right. They began to tumble over and the wine came up as fast as it went down. He got a spade and gave it to me, told me to dig holes at their mouths. So I did. Finally Dr. Downer and I were the only ones left on our feet. The sun was about one hour high was the last thing I recollect. Sometime in the night I waked up and found myself lying on my back, the stars shining in my face. I felt cold. How came I to be lying on the grass? I felt around for my blankets. I began to realize my situation seeing the rest of the company lying as I had left them. I looked around, found my blankets, went to bed.

123

Now this spree was on Christmas day. In the morning when we all got up we felt pretty good but awfully hungry. The old negro sent two of his buckaries out to fetch in a beef for us. They brought in one. We soon had beef and corn meal, ate what we could, thanked him and started for Los Angeles.

John W. Caughey, ed., "The Jacob Y. Stover Narrative," *Pacific Historical Review*, VI (1937), 175–177.

Slave Mart
HORACE BELL

Many ranchos and some other towns used Indian labor. Los Angeles was the only one in which this particular substitute for a hiring hall was in operation.

On the Sunday following I witnessed a sight that if it could be seen now would fill the mind with loathing and disgust. At the time referred to, 1851–52–53, the Mission Indians were numerous. They had only been emancipated from the rule of the Mission fathers a few years prior to the advent of the Americans, and their number at the time seemed without limit.

These thousands of Indians had been held in the most rigid discipline by the Mission fathers, and after their emancipation by the Supreme Government of Mexico, had been reasonably well governed by the local authorities, who found in them indispensable auxiliaries as farmers and harvesters, hewers of wood and drawers of water, and besides the best horse breakers and herders in the world, an indispensable adjunct in the management of the great herds of the country. These Indians were Christians, docile even to servility, and the best of laborers. Then came the Americans, followed soon thereafter by the discovery of and wild rush for gold, and the relaxation for the time of a healthy administration of the laws, and the ruin of those once happy and useful people commenced. The cultivators of vineyards commenced paying their Indian peons with *aguardiente*, a veritable firewater and no mistake. The consequence was that on being paid off on Saturday evening, they would meet in great gatherings called peons, and pass the night in gambling, drunkenness and debauchery. On Sunday the streets would be crowded from morn till night with Indians, males and females of all ages, from the girl of ten or twelve, to the old man and woman of seventy or eighty.

By four o'clock on Sunday afternoon Los Angeles street from Commercial to *Nigger Alley*, Aliso street from Los Angeles to Alameda, and *Nigger Alley*, would be crowded with a mass of drunken Indians, yelling and fighting. Men and women, boys and girls, tooth and toe nail, sometimes, and frequently with knives, but always in a manner that would strike the beholder with awe and horror.

About sundown the pompous marshal, with his Indian special deputies, who had been kept in jail all day to keep them sober, would drive and drag the herd to a big corral in the rear of Downey Block, where they would sleep away their intoxication, and in the morning they would be exposed for sale, as slaves for the week. Los Angeles had its slave mart, as well as New Orleans and Constantinople—only the slave at Los Angeles was sold fifty-two times a year as long as he lived, which did not generally exceed one, two, or three years, under the new dispensation. They would be sold for a week, and bought up by the vineyard men and others at prices ranging from one to three dollars, one-third of which was to be paid to the peon at the end of the week, which debt, due for well performed labor, would invariably be paid in *aguardiente*, and the Indian would be made happy until the following Monday morning, having passed through another Saturday night and Sunday's saturnalia of debauchery and bestiality. Those thousands of honest, useful people were absolutely destroyed in this way. Vineyards were of great profit in those days, and would be today, if we could recall the times as they were before the conquering Saxon came with his boasted perfection of laws, and his much-vaunted *advance civilization.*

Surely, we civilized the race of Mission Indians with a refinement known to no other people under the sun.

The poor Indians are all gone, the crumbling walls of the old Missions and the decaying trunks of the vineyards, no longer profitable when cultivated with honestly compensated labor, stand silent witnesses of the time long gone by, when the Indian, though compelled to labor, was happy and content in viewing the groaning granaries that assured him and his an ample support.

Horace Bell, *Reminiscences of a Ranger* (Los Angeles, 1881), 34–36.

I Know the "Californians" Well
BENJAMIN HAYES

Arriving in Los Angeles in 1850, Benjamin Hayes began his career as a lawyer and after 1852 as a judge. He was an inveterate contributor to the newspapers, keeper of a diary and a meteorological record, and accumulator of a massive scrapbook collection on local and regional history, a treasure trove for Hubert Howe Bancroft when that collector-historian cast his net in the southern part of the state. Hayes soon was as knowledgeable about Los Angeles as any of the older residents. He is credited as ghostwriter of the report on the Indians referred to in the letter that follows. Of added significance is what this letter reveals about tensions between the new and old Californians.

Los Angeles, January 14, 1853

At this time I wish to say a word or two touching on Indian Affairs. Let me get you to notice the Report of the Indian agent for this District, Benjamin D. Wilson, Esq. I am acquainted, of my own knowledge, with nearly all the facts stated by him concerning the character of these Indians, the country they live in, their troubles for the last three years and the causes of them. I have travelled over a

126

great part of their country and camped in it. My opportunities have been various and constant for observing them. And I have given no little attention to the subject—more I suspect, than any other resident here, unless I except Mr. Wilson.

A man who has never mixed with these Indians, can have no idea of the utter difference between them and those of the Great Plains —whose character for the chase and war has so long baffled the benevolent designs of the Government. This Report ought to be printed by Congress and circulated generally in this State and elsewhere. It presents the true plan for managing these Indians. And the boldness with which he asserts the legal right of the Mission Indians to their property, in the face of the *speculators* in Mission titles, some of them otherwise his bosom friends, might immortalize some men, even of greater ability and in a higher station.

I am partly induced to write this letter—without his knowledge (for I shall not show it to him)—by having heard this evening, that some half dozen worthy men who suppose the whole weight and responsibility of the different officers here is upon their shoulders, think of getting up a sort of recommendation of Don *Antonio F. Coronel*, for this office. I know him intimately, respect him, and would do any thing reasonable to advance his interests. He has been assessor of this county, is rather popular, clever and sprightly, has been active as a Democrat in the two political elections we have had here as yet—supported *me* warmly. But, I cannot conscientiously favor him for this responsible post. He is a Mexican by birth, but has been in California some years; he is not a "native Californian." So that his appointment would be no extraordinary complement to the "native Californians" (as they are called). They might be flattered by something of the kind, for the matter of "nine days" or so; if any letters from here assert differently, I assure you, it's mere *stuff*.

I know the "Californians" well. And all of them who would not associate with the idea of an Indian Agent the sole prospect of *dividing out the Indians by force to work on the ranchos*, would infinitely prefer some competent American to one of their own number, under present circumstances.

Candidly, this office ought to be filled by an American, or somebody who can speak English. This seems to be a *sine qua non*. They are to be reared to the uses of American Civilization which cannot be easily separated from the language in which it expresses itself. Mr. Coronel does not write, read, or speak English. It is no disparagement of his other qualities, to say, frankly, that he has not that degree of *moral courage* requisite for an Indian agent in California. There is an absolute necessity of having men here, of iron firmness, to execute the laws, without respect to local caprices, or interests, or prejudices. I do not believe the Indian intercourse laws can be enforced here, by any but an American against Americans (of whom there may be plenty to violate them). This is a daily experience, in judicial and other proceedings. Generally speaking, a "Californian" will not accept an office to which any similar responsibility is attached. You could not get one, for example, to run for Sheriff or constable—not because he could not be elected; but for the reason, that he naturally shuns civil positions of difficulty or danger.

Besides, if you have such an Agent, all your sub-agents, must be of the same class. Americans will not be under the control of such an Agent. They will either resign, or they will control him; which, I suppose is not the spirit of the law. The last would be the result invariably, and any system whatsoever become full of abuses. I should tremble for the poor Indian subjected to them.

Moreover, grave questions are agitated in relation to the rights of these Indians—and of many white persons—under the old law in force here concerning the Missions, etc. The men who took part in public transactions from 1834 to July, 1846, in California, might be good witnesses, in regard to them, but I will ask in sober earnest, would they be the best judges, or would they make the proper representatives of the rights and interests of others, which their own acts as legislators or otherwise, whether of omission or commission, may have directly affected?

The condition of the Indians during the period referred to, is a black page of history. I believe, Mr. Coronel then was never more than *Alcalde*. But it is readily seen, the Government needs men without even that connection with so unfortunate an epoch of Indian misrule, oppression, and injustice. There is more in this objection than I can conveniently put to paper.

Mr. Wilson is an old mountaineer, and a gentleman in every sense of the word. He is wealthy and independent—and so does not need this office. His wealth has come to him in a measure suddenly, by the rise of property; after many "hard knocks" in the Rocky Mountains and here, before, during and since the war. He has been in some little campaigns formerly against portions of these Indians, and knows them, and they know him well. Before his appointment, the Chiefs visiting the City, habitually came to see and talk with him about their business, as much as if he were their Agent. Notoriously he is a favorite with them—no stranger. His good sense, kindness of heart, knowledge of mountain life, familiarity with all the tribes, and reputation for integrity of purpose, are difficult to combine in any one else that may be recommended from this quarter. . . .

It would be good policy to keep him in this office, at any rate until some efficient plan is put in operation for the benefit of these Indians: the difficulty of making any plan work well is at the beginning. A removal ought not to be made prematurely, or hastily.

Draft, Hayes Scrapbooks, Bancroft Library, XXXIX, 121.

The Washington Birthday Ball
HORACE BELL

Ranger, editor, and spitfire, Horace Bell was a character in his own right. He best survives as raconteur on Los Angeles in the stirring fifties. Some of his stories border on tall tales. This most circulated one, as is true of most of the others, had a hard core of fact.

Soon after my arrival in Los Angeles it was my good fortune to attend a first-class ball at the house of Don José Antonio Carrillo, a first-class citizen, who had been honored with a seat in the Sovereign Congress of Mexico. He had also been the military head of the country, and was at the head of the native California *ton.*

The ball was the first of the season, and was attended by the *elite* of the country from San Diego to Monterey. The dancing hall was large, with a floor as polished as a bowling saloon. The music was excellent—one splendid performer on an immense harp.

The assembled company was not only elegant—it was surpassingly brilliant. The dresses of both ladies and gentlemen could not be surpassed in expensive elegance. The fashions of the *gringo* world had made little innovation on the gorgeous and expensive attire of the country as to the gentlemen, while the ladies were resplendent in all the expense of fashion that could be supplied by unlimited resources. The writer had read Major Emory's book on California, in which, after lauding the California horsemen above the Comanche Indian and the Bedouin Arab, he went on to say that "the ladies excelled in dancing more than did the men in horsemanship."

Being thus prepared, the writer expected to witness reasonably elegant Terpsichorean performances, but the dancing on that occasion was something more than elegant, it was wonderful, while the most dignified and staid decorum was observed to the end of the festivities, which broke up about two o'clock in the morning. . . .

Some two and a half months thereafter we had one of those very elegant and exclusive affairs that ended in blood, its very exclusiveness being the cause of its very sanguinary termination. The ball was given at the house of Don Abel Stearns, a very wealthy American, on Washington's birthday, February 22, 1853, and was a grand and patriotic affair, but very exclusive. Somehow or other two or three gamblers were invited guests at the ball, which gave grave offense to the fraternity in general, among whom were many first class Americans, good and patriotic fellows, who loved their country and venerated the name of the immortal hero in honor of whose memory the grand affair was gotton up. These gentlemen maintained that on national occasions one American was as good as another, and that the whole community were on an equal footing, and that to attempt an exclusive national celebration was tomfoolery of the first order. So about two hundred of them assembled to *bust up* and disperse the exclusive humbug. The first move was to get the old cannon, which was grown rusty for lack of revolutions, and place it in position directly in front of the house and bearing on one of the doors. They then procured a large beam, to be used as a battering ram when the time arrived for the general assault—all of which was done with the utmost silence.

At about midnight, when the patriotic dancing was at fever heat, and everything was hilarious within, the old gun was let off, and the battering-ram was driven with terrific force against the other door. Fortunately the cannon was badly trained, and the charge missed the door. The battering-ram, however, did its work well, and the door burst in with a tremendous crash. It fortunately happened that one game little fellow, who was one of the exclusives, was dancing directly in front of the burst-in door, and had a battery of Colts buckled to him, either of which was nearly as large as himself.

This patriotic exclusive stepped directly to the door and plugged the first gentleman who attempted to enter. Then another, and another, and by this time the affair had assumed all the beautiful proportions of a first-class revolution, and the firing became general. Of the assailants several were shot down, and the assault effectually repulsed; while of the exclusives but one man was wounded, and he the gay and festive Myron Norton, the chivalric vanquisher of the great Largo in that memorable game of billiards heretofore referred to. The brilliant Norton received a gentle perforation, that placed him *hors du combat* for some time thereafter.

For the next few days the angels were on a war footing; the community was divided; the defeated gamblers swore vengeance; the well-heeled exclusives were on the alert, determined not to be taken unawares; a general conflict seemed imminent; on retiring at night doors were barricaded and arms carefully examined; a silent, moody gloom prevailed; the gamblers would meet in groups and menacingly discuss the situation; the business part of the community was greatly alarmed. Confidence was only restored when Don Andrés Pico came out and gave the gamblers to emphatically understand that, on the first hostile demonstration, he would raise the native Californians *en masse* against them, and that he would not be responsible for the consequences. It nevertheless took months to cool off the bad blood engendered by that affair of the 22nd of February, 1853, and for some time individual collisions were of frequent occurrence.

Horace Bell, *Reminiscences of a Ranger* (Los Angeles, 1881), 79–82.

131

Charles Koppel, Pacific Railroad Surveys

View from Fort Moore Hill, 1853

Reminiscences of the Fifties

HARRIS NEWMARK

At the sixtieth anniversary of his arrival in Los Angeles as a pioneer merchant, Harris Newmark was persuaded to set down his recollections. He did so, and then had the good fortune of having Perry Worden take them in hand for verification and amplification from the newspapers and other sources. The result is tremendously informative, the principal source on Southern California from 1853 to 1913, and with an engaging quality that suggested calling it the Pepys' Diary of Los Angeles.

Informality in Court

Jurymen and others would come in coatless and, especially in warm weather, without vests and collars. It was the fashion for each juryman to provide himself with a jack-knife and a piece of wood, in order that he might whittle the time away. This was a recognized privilege, and I am not exaggerating when I say that if he forgot his piece of wood, it was considered his further prerogative to whittle the chair on which he sat!

In other respects, also, court solemnity was lacking. Judge and attorneys would frequently lock horns; and sometimes their disputes ended violently. On one occasion, for example, while I was in court, Columbus Sims, an attorney who came here in 1852, threw an inkstand at his opponent, during an altercation; but this contempt of court did not call forth his disbarment, for he was later found acting as attorney for Pancho Daniel, one of Sheriff Barton's murderers, until sickness compelled his retirement from the case. As to panel-service, I recollect that while serving as juror in those early days, we were once locked up for the night; and in order that time might not hang too heavily on our hands, we engaged in a sociable little game of poker.

More than inkstands were sometimes hurled in the early courts. On one occasion, for instance, after the angry disputants had arrived at a state of agitation which made the further use of canes, chairs, and similar objects tame and uninteresting, revolvers were drawn, notwithstanding the marshal's repeated attempts to restore order. Judge Dryden, in the midst of the *mêlée*, hid behind the platform upon which his Judgeship's bench rested, and being well out of the range of the threatening irons, yelled at the rioters:

"*Shoot away*, damn you! and to *hell* with all of you!"

Storekeepers Pass the Time

When I began business in Los Angeles, most of the storekeepers contented themselves with signs rudely lettered or painted on unbleached cloth, and nailed on the outside of the adobe walls of their shops. Later, their signs were on bleached cloth and secured in frames without glass. In 1865, we had a painted wooden sign; and still later, many establishments boasted of letters in gold on the glass doors and windows. So too, when I first came here, merchants wrote their own billheads and often did not take the trouble to do that; but within two or three years afterward, they began to have them printed.

People were also not as particular about keeping their places of business open all day. Proprietors would sometimes close their stores and go out for an hour or two for their meals, or to meet in a friendly game of billiards. During the monotonous days when but little business was being transacted, it was not uncommon for merchants to visit back and forth and to spend hours at a time in playing cards. To provide a substitute for a table, the window sill of the thick adobe was used, the visitor seating himself on a box or barrel on the outside, while the host within at the window would make himself equally comfortable. Without particularizing, it is safe to state that the majority of early traders indulged in such methods of killing time. During this period of miserably lighted thoroughfares, and before the arrival of many American families, those who did not play cards and billiards in the saloons met at night at each other's stores where, on an improvised table, they indulged in a little game of draw.

Squeaking *Carretas*

Carriages were very scarce in California at the time of my arrival, although there were a few, Don Abel Stearns possessing the only private vehicle in Los Angeles; and transportation was almost entirely by means of saddle-horses, or the native capacious *carretas*. These consisted of a heavy platform, four or five by eight or ten feet in size, mounted on two large solid wheels, sawed out of logs, and were exceedingly primitive in appearance, although the owners sometimes decorated them elaborately; while the wheels moved on coarse wooden axles, affording the traveler more jounce than restful ride. The *carretas* served, indeed, for nearly all the carrying business that was done between the ranchos and Los Angeles; and when in operation, the squeaking could be heard at a great distance, owing especially to the fact that the air being undisturbed by factories or noisy traffic, quiet generally prevailed. . . .

This sharp squeaking of the *carreta*, however, while penetrating and disagreeable in the extreme, served a purpose, after all, as the signal that a buyer was approaching town; for the vehicle was likely to have on board one or even two good-sized families of women and children, and the keenest expectation of our little business world was consequently aroused, bringing merchants and clerks to the front of their stores. A couple of oxen, by means of ropes attached to their horns, pulled the *carretas*, while the men accompanied their families on horseback; and as the roving oxen were inclined to leave the road, one of the riders (wielding a long, pointed stick) was kept busy moving from side to side, prodding the wandering animals and thus holding them to the highway. Following these *carretas*, there were always from twenty-five to fifty dogs, barking and howling as if mad.

La Estrella, The Star

In 1853, there was but one newspaper in the city—a weekly known as *La Estrella de los Angeles* or *The Los Angeles Star*, printed half in Spanish, half in English. It was founded on May 17th, 1851, by John A. Lewis and John McElroy, who had their printing office in the lower room of a small wooden house on Los Angeles Street, near the corral of the Bella Union hotel. This firm later became Lewis, McElroy & Rand.

There was then no telegraphic communication with the outside world, and the news ordinarily conveyed by the sheet was anything but important. Indeed, all such information was known, each week, by the handful of citizens in the little town long before the paper was published, and delays in getting mail from a distance—in one case the post from San Francisco to Los Angeles being under way no less than fifty-two days!—led to Lewis giving up the editorship in disgust. When a steamer arrived, some little news found its way into the paper; but even then matters of national and international moment became known in Los Angeles only after the lapse of a month or so. . . .

Our first Los Angeles newspaper was really more of an advertising medium than anything else, and the printing outfit was decidedly primitive, though the printers may not have been as badly off as were the typos of the *Californian*. The latter, using type picked up in a Mexican cloister, found no *W*'s among the Spanish letters and had to set double *V*'s until more type was brought from the Cannibal or Sandwich Islands!

American Takeover

The Church at the Plaza

The only church in Los Angeles at this time was that of *Nuestra Señora la Reyna de los Angeles*, known as Our Lady, the Queen of the Angeles, at the Plaza; and since but few changes were made for years in its exterior, I looked upon the edifice as the original adobe built here in the eighties of the preceding century. When I came to inquire into the matter, however, I was astonished to learn that the Church dated back no farther than the year 1822, although the first attempt at laying a cornerstone was made in 1815, probably somewhat to the east of the old Plaza and a year or two after rising waters frustrated the attempt to build a chapel near the river and the present Aliso Street. Those temporary foundations seem to have marked the spot where later the so-called Old Woman's Gun—once buried by Mexicans, and afterward dug up by women and used at the Battle of Dominguez Rancho—was long exposed to view, propped up on wooden blocks.

The venerable building I then saw, in which all communicants for want of pews knelt on the floor or stood while worshiping, is still admired by those to whom age and sacred tradition, and the sacrifices of the early Spanish Fathers, make appeal. In the first years of my residence here, the bells of this honored old pile, ringing at six in the morning and at eight in the evening, served as a curfew to regulate the daily activities of the town.

The First Public School

In the summer of 1853, a movement was inaugurated, through the combined efforts of Mayors Nichols and Coronel, aided by John T. Jones, to provide public schools; and three citizens, J. Lancaster Brent, Lewis Granger, and Stephen C. Foster, were appointed School Commissioners. As early as 1838, Ygnacio Coronel, assisted by his wife and daughter, had accepted some fifteen dollars a month from the authorities—to permit the exercise of official supervision—and opened a school which, as late as 1854, he conducted in his own home; thereby doubtless inspiring his son Antonio to take marked interest in the education of the Indians. From time to time, private schools, partly subsidized from public funds, were commenced.

Reminiscences of the Fifties

In May, 1854, Mayor Foster pointed out that, while there were fully five hundred children of school age and the pueblo had three thousand dollars surplus, there was still no school building which the City could call its own. New trustees—Manuel Requena, Francis Mellus, and W. T. B. Sanford—were elected; and then happened what, perhaps, has not occurred here since, or ever in any other California town: Foster, still Mayor, was also chosen School Superintendent.

The new energy put into the movement now led the Board to build, late in 1854 or early in 1855, a two-story brick schoolhouse, known as School No. 1, on the northwest corner of Spring and Second streets, on the lot later occupied, first by the old City Hall and secondly by the Bryson Block. This structure cost six thousand dollars. Strange as it now seems, the location was then rather "out in the country"; and I dare say the selection was made, in part, to get the youngsters away from the residential district around the Plaza.

There school was opened on March 19th, 1855; William A. Wallace, a botanist who had been sent here to study the flora, having charge of the boys' department and Miss Louisa Hayes directing the division for girls. . . . Having thus established a public school, the City Council voted to discontinue all subsidies to private schools.

Zanjas and Water Carriers

Zanja water was being used for irrigation when I arrived. A system of seven or eight *zanjas*, or open ditches—originated, I have no doubt, by the Catholic Fathers [on the contrary by the original settlers of the pueblo]—was then in operation, although it was not placed under the supervision of a *Zanjero*, or Water Commissioner, until 1854. These small surface canals connected at the source with the *zanja madre*, or mother ditch, on the north side of the town, from which they received their supply; the *zanja madre* itself being fed from the river, at a point a long way from town. The *Zanjero* issued permits, for which application had to be made some days in advance, authorizing the use of the water for irrigation purposes. A certain amount was paid for the use of this water during a period of twelve hours, without any limit as to the quantity consumed, and the purchaser was permitted to draw his supply both day and night.

137

Water for domestic uses was a still more expensive luxury. Inhabitants living in the immediate neighborhood of *zanjas*, or near the river, helped themselves; but their less-fortunate brethren were served by a carrier, who charged fifty cents a week for one bucket a day, while he did not deliver on Sunday at all. Extra requirements were met on the same basis; and in order to avoid an interruption in the supply, prompt settlement of the charge had to be made every Saturday evening. This character was known as Bill the Waterman. He was a tall American, about thirty or thirty-five years old; he had a mustache, wore long, rubber boots coming nearly to his waist, and presented the general appearance of a laboring man; and his somewhat rickety vehicle, drawn by two superannuated horses, slowly conveyed the man and his barrel of about sixty gallons capacity from house to house. He was a wise dispenser, and quite alert to each household's needs.

Bill obtained his supply from the Los Angeles River, where at best it was none too clean, in part owing to the frequent passage of the river by man and beast. Animals of all kinds, including cattle, horses, sheep, pigs, mules and donkeys, crossed and recrossed the stream continually, so that the mud was incessantly stirred up, and the polluted product proved unpalatable and even, undoubtedly, unhealthful. To make matters worse, the river and the *zanjas* were the favorite bathing-places, all the urchins of the hamlet disporting themselves there daily, while most of the adults, also, frequently immersed themselves. . . . The Common Council of 1850 prohibited the throwing of filth into fresh water designed for common use, and also forbade the washing of clothes on the *zanja* banks. This latter regulation was disobeyed by the native women, who continued to gather there, dip their soiled garments in the water, place them on stones and beat them with sticks, a method then popular for the extraction of dirt.

Fire Alarms and the Bucket Brigade

It was fortunate indeed that the adobe construction of the fifties rendered houses practically fireproof since, in the absence of a water-system, a bucket-brigade was all there was to fight a fire with, and this rendered but poor service. I remember such a brigade at work, some years after I came, in the vicinity of the Bell Block, when a chain of helpers formed a relay from the nearest *zanja* to the blazing structure. Buckets were passed briskly along . . . a process which continued until the fire had exhausted itself. Francis Mellus had a little hand-cart, but for lack of water it was generally useless.

Instead of fire-bells announcing to the people that a conflagration was in progress, the discharging of pistols in rapid succession gave the alarm and was the signal for a general fusillade throughout the neighboring streets. Indeed, this method of sounding a fire-alarm was used as late as the eighties. On the breaking out of fires, neighbors and friends rushed to assist the victim in saving what they could of his property.

Highway Improvement

As early as 1854, the need of better communication between Los Angeles and the outside world was beginning to be felt; and in the summer of that year the Supervisors—D. W. Alexander, S. C. Foster, J. Sepulveda, C. Aguilar and S. S. Thompson—voted to spend one thousand dollars to open a wagon road over the mountains between the San Fernando Mission and the San Francisco rancho. A rather broad trail already existed there; but such was its grade that many a pioneer, compelled to use a windlass or other contrivance to let down his wagon in safety, will never forget the real perils of the descent. For years it was a familiar experience with stages, on which I sometimes traveled, to attach chains or boards to retard their downward movement; nor were passengers even then without anxiety until the hill or Mountainside had been passed.

The Great Horse Race

The most celebrated of all these horse races of early days was that between José Andrés Sepúlveda's *Black Swan* and Pio Pico's *Sarco*, the details of which I learned, soon after I came here, from Tom Mott. Sepúlveda had imported the Black Swan from Australia, in 1852, the year of the race, while Pico chose a California steed to defend the honors of the day. Sepúlveda himself went to San Francisco to receive the consignment in person, after which he committed the thoroughbred into the keeping of Bill Brady, the trainer, who rode him down to Los Angeles, and gave him as much care as might have been bestowed upon a favorite child.

They were to race nine miles, the *carrera* commencing on San Pedro Street near the city limits, and running south a league and a half and return; and the reports of the preparation having spread throughout California, the event came to be looked upon as of such great importance, that, from San Francisco to San Diego, whoever had the money hurried to Los Angeles to witness the contest and bet on the result.

Twenty-five thousand dollars, in addition to five hundred horses, five hundred mares, five hundred heifers, five hundred calves, and five hundred sheep were among the princely stakes put up.

The wife of José Andrés was driven to the scene of the memorable contest with a veritable fortune in gold slugs wrapped in a large handkerchief. Upon arriving there, she opened her improvised purse and distributed the shining fifty-dollar pieces to all of her attendants and servants, of whom there were not a few, with the injunction that they should wager the money on the race; and her example was followed by others, so that, in addition to the cattle, land and merchandise hazarded, a considerable sum of money was bet by the contending parties and their friends. *Black Swan* won easily.

Harris Newmark, *Sixty Years in Southern California* (Boston: Houghton Mifflin Company, 1916; 3d ed. enlarged, 1930), 55–55, 80–81, 84–85, 92–94, 100–101, 105–106, 115–117, 119–121, 157–161.

Crime and Punishment
LEONARD PITT

There is an abundance of writing about crimes of violence in early Los Angeles and punishment meted out by the regular courts and in many instances by lynchings. The selection by Leonard Pitt which follows is noteworthy because it raises an-

*other dimension, the complicating factor of tensions between
the Hispanic Californios and the ever-increasing gringos, a
theme he discussed at book length.*

Vigilante justice began with a bang in the summer of 1852. In mid-
July of that year the legal authorities delivered to Los Angeles three
Latin Americans wanted for murdering two Yankee cattle buyers.
One of the trio was Doroteo Zavaleta, a soldier's son, born and reared
locally. A clod rather than a depraved character, Zavaleta had stolen
oxen, cattle, and horses from Bernardo Yorba's rancho and wood
from Manuel Garfías' property, for which he was arrested. Zavaleta
broke jail with two Sonorans, one of them Jesús Rivas, a cold-blooded
character. Seeking aid from Zavaleta's brother, the trio fled to San
Juan Capistrano "to go away from this part of the country." There,
however, they chanced upon a pair of American cattle buyers, whom
Rivas decided to rob and kill. Zavaleta later testified that he absolutely
rejected the idea of murder, particularly when his brother agreed to
give them horses for their trip to Mexico. After robbing the Americans of $500 Zavaleta wanted to flee, but Rivas saw the danger of this
plan and committed the final deed. Later he claimed that Zavaleta had
incited the murder and had killed one of the pair.

With decorum unsurpassed in San Francisco, Los Angeles convened its own vigilante committee. Abel Stearns, initiator of the
proceedings, served as chairman; Señor Rojo and Mr. Sanford took
the minutes; and Mr. Dryden translated them. Alex Bell, Francisco
Mellus, and Manuel Garfías selected a jury of seven Yankees and five
Latin Americans (José Antonio Yorba, Andrés Pico, Dolores Sepúlveda, Felipe Lugo, and Julián Chávez). A committee of public safety
(Manuel Requeña, Matthew Keller, J. R. Scott, Lewis Granger, Rojo,
and John G. Downey) took the prisoners' confessions in English and
Spanish. The jury returned a verdict of first-degree murder for
Zavaleta and Rivas, and the next morning the town witnessed its first
"grand" lynching.

Thus ended the first popular tribunal, which for its ethnic makeup
and judiciousness won the approval even of the Californios. Ideally,

Manual Garfías, as an interested party, should not have helped select a jury, and a clever defense lawyer might have empaneled lower-class Latin Americans to offset the obvious class prejudice against the prisoners. It is very likely, though, that a regular jury would have rendered the same verdicts—all the more reason to wonder why the town refused to allow the law courts to function normally.

A second vigilance committee was formed after the murder of the estimable Joshua H. Bean, four months later, on November 7, 1852, near former San Gabriel Mission. This time the entire town, rather than the vigilantes alone, pressed the issue, for Bean was a courageous and popular figure, unlike his notorious brother, Judge Roy Bean, "the Law West of the Pecos." Actually, two bodies convened: a central committee consisting of two gringos and M. C. Rojo, and a committee at large composed of Rojo and six gringos. These were as respectable a group of vigilantes as could be found anywhere. Salomón Pico's name arose in connection with the crime, and rangers arrested and jailed several Sonorans and a young Californian thought to be allied with him—"Eleuterio," the cobbler Cipriano Sandoval of San Gabriel, Juan Rico, Reyes Feliz, and the Indian, Felipe Reid, adopted son of Hugo Reid. Young Reid maintained his innocence, but Sandoval claimed that he had stumbled into him in the darkness, that Reid at first had blurted out his guilt but then denied it and finally had tried to bribe him to seal his lips. Reyes Feliz also pleaded innocence, but so frantically that he confessed a previous crime. For ten days the committee grilled the dazed suspects, separately and together, analyzing and reanalyzing the testimony and seeking corroboration for new points. Although unsure of themselves, the vigilantes nonetheless felt that they had the culprits at hand and rested their case before the town.

The tribunal that meted out justice was utterly chaotic. After hearing the evidence about Reyes Feliz, a "ferocious looking gambler" mounted a chair and moved that Feliz be hanged; the crowd assented. The same verdict was meted out to Sandoval, about whom little was actually known. Reid was turned over to regular officials for disposal, although many suspected him because of his known rivalry with Bean for the attentions of an Indian woman. On Sunday the town climbed toward a gray sky to gather before the gibbet on Fort Hill.

142

The two prisoners were led up by a priest (and accompanied by yet a third Latin American caught attempting murder that very morning when the public's dander was up). Before a silent crowd, Sandoval reasserted that he had no connection with this or any other murder and prayed for the Lord's forgiveness for himself and his tormentors. He kissed the crucifix and then was hanged. Says Horace Bell: "A peal of thunder announced the end of the tragedy," and heavy rain began to fall, whereupon the crowd retired quietly to the local saloons. The words of cobbler Sandoval and the thunder later were to nettle the town's conscience; years afterward, the true killer made a death-bed confession, which belatedly made some Angeleños wary of vigilante proceedings.

The third vigilante action, in 1853, concerned Mexican bandits. At the first rumor that the bandido chieftain Joaquín might be attending a fandango at the Moreno adobe, the pugnacious Texans from El Monte got into fighting regalia and went to investigate. "Immediately taken into custody by an overwhelming array of black-eyed Señoritas," the "Texas rangers" neglected their mission. Additional bandit activity two months later led to the formation of Captain Hope's Rangers. Only five of Hope's twenty-three gringo horsemen were among the town's respectables. Although mainly Texans again, they politely tendered their services to Mexican Mayor Antonio Coronel and gladly accepted a gift of a hundred broken horses from Pio Pico and Ygnacio del Valle. Upon hearing that Joaquín was definitely within city limits, writes the ranger historian Bell, the company sallied forth at midnight to "search every suspicious house and place within the city limits." Men scoured Nigger Alley, Sonoratown, the vineyards, and all nearby suburban huts, but without result, escept that one party retrieved a stolen jackass.

Bandido depredations, even murders, continued. By late August volunteer mounted police numbered a hundred men, including Agustín Olvera, Juan Sepúlveda, F. L. Guirado, and new gringo worthies. When a visiting cattle buyer was murdered by his Sonoran interpreter, Vergara, they pursued the felon for 90 miles, driving him into the clutches of the soldiers stationed at Yuma, who killed him. He was not yet quite dead when another Sonoran, named Senate, killed Marshal Whaling and escaped. With new resolve, the rangers chased from one canyon to another in every direction, seeking the trail of the will-o'-the-wisp, Joaquín.

One night twenty-one unidentified bandidos broke into the home of a Frenchman named Lelong and murdered him. They raided the "Spanish houses" in Sonoratown, abducted some girls to a nearby headquarters, and escaped. By October, "rumors of a Mexican invasion and an expulsion of the gringos" evolved into a state of siege and a business standstill. Finally, rangers trapped eight bandits in a cornfield—one of them a woman—but they had no connection with Lelong's murderer. The district attorney told the town that "it was not our hang" and packed the captives off to their own stamping ground of San Luis Obispo for appropriate treatment.

The recent violent occurrences began to sink down into the endless annals of unsolved crimes, when guilt devolved on two missing Sonorans, Luis Burgos (lately allied with Vergara) and Senate, whose last known act was to stab a man and flee for his life. Judge Hayes feared that putting a reward on their heads would create a "bad state of society" among the Latin Americans, but Sheriff Barton nonetheless offered $500 for the culprits, dead or alive, for the crimes of murder, theft, and rape. The reward was claimed by a Californio who brought in the bodies of Burgos and Senate neatly arranged in a carreta. He offered no explanation, but the key to the whole mystery was discovered soon afterward, when a Sonoran sold a watch that formerly had belonged to Lelong. This was Atanacio Moreno who, under close questioning, confessed to having led the recent bandido troop, including Senate and Burgos, whom he had killed after a falling-out. On April 5 Judge Hayes sentenced Moreno to fifteen years. "He took the sentence with perfect composure," noted the judge. This interrupted (but did not end) the checkered career of a "tall, straight, fine appearing white man, belonging to the best blood of Sonora . . . [who had once] stood well in society, and was highly respected."

Not until February, 1854, after a six-year judicial interregnum, did Los Angeles witness its first bona fide execution. The victim was a Mexican, Ygnacio Herrara, who had "killed one of his own race, about a woman!" Thousands attended the historic event, including many Latin Americans who admitted Herrara's guilt but cursed Hayes's death sentence and wondered if he would henceforth punish gringo killers with equal severity. Hayes himself took the event in stride and merely wrote of the Mexican's repentance and of the prayerful attitude of the entire Catholic population. "At their request, candles were burnt there [at the scaffold] last night and today he was buried with martial music and religious rites."

Plainly, by 1854 the Spanish-speaking of Los Angeles felt oppressed by a double standard of justice such as some of them had previously experienced in the gold mines. One sees here in embryo resentments about "Anglo justice" similar to those that have incited Mexican-Americans in more recent times.

Leonard Pitt, *The Decline of the Californios* (Berkeley and Los Angeles: University of California Press, 1966), 156–160.

Getting Out the Vote
HORACE BELL

Although when he went to print in 1881 Horace Bell dates this particular election day as in 1853, his figure of 5,000 for the Los Angeles population suggests a somewhat later date. In all probability his description was intended to fit an ongoing practice.

Los Angeles polled a very great vote in the happy times of pioneer elections. With her population of 5,000, a greater number of votes were deposited in the ballot-boxes than at present, with our four times greater number of noses, and it will now be the duty of the writer to

145

attempt to explain the modus operandi of getting four or five votes out of each sovereign voter.

May Day election arrived. The sun of Austerlitz rose in all the splendor only known to this sunny clime. Before he cast his first glittering rays on *Gallows Hill,* so styled at the time by some profane people, the whole population seemed thoroughly aroused to the importance of the great event. Anxious looking individuals could be seen with pockets full of tickets, hurrying towards the plaza, the *Nigger Alley* corner of which was the polling place. By 8 o'clock A.M. several old army ambulances, ablaze with banners bearing the name of some candidate, commenced driving up and down the principal streets at a furious pace, while one immense wagon with a full band of Mexican circus performers, drove up and down the streets with a regular force of skirmishers and flankers thrown out, capturing and bringing in to the great wagon American citizens to be used as stepping stones to the fortune of some aspiring local politician. When the wagon was filled to its utmost capacity the music would cease, and the great vehicle would be driven in all haste to the polls, and the captured sovereigns would be taken out and marched up to the ballot-box, and after an immense amount of skirmishing and squabbling, for be it known they were not quietly permitted to vote, as the friends and strikers of opposing candidates made every possible effort to change the ticket on the voters as they stood in line waiting their turn.

The duties of American citizenship were finally discharged, and one might suppose the victims were quietly permitted to depart. Not so, however, they were immediately taken in charge by another detachment of the candidates who had first made capture and duly marched off, for what purpose, or where, only the initiated at that time could know. In a brief space of time, however, the same crowd would return to the polls, and for the second time duly discharge the duties of freemen, and will the writer's veracity be questioned when he asserverates that this herd of captured voters would be voted at least five times during the day, and every one of them would in all probability be Mexican and frequently aboriginal Indians, and in no wise entitled to vote.

The *modus* was in this wise: After voting the first time, which would be under gentle pressure, they would be taken to an improvised barber-shop, and their long hair cropped and being otherwise disguised, and then returned to the polls and voted under an assumed name; they would then return to the shaving place and go through another operation, and a possible whitewashing, another name would be given the citizen, also another drink and another dollar, and another vote would be polled for some enterprising candidate.

Voting in early times used to be a lucrative business, and voters were considered valuable according to the facility offered for disguising one's self. *Old Payuche,* who at this day honors our chain-gang with his valuable services, used to be, as I am informed by an old politician, who is yet in the harness, disguised and voted five times at each successive election. Times have materially changed; at the present time the voters shave the candidates, in place of being shaved, as in the happy times long gone by.

Peter Biggs was in his glory on that election day. His shop and its various branches were crowded all day.

It was astonishing the amount of silver in circulation on that day. Mexican dollars were as abundant as $50 slugs, and more so, a dollar being the price of a vote. The reader will at once inquire, as did the innocent chronicler at the time, why so much strife, so much manoeuvring, such an expenditure of cash, when the annual salary of the mayor, who was at the head of the ticket, was only $500. The Councilmen drew no pay, the marshal's perquisites were small; the assessor also got $500. The explanantion is that this angelic city had a grand domain to be disposed of, the foundation of future jobs, and land operations were to be planned and fixed up with a view to future profit, and that was why such stupendous efforts were made to carry the election in May, 1853. It is not necessary to inform the reader what gentlemen were honored with the people's preference on that memorable day, only, as before stated, the gay and festive hangman was elected marshal, and the people raised *Old Nick* on that occasion. They set a bad precedent, that has been improved and refined, until at this day we have the most skilfully managed elections that could be imagined outside the infernal regions.

Horace Bell, *Reminiscences of a Ranger* (Los Angeles, 1881), 92–95.

The Captivity of Olive Oatman

LOS ANGELES STAR

In 1856 Californians thrilled to the news of Olive Oatman's release from captivity with the Mojaves. On her arrival in Los Angeles the Star *enterprisingly interviewed her and on April 19 gave the story two front-page columns. The San Francisco* Alta California *and* Daily Herald *ran the entire interview on April 23 and the* California Chronicle *and the* Sacramento Daily Union *did so on April 25.*

The Oatmans [Royce Oatman, his wife and seven children] started from Iowa in company with the family of Mr. Thompson, with whom they travelled together as far as Tueson, in Sonora, where Mr. T. resolved to lay by to recruit his cattle and wait for other trains to come up, so as to insure the safety of the road by numbers. But the Oatmans pushed on, impatient to get through, and met their fate on the Gila about two hundred miles from the Colorado. While at Tueson the Thompsons had many opportunities of noticing the terror which the Apaches excited in the people. One evening a Spanish woman arrived in the village, saying she had just escaped from the Tonto Apaches, where she had been a prisoner. She related that a day or two before, the band returned to camp from killing and plundering a party of Americans, and also bringing in prisoners. She was left alone with the threat that if she attempted to escape she would be killed. That night while they were dancing the war dance, she escaped and returned to Tucson. By comparing dates they were satisfied this was the band that attacked the Oatmans. Inquiries were made at the time, but nothing could be learned concerning the captives.

Olive is rather a pretty girl, with a skin as fair as most persons who have crossed the plains. Her face is disfigured by tatooed (sic) lines on the chin, running obliquely and perpendicularly from her mouth. Her arms were also marked in a similar manner by one straight line on each. The operation consisted in puncturing the skin and rubbing a dye or pulverized charcoal into the wounds.

It was about sunset when the attack was made, which resulted in the capture of herself and her little sister, Mary Ann. Olive was thirteen and Mary Ann seven years of age. The Indians stripped her of her shoes and nearly all her clothing—her sister had no shoes on at the time—and they started off with the speed of horses in a northerly direction into a mountainous region. They travelled all night without resting. At noon next day they stopped a few minutes to breathe and then hurried on again until night-fall, when they came into camp. She thinks they travelled a hundred miles. She was barefoot, and the sharp stones lacerated her feet, and her blood sprinkled the whole distance. Whenever she lagged, they would come behind and beat her, to urge her on. Her sister soon gave out, but being small, the Indians carried her in her (sic) arms. The reason of their hurrying on so rapidly, was fear lest they might be pursued.

The clothes left to her were worn out, and fell from her back in two weeks, and then she matted together the bark of trees and tied it around her person like the Indians. It was a slight covering, but it did not leave her entirely exposed.

Among these Apaches Olive supposes they remained one year. At any rate, the same kind of season returned as that when she arrived. Time among the Indians is not noted. If they note it at all, it is only by moons. The country was mountainous, and barren of grass or timber. The Indians live in the small vallies (sic). The girls were treated cruelly by these Indians. They were overtasked, and when they could not understand what was said to them, they were beaten. There was no timber nor running stream. The only fuel to be had was scattered sage bushes, and when it rained the water would collect in the holes of the rocks, and these two little girls were compelled to pack all the wood and water from long distances upon their backs. They felt themselves to be slaves. The Indians told them they should never see their friends again, and concealed them as much as possible. There was no snow, but they suffered from cold in the winter.

The Mohaves and Apaches were friends and sometimes visited each other. It was during one of these visits that the Mohaves learned

149

of the captives and offered to purchase them. The Apaches consented and received in exchange a few pounds of beads, two horses, and two blankets. They were ten days travelling, "like horses" as she describes it, to the Mohave villages, barefoot and over a rough mountainous country, each day stopping a short time at noon to rest. She thinks they travelled 350 miles in a northwest direction. On this journey they eat *(sic)* nothing until the fourth day, when they received a piece of meat about as large as her hand, and this kept them alive. There were no roots nor berries, and they dared not ask the Indians for food. The Indians would kill such game as came in their way, but they did not offer it to their captives. She describes them as being too lazy to exert themselves to procure food, and only killing such game as chance brought to them. Her days had thus far been dark, and she was almost ready to despair. Not an act of kindness, nor a word of sympathy or hope had been addressed to her by her captors, who treated her and her sister as slaves.

Arrived among the Mohaves, the Chief, whom she calls *Espanesay*, took them into his own family, and they were treated in every respect as his own children. Two blankets were given to them for covering; food was divided with them; they were not obliged to labor, but did pretty much as they pleased. Lands were allotted to them, and they were furnished with seeds, and raised their own corn, melons and beans as the Indians did.

There is little or no rain at the Colorado, and the Mohaves depend upon the overflow of the river for the irrigation necessary to germinate and ripen their harvests. Sometimes there is no overflow of the river, and much suffering follows. The Indians are too indolent to plant more than will suffice for their actual necessities. Three years ago there was no overflow, and a famine was the consequence, in which many perished. It was in this famine that Olive suffered her greatest grief. Her little sister, Mary Ann, had endured all her captivity with her. They supposed that they were alone of their family; they had suffered together the cruelties of the savages; but they had not been separated. They could sympathize and cheer each other in their dreariness, and sometimes they would whisper together a faint hope of future redemption. But now came the trial. The child wasted away by degrees—she knew that she was to die, and talked calmly of death to Olive. She had no disease, but there was no food—and she wasted miserably in the famine that desolated the tribe. Olive herself was near perishing, but the strength of her constitution saved her life. She speaks of the Chief's wife in terms of warmest gratitude. A mother could not have expressed more kind hearted sympathy than did this good woman whose gentle treatment saved her life. This woman had laid up seed corn to plant, and which even the dying groans of her own people could not make her bring out. When she saw Olive's distress, she ground this corn between stones, made a gruel and fed it to her, not reserving any even to herself.

The Mohaves always told her she could go to the white settlement when she pleased, but they dared not go with her, fearing they might be punished for having kept a white woman so long among them, nor did they dare let it be known that she was among them. She could not go alone, for she did not know the way, and she despaired of ever again seeing her friends. Hope almost died within her. For three long years she mourned her captivity; though well treated she was restrained, for she knew not how to extricate herself. What were her sensations, during all this time, must be imagined; for she is not, as yet, able to express her thoughts in language.

Before the arrival of the Indian messenger charged to release her, she heard of his departure from the Fort, by an Indian runner. Her joy was very great, but she forced herself to appear indifferent, lest the Indians should still restrain her. She had little confidence in their sincerity, when they gave her permission to. leave them, because they refused to go with her, and they knew she could not go alone.

At length, Francisco, the Yuma, arrived with the requisition from Col. Burke for her delivery. The packet was examined by the Indians, but no one understood it. It was put into her hands to explain. It was written in a bold, round hand, the letters being a third of an inch long. It was the first word of English she had seen for five long, weary years, and she could not restrain her emotion. The cold chill of Indian reserve seemed to melt away, and she saw before her mind the old home scenes; and happy voices seemed to welcome her return. She readily deciphered the meaning of that rescript, and communicated it to the assembled Indians. Accompanying it were six pounds of white beads, four blankets, and some other trinkets, to be given in exchange. These were accepted, and the Chief told her she was at liberty to depart for her friends. Many of the Indians, however, objected to her going, fearing they would be punished as her captors. The Chief's wife, the kind woman who saved her life in the famine, cried a day and a night as if she were losing her own child, and then gave her up. With the guide she started for the Fort with a light heart, on foot, as usual. She was ten days on the road, travelling with greater speed than ever before. This time the days were short to her, and so great was her mental excitement, that she knew neither weariness nor hunger. The trail was tortuous and rough, leading through mountains and gorges, and several times she was compelled to swim the Colorado. This time, too, her feet were protected from the sharp stones by sandals, such as are worn by the Indians.

During all her captivity she does not remember to have seen a wild flower, or shrub. If there were any, her mind was so absorbed with her own misery, that she did not observe them. Among the Mohaves there is no food except what is raised—that is, corn, wheat, melons, and beans. A few fish are caught from the river; a small bulb, resembling a brodeia, is taken from the ground, which is boiled or roasted. This bulb is almost tasteless, and is found in such small quantities that a whole day is required to gather enough for a meal. There (are) no berries nor fruit trees of any kind. . . .

She converses with propriety, but as one acting under strong constraint; and she has not forgotten the instructions of her childhood. She reads well, writes a fair hand, and sews admirably; though in her captivity she saw no implement nor instrument of civilization. She is very ambitious to learn, and spends most of her time in study.

An interview reported in the Los Angeles *Star*, April 18, 1856; reprinted in William B. Rice, *The Los Angeles Star* (Berkeley, 1947), 278–284.

A Most Lovely Locality
WILLIAM H. BREWER

William H. Brewer was a member of the team sent in 1860 by Yale University to make a geological survey of California. Its work stressed the Sierra Nevada, but parties were deployed in other parts of the state. Brewer's book-length journal, more broadly descriptive, was an extra dividend from the survey.

In Camp at Los Angeles, December 7.

Well, we are in camp. It is a cold rainy night, but I can hardly realize the fact that you at home are blowing your fingers in the cold, and possibly sleighing, while I am sitting here in a tent, without fire, and sleeping on the ground in blankets, in this month. We are camped on a hill near the town, perhaps a mile distance, a pretty place.

Los Angeles is a city . . . nearly a century old, a regular old Spanish-Mexican town. . . . The houses are but one story, mostly built of *adobe* or sun-burnt brick, with very thick walls and flat roofs. They are so low because of earthquakes, and the style is Mexican. The inhabitants are a mixture of old Spanish, Indian, American, and German Jews; the last two have come in lately. The language of the natives is Spanish, and I have commenced learning it. The only thing they appear to excel in is riding, and certainly I have never seen such riders.

Here is a great plain, or rather a gentle slope, from the Pacific to the mountains. We are on this plain about twenty miles from the sea and fifteen from the mountains, a most lovely locality; all that is wanted naturally to make it a paradise is *water*, more *water*. Apples, pears, plums, figs, olives, lemons, oranges, and "the finest grapes in the world," so the books say, pears of two and a half pounds each, and such things in proportion. The weather is soft and balmy—no winter, but a perpetual spring and summer. Such is Los Angeles, a place where "every prospect pleases and only man is vile."

As we stand on a hill over the town, which lies at our feet, one of the loveliest views I ever saw is spread out. Over the level plain to the southwest lies the Pacific, blue in the distance; to the north are the mountains of the Sierra Santa Monica; to the south beneath us, lies the picturesque town with its flat roofs, the fertile plain and vineyards stretching away to a great distance; to the east, in the distance, are some mountains without name, their sides abrupt and broken, while still above them stand the snow covered peaks of San Bernardino. The effect of the pepper, fig, olive, and palm trees in the foreground, with the snow in the distance, is very unusual.

This is a most peculiar climate, a mingling of the temperate with the tropical. The date palm and another palm grow here, but do not fruit, while the olive, fig, orange, and lemon flourish well. The grapes are famous, and the wine of Los Angeles begins to be known even in Europe.

We got in camp on Tuesday, December 4. We had been invited to a ranch and vineyard about nine miles east, and went with a friend on Tuesday evening. It lies near San Gabriel Mission, on a most beautiful spot, I think even finer than this. Mr. [Benjamin D.] Wilson, our host, uneducated, but a man of great force of character, is now worth a hundred or more thousand dollars and lives like a prince, only with less luxury. His wife is finely educated and refined, and his home to the visitor a little paradise. We were received with the greatest cordiality and were entertained with the greatest hospitality. A touch of the country and times were indicated by our rig—I was dressed in colored woolen shirt, with heavy navy revolver (loaded) and huge eight-inch bowie knife at my belt; my friend the same; and the clergyman who took us out in his carriage carried along his rifle, he said for game, yet owned that it was "best to have arms after dark."

Here let me digress. This southern California is still unsettled. We all continually wear arms—each wears both bowie knife and pistol (navy revolver), while we have always for game or otherwise, a Sharp's rifle, Sharp's carbine, and two double-barrel shotguns. Fifty to sixty murders per year have been common here in Los Angeles, and some think it odd that there has been no violent death during the two weeks that we have been here. Yet with our care there is no considerable danger, for as I write this there are at least six heavy loaded revolvers in the tent, besides bowie knives and other arms, so we anticipate no danger. I have been practicing with my revolver and am becoming expert.

Well, to return to my story, and to Mr. Wilson's. We found a fine family, with two lovely young ladies. The next day, Wednesday, December 5, we went up into the mountain, followed up a canyon (gorges are called *cañons* or canyons), and then separated. I climbed a

154

hill 2,500 or more feet, very steep and rocky, gathered some plants, and had one of the most magnificent views of my life—the plain, and the ocean beyond. The girls went with us into the canyon, but did not climb higher. After our climb and a lunch, a ride of eight miles over the fields (for no fences obstruct the land) brought us back; then dinner and return here. We had a delightful time—I ought to say "we" were the field assistant Mr. Ashburner and I. We will try to visit them again when Professor Whitney comes.

It is cold, wet, cheerless, so good night! Rain patters on the tent and dribbles within.

William H. Brewer, *Up and Down California in 1860–1864* (New Haven: Yale University Press, 1930), 12–15.

The Passing of the Cow Counties

ROBERT GLASS CLELAND

On the northern Plains, a quarter century after the floods and the Great Drought here described, a legendary Great Blizzard would administer a severe setback to another flourishing cattle industry. Statistically southern California's Great Drought was a worse disaster. As Cleland elaborates in the book quoted from, several other adversities were belaboring these once fabulously prosperous rancheros. The gold mines were playing out and the price incentive for the long drives to San Francisco and the mines just about disappeared. These rancheros had shown great talent for spending whatever came to hand but not for saving or investing. They were at heavy expense in the frequently forlorn effort to defend the Spanish or Mexican titles to their ranchos, and for twenty years they were ground down by indebtedness at interest compounding at 3 or 4 or 6 per cent a month.

155

American Takeover

Normally, California was an ideal cattle country; and to the owner of flocks and herds no land could have been kinder or more consistently benign. Year by year the ranges responded to the miracle of the fall rains, and the springing grass spread an inviting carpet over endless miles of valleys and rolling hills. Usually the rains ceased in April; but, throughout the cloudless months of summer, cattle found an abundance of nutritious pasture in the dry alfilaria and bur clover which covered the ranges.

Despite nature's traditionally benevolent rule, however, southern California was not immune to occasional visitations of flood or drought. A succession of such disastrous seasons, each one worse than its predecessor, began in 1862 and continued until the fall of 1865. Never before or since has southern California suffered, at least relatively, as it did during those three years; but out of the land's misfortunes came a major economic revolution.

The series of ills started with an unprecedented rain. The storm set in shortly before Christmas and continued almost without cessation for a month. During that time rain fell so continuously and in such tropical proportions, that the editor of the Los Angeles *Star* remarked: "On Tuesday last the sun made its appearance. The phenomenon lasted several minutes and was witnessed by a great number of persons." The prolonged rains caused floods which paralyzed business everywhere, drowned thousands of head of cattle, and destroyed possibly a fourth of the state's taxable wealth. . . .

Rivers were formed in every gulch and arroyo, and streams poured down the hillsides. The Los Angeles River, already brimful, overflowed its banks, and became a fierce and destructive flood. The embankment lately made by the city for the water works was swept away—melted before the force of water. The Arroyo Seco poured an immense volume of water down its rugged course, which, emptying into the river, fretting and boiling, drove the water beyond all control. . . . The vineyard of Mrs. T. J. White was the first to suffer. Almost instantly about 5,000 vines were washed away, besides several acres of land used for pasture. The destruction continued the next and following days, until a great breadth of land was washed away, which had been planted with orange and all other kinds of the most valuable fruit trees. . . .

"A rumour prevailed in town yesterday," the *Star* reported, "that

156

the flourishing settlement of Anaheim has been completely destroyed by the flood. We hope it is not so." Another report was that almost the entire property in the San Bernardino Valley had been destroyed.

From Agua Mansa on the Santa Ana, Judge Benjamin Hayes wrote: "A dreary desolation presented itself to my eye, familiar buildings overturned or washed away; here only a chimney, there a mere doorpost or a few scattered stakes of a fence, stout and lofty trees torn up, a mass of drifted branches from the mountain canyons, and a universal waste of sand on both banks of the river, where a few months before all was green and beautiful. . . ."

The great flood of 1861–62 was followed by two years of unparalleled drought. Almost no rain fell during the ensuing fall or winter; and, by spring, cattle on many of the southern ranges were beginning to be in desperate straits. "We have had no rain yet," wrote a ranch foreman to Abel Stearns in February, 1863, "there is no grass and the cattle are very poor; your Rancho men report a great many dying. Should we have no rain your cattle buyers will get nothing but hides and bones. . . ."

To make matters worse, the late spring brought a succession of hard, scorching winds from the desert; and millions of grasshoppers swept across the country like a devastating fire. A few rancheros were fortunate enough to find pasturage for portions of their herds in the mountains; one of the Wolfskills sent 3,000 head of stock to the Mojave River; the Yorbas and some other owners even drove cattle far below the border line into Lower California.

But far grimmer and more ruthless than the country's multiplied economic ills, was the virulent epidemic of smallpox which broke out in widely scattered localities and ravaged the whole of southern California. . . . The country had few physicians, all of whom resided in the larger towns, and consequently most ranch settlements and Indian communities were without medical attendance. Vaccine could be secured only by steamer from San Francisco. . . .

"We are all badly scared about small-pox," wrote Cave Coutts from the remote Rancho Guajome, "[we] keep a sentinel posted to give notice of the approach of anyone, and have to know all about them before they can come nearer than the corral. Many around do the same thing. . . ."

All through the long, dry summer, southern California ranchers looked to the coming of the fall rains to save them from ruin; but the fall slipped into winter, and the winter into spring, while the parched earth waited in vain for relief, and the cattle died by the thousands on sun-baked ranges and beside waterless streams and sand-choked springs.

"Do you remember what kind of a season it was in the latter part of the Fall of 1863 and the winter of 1864?" Don Juan Forster was asked in the trial of *Forster* vs. *Pico*. "The climate was very dry," he replied. "It was a most miserable drought that time. There was no moisture and our cattle died off in great numbers. About that winter the whole country from North to South became almost depopulated of cattle. . . . Before the year 1864 had passed away there was a perfect devastation—such a thing was never before known in California."

The carcasses of dead cattle lay in heaps about the parched water holes and *cienagas*, and beside creeks and streams from which every trace of moisture had disappeared. A drover described the twenty miles of once rich grazing land between Los Angeles and Wilmington, as "a regular mass of dead cattle," and the editor of the *Southern News* drew a despairing picture of the great ranchos and their now almost vanished herds. "The cattle of Los Angeles County are dying so fast in many places, for want of food," he wrote, "that the large rancheros keep their men busily employed in obtaining hides. Thousands of carcasses strew the plains in all directions, a short distance from this city, and the sight is harrowing in the extreme. We believe the stock interest of this county, as well as the adjoining counties, to be 'played out' entirely."

Out of the drastic losses inflicted by the Great Drought emerged a new economic order. Forbidding heaps of bones and skeletons, everywhere bleaching in the sun, symbolized the ruin of the universal industry of southern California. Thereafter, the "cow counties" lost their distinctive appellation. The day of unfenced ranchos, of enormous herds of half-wild cattle, of manorial estates, and pleasure-loving *paisanos*, came to its inevitable close. But, in its passing, something of color and romance faded forever from the California scene.

Robert Glass Cleland, *The Cattle on a Thousand Hills* (San Marino: Huntington Library, 1941), 168–183.

An American City Emerges

"As we rounded the point at the lighthouse, and entered the Santa Barbara
Channel, almost in a ship's length we had run out of the fog and had entered
into the sunshine. The cold north wind, which had been whistling through
the rigging and chasing us down the coast for three hundred miles, died
away. The rough sea calmed to a glassy swell. As we sailed on, hour after
hour, over a summer sea, I realized that I had entered into that Southern
California of which I had heard."

J. P. Widney

J. Albert Wilson, History of Los Angeles County (1880)

Wolfskill's orange grove

5

An American City Emerges

In 1871 a shooting scrape in Chinatown expanded into a mass assault on the Celestials in which nineteen were killed, many in execution style. Nevertheless, the era of violence was winding down. Three years later, when the celebrated bandido Tiburcio Vásquez was captured, instead of a lynching he drew a stream of visitors to the jail and was routinely forwarded to San Jose to stand trial.

Other changes were taking place. Rancho life, as baronial as before, persisted in the backcountry, as Mary Austin tells in her cameo description of Ranchos Tejón. But experimental plantings tremendously expanded the list of potential products, and the southern California countryside was moving to wheat and barley plantings, orange groves, vineyards, and bee ranches. Some of these operations were on a large scale but most functioned as single-family farm units.

The town steadily took on characteristics of its American counterparts. In its celebration of the centennial of independence some reminders of the intercultural heritage were to be seen, but the Indian element in the parade was in the nationwide stereotype as were most of the trade and industry displays and the oration that climaxed the literary exercises. Sarah Bixby-Smith's recollections of her childhood corroborate.

In September 1876 Angelenos exulted over the joining of the rails at Lang, north of the Saugus tunnel. Via the Tehachapi crossing and Lathrop Junction, Los Angeles hooked up with Reno, Omaha, and Chicago, and with San Francisco. In the preceding eight years it had acquired more than 200 miles of local trackage raying out in all directions. It was by rail that much of the county could join in the Fourth of July celebration.

Safety, through the decline in violence; access, with trains supplementing freight wagons, stages, and coastal steamers; irrigation,

161

greening hitherto arid wastes and thereby improving the ecology and the attractiveness; the climate, now touted as a health benefit as well as caressing; and diversification, especially in the broadening of the economic base—these were among the stimulating factors. The returned tourist was an even more effective advertiser.

Arrival of a competing railroad and of a bevy of skilled and unscrupulous real estate promoters touched off a spectacular real estate boom. Subdividers staked out sixty new towns and numerous additions to the older ones. Mammoth resort hotels and sanitariums were built. Orange groves were marked off into 25-foot lots. Newcomers poured in by the train load. Suddenly in 1887 Los Angeles had seven or eight times as many people. Old residents now turned speculator and helped bring on a crash in 1889, in the course of which thousands deserted Los Angeles and southern California.

This combination of boom and bust was a major crisis. As a turning point, the boom was far more significant than the bust. A new era opened—the era of the health-seeker, the tourist, the orange, the beginnings of oil production, the railroad bringing people in and taking local produce out, the promoter, and the tempting thought of the unearned increment available in the profit sure to come in southern California real estate.

The nineties were less ebullient than the late eighties but population continued to mount as did the indexes of oranges shipped, oil produced, lumber unloaded, college students enrolled, and retailers, doctors, and lawyers in business. Los Angeles had emerged as unquestionably a city and the hub of a burgeoning region.

The Centennial Parade
July 4, 1876

J. J. WARNER, BENJAMIN HAYES, J. P. WIDNEY

Exhilarated by their centennial as a nation, Americans en-thusiastically celebrated the Fourth of July in 1876. Appro-priately the festivities centered in Philadelphia. Los Angeles, ninety-five years after the founding of the pueblo and thirty since the raising of the Stars and Stripes, marked the occasion with a parade, "literary exercises," and a commissioned cen-tennial history by pioneer settler J. J. Warner, forty-niner Ben-jamin Hayes, and recent-comer Dr. J. P. Widney, who was on hand sixty years later to add a preface to the second printing of this classic.

The parade description that follows was summarized in the centennial history from newspaper accounts. There also appeared the Centennial Poem, the Centennial Oration, and a resumé of the literary exercises. The parade in particular re-flects the community which then consisted of seven or eight thousand Angelenos and about twice that many more residing in the rest of the county.

The Procession

There were crowds of people coming into the city by car and carriage, buggy and wagon. They were coming on horseback and a-foot, and they continued to come. They came by train from all parts of the county: Tustin City, Richland, Anaheim, Wilmington, Santa Monica, San Fernando, Spadra. . . . The streets were crowded at an early hour. Every window along the line of march was crowded, every balcony had its throng of eager lookers on. There never was such a crowd in the city before. With one or two exceptions everybody was on good behavior. . . .

From Fifth and Fort [Broadway] the line of march went to the Aliso Mills, the Plaza, and down Main to the Round House Gardens and was over thirty minutes in passing.

The column was led by Major H. M. Mitchell and his aides. Then came the Opera House Band, followed by the officers of the first division. They were followed by the Los Angeles Guard, Capt. Bailey commanding, and the Los Angeles Rifleros, Capt. Pantalean commanding. Next came the magnificent car appropriated to the Goddess of Liberty, who was personated in a very queenly manner by Miss Carrie Cohn. She was attended by Miss Lulu Lehman, representing Peace, and Miss Ally Carpenter, representing Plenty.

The Veterans of the Mexican War turned out strong . . . General George Stoneman, President, and 39 men.

Next in order came the French Benevolent Society. A very beautiful feature of the splendid display made by our patriotic French fellow citizens was a triumphal chariot, elegantly adorned, in which were seated three young ladies, Miss Mary Lache, Miss Blanche Crowley and Miss Leonie Dupuytren. They represented the Goddess of Liberty, the second France, and the third America. . . . Carriages with the President of the Day, Orator, Poet, Chaplain and invited guests followed.

Then came the marshall of the second division, Mr. Otto Von Ploennies with his staff. The 38's followed; there were fifty men on the ropes and they looked splendidly. The Pioneers wore handsome blue caps and hats. The uniform of the 38's is a red shirt with blue hats. The hose carriage was covered with a blue canopy under which reclined Master George Kuhrts in uniform, as a representative of a hoseman. The steamer, fairly gleaming with a wealth of floral decorations, followed, drawn by six fine horses.

The hook and ladder truck, also very tastefully decorated, presented a very fine appearance, drawn by fifteen men in uniform.

Confidence Engine, No. 2, followed, drawn by six horses, richly comparisoned in red, white and blue housings. A finely decorated canopy surmounted the splendidly trimmed steamer in which Miss Emily Smith sat, personating America. . . .

A triumphal car upon which Confidence Engine Company seemed to have bestowed great pains followed. It was covered by an ornamental canopy beneath which sat Miss Hattie Furman, representing Columbia, and Miss Mamie Furman personating Uncle Sam; Henry Dockweiler, jr., an exempt fireman reclining on a coil of hose. At one corner of the canopy stood Master John Foster in the guise of "Mose," [black-faced], plug hat and all, at another, Master Harry Fanning as "Young Continental," in appropriate costume, at another Master Willie Gard as the representative of the 38's, and at the other Master Isadore Dockweiler as one of the Confidence boys. . . .

Wilmington hook and ladder truck followed and made a manly feature in the grand procession.

The Junta Patriotica de Juarez and Turner rifles followed, making a very fine display. A number of carriages containing the Directors of the Junta Patriotica and private citizens followed.

The Third Division was led by Marshal Eugene Meyer and his aids. . . . This division consisted of the following orders: Knights of Pythias, Independent Order of Odd Fellows, Improved Order of Red Men, Ancient Order of Hibernians, Irish Literary Society, and Irish Temperance Society. . . . A pleasing feature of this Division was a car containing thirteen young Misses representing the thirteen original colonies.

The Fourth Division, Mr. F. Guirado and staff, now wheeled into line. The leading feature was the car of state, containing thirty-eight young ladies representing the States of the Union. The car was a triumph of decorative art. . . .

The Butchers' association, making a fine display, followed, and the inevitable forty-niners on their mules attracting their full share of attention, and half a dozen representatives of the noble red man of the forest, who, with their lay figure of Capt. Jack of the Modocs, contributed not a little to the hilarity of the occasion. . . .

The long line of trades display presented itself, preceded by a handsomely decorated wagon representing the Philadelphia Brewery.

Page & Gravel followed with an immense van in which a dozen or more artisans were plying the different branches of wagon making and blacksmithing. . . . Next the Asbestine Stone Company with specimens of their excellent handiwork. Then Cameron's display, comprising fish, flesh and fowl, and on the whole, unique and amusing. Then a wagon with specimens of B. Aphodl's cooperage, with an immense wine vat marked "A. Pelanconi, wine dealer." Then a fine display of Halliday's standard windmills.

Next a wagon from the Grange store laden with all sorts of toothsome delicacies. Then a laundry wagon driven by a lady, whose name we did not learn. Next came a fine display by the Adams Windmill Company. Then a wagon from Coulter & Harper's hardware store containing a little of everything in the housekeeping line from a stove to a nutmeg grater. Next came Trapp's fruit wagon with the motto, "Home Produce;" a good idea. Then Reinert's cooperage made a fine display with the legend, "Show us a leak in the Union and we will tighten it." W. M. Stoddard followed with a long line of wagons, carryalls and buggies. Then the Los Angeles Soap Company with specimens of their handiwork. Dotter & Bradley followed with a very handsome canopied wagon which contained a number of elegant specimens of their own manufacture of furniture. J. T. Woodward & Co., of the Los Angeles Broom Factory, made a very fine display of broom ware, all of which is manufactured in this city. The Centennial broom was a feature of the display. Next the New York Brewery, then the Los Angeles Steam Coffee Factory, and after them the Sewing Machine Companies. A long line of citizens on horseback and in carriages followed, and the most magnificent pageant Los Angeles has ever witnessed came to an end as far as the passing of the procession was concerned.

The procession broke ranks at the Round House, and the Literary Exercises of the Day took place. Seats were prepared for about fifteen hundred people and they were all occupied, and hundreds listened throughout standing.

Literary Exercises

After "Hail Columbia" by the band and an "impressive and appropriate prayer" by Rev. T. T. Packard, General Phineas Banning delivered a short address "replete with patriotic sentiments." The hymn "America" was sung by gentlemen from the different church choirs of the city. Professor Thomas A. Saxon read the Declaration of Independence. The choir sang "Red, White and Blue." The Poet of the Day recited the Centennial Poem, the band played "Dixie," and John G. Eastman took over as Orator of the Day. . . .

His magnificent effort soared to this peroration:

"Sir, we are now a great people, standing at the head of the governments of the world. Our navy floats in every water; in all progress that characterizes civilization we bow to none. In all that tends to make a nation great, we have made a glorious history. True, some of its pages bear the stain of tears and blood, and evidence of our follies find a place upon the record, yet it is grand as human record ever has been, and if we profit by the lessons our follies have taught us, devote our lives and intelligence to the establishment of a higher nationality, a broader patriotism, a more self-sacrificing devotion to our common country, when, in another century, our children's children shall meet to celebrate our governmental birth, America shall be the pride and boast of the free, the Queen of the earth."

After listening with rapt attention throughout, the audience burst out in a roar of enthusiastic applause. Following a few remarks by Los Angeles' one and only consul, Jacob A. Moerenhaut, representing France, Rev. A. W. Edelman pronounced the benediction, which closed the exercises.

J. J. Warner, Benjamin Hayes, and J. P. Widney, *Historical Sketch of Los Angeles County, California* (Los Angeles, 1876), 142–159.

Childhood Recollections
SARAH BIXBY-SMITH

In rural America of the single-family farm, the family lived on the farm. In the sheep and cattle country, on the contrary, the home of the ranch family frequently was in town. Los Angeles was so favored, as Sarah Bixby-Smith's recollections attest. The scene she describes was thoroughly Americanized.

Los Angeles was about ninety years old and I about one when we first met, neither of us, I am afraid, taking much notice of the other. For over twenty years San Francisco had been a city, a most interesting and alive city, making so much stir in the world that people forgot that Los Angeles was the older; that her birth has been ordained by the governor and attended with formal rites of the church and salutes from the military way back in 1781, when the famous revolution on the east coast was just drawing to a successful close. Until the stirring days of '49, San Francisco was insignificance on sand hills. Then her rise was sudden and glorious and the Queen of the Angels was humble. But she was angelic only in name. She was a typical frontier town with primitive, flat-roofed dwellings of sun-dried bricks, much like those built in ancient Assyria or Palestine. Saloons and gambling houses were out of proportion in number, and there were murders every day. The present crime wave is nothing in comparison.

My father first saw Los Angeles in January, 1854, when he was camped with his sheep on the Rancho San Pasqual; his arrival was a few months later than that of Mr. Harris Newmark, who, in his book *Sixty Years in Southern California*, so vividly describes the village as he found it.

By the time I knew it there had been a great change. There were some sidewalks, water was piped to the houses, gas had been introduced; several public school buildings had been built; there were three newspapers, *The Star*, *The Express*, and *The Herald*. The public library had been founded—it occupied rooms in the Downey Block where the Federal Building now stands. Compared with what it had been twenty years before, Los Angeles was a modern, civilized city; compared with what it is now, it was a little frontier town. At school I once learned its population to be 11,311.

We lived first on Temple Street, near Charity. Once Los Angeles boasted Faith and Hope Streets as well, but only Hope remains, for Faith has turned to Flower, and Charity masquerades as Grand.

Next door to us lived a Jewish family whose girls sat on the front porch and amazed me by crocheting on Sunday. I had not known that any Jews existed outside the Bible. Perhaps this family was the nucleus for the present large colony of Hebrews that now fills the neighborhood.

168

Childhood Recollections

Temple Street was new and open for only a few blocks. Bunker Hill Avenue was the end of the settlement, a roof of scattered houses along the ridge fringing the sky. Beyond that we looked over empty, grassy hills to the mountains. . . .

The second year we moved to the Shepherd house, (so-called because of its owner). This house still stands at the top of the precipice made by the cutting of First Street between Hill and Olive Streets. . . .

After a couple of years we built our own house in the same neighborhood on the south-east corner of Court and Hill Streets. It began as a seven room cottage, white with green blinds to suit father. Later the roof was raised and a second story inserted and the house painted a more fashionable all-over gray, to suit the ladies. . . .

At the time we built there seemed to be but two styles of architecture in vogue, one square on a four room base and the other oblong on a six room plan, the narrow end being to the street, with one tier of rooms shoved back a little in order to provide a small porch—we chose the latter. Every such house had a bay window in the projecting end, that being the front parlor, and all windows visible from the street must have yellow, varnished inside blinds.

One evening while the building was going on we went over as usual for our daily inspection and noted that the newly set studding marked the coming rooms. The connecting parlors seemed small to our eyes and tastes not yet trained to apartment and bungalow court proportions, so on the following morning father ordered out the wall between proposed front and back parlor, and our large sitting room —living room it would be called today—was ordained. It was unusual in Los Angeles where the prevailing mode demanded the two parlors. This room was large enough, 18' X 33' to stand the height of the ceiling, fourteen feet. Wide, high double-doors opened into the hall, opposite similar ones into the reception room, giving a feeling of spaciousness to the house.

The furnishing was of necessity more or less that which it is now customary to damn as mid-Victorian—walnut furniture and a wealth of varying design in carpet, curtains, upholstery, wall-paper; but the whole in this case was kept in harmony by a key color, a medium olive, relieved by soft shades of rose and tan. Even the woodwork was painted to match the ground color of the walls, instead of glistening in

169

the usual glory of varnished redwood or yellow pine. Everything was in good taste except a fearful and wonderful ceiling that was wished on us by the local wallpapering nabob. How fortunate that the walls were so high it was almost out of sight!

Over our heads were the two plaster of paris centerpieces from which lighting fixtures sprang, first hanging lamps with prismatic fringes, later gas chandeliers. These fruits and flowers were tinted and gilded. Around them was a cream colored sky, set with golden stars, small ones, not planets—limited in extent by an oval band of brocaded red velvet, this being the pet aversion of Aunt Martha. Outside this pale there was a field of metallic colored paper with an all-over design like chicken wire; next came a border of flowers and something modest to connect the whole artistic creation with the side wall.

We had a ceiling, but there were many things characteristic of the period that we did not have. We never had a "throw," nor a gilded milking stool with a ribbon bow on one leg; we never had a landscape painted on the stem of a palm leaf, nor oranges on a section of orange wood; we did not hang in any door a portiere made of beads, shells, chenille ropes or eucalyptus seeds, all of which things were abroad in the land.

The room contained four bookcases, a rosewood square piano, a large table, a sofa and several easy chairs. From the walls looked down upon us Pharoah's Horses, The Stag in the Glen, and the Drove at the Ford (suitable subjects the vogue provided for a family dependent upon livestock), but these were not all, for there were a few reproductions of old masters, a fine portrait of grandfather in his youth, and a picture of the sweet-faced mother who had gone to Heaven, as we children said.

At one end of the room was a white marble mantel with a large grate, always annoying us by its white patchiness in the low toned room, but contributing cheer with the coal fire that, through more than half the year, burned all day long. Los Angeles had no furnaces in those days, but the family was suited by the single fireplace, for one could choose the climate he wished from torrid zone near the grate to arctic in the bay window, where the goldfish circled their watery globe.

The room was the center of a happy family life, where, of an evening, all read by the light of the student lamp, or indulged in games, dominoes, authors, crambo, or logomachy, sugar-coated ways of getting training respectively in addition, names of books and writers, verse-making and spelling. Father rarely went out, and after the reading of his evening paper might join a lively domino tournament or amuse himself with solitaire.

Until the very last years of his life he busied himself at odd jobs about the house. Sometimes it would be a session with the grandfather clock, sometimes it would be chopping wood. He had the willow brought up from the ranch in long pieces, which he cut and stacked under the house. He raised chickens and at first cared for a horse and cow. Later we kept two horses, dispensed with the cow, and had a man for the livestock and garden and to drive us about town. We did not have a dog regularly but always cats, classical cats. Aeneas was very long-legged and Dido lived with us a long time. I think it was she who went every evening with father for his after dinner walk and cigar.

One Thanksgiving time the wagon from the ranch came, bringing us a couple of barrels of apples, a load of wood and a fine turkey for the feast day. Imagine our dismay, one afternoon, to see it mount up on its wings and soar majestically from our hill top backyard down to the corner of First and Broadway below. He escaped us but, I presume, to some one else he came as a direct answer to prayer. . . .

The location of our home on the brow of a hill was chosen because of the view and the sense of air and space. Below us was the little city, the few business blocks, the homes set in gardens on tree-shaded streets, the whole surrounded by orchards and vineyards. On clear days we could see the mountains far in the east and the ocean at San Pedro, with Santa Catalina beyond.

One very rainy winter, possibly '86, we watched the flood waters from the river creep up Aliso Street and into Alameda: we saw bridges go out and small Aguierre, a young policeman, won the admiration of everyone when he rode his black horse into the torrent and rescued flood victims from floating houses and debris in midstream. One of the girls in my room at school lost all her clothing except what she wore, and we had a "drive" for our local flood-sufferer.

This was a very different river in summer. I once saw a woman whose nerves had been wracked by dangerous winter fordings when the water swirled about the body of the buggy, get out of her carriage, letting it ford the Los Angeles river while she stepped easily across the entire stream. She had a complex, but she didn't know that name for her fear!

Beyond the river and up the hill on the other side stood, stark and lonely, the "Poor House," the first unit of the present County Hospital. Many a time when the skies forbore to rain I had it pointed out to me as my probable ultimate destination; for, after the bad middle years of the seventies when to a general financial depression was added a pestilence that killed off all the lambs, and to that was added a disastrous investment in mines, the firm of Flint Bixby & Co. was sadly shaken, and it was of great moment whether or not sufficient moisture should come to provide grass and grain for the stock.

Sarah Bixby-Smith, *Adobe Days* (Cedar Rapids, Iowa: *The Torch Press*, 1925), 128–143.

Vagrant Rivers
BERNICE EASTMAN JOHNSTON

From the Salinas to the Los Angeles and beyond, California is famous for its upside-down rivers and their dusty crossings. A companion feature is the alluvial cone that such a river builds up after issuing from the mountains and its uncertain course, in some instances all the way to the sea. The display performance was in 1905–1907 when the Colorado left its bed to flow into Salton Sink. Similarly, within the short span of its recorded history, the Los Angeles River for a time used its alternate channel by Ballona Wash to Santa Monica Bay.

Not even an Indian could always outguess such prima donnas as those tempermental rivers which the Spanish were finally to name the

172

Santa Ana de los Temblores, the San Gabriel, and the Porciún-cula. . . .

Following the floods of 1914, when it became obvious that these streams must yield to a civilizing restraint, interviews were held with the old settlers still able to recall the storms of earlier decades. The report thus gathered could compete in suspense with mystery fiction, as one after another of these long-time residents told which way the waters ran after too copious winter rains, such as those of 1814, '24, '51, '67, '87, and '89. From it we learn what to us is startling information.

With few exceptions old residents recalled that, until the floods of 1824–25 sent it careening off through the lowlands to the south, the Los Angeles River ran below a high bluff between the present Main and Los Angeles Streets, turning westward on its meandering way to the "cienegas," the great marshlands that lay between the Baldwin and the Beverly hills. This course can be traced roughly today by observing the trend of the low ground in the region of Venice, Adams, and Washington, between La Brea and La Cienega Boulevards, in the present city of Los Angeles.

From some unknown prior date, or perhaps always until the winter of 1824–25, this was the course the Los Angeles River followed to its mouth in the Santa Monica Bay. Thereafter, during every major storm, until a deep, concrete-lined channel formed a strait-jacket for its deceptive strength, this was the way it threatened to take and deep sands exist to prove its right to such a course. "The river needed to rise only a few inches to send it down the old channel," reported one old resident. In 1867 this actually happened and for a while the water stood like a great lake all the way to the "cienegas." From that point to the sea the course had been that of the stream the Spanish were to call "La Ballona," although the low ground southward to the Dominguez country sometimes coaxed the overflow in that direction.

La Ballona's upper reaches are now tucked away underground and it emerges for its last few miles as a mere creek with straight and unlovely concrete banks. Its present exit to the sea can only suggest the broad delta of those other days, when the drainage of the great San Fernando Valley came on a long, roundabout journey to merge with the flow from myriad canyon rivulets and spring-fed brooks from the

173

Hollywood, Beverly and Baldwin hills. Streams now long forgotten added their volume, like those which carried the overflow from the pools of the present MacArthur Park, or the "King's Waterway," sometimes called "San Juan de Reyes," which ran down Grand Avenue. . . .

The San Gabriel River had its own dark history. It carried a great volume of the run-off from many a mountain canyon around by Azusa and then to the east of El Monte, "down Basset way," as old residents phrased it. From the pass which we call the Whittier Narrows it ran a long south-westerly course to empty into San Pedro Bay by a choice of exits in a wide fan. One of these coincided almost exactly with the present mouth of the Los Angeles River. The Rio Hondo of those days was a creek of only a couple of miles through which the overflow from the swamps below El Monte reached the San Gabriel. How the Rio Hondo fell heir to most of the sources and a considerable portion of the main channel of the present stream, to become the principal tributary of the Los Angeles River, is again a story of the vagaries of the winter storms and of disturbances of nature by ambitious white farmers. . . .

Across much of the land between the modern city and the seaports to the south, except for an occasional cluster of hills, there lay a vast forest, undergrown with almost impenetrable thickets and laced with hidden pools and swamps. Well into the Spanish era, when half-wild cattle and horses found hiding places in this jungle of sycamores, willows, alders, wild grape vines and bramble bushes, only a few trails penetrated it and these were made hazardous by prowling grizzly bears.

Willows helped to secure the land, but sometimes when they were planted in rows to mark a boundary they diverted an accumulation of flood waters into ever-deepening ditches which soon became the jagged washes of an eroded land. Still later railroad bridges, and projects such as the ditch which was hopefully dug in Civil War times in an attempt to develop a water supply for Drum Barracks at Wilmington, acted toward the same end. Thus were formed deep cuts such as the Dominguez Wash which earlier had been but a long swale, marked by "cienegas," lakes and pools. After the floods of 1824–25 and 1832 the greater part of the marshlands north of Wilmington and Long Beach

174

drained away through these newly defined channels. In the stage-coach era travelers wrote of crossing the plains between San Pedro and Los Angeles. The forest had disappeared.

Bernice Eastman Johnston, *California's Gabrielino Indians* (Los Angeles: Southwest Museum, 1962), 77–81.

Madame Modjeska's Utopian Dream

ROBERT V. HINE

California produced a spate of utopian colonies. Madame Modjeska's fling in Santiago Canyon embraced more notables than most and was more short-lived.

In Cracow, Poland, Count Charles Bozenta Chlapowski and his actress-wife, Helena Modjeska, were frequently entertaining a circle of intellectual radicals bitter over Russian domination of their home-land. From this coterie one winter evening in 1875, after a period of excessively oppressive censorship and a siege of ill health for Madame Modjeska, a scheme of emigrating to America was hatched, and in the elated conversations that followed the plan narrowed to the establishment in California of a utopian colony on the model of the earlier Brook Farm in Massachusetts. Serious meetings through the winter carried the enterprise nearer maturity. The members drafted statutes, vowed to obey their own laws, and pooled financial resources. Madame Modjeska reflected the group's enthusiasm when she described her dreams of California:

"Oh, but to cook under the sapphire-blue sky in the land of freedom! What Joy!" I thought. "To bleach linen at the brook like

175

maidens of Homer's 'Illiad'! After the day of toil, to play the guitar and sing by moonlight, to recite poems, or to listen to the mockingbird! And listening to our songs would be charming Indian maidens, our neighbors, making wreaths of luxuriant wild flowers for us! And in exchange we should give them trinkets for their handsome brown necks and wrists! And oh, we should be so far away from everyday gossip and malice, nearer to God, and better."

The group which eventually left Poland for California consisted of Count Chlapowski, Madame Modjeska, and Rudolphe (later Ralph) Modjeska, son of her first marriage; Henryk Sienkiewicz, whose fame as an author rests on his later work, *Quo Vadis?* ; Julian Sypniewski, his wife and two children; Paprocki, a painter; and Anusia, a flighty girl of sixteen who had been hired to care for the children. In the early spring of 1876 the group sent two of its members, Sienkiewicz and Sypniewski, to explore the land of southern California. After investigation, the committee chose the area of Anaheim because many citizens of that town spoke German, a familiar language for the Poles. Sypniewski returned to Poland with glowing accounts; Sienkiewicz waited in California at Anaheim Landing writing letters which were no less enticing. In July, 1876, the little band sailed aboard the *Donau* from Bremen. They landed in New York, stopping long enough for an excursion to Washington where they eagerly received boxes of pamphlets on farming from the Department of Agriculture; proceeded to the Isthmus on a steamer which suffered an explosion from a bursting boiler; journeyed from Panama to San Francisco on an antique side-wheeler; and finally entrained for Los Angeles. Reuniting with Sienkiewicz, they made the last lap of their journey in wagons to the ranch near Anaheim.

After the long trek and the glowing prospects, the immigrants arrived at their utopia to find a wooden house of two bedrooms, a dining room, and a parlor with an upright piano and a sofa. To Modjeska "the commonplaceness of it all was painfully discouraging." Sypniewski and his family took the large bedroom; Chlapowski and his wife, the small one; Ralph slept on the parlor sofa; Anusia, in a nook of the kitchen; and Sienkiewicz and Paprocki made shift in the barn.

Utopia suffered problems from the very first morning. Madame Modjeska, who in the assignment of tasks had drawn the kitchen, soon learned that even breakfast for a group of intellectual Poles was no simple affair. Each one wanted something different. Tea, coffee, milk, chocolate, and wine-soup had to be served every morning, to mention the drink alone.

The first day's work in the fields was glorious—Nature's sons and daughters returning to her bosom. But on the following morning lame backs and sore arms kept Nature's children abed. In the weeks that followed, when muscles reacted better but the spirit lagged from toil and homesickness, the whole colony often took to its buggies for a picnic or a drive to Anaheim Landing. It required the combined efforts of three men to kill a turkey on the occasion of a festive dinner. Even Sypniewski, the sole possessor of agricultural experience, had gained his knowledge in a fundamentally different soil and climate.

Trouble came and agricultural reverses, but the colony never lost its high spirits. A visitor reported that he found the men practicing Wagner while a mule and a cow died from improper feed. Another neighbor, Lyman Busby, once said, "You ought to have seen how jolly they used to be when everything on the farm was drying up in the sun and the animals were all sick and dying." Sienkiewicz came gradually to divorce himself from the agricultural labor, setting up a table under the trees in a far corner of the ranch where he read, smoked, and wrote most of the day.

After six months on the new Brook Farm, the colony counted $15,000 spent and almost nothing returned. "We all came to the conclusion," wrote Modjeska, "that our farming was not a success.

"We had several cows, but there was no one to milk them, and we had to buy milk, butter, and cream from the neighbors. We had chickens, but our fine dogs made regular meals of the eggs. We had a vineyard, which yielded beautiful muscat grapes, but there was nobody to buy them, and often people would come and fill their wagons with them without more ado; they said that such was the custom of the country. . . . Our winter crop of barley was fast disappearing in the mouths of the neighboring cattle, although I tried myself to shoot at the latter with my revolver."

In the spring of 1877 the actress laid down her gun and her skillet, perfected her English, and returned to the stage, paving the way for those triumphs with Edwin Booth and Otis Skinner which placed her so prominently in the history of the American theater. Money from the sale of the farm provided return passage for the other homesick colonists. Madame Modjeska and her family, however, remained in America, building a summer house surrounded by her Forest of Arden in Santiago Canyon, only a few miles from the site where the rudeness of agricultural reality had disrupted a captivating utopian dream.

Robert V. Hine, *California's Utopian Colonies* (San Marino: Huntington Library, 1953) 137–140.

Ranchos Tejón

MARY AUSTIN

In The Land of Little Rain *and* The Flock *Mary Austin captured for all time an evocation of the sickle of desert and oases that sweeps around the southern end and eastern side of the Sierra Nevada. Her theme is the environment and the life it constrained and supported. This area now can readily be claimed as a hinterland of Los Angeles. At the time of which she writes, Los Angeles was the entrepot for the wool from Ranchos Tejón.*

This year at Button Willow they sheared the flocks by machinery, which is to say that the most likable features of the old California sheep ranches are departing. That is why I am at the pains of setting down here a little of what went on at the Ranchos Tejón before the clang of machinery overlays its leisurely picturesqueness.

When Mexico held the state among her dependencies she gave away the core of it to the most importunate askers. A good lump of the heart land went in the grants of La Liebre, Castac, and Los Alamos y Agua Caliente, to which Edward Fitzgerald Beale added in '62 the

178

territory of the badger, called El Tejón. This principality is three hundred thousand acres of noble rolling land, lifting to mountain summits and falling off toward the San Joaquin where that valley heads up in the meeting of the Sierra and Coast Ranges. The several grants known as Ranchos Tejón dovetail together in the high, wooded regions where the Sierra Nevadas break down in the long, shallow passage of Cañada de las Uvas (the Grapevine).

Beginning as far south as the old Los Angeles stage road, which enters the grant at Cow Springs, the boundary of it passes thence to Tehachapi; northward the leopard-colored flank of Antelope Valley heaves up to meet it. Here begins the Tejón proper, crossing the railroad a little beyond Caliente, encompassing Pampa on the northwest; from hence trending south, stalked by blue mirages of the San Joaquin, it divides a fruitful strip called since Indian occupancy the Weed Patch, and coasts the leisurely sweep of the Sierras toward Pastoria. This guttering rift lets through the desert winds that at the beginning of Rains fill the cove with roaring yellow murk. About the line of the fence, bones of the flock overblown in the wind of '74 still stick out of the sand. Hereabout are the cleared patches of the homesteaders, where below the summer limit of waters the settlers play out with the cattlemen and the sheep the yearly game of Who Gets the Feed. Thence the boundary runs west to Tecuya; here the oaks leave off and the round-bellied hills of San Emigdio turn brownly to the sun. Castac, which is to say The Place of Seeping Springs, basks obscurely in the shallow intricacies of cañon behind Fort Tejón, finding the border of La Liebre a little beyond the brackish lake, wholly to include the ranch of the cottonwoods and warm water, otherwise Los Alamos y Agua Caliente. Beginning at Pampa, a fence rider should encompass the whole estate in a week and a day. For those so dry-as-dust as to require it there is an immense amount of stamped paper to certify the time and manner of Beale's purchases, but I concern myself chiefly with the moment when he married the land in his heart, coming first out of the dark, tortuous cañon of Tejón, not the fort cañon, but that one which opens toward the ranch house, and looked first on the slope and swale of the basking valley. . . .

I suppose that Beale was the first official to discover, or to give evidence of it, that it is wiser for Indians to become the best sort of In-

Voyage de la Pérouse (1797)
First published drawing of California quail

dians rather than poor imitations whites. That part of the estate known as Rancho el Tejón had been an Indian reservation, gathering in broken tribes from Inyo, from Kern and Tule rivers and Whiskey Flat, prospering indifferently as Indians do in the neighborhood of an idle garrison such as Fort Tejón. Beale, being made superintendent of Indian Affairs, began to prove the land and draw to him in devotion its swarthy people, and the Reservation being finally removed to Tule River, there passed to him with the purchase of El Tejón, the wardship of some dozens of Indian families. Such of them as longed homesickly for their own lands melted from Tejón like quail in nesting time, by unguessed trails, to the places from which they had been drawn, and to those remaining were accorded certain rights of homebuilding, of commons and wage-working, rights never abated nor forsworn during the lifetime of Edward Beale.

There were notable figures of men among these Tejón Indians; one Sebastian whom I have seen. Born a Serrano in the valley of San Gabriel, he was carried captive by the Mojaves, one spark of a man child saved alive when the hearth fires were stamped out in war. He being an infant, his mother hid him in her bosom; with her long hair

180

she covered him; between her breasts and her knees she suckled him in quietness until the lust of killing was past. Among the captive women he grew up, and escaping came to know the country about Kern River as his home. Here when Frémont came by, exploring, the river was at flood, a terrible, swift, tawny, frothing river, and no ford. However, there was Sebastian. This son of a chief's son stripped himself, bound his clothing on his head, swam the river, brought friendly Indians, made fast a rope across, brought the tule boats called "balsas," ferried over the explorers, and got from Frémont for his pains—nothing; a rankling slight until the old man died. But between Sebastian and Beale grew up such esteem from man to man as lasted their lives out in benefits and devotion. . . .

Between the point of San Emigdio and the Weed Patch there is a moon-shaped cove, out of which opens, westerly, the root of the cañon by which Frémont and Kit Carson came through. The ranch house sits by the water that comes down guardedly between tents and tents of wild vines. Below the house by the stream-side the Indian washerwomen paddle leisurely at the clothes and spread them bleaching in the sun. Silvering olives and mists of bare fig branches slope down the blossomy swale; deep in the court between the long adobes, summer abides, and yearly about the fence of the garden the pomegranates flame. The beginning of all these, and the oranges, Jimmy Rosemeyre brought up from the Mission San Fernando. . . .

Straight out from the ranch house runs the road to Castac and La Liebre. It turns in past the house of José Jesús López, and runs toward Las Chimeneas. Here, to the left, is the camel camp. Nobody much but Jimmy Rosemeyre and the Bureau of Animal Industry knows about the camels that the government, by the hand of Lieutenant Beale, undertook to domesticate on the desert border. Twenty-nine of them, with two Greeks and a Turk, came up by way of The Needles, across the corner of Mojave to Tejón. There I could never learn that they accomplished more than frightening the horses and furnishing the entertainment of races. They throve—but no American can really love a camel. Whether they admit it or not, Bureau of Animal Industry is balked by these things. Nothing remained of them at Tejón but tradition and a bell with the Arabic inscription nearly worn out of it by usage, cracked and thin, which Jimmy Rosemeyre, in a burst of generosity, which I hope he has never regretted, gave to me. Hanging above my desk, swinging, it sets in motion all the echoes of Romance.

The road runs whitely by Rose's Station. Los Angeles stages used to stop there, but I like best to remember it as the place where Jimmy Rosemeyre had a circus once, in the time when circuses traveled overland by the stage-roads from camp to roaring camp. . . .

The spirit of Tejón in General Beale's life much resembled the best of mission times. The measure of regard which he won from the Indians was paid for in respect for usages of their own; as you shall hear and judge in the case of the *Chisera.*

A *Chisera* you must know is a witch, in this instance a rainmaker. In a dry year the General put the Indians to turning the creek into an irrigating ditch to water the barley. Said they:

"Why so much bending of backs and breaking of shovel handles? There is a woman at Whiskey Flat who will bring rain abundantly for the price of a fat steer."

"Let her be proven," said the General, like Elijah to the prophets of Baal.

The *Chisera* wanted more than a steer—beads, calico, the material for a considerable feast, all of which was furnished her. First the Indians fed and then the *Chisera* danced. She leaped before the gods of Rain as David before the Ark of the Lord when it came up from Kirjath-jearim; she stamped and shuffled and swung to the roll of the hollow skins and rattles of rams' horns; three days she danced, and the Indians sat about her singing with their eyes upon the ground. Day and night they sustained her with the whisper and beat of their moaning voices. Is there in fact a vibration in nature which struck into rhythm precipitates rain, as a random chord on the organ brings a rush of tears? At any rate it rained, *and* it rained, and it *rained!* The barley quickened in the field, a thousand acres of mesa flung up suddenly a million sprouting things. Rain fell three weeks. The barley and the wheat lay over heavily, the cattle left off feeding, the budding mesa was too wet to bloom.

"For another steer," said the *Chisera*, I will make it stop."

So the toll of food, and cloth, and beads was paid again, and in three days the sun broke gloriously on a succulent green world. It is a pity, I think, that the *Chisera* is dead. . . .

Ranchos Tejón

There were once great grizzlies at Tejón, but mostly the bears are of the variety called black by scientists because they are dark brown, or even reddish when the slant light shows them feeding on the mast under the oaks or gathering manzanita berries on the borders of hanging meadows, wintry afternoons. Black enough they look, though, lumbering up the trail in the night or bulking large as their shadows cross the herder's drying fire. Pete Miller is the official bear-killer of the Ranchos Tejón, though his account of the killings are as short as the items in a doomsday book.

"Tell me a bear story, Pete," say I, sitting idly in the patio about the time of budding vines. Says Pete, "The herder was sleeping in a tapéstre—that's a bed on a platform in a tree. He said the bears bothered him some. But he was an all-right fellow; he wanted me to sleep in the tapéstre and let him sleep on the ground. Along in the night we heard the sheep running. It was dark as dark, a thick dust in the corral, and big lumps of blackness chasing around among the sheep. We couldn't see to shoot, but there were oak poles smouldering in the fire. We whacked the big lumps over the head with them. Leastways we aimed to whack 'em on the head, but it was pretty dark. I guess we scorched 'em considerable by the smell. There was one wallowed in the creek to put himself out. Seemed as if that corral was full of bears, but in the morning when we counted the tracks there were only four."

But think of knowing a man who could whack four big California bears over the head with a fire-brand!

There was never anything to equal the spring shearing at old Tejón; when there were eighty thousand head to be clipped, you can imagine it was a considerable affair. Seventy-five or eighty Indians bent backs under the sheds for five or six weeks at a time, and Nadeau's great eight-ox teams creaked southward to Los Angeles, a hundred and twenty miles, with the wool. All this finished with a fiesta lasting a week, with prizes for races and cockfights, with monte and dancing, and, of course, always a priest at hand to take his dole of the shearing wage and confess his people where the altar was set out with drawn-work altar-cloths and clusters of wild lilies in the ramada, that long two-walled house of wattled brush that served the Indian so well. . . .

If you ask me at a distance from its mirage-haunted borders, I should be obliged to depreciate the holding by one man of so large and profitable a demesne as the Ranchos Tejón, Castac, La Liebre, Los Alamos y Agua Caliente, but once inside the territory of the badger I basely desert from this high position, frankly glad of so wide a reach of hills where mists of grey tradition deepen to romance, where no axe is laid wantonly to the root of any tree, and no wild thing gives up its life except in penalty for depredation. Most glad I am of the blue lakes of uncropped lupines, of the wild tangle of the odorous vines, of the unshorn watershed; glad of certain clear spaces where, when the moon is full and a light wind ruffles all the leaves, soft-stepping deer troop through the thickets of the trees.

Mary Austin, *The Flock* (Boston, Houghton Mifflin and Company, 1906) 215–250.

A Health Rush Begins

JOHN E. BAUR

In the 1870s the medical profession freely prescribed a change of climate for a long list of complaints and disorders. By that time Los Angeles and its environs were accessible by rail and sufficiently "civilized" to be eligible for health seekers. Shortly after 1900 doctors became more inclined to cure the sick where they were, but by that time, according to John E. Baur's calculations, a quarter of the population of southern California was attributable to the health rush.

In the 1860s Los Angeles was still a frontier town with a notoriety for its outlaw element. More Mexican than Anglo-Saxon in culture, this "Queen of the Cow Counties" had been changed but little by the great gold rush. Now, settlers were beginning to arrive for whom Los Angeles and the county it headed promised peculiar benefits. These were the health seekers. Hope had brought them west. Yet, in their long-sought haven, sanitary conditions, basic for their recovery, were still abominable, for many residents used the irrigation ditches for washing and bathing. Dust, filth, and poor accommodations did not unduly deter the coming of invalids. One of the earliest to arrive was General James Shields, who, having just completed his term in the United States Senate, in midsummer, 1860, arrived by overland stage. A wound received thirteen years before at Cerro Gordo during the Mexican War prompted Shields's coming. The long trip proved worth while, for he remained to become a prominent "old settler."

The new transcontinental stage which carried the general to Los Angeles brought but a trickle of health seekers. A substantially larger number came by sea. Although probably there were still only a few score of health seekers in town by 1869, by that year Angelenos were complaining of the influx of indigent invalids for whom their community could provide neither adequate housing nor a steady livelihood. When the celebrated Pacific railroad was completed in May of 1869, it began to turn the migration into a rush which would last more than thirty years.

In January of that year, an editorial in the Los Angeles *Daily News* entitled "Wonderful Growth and Improvement of Los Angeles County" declared that "the great desideratum, a genial and healthful climate, constitutes the chief attraction." At the time, the boast was nearly accurate. Already unpleasant results could be cited; one physician said that he had never seen in any other state so much suffering from pulmonary diseases as he had found in southern California. "Oh! what a lot of coughing suffering mortals are coming here! Many too late. One man died in sight of the harbor," exclaimed D. M. Berry in Los Angeles during 1873. During the 1860s Phineas Banning's crude port facilities at Wilmington had served hundreds of health seekers, and his stages provided their first transportation from harbor to the inland towns.

This increasingly large migration for health could not have occurred at any earlier date, and the reasons for its occurrence changed within a generation. Before this period, the American standard of living had not been high enough for such a mass movement of invalids across the continent. Los Angeles, until the eighties a village surrounded by dry mustard fields and based on a vineyard and fruit economy, was hardly the place most of these people would have chosen had they been well. By the 1880s, however, the town was rapidly becoming a city in miniature, and railroads were ending its isolation. The promise of health had already played a noticeable part in making these fundamental changes, for although the health seekers constituted a minority of the newcomers, that minority was an active one, and either directly or indirectly it influenced a growing number of well people to migrate to California, many of these latter individuals being members of the invalids' families. By the nineties the sick had become as typical as the palm or orange. A tubercular described the result in Los Angeles:

"At every street corner I met a poor fellow croaking like myself. I strolled into the Plaza, there to imbibe the exhilarating effects of a community with broken lungs in all stages, and the inspiring comfort of a vocabulary like this: 'Well, how do you feel today? Did you have a good night? Are you trying any new medicine?' 'O, the pain in my side is very bad.' 'Do you cough much now?' Fancy how helpful to an invalid! Then, at the boarding house opposite ours, one would come on to the porch muffled in shawls, a parchment face and sunken eyes, cough, cough, cough, leaning over the hand-rail another fellow with spindle legs and shrunken form; another joins them and still another, feebly walking to and fro, alive to save funeral expenses."

On the streets and in the trolleys or at the post office, where they invariably awaited cheering letters from home, one could meet these desperately ill yet courageous people with their "hollow eyes and still more hollow cough."

From their first arrival, the invalids created a housing shortage in Los Angeles, one of the first situations of this kind the quiet little pueblo had experienced. Their very numbers stirred up considerable action, and the picturesque Mexican community began to disappear before the inrush. Beginning its campaign in 1874, the Los Angeles *Herald* determined to obtain new hotels and end the crisis. The "city," as even then residents chose to call Los Angeles, was in a "catyleptic sleep" and was complacently permitting San Diego and Santa Barbara to build hotels and capture its potentially profitable health seekers. A 300-guest hotel, the *Herald* said, could be built for $175,000.

A Health Rush Begins

Yet, in 1882 one health seeker noted that there still was urgent need for a good family hotel. Invalids were leaving for other towns because of this lack. Not all of them, however, were frightened off by poor accommodations, for the average had a strong backbone to accompany his weak chest and was willing to endure numerous hardships if there was the slightest hope of recovery. That same season the sick had filled all the available hotels and rooming houses, and many private families were taking in boarders for the first time. Real-estate men were reporting that houses had been bargained for before the foundations had been laid, and other observers concluded that health seekers currently constituted the major portion of the American population. Whether this was a valid assumption or not, their numbers were certainly greater than had been expected. Chief headquarters for the health seekers of the early eighties were the city's two leading hotels, which, unfortunately, housed only 250 guests.

Until later in the eighties, amenities were rare. The lack of them was bad publicity for Los Angeles. In one of its numerous editorials for better hotels, the *Herald* cried, "Let in the Sunshine and Stir Up the Fire!" Too many badly lighted rooms were being designed, despite ample evidence that: "A large portion of the patrons of our hotels and boarding-houses, especially during the Winter months, are invalids, and persons in feeble health—persons who wish, and are willing to pay for comfort. The constant complaint among them is that they are compelled either to remain shivering in their rooms or else crowd around the public fire in office or parlor." Hotel builders should watch the sun to determine at what hour it shone in certain directions and then construct their rooms accordingly. Flues should be used instead of pipes. In conclusion, the newspaper advised, "publish these facts —'fire and sunshine in all the rooms of the house'—and every steamer will bring you guests; you cannot drive them away."

Only slowly was the housing problem remedied. While hunting quarters for an invalid friend in 1882, Dr. Norman Bridge could not find a single house in all Los Angeles providing means for heating in every room, except by gas or kerosene stoves, the fumes of which stayed in the rooms. Most places had only a kitchen stove or a single fireplace, usually found in the parlor. "They look upon you with horror and consternation here when you ask for a fire," observed a

187

health seeker in 1886. His request eventually materialized as a small fireplace "the size of your thum-nail."

At the time, the diet offered an invalid in Los Angeles was far from ideal, the abundance of food notwithstanding. Restaurant meat, bread, and cream were generally inferior, certainly not to be recommended for a tubercular who needed the best of nutritious meals. In boarding house, hotel, or restaurant, the sick had to accept the menu offered to the general public, for there were no health-food restaurants until after the turn of the century. Although visitors might vary widely in their praises of and complaints against Los Angeles, they almost uniformly condemned the city's twin shortcomings, poor heating and unsatisfactory meals. Confronted with these problems as well as a climate which offered less than the perfection they sought, it is no wonder that some health seekers were not surprised to find on a tombstone in Fort Hill Cemetery the inscription "Translated to a More Genial Clime."

John E. Baur, *The Health Seekers of Southern California* (San Marino: Huntington Library, 1959), 33–37.

Water Rights in Condominium
J. A. ALEXANDER

A Canadian engineer, George Chaffey, opened a new era of irrigation in southern California. His major exploit was diverting water from the Colorado to convert desert land into the highly productive Imperial Valley. At Etiwanda on the Cucamonga Plain in the early eighties, he capitalized on the underground as well as the surface streams, used cement pipes for efficient delivery to each ten-acre plot, and added the garnish of generating electric power. Assisted by L. M. Holt, editor of the Riverside Press and Horticulturist, he installed a mutual water company system in which ten shares in the water supply were tied to ownership of each ten acres in the irrigation district. This holding of water rights in condominium, along with gravity flow and cement pipes, made irrigation workable.

The Garcia Ranch, situated on the Cucamonga Plain, fourteen miles west of San Bernardino, beginning at the foot of the Sierra Madre Range and extending four miles down the plain, was the site of the first irrigation colony established by Chaffey Brothers. The younger brother was attracted by the quality of the land, which he found to be eminently suited for subdividing into small fruit farms. He foresaw that these would sell readily to home seekers from the East and from Canada, who were beginning to flock to California, drawn by the marvellous climate and unlimited supply of land. The soundness of his judgment was vindicated by the success which attended the first venture of Chaffey Brothers.

George Chaffey was attracted by the water supply flowing down three small neighboring canyons from the mountains, and by the water rights attached to the Garcia property. He perceived an opportunity for creating, by a small expenditure on water works, a new irrigation colony on land given over to cactus, sage brush and manzanita. The water right dated from 1867, when George Day, occupying land close against the foot of the mountains, watered it from the canyon which now bears his name, and filed on all the waters passing down it. This water right was extended by successive filings by Day, Wm. B. Pierce and one Smith, till, in 1873, a right had been established by filing and use to the waters of Day's, Middle, and Young's Canyons. These rights and utilizations became consolidated and in part attached to what was later known as the Garcia Ranch.

Late in 1881 Chaffey Brothers . . . made their way to the home of Capt. J. S. Garcia. They . . . arrived just in time to sit down to Thanksgiving Day dinner. Afterwards they went up into the canyons to inspect the water supply. The water was very low that season, and of the supply in sight the Captain owned one hundred inches. George Chaffey was delighted with the possibilities he saw opening before him. Drawing Capt. Garcia aside, he offered to buy 1000 acres with the water right at a price in the vicinity of a dollar-and-a-half an acre. The bargain was clinched on the spot. This, with five hundred acres of an adjoining property, formed the original Etiwanda Colony, which, in 1888, comprised nearly 2500 acres.

Work on the new colony was begun immediately. The rapid progress made demonstrated that the brothers had a magical gift for getting things done. The first survey was completed early in 1882. The land was divided into ten-acre blocks, with the water brought in cement pipes to the highest corner of each lot. . . .

Though Etiwanda was a small settlement compared with the projects undertaken by George Chaffey in later years, it is in many respects the most notable irrigation colony in Western America. It was the first California irrigation settlement watered by a cement pipe line system. In introducing this method of bringing the water to the field ditches, George Chaffey made irrigation history.

But Etiwanda is more notable still for having occasioned the creation of the Holt-Chaffey Mutual Water Company system, the model on which nearly all future Californian irrigation companies were based. . . .

The inadaptability of Californian riparian law, inherited from England, had proved a serious obstacle to the development of irrigation in the West, causing interminable litigation and consequent loss and delay, enriching attorneys and impoverishing and disheartening irrigators. . . . Each land owner claiming water simply put in a ditch to bring it to his land, regardless of the rights or wishes of those lower down the stream. In early days, when claimants were few, this haphazard plan worked, but later, when numbers were clamoring for water, those near the source of distribution held the upper hand and, often feeling no responsibility towards the luckless ones lower down, took their fill regardless of those who went without.

George Chaffey's scientific mind rebelled against this untidy system, with its endless disputes and losses. (L. M.) Holt believed he had found the solution in a system by which all the water available for the irrigation of a definite area would be owned by all who constituted the colony, the ownership of each individual to be proportionate to his holding of land. . . .

Stripped of technicalities, the idea was: A water company was organized, its stock consisting of one share for every acre of land comprised in the colony. Each purchaser of land received one share in the water company for every acre held. The water rights were sold to the water company by the vendors, the Chaffey Brothers, who had, of course, purchased the water rights with the property. They received in return for the water right all the shares in the water company, these to be transferred pro rata to the purchasers of land. Thus ten shares in the water company would be transferred to the purchaser of each ten-acre lot. The effect of this was that the water company would assume responsibility for the distribution of water to each ten-acre tract, irrespective of nearer or remoter location and no one was entitled to more than his proportionate share. . . .

Early in 1882 the Etiwanda land was advertised in the East and Canada, and settlers immediately began to come in. . . . The wild country must have looked forbidding enough to the stout-hearted pioneers who first settled Etiwanda. Bears and mountain lions were unwelcome visitors to the infant settlement. Rabbits were a pest, but the packs of coyotes making chicken-raising impossible were worse. Excepting *El Camino Real* and the old Santa Fe Trail there were no roads. Disappointments with the products of the soil were frequent at first, but to-day, its old-time desolation and isolation gone forever, Etiwanda is a most prosperous colony—its network of beautiful shady avenues and smiling orchards a monument to the courage and tenacity of the first settlers, no less than to the vision of its founders.

Grape, orange, and lemon have brought great prosperity to Etiwanda, and for over a generation it has been producing large quantities of high-class fruit. The earliest settlers could not at first afford to pay nurserymen a dollar each for citrus trees, but vines put them on their feet, and they found later that oranges did splendidly in that frostless region. In a few years, hundreds of acres were under citrus trees. Vines proved very profitable after the first decade, when better marketing facilities were available. Now Etiwanda produces magnificent field-packed table grapes, Thompson's seedless and sultana raisins. It has long held a high position in the Californian fruit industry as a prize-winning colony.

George Chaffey, with that long-range vision which penetrated into the future, foresaw that electric energy would entirely change conditions of living within a generation, and he determined to be a pioneer of electricity in Southern California. As a preliminary experiment he installed electric light at Etiwanda which became the first place on the Pacific Slope at which hydro-electric current was developed. He was the first engineer in Western America to file on mountain streams for electric current. At the head works he installed a small dynamo operated by the down-rushing torrent. This provided electricity for an arc light placed in 1882 on top of the old ranch house in which George Chaffey was then living. The strange white beam which flashed across the mountain slope aroused more than Statewide curiosity and interest. Seen as far away as Riverside, it proved an effective advertisement for the Chaffey enterprise.

J. A. Alexander, *The Life of George Chaffey* (Melbourne, 1928), 32–37.

Steel Ropes into the Howling Wilderness

ROBERT C. POST

This thumbnail history of the Second Street Cable Carline compresses a chapter in Robert C. Post's book-length study of Los Angeles streetcars from their beginnings in the 1870s to consolidation decades later in the hands of Henry E. Huntington. This railway had the character of an infringement on a San Francisco monopoly. It also illustrates a fundamental of the period: that the pay-off at the real estate office was treasured more than the pay-in at the fare box.

192

Historical Collections, Security Pacific National Bank

Second Street cable car.

Signs of modern times began to show up in Los Angeles soon after the Civil War—such things as gaslights in 1867, then a railway line from the harbor, iron water mains, a stretch of street paving, and in 1874 a streetcar. The town's first traction magnate was Judge Robert M. Widney, who set a gay little four-wheeler to plying Spring Street and Sixth out to Figueroa—then called Pearl Street. Next year, Isaias W. Hellman and John G. Downey financed a more substantial line on Main Street and Washington. By the early 1880s Angelenos could go many places aboard horsecars: to the S.P. Depot north of the Plaza, to East Los Angeles and Boyle Heights beyond the river, and down to Agricultural Park (today's Exposition) in the southwest. Still, one large sector remained deprived of public transit—Bunker Hill, just west of the business district, and the rolling country beyond all the way to the city limits. Here were broad vistas of tall grass and wild-flowers and scarcely a building to be seen. The papers liked to call it a "howling wilderness." That was a bit melodramatic, although, true to the words of James Miller Guinn, it was territory "not exempt from the coyote's nightly wail."

One wagon road went out this way, Temple Street. Temple had no carline, for its grades would have taxed even the hardiest streetcar horses unbearably. But there was an alternative to horsecars. In San Francisco, in 1873, an engineer named Andrew Hallidie had devised a way to impel streetcars with an underground wire rope. Soon cable cars were running up and down half a dozen of the Bay City's most formidable hills, and Hallidie's partisans pronounced his innovation "the true solution of economical, metropolitan rapid transit." If in San Francisco, some Angelenos began wondering, why not here? Why not up and over Bunker Hill?

Cable railways had horsecars beat in safety, operating economy, and speed (six miles an hour or more, even uphill). To be sure, they were costly to build, five or ten times more per mile than horse railways. But the men most interested in cable cars for Los Angeles were an optimistic bunch, and gamblers, too—real estate speculators, mostly. In many cities "the heights" were prime residential property. Obviously the entire west side was ripe for subdivision. All that was needed was transportation.

In late 1884 a representative of Hallidie's company came to town, rented an office in the Nadeau Block, and set about marshaling capital for two lines, one on Temple, the other on Second Street. The Second Streeters responded more quickly, getting the necessary funds together and completing a survey even while awaiting their franchise from the City Council. The day it came through they advertised for grading bids, and work was underway on the Second Street Cable Railroad by March, 1885. While there was some San Francisco money in the enterprise, and tradesmen around the Spring Street terminus invested too, the company's prime backers were Henry Clay Witmer and a group of his associates who controlled the Los Angeles Improvement Company—and, through that, 1,400 building lots.

The carline cost roughly $100,000. This included 6,940 feet of track from Spring to Texas Street (Belmont Avenue), rolling stock, and a powerhouse at Boylston Street equipped with a 75-horsepower Corliss steam engine. Grading was particularly expensive, for Second Street did not even exist west of Hill; great cuts had to be made at two places, a massive fill at another. Even so, the ultimate profile embodied grades of more than 25 per cent (up a foot for every four feet ahead), steeper than any other American line ever built. The roadbed was costly too, though that was normal. Cable railway engineering entailed digging a large trench for the yoked conduit that carried the steel rope along on a maze of pulleys, sheaves, and idlers. All went well enough, and construction was completed in late summer, 1885.

The first runs "over the hill" took place on October 8. There were three open-sided cars equipped with operator's controls (but called "dummies" nevertheless), and three colorful trailers with seating for twelve. A man from the *Times* reported that the passengers seemed "delighted" at how rapidly and smoothly the cars glided along. Indeed, the sheer novelty—streetcars moving without the clop clop that always before had signalled their approach—was a major attraction and patronage topped the owners' fondest hopes.

What truly mattered to them, however, was not the cars but their lots. Promotional lures included bounteous picnic lunches, and typical advertising ran:

PURE AIR—NO FOGS
CHEAP LOTS IN THE WESTERN ADDITION OF THE CABLE ROAD

Batches of a hundred were marketed for one, two, or three hundred dollars, depending mainly on the distance from the carline. Terms were 25 per cent down, the balance in two years at 7 per cent interest. By the end of 1886 all but 52 of the lots had been sold, and many were being built on. The new homes, especially those on Crown Hill at the western terminus of the line, helped fire the excitement of boomtimes. On the eastern end, business was thriving at Second and Spring, now becoming the town's main intersection.

And the carline was doing well too. Witmer had pegged the break-even point at 600 revenue passengers per day; by the end of 1886 patronage was more than double that and the company even paid a dividend. Nevertheless, he and his associates did not want to stay in the transit business, and in January, 1887, they sold out. The price was $130,000, the buyer James McLaughlin, son-in-law of Senator Cornelius Cole. McLaughlin also had building lots to sell, only they were farther out, beyond the far terminus of the cable line in Colesville—now, Hollywood. He immediately began a steam railroad extending to Colesville, and had two miles of this Cahuenga Valley Railroad in operation by midyear. He also bought new equipment for the cable line, upgraded service, and refurbished City Park, an on-line beer garden that Witmer had tossed into the deal. McLaughlin planned much else, including double-tracking the entire line and extending the steam road all the way to the sea at Santa Monica. But in the late summer of 1887 the Great Boom began to fade out, and any such investment quickly lost its appeal.

Then a whole series of natural calamaties hit. Torrential rains the next winter often washed so much silt into the cable conduit that operation literally ground to a halt. In January, 1888, the frazzled cable had to be replaced. A new one arrived at the railroad station soon enough, but the wagon sent out to pick it up became mired due to its ponderous load. The *Herald*, which took real delight in such misfortunes, jeered that the carline was closed because its rope "was, stuck in a mud hole." That shutdown lasted two weeks, others nearly as long.

Next came legal problems. In September, 1889, the Cahuenga Valley Railroad was enjoined from operating its locomotive inside the city limits, on account of its noise and soot. A month later McLaughlin quit running the cable line, pleading that it was in the red despite his investment of $200,000. He needed the revenue provided by the connection with the Cahuenga Valley, and was willing to extend the cable line to the city limits and reroute the railroad to a new junction point. But the City Council refused to approve a new franchise, allegedly because McLaughlin had suggested in public that certain councilmen could be "bought." Whatever the case, his position regarding the carline was clear: no franchise, no extension, no resumption of service.

The stalemate persisted. After Christmas eve, however, it became academic. That night a great downpour—said by many to have been the heaviest of all time—sent a flood rushing down from Echo Park which swept away a long segment of track. Then a huge cave-in completely buried the right-of-way from Flower to Figueroa.

By 1890 the moribund company was deeply in debt. Even had he received his franchise, McLaughlin's capacity to make repairs and build an extension was doubtful. Later the property was foreclosed to satisfy a $10,000 judgement. Rumors persisted that out-of-town cable men planned to buy the bankrupt property, rehabilitate it, and resume operation. But the steel rope rumbled beneath Second Street for only four years, 1885–1889, and never again thereafter. One of the earliest cable car lines in the country (eventually there were more than sixty), the Second Street Cable Railroad Company was the very first to suffer outright abandonment.

In the meantime, another cable road had come to the western hills, on Temple Street, that served much the same territory. An extensive city-wide system had also been opened. This system, all $2.5 million worth, was ignominiously junked in favor of trolley cars after just a few years. The Temple Street line, on the other hand, survived until 1902 and was the last non-electric carline in the city. The man who bought it and ended cable operation was Henry E. Huntington, whose name was to become synonymous with electric railways in and about Los Angeles. Everybody remembers the Los Angeles Railway and the Big Red Cars of the Pacific Electric. The Second Street Cable Railroad is forgotten, as are James McLaughlin and Henry Witmer. Oh, there is still a Witmer Street close by the Harbor Freeway. But there is surely no Witmer Beach, Witmer Boulevard, Witmer Park, Witmer Memorial Hospital, or Witmer Library.

Yet Henry Huntington was not unique—only the most important of those entrepreneurs who determined Los Angeles' residential pattern by cultivating a taste for uncrowded living. Others did much the same thing as he did on a smaller scale. Notwithstanding their resemblance to the Toonerville of cartoon fame, it was the little outfits such as the Second Street company that anticipated the Pacific Electric long before Huntington ever saw Los Angeles. In 1890, the resident of Crown Hill was no less a suburbanite than the resident of Pasadena or Santa Monica in 1910 or 1920.

The difference between Henry Witmer and Henry Huntington, then, was one of degree not of kind. The difference between the sort of streetcars they operated, though, ran much deeper. There are still trolleys in nearly a dozen North American cities. Cable cars survive in only one, San Francisco. But next time you ride a cable car up Nob Hill or Russian Hill, recall that not so long ago such delightful contrivances also carried Angelenos to the heights, to the realm of Pure Air—No Fogs.

Condensed from Robert C. Post, *Street Railways in Los Angeles* (M.A. thesis, UCLA, 1967), 84–119.

The Condition and Needs of the Mission Indians

HELEN HUNT JACKSON

Helen Hunt Jackson became the most vocal friend of the California Indians. Her Century of Dishonor *excoriated federal Indian practices. After she and Abbot Kinney filed their Report on the Conditions and Needs of the Mission Indians, she translated this message into one of the most widely read of California titles, the novel* Ramona. *The selection that follows is from the* Report. *In the tally of Indians surviving in southern California the Gabrielino are not mentioned. A few probably were included in the Serrano count, others had gone north, but no coherent group remained.*

The term "Mission Indians" dates back over one hundred years, to the time of the Franciscan missions in California. It then included all Indians who lived in the mission establishments, or were under the care of the Franciscan Fathers. Very naturally the term has continued to be applied to the descendants of those Indians. In the classification of the Indian Bureau, however, it is now used in a somewhat restricted sense, embracing only those Indians living in the three southernmost counties of California, and known as Serranos, Cahuillas, San Luisenos, and Dieguinos; the last two names having evidently come from the names of the southernmost two missions, San Luis Rey and San Diego. A census taken in 1880, of these bands, gives their number as follows:

Serranos	381
Cahuillas	675
San Luisenos	1,120
Dieguinos	731
Total	2,907

198

This estimate probably falls considerably short of the real numbers, as there are no doubt in hiding, so to speak, in remote and inaccessible spots, many individuals, families, or even villages, that have never been counted. These Indians are living for the most part in small and isolated villages; some on reservations set apart for them by Executive order; some on Government land not reserved, and some upon lands included within the boundaries of confirmed Mexican grants.

Considerable numbers of these Indians are also to be found on the outskirts of white settlements, as at Riverside, San Bernardino, or in the colonies in the San Gabriel Valley, where they live like gypsies in brush huts, here to-day, gone to-morrow, eking out a miserable existence by day work, the wages of which are too often spent for whiskey in the village saloons. Travellers in Southern California, who have formed their impressions of the Mission Indians from these wretched wayside creatures, would be greatly surprised at the sight of some of the Indian villages in the mountain valleys, where, freer from the contaminating influence of the white race, are industrious, peaceable communities, cultivating ground, keeping stock, carrying on their own simple manufactures of pottery, mats, baskets, &c., and making their living,—a very poor living, it is true; but they are independent and self-respecting in it, and ask nothing at the hands of the United States Government now, except that it will protect them in the ownership of their lands,—lands which, in many instances, have been in continuous occupation and cultivation by their ancestors for over one hundred years.

From tract after tract of such lands they have been driven out, year by year, by the white settlers of the country, until they can retreat no farther; some of their villages being literally in the last tillable spot on the desert's edge or in mountain fastnesses. Yet there are in Southern California to-day many fertile valleys, which only thirty years ago were like garden spots with these same Indians' wheat-fields, orchards, and vineyards. Now, there is left in these valleys no trace of the Indians' occupation, except the ruins of their adobe houses; in some instances these houses, still standing, are occupied by the robber whites who drove them out. The responsibility for this wrong rests, perhaps, equally divided between the United States Government, which permitted lands thus occupied by peaceful agricultural communities to be put "in market," and the white men who were not

199

restrained either by humanity or by a sense of justice, from "filing" homestead claims on lands which had been fenced, irrigated, tilled, and lived on by Indians for many generations. The government cannot justify this neglect on the plea of ignorance. Repeatedly, in the course of the last thirty years, both the regular agents in charge of the Mission Indians and special agents sent out to investigate their condition have made to the Indian Bureau full reports setting forth these facts.

Our Government received by the treaty of Guadalupe Hidalgo a legacy of a singularly helpless race in a singularly anomalous position. It would have been very difficult, even at the outset, to devise practicable methods of dealing justly with these people, and preserving to them their rights. But with every year of our neglect the difficulties have increased and the wrongs have been multiplied, until now it is, humanly speaking, impossible to render to them full measure of justice. All that is left in our power is to make them some atonement. Fortunately for them, their numbers have greatly diminished. Suffering, hunger, disease, and vice have cut down more than half of their numbers in the last thirty years; but the remnant is worth saving. Setting aside all question of their claim as a matter of atonement for injustice done, they are deserving of help on their own merits. No one can visit their settlements, such as Aqua Caliente, Saboba, Cahuilla Valley, Santa Ysabel, without having a sentiment of respect and profound sympathy for men who, friendless, poor, without protection from the law, have still continued to work, planting, fencing, irrigating, building houses on lands from which long experience has taught them that the white man can drive them off any day he chooses. That drunkenness, gambling, and other immoralities are sadly prevalent among them, cannot be denied; but the only wonder is that so many remain honest and virtuous under conditions which make practically null and void for them most of the motives which keep white men honest and virtuous.

Helen Hunt Jackson, *A Century of Dishonor: A Sketch of the United States Government's Dealings with Some of the Indian Tribes* (Boston, 1885), 458–474.

The Great Southern California Boom

T. S. Van Dyke and Glenn S. Dumke

The real estate speculation that reached its hectic peak late in 1887 outreached anything this 106-year-old city had seen. Suddenly there were five or six times as many persons in town. In the latter half of the year the post office handled the mail of 200,000 transients, more than twice the number of Argonauts in 1849. When bust followed on the heels of the boom, T. S. Van Dyke, participant as well as observer, looked back in dismay and fervently hoped that the folly would never be repeated. Glenn S. Dumke, a modern scholar, aware that the pattern of Los Angeles has been to grow by spurts, though not discounting the absurdities, sees much that was constructive.

A Rueful Appraisal

"I wouldn't have missed it for all I have lost. It was worth living a lifetime to see."

So said to the author last year one of the ex-millionaires. And in truth he was not far from right. One who has not, as an actor, been through a first-class "boom" has missed one of the most interesting points of view of human nature.

Now that we have had plenty of time to look back upon the great boom that raged so long in the six southern counties of Southern California and gauge its immensity, we can see that it had never its like on earth. There have indeed been times of wilder excitement, when property has changed hands oftener in twenty-four hours and brought perhaps higher prices, but they were limited to a single point or to a brief period, and nearly always to both. But this boom (for convenience we will drop the quotation marks hereafter) lasted nearly

Los Angeles Convention and Visitors Bureau

Baldwin Cottage, built in 1881

two years, embraced a vast area of both town and country, and involved an amount of money and players almost incredible to even those who were in it.

There was nothing in this analogous to any South Sea Bubble, or

202

oil or mining stock swindle, or any other of the great humbugs of the past. The actors in this great game were not ignorant or poor people, and from end to end there was scarcely anything in it that could fairly be called a swindle. What few misrepresentations there were, were mere matters of opinion such as no one of sense ever relies on, any more than he does on the assurance that he will double his money within so many days. With a very few exceptions the principal victims were men of means. Most of them, and certainly the most reckless of them, were men who in some branch of business had been successful. Very many of them were "self-made men" who had built up fortunes by their exertions, and were supposed to know right well the value of a dollar, and to have some idea of the value of property. All had the amplest time to revise their judgments and investigate the conditions of the game. The country all lay open, was easily and quickly traversed, and the advantages or disadvantages of any point could be readily seen. Over and over again the shrewdest of them did revise their judgments, debated with themselves the question whether they were fools or not, and the more they debated the more they were convinced that they were underestimating instead of overestimating the situation. And some of the silliest of the lot were men who, during the first three fourths of the excitement, kept carefully out of it, and did nothing but sneer at the folly of those who were in it.

The history of such a craze seems worth writing. Much has, of course, been told about it; but no one, unless he had a hand in it and could see its inside working, can tell of it in its most important phases, and nothing would be history that did not follow the results of the folly to their end.

To the people of the older States much of this will seem mere burlesque, and they will toss it aside as unworthy of belief. But the Californian will say that instead of being an exaggeration many interesting facts have been suppressed, probably because the writer dare not tell them. But enough has been told to interest all who were in it, though it will awaken many a painful recollection, and enough to warn any one who will study it from ever gambling on a margin on any prospects, no matter how good a judge he may think himself of booms and conditions of growth. Of course no warning will have any effect upon the great majority; but one thing is certain—the Californians want no more booms. A steady and substantial growth they do want, are having now, and will continue to have if Eastern boomers do not again set them crazy. They want nothing that will again check true development as the great boom did, and will advise all who think of coming to California to read this brief sketch of the greatest piece of folly that any country has even seen.

T. S. Van Dyke, *Millionaires of a Day* (New York, 1890), 1–4.

A Carefully Measured Conclusion

No precise date can be given for the end of the boom. . . . Loans were extended, week by week and month by month, and deficiency judgments were remarkably few in number. As a result, the collapse was milder in its effects than might have been expected. There was no widespread suffering or want. . . . Pasadena had soared highest in the balloon of inflation, when the drop came she struck bottom the hardest. . . . Glendale stagnated in economic doldrums for many months, the new hotel lay empty, and the Improvement Society died a quick death, but the town was permanently benefitted by the interested activity of many prosperous businessmen who had invested in Glendale property. . . . [In Monrovia] the nadir of the depression was perhaps reached when the "garbage wagon was discontinued and the city marshal instructed to employ a wagon once a week," . . . but in 1889 signs of reviving activity were evident in the construction of a new bridge over the San Gabriel River and in the establishment of a telegraph office. . . .

The effects of the crash on individuals were often disastrous. "Lucky" Baldwin, patriarch of Santa Anita, left landpoor by the boom's failure, was forced to withdraw temporarily from his beloved horse racing, and for a time found difficulty in paying his employees. . . . The Los Angeles *Times* on June 9, 1887, told of a Pasadena citizen who took strychnine because he had "sold some property too cheap. . . . "

Yet the boom was not entirely detrimental. The economic flurry was California's characteristic mode of development, and, like the comber carried by a rising tide, it always receded—but never quite so far as its starting point. Joseph Netz argued that "the great real estate boom of 1887 was not built wholly on air. . . . Our real estate boomers went a little faster than the country, that was all. . . . "

L. M. Holt of Riverside noted: "During this wild speculative craze many solid improvements were established that have since been turned to good use in building up the country and making it attractive to eastern people who are seeking homes in our midst. There is no section . . . where good cement sidewalks in cities and towns begin to compare with those of Southern California. There is no other section where cities and towns have so good a supply and system of domestic water service, it frequently being found that the domestic piped water system under pressure is established before there are people to use the water. There is no other section where there are so many rapid transit motor railroads."

The boom greatly affected the caliber of southern California's population. . . . Los Angeles had less than 6,000 citizens in 1870, but the census of 1890 credited it with more than 50,000 permanent residents. Pasadena increased in size more than tenfold during the boom decade. . . .

A basic reason why the boom's collapse did not utterly ruin southern California's economy was the conservative policy of the banks. . . . Deposits reached $5,500,000 in 1886, $8,000,000 in January of 1887, and $12,000,000 before the end of that year. . . . In 1887 loans amounted to 80 percent of deposits; in January, 1887, to 62½ per cent; and by July, 1887, were below 50 per cent. . . .

"With all its faults and failures, with all its reckless waste and wild extravagance," observed James M. Guinn, "our boom was more productive of good than of evil to Southern California." True, the flurry overemphasized realty speculation at the expense of more productive development, caused bankruptcies and failures when it collapsed, and was responsible for an artificial level of economic activity which might have been very dangerous to the region's future welfare. But, in general, benefits exceeded harmful effects. The boom brought people to California in ever increasing numbers, and they themselves were the foundation for a greater economic structure. It enlarged transportation facilities and municipal development, settled hitherto barren areas, completed the breakup of the ranchos, and was largely responsible for southern California's modern publicity consciousness, which has done much to develop the southland.

Even in their most extravagant predictions, boom promoters proved to be true prophets, for Los Angeles realty valuation and activity have long since overtopped the highest boom levels. The depression following the boom was not a bad one, for, as a contemporary [our friend, T. S. Van Dyke] put it; "when millions of hands have been hanging idle in the east, every hammer and saw in the city has been busy, and business houses, fine residences and neat cottages are still rising as fast as ever."

The boom was significant, not only for its color, picturesqueness, and uproarious enthusiasm, but also because it wiped out forever the last traces of the Spanish-Mexican pastoral economy which had characterized California since 1769. The gold rush made northern California a real part of the United States; the boom of the eighties did precisely that for the south. Where once the "cattle of the plain" had grazed in silence over rich acres, now the American citizen built his trolley lines, founded his banks, and irrigated his orange groves. The boom was the final step in the process of making California truly American.

Glenn S. Dumke, *The Boom of the Eighties* (San Marino: Huntington Library, 1944), 260–276 passim.

Specter of No Growth

"One thing is certain: in arid lands man's progress has been no faster than his ability to meet his water needs."

—Remi Nadeau

San Fernando Valley before the water came

6

Specter of No Growth

In the 1890s practically every southern Californian accepted the growth ethic. Today's rule of thumb that we simply must have an economy growing at 4 or 5 percent a year if we are to have prosperity, employment, and a tolerable society was yet to be formalized, but turn-of-the-century Angelenos would have agreed. Understandable then is their concern when it appeared that the underpinnings of Los Angeles growth were threatened.

Using what Dana called the worst port along the coast, Los Angeles had been the principal loading point in the hide trade. Looking toward the twentieth century, everyone could see that it was imperative to build a respectable harbor. Los Angeles also would have to prevent that harbor falling under the monopoly of one railroad, the Southern Pacific.

Although great proficiency had been shown in growing oranges, it was mandatory to improve, almost, in fact, to create, an adequate and reliable market.

Once the only municipality in the vicinity, Los Angeles now was ringed and enfiladed by scores of towns. Its role as the business center required metropolitan rapid transit, or so it was believed.

The Los Angeles River with its fabulous natural storage basin underlying the San Fernando Valley had served the water needs of the growing population for a dozen decades and more. But for the needs even modestly forecast some additional source would have to be tapped.

The Chamber of Commerce took in hand the task of persuading Congress to underwrite surveys, the necessary dredging, and the building of breakwaters to give Los Angeles a port. Midstream the harbor advocates collided with Collis P. Huntington whose objective was a port that the Southern Pacific could control. The rather small city scored a political victory over the really big corporation.

The citrus growers, observing that the profits if any went to the middlemen, experimented with various remedies. At length most of them lined up in the California Fruit Growers Exchange under the Sunkist brand. The association undertook to enforce quality controls. Eventually it provided miscellaneous services to members, such as furnishing boxes at cost. The essence of its program was to control delivery all the way to the retailers and through advertising to build demand for oranges not just in the Christmas stocking and not just any orange, but the Sunkist brand year round. The Exchange was the first and one of the few agricultural cooperatives to score a real success.

Henry E. Huntington entered the streetcar business as an investment. Moving on to the Pacific Electric, he was charged with deploying new trackage to serve his real estate developments, a charge not altogether fair because he was in the transportation business too. Within a few years his big red cars ran to San Fernando, the beach towns, the harbor, Newport, Riverside, San Bernardino, and to a host of intermediate communities. The service was rapid, comfortable, and inexpensive. Few metropolises were so farflung as Huntington's Pacific Electric empire. Few if any were so well served. But then in 1925 or thereabouts, automobiles menaced the crossings and so clogged the streets near the Los Angeles terminals that schedules were impossible. Phaseout was gradual, then rapid.

The neatest miracle worked by this generation was in outdoing the Romans with a 250-mile aqueduct across a flank of the Mojave Desert. Following a divining rod to the eastern slope of the Sierra Nevada, Fred Eaton, J. B. Lippincott, William Mulholland, and their associates quietly bought up water rights in Owens River, importuned the President for a right of way across government land and, for $25 million, constructed a gravity-and-syphon-flow conduit to bring this life-giving water to the City of Los Angeles. This water would take care of the needs of one and a half to two million Angelenos to come.

To this day a two-barreled criticism persists: that Owens Valley was raped and returned to sagebrush, and that a syndicate, some members of which had advance information on the plan, made a killing in San Fernando Valley land where much of the water was put to use. By any standards the design and construction of the aqueduct was a marvel of the age. As to dispelling the specter of no-growth, the bringing in of the Owens River water was worth more than the harbor, the Sunkist brand, or the Pacific Electric.

These four causes, compelling though they were, did not consume all available energy. Another, the mission myth, which John O. Pohlmann calls the desire for history and tradition, drew a substantial amount of attention and made an impression on the southern California scene. It aided among others the tourist industry, a southern California enterprise suffused with optimism.

The Fight for a Free Port

GLENN CHESNEY QUIETT

Glenn Chesney Quiett explains the spectacular development of the West in the latter half of the nineteenth century in terms of the men who built and ran the Union Pacific-Central Pacific and the successor lines thrown across to the Pacific. Thereby they also performed prodigies in helping along the region. In the contest to see whether the harbor to be created for Los Angeles would be monopolized by one railroad or served competitively, the railroad magnate, Collis P. Huntington, comes off as the villain.

The prospect of making a really great port for Los Angeles was not bright, and certainly no one in the harbor cities of San Francisco or

San Diego would have considered it seriously. The sea-going aspiration of Los Angeles, Queen of the Cow Counties, was a joke. But the people of the community were in earnest. . . . Whenever a Representative or Senator arrived within hailing distance of Los Angeles, the Chamber of Commerce would seize him and transport him to the harbor. . . . One such visitor was Senator William P. Frye of Maine, of the Committee on Commerce, and as he stood on the barren San Pedro headlands after the 30-mile ride from Los Angeles, his reaction was not much more favorable than that of young Dana on his first trip.

"Why, where are all the ships?" inquired the Senator from Maine. "As near as I can make out, you propose to ask the Government to create a harbor for you almost out of whole cloth. The Lord has not given you much to start with, that is for certain. It will cost four or five millions to build, you say; well, is your whole country worth that much? . . . Well, it seems you have made a great mistake in the location of your city. If you Los Angeles people want a harbor, why not move the city down to San Diego? There is a good harbor there."

Despite the unfavorable opinion of the Senator from Maine, in 1890 Congress was induced to grant $5,000 for a survey of a deep-water harbor project for Los Angeles, and a commission came west to examine the possible sites and to hold public hearings. Although there is no natural deep-water harbor along the coast near Los Angeles, there are several points where artificial harbors might be constructed. One of these is Santa Monica, developed by Senator John P. Jones of Nevada. . . . Another possibility was Redondo, near-by, where the Portland capitalist Captain John C. Ainsworth had built a wharf, connected by a narrow-gage railway with Los Angeles. The third was the old port of San Pedro, served by the Southern Pacific, where the Terminal Railroad Company also had acquired trackage rights with the purpose of permitting other railroads to use its tracks to get access to the harbor. The Congressional commission, having considered the various sites, decided San Pedro to be the most desirable, estimating that a favorable deep-water harbor could be made there by spending about $4,000,000 for a breakwater.

Now the people of Los Angeles were ready to go forward. . . . But they reckoned without Collis P. Huntington, who had become interested in getting a port for Los Angeles when the Southern Pacific began to fear competition. . . . In 1892 he informed the Senate that the San Pedro harbor was not suitable because the ground was so rocky that piles could not be driven into it, and that the railroad was therefore abandoning its wharf there and building at Santa Monica. A board of five Army officers was appointed to examine the proposed sites, and again the decision was in favor of San Pedro. But Huntington went on building his million-dollar pier at Santa Monica, and his representative, addressing a Los Angeles Chamber of Commerce banquet, suavely remarked, "Somewhere on your border there is to be a harbor, and I am asked a question regarding Santa Monica, and the intentions of our people. To be frank with you, I will say that their intentions seem entirely apparent. They are making a wharf there for deep-water vessels. They must intend to land at the wharf with deep-water vessels."

At this point, Harrison Gray Otis, owner of the Los Angeles *Times*, entered the controversy, putting his newspaper actively behind the San Pedro project and declaring that Congress should not appropriate money, against the advice of its experts, for a harbor that would benefit only one corporation. Huntington added to the general unrest by declaring:

"You people are making a big mistake in supporting this San Pedro appropriation. The Rivers and Harbors Committee of the House will never report in favor of that place—not in a thousand years. I know them all and I have talked to them about the matter. Now, I propose to be frank with you people. I do not find it to my advantage to have the harbor built at San Pedro and I shall be compelled to oppose all efforts to secure appropriations for that site; on the other hand, the Santa Monica location will suit me perfectly, and if you folks will get in and work for that, you will find me on your side—and I think I have some little influence at Washington—as much as some other people, perhaps."

He concluded his talk by banging on the table and saying: "Well, I don't know for sure that I can get this money for Santa Monica; I think I can. But I know damned well that you shall never get a cent for that other place."

The Chamber of Commerce objected, the Santa Fe protested that it would not have free access to Huntington's harbor, the Senate voted to postpone action for a year, and the New York *World* inquired, "Is this a government for the people, or a government by Mr. Huntington, for Mr. Huntington? The question may as well be settled in the Santa Monica-San Pedro controversy as anywhere."

In Los Angeles the Free Harbor League was organized, and there was a campaign to get citizens to write their old Congressmen "back east," inquiring how long a crafty corporation could defraud the people of their right to a free harbor. . . . But . . . when the Rivers and Harbors bill was reported to the House, the people were astounded to find an item of $2,900,000 for a breakwater at Santa Monica. . . . The fight was carried to the Senate by Senator Stephen M. White, where, over Huntington's opposition, another commission was appointed which was to decide where the $2,900,000 appropriation was to be spent. Again the decision was in favor of San Pedro. So, ironically enough, the money wangled out of an economy Congress by the powerful Huntington was appropriated for the benefit of the rival harbor.

Far from being licked, however, Uncle Collis persisted in his obstruction, hoping to throw the matter back into Congress. . . . Finally, in 1898, when the item making an initial appropriation of $400,000 for the construction of San Pedro harbor was reached in the appropriation bill in the House, Charles H. Grosvenor of Ohio rose to say that private enterprise—meaning Mr. Huntington—would build a harbor free of charge in the immediate vicinity—meaning Santa Monica—and he suggested that the appropriation be postponed. Whereupon Harry A. Cooper of Wisconsin rose and said:

"This matter of San Pedro harbor is to me in many respects the most astonishing I have ever encountered since I have had a seat in this House. I do not believe it ever had its counterpart in the legislative history of the country. . . . Is it not strange that after two boards of Engineers had said that San Pedro was the only place to improve, nevertheless, the provision was inserted in the bill of the last session for the improvement of Santa Monica? . . . It is time that people who propose to fight as they have, violating every precedent, should be taught a lesson that the patience of the American people on this subject has been exhausted."

Thus ended the free-harbor fight. . . .

The port of Los Angeles, wrested from an unfavorable coastline by an ambitious people, is now [1932] one of the nation's greatest. A maze of wharves and terminals lines its shores, and it is open to every railroad that enters the city.

Glenn Chesney Quiett, *They Built the West* (New York: D. Appleton-Century Company, 1934), 288–293.

Sunkist Advertising— The Iowa Campaign

JOSEPHINE KINGSBURY JACOBS

Josephine Kingsbury Jacobs has surveyed in depth fifty years of public relations programming for the merchandising of California citrus crops. Oranges were brought in by the Spaniards, but the first businesslike planting was William Wolfskill's grove. This selection picks up the story at a crucial moment in 1907. Earlier mishaps had convinced the main corps of growers that they must orchestrate the delivery of their fruit to jobbers throughout the nation. Their president, Francis Q. Storey, had urged an advertising program, and now, aided by a matching grant from the Southern Pacific, the California Fruit Growers Exchange had opportunity to make the noble experiment. Later there would be public relations additives—the trademark "Sunkist," individual wrappers, prizes such as a spoon with which to eat a Sunkist orange, and, best of all, the vitamins. But it was the Iowa campaign that broke the resistance of the growers to advertising.

Should you ask me, whence these stories,
Whence these legends and traditions,
With the odor of the roses
With the brightness of the sunshine,

215

Specter of No Growth

With the rushing of great rivers,
Leaping headlong from the mountains?
I should answer, I should tell you,
From the richest land 'neath Heaven,
From the snow-capped hills of purple,
From the broad and fertile valleys,
Where the orange and the lemon
Grow amidst the peace and plenty.
This they say—the happy dwellers,
In that land of flowers and gold—
That the orange is the symbol
Of their health and wealth untold.
All the brightness of the sunshine,
All the sweetness of the flowers,
All the glow of hidden gold fields,
All the dew from healing herbs,
Are by cunning nature blended
In this fruit of golden hue.
If long life you would be having,
Knowing naught of human ills,
Daily eat at least one orange,
Brought from California's groves.

This prize-winning "poem" set the tone of the first concentrated advertising campaign of the California Fruit Growers' Exchange in 1907. Special trains steamed into Iowa bearing the golden globes of health from the glorious land of California to enrich the lives and loosen the purse strings of the farmers with the slogan, "Oranges for Health—California for Wealth."

Railroad cars carrying citrus had been prominently labeled with banners purchased by the Exchange as early as 1895, and within four years 10,000 banners were ordered to mark all citrus cars. . . . Advertising in standard consumer magazines was discussed by the Board of Directors at least as early as 1904. Lord & Thomas advertising agency developed an elaborate presentation for a lemon campaign but was rebuffed by growers unwilling to commit themselves to an outlay of $30,000. Armed with the offer from the Southern Pacific, Story could convert even the most recalcitrant directors who protested the extravagance but could not resist the offer of free advertising. Lord &

Thomas was given the account . . . launched with a maximum budget of ten thousand dollars, which marked the beginning of Sunkist and the glorification of the orange. . . .

Although a maximum expenditure of $10,000 had been authorized, only $7,000 to $8,500 was actually spent by the Exchange. . . . The larger figure includes the cost of a carload of oranges given away as prizes in essay and poetry contests in the schools. In addition to the Iowa efforts, the London agent was authorized to spend $300 for advertising in English markets.

Three colors adorned the full page advertisement which initiated the newspaper campaign on March 2, 1908, in the Des Moines *Register and Leader*. A J. M. "Ding" Darling cartoon of little Miss California feeding an orange to a little boy Iowa was the feature illustration with orange and green sprays of fruit and leaves around the border of the page. The headline proclaimed Orange Day in California and Orange Week in Iowa with special sales of fresh fruit. Eating of the whole orange was the primary use featured with a mention of the use of fruit in desserts. . . .

As part of the campaign, the Southern Pacific ran special fruit trains to Iowa. Newspapers furnished so much free publicity that an Exchange official estimated it totaled in value the combined expenditures of the cooperative, the railroad, and the jobbers.

G. A. Charters, the eastern agent of the Exchange, suggested that these trains carry a messenger who would send frequent wires to the offices on the progress of the train. These wires would be supplied to newspapers as news items. One of his subordinates later claimed to have gone to the telegraph office for books of receiving blanks with which to copy one telegram and make each newspaper think it was getting the original. He noted that "Charters thought I was crazy." Such independent and irresponsible activities seem to have been a bit unusual in the entire Exchange program. The Des Moines manager travelled with the jobber salesman by horse and buggy from grocery to grocery and used the sturdy cardboard placards designed for railroad car banners for his display materials. . . .

The five month campaign was carefully checked for results. Orange sales in the rest of the country rose by 17.7 per cent while sales in Iowa gained by 50 per cent. The general manager reported to the

Board of Directors that the total advertising costs for the 1907–1908 season had been only $.00105 per box and concluded that "it is believed that the consumption of your fruits can be very largely increased without any material reduction in the price . . . by an extension of the advertising methods which you have already proven profitable." The success of this first major excursion into advertising led the directors to approve a budget of $25,000 for expansion of the territory to be covered by publicity in the 1908–1909 season.

Josephine Kingsbury Jacobs, *Sunkist Advertising* (Ph.D. diss. UCLA, 1966), 1, 20–25.

Pacific Electric

FRANKLIN WALKER

As the leading critic of California literature, Franklin Walker inexorably has dwelt mainly on writers associated with the northern provinces. His San Francisco's Literary Frontier *covers the outburst of creative writing touched off by the gold rush, and he has written in depth on Prentice Mulford, Frank Norris, and Jack London. From that mainstream he made one digression,* A Literary History of Southern California, *a most revealing cultural history of this region up to 1915. The paragraphs that follow account for the construction of the Pacific Electric network and credit its impact on southern California life.*

By the time America entered World War I, Southern California had come to be one of the principal playgrounds of the nation, unpretentious on the whole, and quite naive. It was a sort of middle-class Methodist paradise, with enough sunshine and oranges to give color, enough innovations in the way of airplanes and automobiles and cafeterias to lend excitement, and enough ruggedness—with its jack rabbits and stingarees and hiking trails and surf bathing—to provide adventure. As good a way to get a glimpse of those days as any other is to follow the experiences of the comic characters in the humorous book called *Tourist Tales of California*, by Sara White Isaman, published in 1907. In a monologue delivered in "hick" dialect (later made "literary" by Will Rogers, mayor of Beverly Hills), Aunt Pheba Harrison tells her niece about the experiences she and Uncle Hiram had when they sold the Nebraska farm and went to Southern California to see the sights. After a trip west in a tourist coach, in which they boiled coffee and baked potatoes on the little stove at the end of the car, they found California sunshine to replace Nebraska snow, explored the mysteries of an apartment with a disappearing bed, and visited cafeterias where one bought twice as much as he could eat. They had their difficulties trying to devour tamales with the shucks on, sampling olives straight from the tree, and fighting the fleas at the beach. They made a trip up Mount Lowe on the funicular, explored Orange Grove Avenue and Busch Gardens in Pasadena, visited the old mission at San Gabriel, walked the pike and went in swimming at Long Beach, ate at the ship restaurant and had their fortunes told at Venice, got seasick going to Catalina Island, and gawked at the ostrich farm, the alligator farm, and the fiesta of flowers. Finally, they bought a house out Westlake Park way, picked up an automobile, which snorted and coughed its way to the Nebraska State picnic, and made arrangements to rent a cottage at the beach for the summer. At the end of the book they were polishing up their language, planning to take in a little culture, and talking with the enthusiasm of the newly converted Southern California booster.

One of the phenomena that aroused most enthusiasm in Uncle Hiram and Aunt Pheba was the remarkable public transportation system always ready to carry them on the grand tour.

> Then we felt so glad and free,
> We started out to see
>   Los Angeles, the good old tourist town;
> From the ocean to Mt. Lowe
> Sight seein' we did go—
>   Rode them trolley cars for miles and miles around.

For these were the days of the Big Red Cars, when Southern California boasted one of the best electric interurban systems in the nation, or, for that matter, in the world, and the mournful hoot of the red cars was as omnipresent, as insistent, and as exciting a part of the land as the crash of the breakers at Santa Monica. Henry Huntington's interurbans were a great boon and a dominating factor in the Southern California of the early part of the twentieth century. This was the era of the Pacific Electric.

Back in the 'seventies, when Robert Widney introduced the horse-car to Los Angeles, he had been forced to redesign the carriage in order to keep the vehicles on the track when they took the curves. In contrast was the equipment of the Pacific Electric, which, in 1913, inspired a publicity man to write an article for *Sunset Magazine* titled "The Red Car of Empire." In this panegyric he grew lyrical about "the crimson chariot," "the red car with the invisible wings," "the flitting red car" which said to the suburban dweller: "'I'll just wipe distance off the map, and your life shall be one long cocktail of orange blossoms, ocean beaches, and Spring Street.'" Other statements in his article were perhaps less poetic but somewhat more informative.

"Los Angeles is the center and heart of the most highly developed interurban electric system in the world. . . . Within a radius of thirty-five miles of Los Angeles, there are forty-two incorporated cities and towns with countless country homes between. All these are literally of one body, of the healthiest and most rapidly growing body in America. The arterial system that holds them together is the double trackage of the interurban electric road. The red corpuscles that race to the end of every farthest vein to proclaim and carry the abundant life are the flitting crimson cars."

By the time this description was written, the up-to-date system developed by Henry E. Huntington between 1900 and 1910 had been expanded by acquisition of all the interurban lines in the area. It covered more than a thousand miles, with tracks going out from Los Angeles north as far as San Fernando, east as far as Riverside, south as far as Newport Beach, and west to the ocean. (Henry E. Huntington had once had dreams of sending the red cars up to Santa Barbara and down to San Diego, but these never came true.) The hundred million dollar corporation carried 225,000 persons 73,000 miles a day in its 600 cars, at between one-half and three-quarters of a cent a mile. It transported mail, sugar beets, oranges, tourists, and commuters who wanted "to sleep in the woods and have an office in the city." Yet at the same time it kept something of the small town quality and was genuinely proud to boast that it once held up the departure of a car while a widow rustled the dozenth egg in order to earn her mite and support her wee babe. It was unquestionably a first-class transportation system, far superior to anything the Southern Californian grumbles at today. As such it exercised an important influence on the pattern of the developing Los Angeles, which came to have loosely knit residential districts far removed from the business areas. . . .

Both tourists and residents used the red-car system generously for recreation and education. Groups frequently chartered private cars for Sunday-school picnics, singing trolley parties, and moonlight streetcar excursions. It was great fun to return from a weiner roast at Redondo on the *Mermaid*, poppies barely visible along the tracks in the moonlight, and youngsters out on the wicker seats in the open section in the back of the car, singing "Down Went McGinty" and "After the Ball." One could always make the round trip to any of the beaches for fifty cents, and the famous daylong tours were not expensive. These rivaled the earlier Santa Fe Railway excursion trips on "The Old Kite Route," which went from Los Angeles along the foothills to Redlands and back to Los Angeles via the Santa Ana Canyon and the Fullerton valley—"No scene twice seen on the kite-shaped track." The Pacific Electric daily offered three "specials": the Balloon Trip, a swing down to the beach at Santa Monica, then through the boom towns of Venice, Manhattan Beach, and Hermosa Beach, on to Redondo, and back by way of Culver City; the Old Mission Trip, which mixed orange trees and ostriches with Mission San Gabriel; and the Triangle Trip, down to Long Beach, Balboa, and Santa Ana, with glimpses of forests of oil derricks, fields of sugar beets (the agricultural enthusiasm of the moment), and groves of almonds, lemons, and oranges. Best of all, there was the Orange Empire Excursion, run only twice a week, which took one to San Bernardino, Redlands, and Riverside. The high points of this expedition were the trip by tally-ho up to Smiley Heights near Redlands and the stop for lunch at Riverside Inn.

Henry E. Huntington built up his Pacific Electric empire rapidly and solidly, with the same shrewdness that had been shown by his more famous uncle, Collis P. Huntington, the most ruthless and most efficient of the Big Four, a man known throughout the country as "the Colossus of the Pacific." Born in Oneonta, New York, in 1850, the year his Uncle Collis reached California, the keen, acquisitive nephew hitched his wagon to the family star not long after the first transcontinental railroad was completed, and, after years of able administration in the Eastern branches of the Huntington empire, had come West as Collis' right hand man on the West Coast. He was more than an able lieutenant, for the childless uncle treated him almost as a son. (The family relationship was actually closer than that of nephew-uncle; Henry Huntington's first wife was the sister of Collis' adopted daughter; his second wife was Collis' widow.) One of his early duties in the West, the reorganization of San Francisco's traction system in the 'nineties, was, as it turned out, training for his later career. For after his uncle's death in 1900, Henry Huntington soon became the owner of the Los Angeles street railways, the developer of the Pacific Electric system, and the most extensive landowner in Southern California.

Less than ten years after Collis Huntington's death Henry Huntington retired from active business affairs and started to accumulate the finest private library of his day, which was to become an almost unparalleled storehouse of documents and books dealing with English and American history and culture, and to build up one of America's best art collections, which would include a peerless group of eighteenth-century English paintings. Such was the man who made the Pacific Electric the symbol of the period.

Franklin Walker, *A Literary History of Southern California* (Berkeley and Los Angeles: University of California Press, 1950), 229–235.

"The Rape of Owens Valley"
MORROW MAYO

Morrow Mayo's Los Angeles *is a scintillating, usually light-hearted, sometimes cynical, but most discerning report on the*

"The Rape of Owens Valley"

past of Los Angeles and its state of being in the last year of Hoover's presidency. For six years Mayo had practiced his trade as journalist in San Francisco and Los Angeles and had published many interpretive essays. On the Chinese Massacre and some other episodes he was critical, but it was only against those who masterminded the capture of Owens River that his outrage boiled over.

Certain basic facts are well established: recognition by a few men that more water was needed; a large quantity of fine water wasting into Owens Lake; a long but downhill course from Owens Valley to the city; undercover work, with the newspapers pledged not to break the news; a syndicate, including the most influential newspaper owners, which took options on large blocks of San Fernando Valley; a federal reclamation project planned and then abandoned; high officials in Washington giving the city all sorts of variances for the water transfer. But for proof of conspiracy and dominance throughout by the San Fernando syndicate, Mayo had to rely on coincidence rather than solid documentary proof.

Department of Water and Power

Owens Valley water entering the aqueduct

223

Specter of No Growth

From an airplane Los Angeles today resembles half a hundred Middle-Western-Egyptian-Italian-English-Spanish communities, repainted and sprinkled about. Its population is about 1,400,000. It is, and has been for ten years, the largest city in America in area, and people often wonder why. The answer is Water.

Water is scarce in southern California—so scarce that since 1913 Los Angeles has obtained its main supply from a source two hundred and fifty miles away. Since then, whenever a new town has bloomed ten, fifteen, or twenty miles away and reached the point where the water-supply from its artesian wells and underground streams has become inadequate, Los Angeles has given it a drink and taken it under the motherly wing. That is the way in which ungrateful Hollywood and a score of other towns were saved from dying of thirst, and that is the way in which Long Beach, Beverly Hills, and Pasadena would probably have been annexed by now but for their threat to defeat the building of the new aqueduct from the Colorado River when the Hoover Dam impounds its waters.

As a result of these repeated annexations the sunshine metropolis now winds in and around southern California from the mountains to the sea, squirms through "bottle necks," attaches itself to its Wilmington and San Pedro by means of a "shoe-string" district a half-mile wide and fifteen miles long, drapes itself over deserts, mountains, and sand-dunes, and altogether sprawls grotesquely over 442 *square*-miles—a "municipal" area three times the size of Chicago—including leagues of farms and virgin soil. The result, *legally*, is "Los Angeles." It must be obvious, however, that all this vast area is no more one "city," properly so called, than, say, Merced, California, would be one "city," the largest on earth, if it should suddenly annex Yosemite National Park.

How Los Angeles got this way—how it got the water which it uses as a club—is a story of business beside which Teapot Dome pales into insignificance. It constitutes one of the most dramatic epics ever enacted in America.

Two hundred and fifty miles northeast of Los Angeles, in Inyo County, near the Nevada line, there is a long, slender arid region, about ten miles wide and one hundred miles long, known as Owens Valley. This is Mary Austin's original "Land of Little Rain." In its natural state the valley supports little life except cactus, sagebrush and chaparral, tarantulas, horned toads and rattlesnakes. But this desert valley has one freakish, inexhaustible, priceless treasure, bestowed upon it when it was created by the geological convulsion which threw that chain of mountain peaks (the highest in America) into the air on one side of it, and the Inyo and White Mountains on the other. Right down through the center of this arid valley runs Owens River, a life-giving, permanent stream, fed by the melted snows of the High Sierras—including the melted snows of Mount Whitney, towering twelve thousand feet above it, a permanent supply of pure, fresh water. This strange river terminates at the southern end of the valley in a saline lake which has no outlet. . . .

Eleven months a year, except right along the banks of Owens River, the valley *in its natural state* would be as dry as the Mojave Desert.

But seventy years ago homesteaders selected this region, because of its permanent river, as one of the potentially richest sections in California. It would take water and work and time to make something out of this God-forsaken country; but these struggling, pioneer men and women were not afraid to work. . . . There was something heroic about them, as there is something heroic about people everywhere who grapple with Nature, against terrific odds, in an effort to tame and civilize it.

Slowly the desert bloomed—two narrow, cultivated strips on each side of the river—two strips gradually widening as the water was led out from the stream, acre by acre. Orchards began to bear; wheat, corn, and clover grew in the fields; cattle grazed in pasture-land. Farther and farther from the river homesteaders took up land. Finally, there were flood-diversion canals running down from the hills, and irrigation ditches running out five miles from the river, with home-steaders living near them, and all working to build up the country, to keep the canals open and clean, the water moving.

Gradually a part of this desert was transformed into a rich agricultural valley. Along the river a series of little towns sprang up and prospered—Bishop, Independence, Laws, Manzanar, Lone Pine, and others. Unproductive acres blossomed into prosperous ranches, desert shacks into fine farmhouses, flanked by barns, silos, shade trees, and flowers. Roads and schoolhouses were built. A railroad came up from Los Angeles. There were eight thousand people in Owens Valley. Their agricultural exhibits were among the finest at the State fairs. Specifically, they were the best in California and captured first prizes year after year, in hard grain, in apples, in corn, and in honey.

Two hundred and thirty miles south of Owens Valley, *twenty miles northwest of Los Angeles*, there was another arid valley of about a hundred and fifty thousand acres, San Fernando Valley, where the land got little water, and which, in its natural state was virtually desert land.

Some time between 1899 and 1903, when Los Angeles was growing hand over fist—and the orange-growers were beginning to drain the Los Angeles River and the artesian wells—a select group of public-spirited Los Angeles business men, bankers, and real-estate operators hit upon a great idea. Just who conceived it I do not know, but he was a genius. It was a fantastic scheme, but they were Men of Vision. They decided to buy up the worthless San Fernando Valley land, acquire control of the Owens River, and then frighten the taxpayers of Los Angeles into paying for a huge aqueduct to bring the water down two hundred and fifty miles over mountain and desert—to give Los Angeles an added water-supply and, incidentally, to use a great portion of the water to irrigate the San Fernando Valley and thus convert that desert region into a fertile farming section, just outside the city. It was a bold, tremendous enterprise, a piece of business in the grand manner. For several years the little group conspired secretly, and eventually they worked out and perfected their scheme.

In 1903 the United States Reclamation Service became suddenly interested in Owens Valley. J. B. Lippincott, chief engineer of the U.S. Reclamation Service in California, appeared on the scene and began to explain to the ranchers that a benevolent Government was working out a plan to place about two hundred thousand additional acres of their desert valley land under irrigation, for the purpose of further promoting settlement, prosperity, and development. The people of Owens Valley were overjoyed.

Meanwhile down in Los Angeles a small real-estate syndicate began buying up San Fernando Valley land at five, ten, twenty, fifty dollars an acre.

The U.S. Reclamation engineers working under Lippincott went into Owens Valley, "made extensive investigations, tested the soil, measured the area of farming lands, determined the duty of water in the soil and climate, surveyed sites of proposed storage dams," and otherwise went ahead with the Federal project. Lippincott told the farmers and mutual water companies that they should co-ordinate their forces with the Government in order to advance the Government's plans; that is, they should pool their interests, and turn over their rights and claims to the Government, so that Uncle Sam could get the whole thing in hand at once and go ahead. By doing this, he said, when the project was completed, they would be able to get the water-improved lands, most of which they already owned, for the actual cost of the development, estimated at twenty-three dollars an acre. If for any reason the Government should not go through with the project, their priority rights would of course be returned to them, the Government would restore all reservoir and power filings to their former status, and furthermore the Reclamation Service would turn over to the valley people all charts, maps, surveys, stream measurements, etc., so that in any case the farmers stood to gain by the transaction. The trusting citizens thereupon surrendered their claims and locations to the Federal Government, and every co-operation was given the National Reclamation Service by the people of Inyo County. These ranchers were naive, unsophisticated people; that is, they had faith in the Federal Government.

In 1899–1900 Fred Eaton was Mayor of Los Angeles. In 1904 Mr. Eaton, representing himself as Lippincott's agent, went into Owens Valley and began taking options on land which was riparian to the Owens River. He was in possession of the United States Reclamation Service maps and surveys (the property of the Federal Government), and the ranchers believed that he was obtaining the lands for the Government. In obtaining these options Eaton followed what is known as the "checkerboard" or "spot-zone" system; that is, he followed the irrigation canals from the river, obtaining options, if possible, on every other ranch on each side.

The following year Eaton returned to the valley, acquiring more land, and bringing with him William Mulholland, chief of the Los Angeles Water Department, and a group of Los Angeles bankers. The presence of these bankers aroused the suspicions of the Owens Valley ranchers for the first time; the presence of the bankers, plus vague rumors which now began to reach the valley, that somebody down in Los Angeles, two hundred and fifty miles southward, was after their water. At the same time Lippincott began to hint that the reclamation project might be abandoned. . . .

By this time Eaton had obtained options on considerable riparian land along the river and elsewhere. He thereupon exercised his options and bought the land. Lippincott then announced definitely that the reclamation project had been abandoned by the Government. He resigned from the United States Reclamation Service and took a job with the Los Angeles Water Department, as assistant to Mulholland, turning over to the city all maps, charts, field surveys, stream measurements, etc. This data told the story of what could be done and what had been planned for Owens Valley, *and gave also the ownership, value, and status of every piece of land in the valley.* At the same time this information was denied to the people of Owens Valley. It was subsequently proved, and very shortly, that Lippincott had been receiving a salary from the city of Los Angeles while still a government officer and while he was ostensibly promoting the mythical Federal reclamation project in the valley. . . .

Not a word of all this had appeared in the Los Angeles papers. For three years the people of Los Angeles were kept in ignorance while the scheme was being hatched. The city of Los Angeles was to get an aqueduct, but the city—even the City Council—was unaware of it. Only the little group of leading citizens and the newspapers (let in on the deal for fear that they might expose it) knew what was going on. For three years the newspapers suppressed the news. By July 1905, however, the time was ripe for printing it. Eaton now owned much of the land riparian to Owens River and was ready to deed it to the city. The syndicate now owned virtually all of near-by San Fernando Valley. Money was needed to pay Eaton, to gain control of the full flow of Owens River, and to bring the water down to Los Angeles. The papers agreed to break the story simultaneously, part in the morning and part in the afternoon papers. . . . But [on July 29, 1905] the *Times* came out with the scoop of the century plastered all over its first three pages.

[According to Louis Sherwin, a former editorial writer on the *Times*], "The city had for years been quietly preparing to build an

228

enormous aqueduct from the Owens River Valley. In order that the poor, down-trodden farmers in that region should not get wind of the project and hold the wicked city up for blackmail, all the Los Angeles papers had agreed to suppress the news until the necessary land had been acquired." . . . The real reason the whole matter was kept secret was that the conspirators did not want *the people of Los Angeles to get wind of the San Fernando scheme.* . . .

There was not the slightest need for conspiracy. Enough water comes down from the High Sierras each year, ninety-nine per cent of it wasted, to supply the needs of half the people in the State of California. There was not the slightest reason why the people of Owens Valley, the Federal Government, and the Angel City should not have co-operated on the entire project. All that was necessary to give Owens Valley twice as much water as it was getting, and Los Angeles twice as much as it has ever received from its aqueduct, was to build a storage reservoir [in Long Valley] above Owens Valley.

But the San Fernando land-grabbers and the politicians of the Water Department, whom they controlled, had no time to waste upon such a public project. The city (that is, the small group who ran it) simply announced that it was going to stick an aqueduct into the Owens River and divert *all* that life-giving water to Los Angeles, two hundred and fifty miles away, and furthermore that it was out to buy, and proposed to acquire, some seventy thousand additional acres still owned by the ranchers in order to gain full control of the river. . . .

Protest after protest rained upon [President] Roosevelt, the Secretary of the Interior, and the United States Senators, but without avail. The way had been greased. A Bill was prepared granting to Los Angeles a free right of way for an aqueduct on government lands through Inyo, Kern, and Los Angeles counties.

At the same time Los Angeles, through the press, through pamphlets, and otherwise, began to impress upon its citizens, most of whom were newcomers, the need for an immediate supply of water. Unless they voted bonds for building an aqueduct and getting water from Owens River, they were told that the country would soon dry up. Water was run into the sewers—"for purposes of necessary sanitation, to flush the system"—decreasing the supply in the reservoirs. The people were forbidden to water their lawns and gardens.

This drought, artificial or real, lasted throughout the dry summer months; lawns in the city turned brown and flowers died.

On election day the people of Los Angeles voted the aqueduct bonds—twenty-two and a half million dollars' worth—to build an aqueduct from Owens River and to defray other expenses of the project to bring Los Angeles a domestic water-supply.

With this money in hand the city "acquired" all the land that Eaton had acquired in Owens Valley, and Mulholland started to build the longest aqueduct in the world. Los Angeles, to be sure, did not yet own all the water-rights in Owens Valley; and there was no assurance that it could acquire it. Ranchers still owned much of it. Moreover, all of Owens Valley was homestead land, and homesteaders were still moving into the valley and acquiring their share of the water rights. However, as it soon appeared, there was a way to take care of *that*.

In 1906 the Honorable Gifford Pinchot (now Governor of Pennsylvania), at that time chief of the United States Forest Service under Roosevelt, issued an order transforming a great portion of the desert land of Owens Valley into a *Federal forest district!*—thereby withdrawing approximately two hundred thousand acres of land from its homestead status. . . .

Meanwhile the Los Angeles Aqueduct Bill was being rushed through Congress. In the presence of Secretary of the Interior Hitchcock, Chief Forester Pinchot, and Director Walcott of the Geological Survey, President Roosevelt . . . approved, with the prohibition against the use of the water by the municipality for irrigation struck out. . . . He had hardly signed it before the syndicate which owned San Fernando Valley began to advertise that the aqueduct would go through the valley and that early investors in the thousands of acres of dusty stubble fields there would make lots of money with the use of Owens River water on that land.

In the meantime, Los Angeles started devastating the ranches which it had acquired in Owens Valley, by withholding water from them; and also it began to force the other ranchers to sell out. . . .

The engineering project which Los Angeles planned and executed, indeed, is the most remarkable in engineering history. It is the only project of comparable size in the world which did not provide for the storage of water near the source. Not a gallon of water storage has been provided by Los Angeles at Long Valley or at any other of the adaptable sites above the former diversion points of Owens Valley irrigation.

In short, the nose of the aqueduct was simply stuck into the Owens River, diverting the water, while pumps were installed in the ground to suck into the aqueduct water from all the surrounding farming land. In other words, the water was simply stolen from one valley, already under cultivation, and distributed upon another, uncultivated valley 233 miles away.

It takes some time to destroy an agricultural section. It took Los Angeles fourteen years to ruin Owens Valley. The aqueduct was completed in 1913. In the early spring of 1927 there appeared a full-page advertisement in most of the large California papers beginning: *"We, the farming communities of Owens Valley, being about to die, salute you!"* The ranchers were giving up the ghost.

As I write, the New York *Times* of August 26, 1932 lies before me, containing one of Will Rogers' syndicated dispatches. I quote the first paragraph: "Bishop, Ca., Aug. 25—Ten years ago this was a wonderful valley with one-quarter of a million acres of fruit and alfalfa. But, Los Angeles had to have more water for the Chamber of Commerce to drink more toasts to growth, more water to dilute its orange juice and more water for its geraniums to delight the tourists, while the giant cottonwoods here died. So, now, this is a valley of desolation. . . ."

Today there is a saying in California about this funeral ground, which may well remain as its epitaph:

"The Federal Government of the United States held Owens Valley while Los Angeles raped it."

Morrow Mayo, *Los Angeles* (New York: Alfred A. Knopf, 1933), 220–246.

"There It Is—Take It"
REMI NADEAU

Coming from an old Los Angeles family, Remi Nadeau has written at length about this city. His City Makers *were*

Angelenos, as were most of his Water Seekers. They are prominent also in his California, The New Society and of course in Los Angeles: From Mission to Modern City. The construction project here eulogized was most remarkable. Part of the way, an open or covered concrete ditch following the contour line was all that was needed. But there were mountain spurs to surmount or tunnel through and barrancas and canyons to cross. Here the resort was to great syphons and inverted syphons the likes of which had never been seen. The work site moved over a forbidding desert to which water and all else had to be freighted. Locomotives and improvised track helped. Caterpillar tractors were tried, but in the real crunch mulepower was relied on. To place the heaviest syphon sections, 52-mule-team purchase had to be applied. Completion on time and within budget was one of the wonders of the world.

Department of Water and Power

Deadman syphon under construction

It had already been announced that the long-heralded ceremony for the aqueduct completion, scheduled for July before the Sand Canyon break, would be held on November 5, 1913. While the reservoirs on either side of Elizabeth Tunnel were allowed to fill, the people of Los Angeles made ready to celebrate the event with typical Southern California enthusiasm. An impressive aqueduct display was built at Exposition Park, formal dedication ceremonies were prepared at the man-made cascade north of the San Fernando reservoirs, and a final grand parade was planned for downtown Los Angeles.

No less exuberantly did Los Angeles—and all of California—turn to William Mulholland in the hour of his greatest triumph. The aqueduct was recognized across the country as the finest in America and second only to the Panama Canal as an engineering feat. The Chief was showered with honors, introduced everywhere as "the Goethals of the West" or "California's Greatest Man." Engineering societies gave him high awards and congratulations, while the University of California conferred on him an honorary doctor's degree.

Early in 1913, as a new mayoralty campaign loomed in Los Angeles, publisher E. T. Earl of the *Express* began campaigning for Mulholland as the city's next mayor. General Otis of the *Times* then wrote to Mulholland that for once Earl had made a suggestion with which he could agree. A committee of determined Angelenos waited on the water chief at his office and one by one recited to him the superlative qualifications which made him exactly suited for the city's highest office. Mulholland was clearly moved by their words. But when they had finished he solemnly put an end to the entire affair with a startling but typical reply:

"Gentlemen, I would rather give birth to a porcupine backwards than be mayor of Los Angeles."

In his hour of success Mulholland was burdened with sorrow over the protracted illness of his wife, Lillian. . . . But though his wife's health weighed heavily on on him, Mulholland's thoughts undoubtedly turned to the significance of the new aqueduct as his staff automobile carried him northward on that historic day. The waters of Owens River, he knew, had not come too soon. Though the city's own water system from the Los Angeles River had been successfully stretched to cover the increased customers, some half-dozen private

233

water companies in the suburbs had been unable to meet demand during the hot days of the previous summer. There were instances where citizens had stayed up till early morning with their faucets wide open to catch enough drippings in pails for domestic needs the next day.

The nightmare of water famine would now be over; Mulholland himself would turn the waters of Owens River into San Fernando Reservoir. From there water mains were almost completed to carry the vast new source to city water taps, with enough left over to irrigate a valley and provide for a population growth of two million.

At the San Fernando cascade Mulholland found a crowd of some forty thousand exuberant citizens, who had ridden from every point in the Southland by carriage, auto, and train. Climbing to the platform amid a welcoming ovation, he wearily took his seat among the notables of Los Angeles. Immediately the ceremony began. The first speaker, a California congressman, opened with a declaration that captured the entire significance of the event.

"We are gathered here today to celebrate the coming of a king—for water in Southern California is king in fact if not in name."

At length the chairman introduced "the Honorable William Mulholland—the man who built the aqueduct." As though they had been holding themselves in readiness for this moment, the people rose to their feet, clapping and cheering, throwing handkerchiefs and hats in the air. Mulholland trudged forward from his seat, bent and tired, without notes or any idea of what he would say. But after gazing for a moment at the vast assembly, he opened with generous praise for all the men who had built the aqueduct, from his top advisers to the humblest laborers.

"This rude platform," he concluded, "is an altar, and on it we are here consecrating this water supply and dedicating this aqueduct to you and your children and your children's children—for all time!"

He shuffled back to his seat in the midst of another ovation. A silver loving cup was presented to him, and another to Lippincott, who made a short speech of his own. Mulholland then stepped to a flagpole on the grandstand and unfurled the Stars and Stripes—an act that was the prearranged signal for the engineers at the top of the cascade to turn the great wheels and release the water. Instantly the crowd sent up its cheers once more. Army cannons boomed, a brass band played furiously.

Mulholland scarcely heard the pandemonium. His eyes were fixed on the gates above, half in wonderment, as though he feared the precious water might not appear. With painful slowness the metal gates rose. A trickle of water emerged and started downward. It grew to a stream, then to a raging torrent, churning and sparkling down the cascade. Just above the grandstand it sprayed over a rise in the incline and roared past toward San Fernando Reservoir.

The Chief took his seat with a sigh that was almost a sob. For a moment he closed his eyes. The tired spirit gave way to a smile. He threw back his head and laughed aloud.

"Well, it's finished!"

Without waiting for the scheduled presentation speeches, by which Mulholland was to turn the aqueduct over to the city, the multitude stampeded to the side of the cascade to watch the seething torrent. Mulholland and Mayor H. H. Rose, who was to receive the water for the city, were left virtually without an audience. With the roar of the water and his own emotion all but stifling his voice, Mulholland turned to the mayor and made the five-word speech that has become famous:

"There it is. Take it."

Remi Nadeau, *The Water Seekers* (Garden City: Doubleday & Company, 1950), 60–63.

Abbot Kinney's Venice

Franklin Walker

A community into which new residents are moving collects several invisible dividends. Laborers arrive full grown, their nonproductive years paid for, and ready to take their places in

235

the workforce. Children come half-educated at the expense of the sending state. Young adults ready to practice one of the professions may be the best bargains, unless it is those in mid-career, tested and experienced, and bringing along a medium to large fortune. Los Angeles and environs were beneficiary of many such recruits. Here Franklin Walker pictures one who put his mark on the scene.

Venice was the product of the curious mind of Abbot Kinney, Helen Hunt Jackson's fellow commissioner, who has been described as "a student of law and medicine, commission merchant, botanical expert, cigarette manufacturer, and member of the United States Geological Survey." Ever since Kinney had inherited half of the Sweet Caporal fortune before he was thirty, the blue-eyed sorrel-thatched adventurer had been looking for interesting things to do. For a while he roamed in Africa and Asia; then, in 1880, he settled near Pasadena, on the ranch which he named Kinneyloa—"Kinney" for himself and "loa" the Hawaiian word for hill. After touring the Indian country with Mrs. Jackson, he became an enthusiast for marriage, and, finding a mate—whom he called another Helen Hunt Jackson—in the daughter of a San Francisco judge, proceeded to illustrate the theories of "creative reproduction," which he had put forth in his *Tasks by Twilight*, by fathering nine children. In the meantime and in between he helped to develop Yosemite as a national park, aided in securing the local enactment of the Australian ballot law, furthered the establishment of federal forest reserves, pioneered in the use of the eucalyptus tree in California, helped to found public libraries at Pasadena and Venice, and edited and published a local agricultural journal titled *Los Angeles Saturday Post; Fruit, Forest, and Farm* (1900–1906).

When Mrs. Jackson pictured Kinney in her story for children, *The Hunter Cats of Connorloa*, she described him as a wealthy retired man, finding pleasure in writing and science. As he once put it, he believed in culture and familiarity with literature as a means of development of a well-rounded character but not as a sole outlet for one's mental energies. In addition to helping with the report on the California Indians, he wrote books titled *Under the Shadow of the Dragon, Money, Protection vs. Free Trade, The Australian Ballot, The Eucalyptus, Forest and Water, The Conquest of Death, and Tasks by Twilight.* The last two are perhaps the most interesting, because they were manuals of social philosophy and sex education for his growing family; he felt that the two most important principles to be followed in improving society were the recognition of the right of the individual to enjoy what he earned and the exercise of creative reproduction. Pledged to a sort of modified Lamarchian evolutionary theory, he believed it possible to improve the race by persuading the best folks to mate with the best folks, to live well in a congenial environment such as Southern California, and to produce many children better than themselves.

In developing his Venice of America, Kinney entertained the optimistic idea that he could create a center of culture overnight by providing the surroundings that would attract settlers of taste and ability. As Newmark put it, "the dreams of his prime became the realities of his more advanced age"; as the doge of a new Venice, he would provide select entertainment for the cultured, good music for the masses, laboratories for the scientist, and a wholesome playground for the children. Characteristically, he threw all his resources into developing Venice once he decided on the venture.

Promptly, sixteen miles of canal were dredged, weeping wilows and gum trees were planted, and Italian villas were built. Gondolas and singing gondoliers were brought from the old Venice, as were pigeons, whose descendants still beg popcorn near the dismantled pier. The architecture of Windward Avenue, with the second stories of its Italian Renaissance buildings projecting over arcades, was intended to conform with that of the square of St. Mark, and a St. Mark's Hotel further carried out the motif. The art galleries included an Oriental building with a permanent Japanese display sponsored by the local Nisei; the aquarium was designed as a laboratory for studying Pacific marine life; the pier with its ship cafe was one of the best on the Coast, with a concert pavilion at its ocean end where Ellory's Famous Italian Band played and Madame Johnstone Bishop and other fine singers sang to the accompaniment of the great organ. A Chau-

John Palmer

Last days of Venice pier

tauqua was inaugurated, bringing men of letters and scientists and musicians. Kinney hoped that there would be created a true folk university. Other plans included a deep-water harbor (Redondo and Santa Monica also talked in such terms) which would accommodate the largest ocean-going vessels.

But Venice was not able to survive on culture alone, much as Kinney had hoped it would. Even such stellar attractions as Benjamin F. Mills, the well-known liberal religious leader and evangelist, and Sarah Bernhardt, whose private train stood for two days in Venice while the actress played "Camille" at the end of the pier, failed to bring all the moneyed settlers he had envisaged. However, if Venice did not entirely meet the desires of the old folk from Iowa, it soon came to be a paradise for the children. Concessions from a Midway Plaisance in Portland, Oregon, and the huge Ferris wheel from the Chicago Fair, a big warm salt-water plunge, a miniature train, and a shoot-the-chutes added to cultured Venice a section which was probably the most pleasurable fun house America was ever to see. It was a Coney Island without a blasé person in sight, a carnival without a hangover. For perhaps ten years it retained its character, but changing tastes, social deterioration, annexation to Los Angeles, and local option gradually brought the serpent into Eden. When the day came that one could get a drink at Venice when he could get it nowhere else, the resort was doomed.

Today (1950) it is little more than a slum at the edge of the water, although plans have been made to turn it into a municipal recreation center. Most of the canals have been filled in, because of their threats to sanitation; oil derricks have replaced Venetian villas; the miniature train no longer toots its whistle; the pier has been razed; the ship cafe is gone; the Renaissance palaces on Windward Avenue look like the tin shacks they really are; and the gondoliers' sons are no doubt running Bingo games. The oldtimers in the local "greasy spoons" maintain that Venice went to pieces because Kinney's sons did not have the vision of their father, that "creative reproduction" failed to produce results. A much sounder explanation, however, lies in a changing world rather than in a eugenic failure.

Franklin Walker, *A Literary History of Southern California*, (Berkeley and Los Angeles: University of California Press, 1950), 235–238.

The Missions Romanticized
JOHN O. POHLMANN

Beginning in the 1890s southern Californians advanced an idyllic picture of the mission regime that had operated several score decades earlier. The picture, as John O. Pohlmann points out, was at variance with most observations by visitors in the mission period and with the understanding of pioneer settlers, forty-niners, and most residents in the earlier decades of state-

hood. The mission era, he concedes, "may yet prove to be one of the more interesting if not inspiring periods of California history, but for most people the reality remains thoroughly obscured by the romantic haze of the mission myth."

Shadows cast by the old missions have given California one of its oldest and most durable legends. The essence of the nostalgic tale is that the missions, founded by one of California's greatest heroes, Junípero Serra, were spectacularly successful in Christianizing and civilizing a mass of stupid, ignorant, and savage Indians. In the words of John Steven McGroarty, author of the Mission Play, the Franciscan padres "took an idle race and put it to work—a useless race that they made useful in the world, a naked race and they clothed it, a hungry race and they lifted it up into the great white glory of God."

When the chain of twenty-one missions, "Father Serra's Rosary," was at last completed, according to McGroarty, "California was the happiest land the world has ever known. There was peace and plenty, and hospitality became a religion. . . . Song and laughter filled the sunny mornings. There was feasting and music, the strum of guitars and the click of castanets under the low hanging moons. Toil was easy and the burden of existence light. It was a sheer Utopia. Nothing like it ever existed before, nor has any approach to it existed since."

The serenity of this idyllic setting, according to the legend, was abruptly shattered by Mexico's greedy and unnecessary decision to secularize the thriving mission establishments. . . . But although the mission myth and Serra's spectacular rise to fame were to be intimately connected, neither exerted much appeal upon the popular romantic imagination prior to the 1880s.

On the national level, and in California as well, the intense emotions aroused by the Civil War and Reconstruction dictated that no institution even remotely resembling the ante-bellum slave plantation could become the focal point for a widespread romantic legend. . . . The gold rush and the subsequent excitement centering in bustling, cosmopolitan San Francisco supplied a rich body of history and folklore whose appeal has only slightly diminished over the years.

Because their city was the cultural and economic capital of the Pacific Coast, San Franciscans were understandably concerned primarily with the contributions and traditions established by people who had participated in their city's recent growth. Few subjects could have been further from popular interest or seemingly less relevant to daily existence than stories about virtually extinct mission Indians or long since departed Franciscan padres. . . .

Even in southern California, the Franciscan missions were generally considered more with contempt than admiration. As an extreme example of this negative interpretation, Thompson and West's *History of Los Angeles County* (1880) regarded the decaying remains of the missions as "mute witnesses against a time when man oppressed his fellow, and enslaved his body, under specious pretense of caring for his soul. . . ."

In the 1880s Los Angeles was in the process of completing the transition from Mexican pueblo to American city. The spectacular but also traumatic real estate boom of 1887–1888 was precipitated by competition between the well established Southern Pacific Railroad and the newly arrived Santa Fe which took the form of a ticket rate war. The boom also witnessed the final dispossession of the rancho elite who had become the principal landowners after secularization. And in the process, according to historian Glenn Dumke, the last vestiges of the old Spanish and Mexican civilization were forever submerged by the influx of immigration. Ironically, without the influx of these same immigrants and those who followed during the next three or four decades, California's mission myth would have had no raison d'être.

The desire for "history" and tradition has been one of the more notable aspects of American civilization, especially in those regions not blessed by either. Although real estate boosters and tourism promoters generally failed to exploit the mission's romantic potential during the boom of the 1880s, the collapse of the boom dramatically emphasized the shallow foundations upon which the region had rested its hopes. For many who survived the shock, their immediate concern was with the potentially lasting negative publicity rather than with the spectre of some similar occurrence in the distant future. For people concerned about the image of southern California's stability and its permanent development, what better tactic could have been devised than to create and project the appearance of security by enthusiastically emphasizing supposedly long-standing traditions —cultural, agricultural, architectural, educational, spiritual, and hospitable? Not surprisingly, as early as 1893 the first of many books popularizing the mission romance for tourists contended that preservation of the Franciscan missions would provide evidence of California's stability.

The process of creating artificial traditions, which Franklin Walker has termed "cultural hydroponics," focused upon the "Spanish" past and primarily upon the Franciscan missions. Its outstanding figures included four professional writers, several clubwomen, a furniture designer, and a hotel proprietor: Helen Hunt Jackson, staunch Massachusetts Calvinist, journalist, poet, novelist, and ardent defender of the American Indian; Charles Fletcher Lummis, editor, journalist, folklorist, energetic organizer of mission preservation, spokesman for Indian rights, and crusader to restore the tarnished image of Spain's New World endeavors; George Wharton James, professional enthusiast, lecturer, defrocked clergyman, ethnologist, self-styled explorer, journalist, editor, photographer, sometime-eccentric and sometime-hack writer; John Steven McGroarty, converted Catholic, newspaper writer, author of the *Mission Play*, California poet laureate, and United States Congressman; Mrs. Armitage S. C. Forbes, leader of the movement to "restore" El Camino Real, the fabled "King's Highway" popularly believed to have connected all the missions, and designer of the familiar mission bell markers which trace the supposed "Pathway of the Padres"; Gustav Stickley, creator of a "modern" style of furniture which paradoxically gained enormous popularity under the misnamed label of "mission furniture"; and Frank Miller, owner, manager, and developer of Riverside's "world famous" Glenwood Mission Inn. . . .

From the late nineteenth century until the Great Depression, the image of the Franciscan mission was California's most conspicuous and influential cultural symbol. According to an early student of the mission revival, writing in 1915 at the apex of the padres' popularity, the mission had "almost become the symbol of California." Even more authoritative are the words of Lummis, foremost champion of mission preservation and the first to realize the missions' potential for commercial exploitation. After more than two decades of intimate association with the old Franciscan monuments, Lummis noted in 1916 that more had "been written about our missions than about our climate, gold, oranges, oil, population and progress all put together. . . ." More pictures of the missions were sold, according to Lummis, "than of any other feature of California," and more tourists visited the missions in automobiles "than visit the historic landmarks of any other State of the Union."

Much more than mere historical landmarks, the missions influenced and were in turn exploited by people in such diverse fields as architecture, advertising, household furniture, highway construction, education, booster activities promoting tourism and/or real estate, civic nostalgia, photography, painting, poetry, journalism, theater, the writing of history and historical novels, and the preservation and restoration of other historical landmarks in addition to the missions themselves. Even today the influence continues, albeit considerably diminished by competition from such attractions as Hollywood, Knott's Berry Farm, Disneyland, Marineland, professional sports, and the ubiquitous television set which proliferated following World War II.

Adapted from John O. Pohlmann, *California's Mission Myth* (Ph.D. diss., UCLA, 1974), 1–9.

Autos and Movies and Oil

"You have to begin with the singular fact that in a population of a million and a quarter, every other person you see has been here less than five years. Practically, therefore, the whole population is immigrant."

—Garet Garrett

In 1922 the Los Angeles Philharmonic Orchestra began programming summer concerts in a natural amphitheater in the Hollywood Hills. To outlanders nothing better symbolized the southern California nirvana than these symphonies under the stars.

7

Autos and Movies and Oil

Freed from the constraints that had threatened, Los Angeles mush-roomed. The pattern of growth was lateral, which is to say sprawl. Builders were active, but the subdividers kept well in advance. Los Angeles thus had an abundance of vacant lots as playgrounds for its children. In and around the city it retained enought good farm land to allow the county to lead all others in the nation in value of production.

Los Angeles was unashamedly bucolic. It drew from New York and the Atlantic states but more especially from the midwestern heart of the continent. These newcomers far outnumbered the oldtimers. Accents such as the orange and the pepper trees were distinctive, but many an observer saw the ways of small-town America reproduced all over the place.

The Panama-California Exposition in San Diego in 1915 and the mission cult gave something of an impetus to so-called Spanish and mission architecture. More pervasive was the popularity of the bungalow (the word is from bengalese) or, as often rendered, the California bungalow. Here was a structure that could be simple and inexpensive or as regal as one wished. It suited the land, the climate, and the life-style. It was preeminently a single-family residence, called for a garden setting, and that meant extensive lateral spread.

Along with the bungalow, the automobile was a key component of the Los Angeles that was a-building. Ubiquitous as the streetcars and interurbans were, a car in every garage was recognized by the first Californian in the White House, Herbert Hoover, as a sure-fire slogan. Jackson A. Graves's excursion in 1910 was a hint of what was to come. So perhaps were Mack Sennett's Keystone Cops. The picture industry never employed more than a small fraction of Angelenos, but by the twenties Hollywood had become the tone-setter.

247

Autos and Movies and Oil

The bombing of the Los Angeles *Times* is given much credit for entrenching the open shop in Los Angeles for decades to come. Some oversimplification exists, because the idea was comfortable to most of the people who were moving to Los Angeles. They were amenable also to the blandishments of Sister Aimee, the fast talk of the real estate promoters, and the enticements into speculation by C. C. Julian and his high-flying successors in what they preferred to call the Julian scandal.

Thanks to Edward L. Doheny's probings, Los Angeles became an oil producer in the 1890s in a strip between Elysian Park and Vermont Avenue. More oil was struck to the east and to the west and in 1904 the new Salt Lake field came in at what is now the Farmer's Market neighborhood. All this well drilling was on front lawns and in backyards, cheerfully put up with by the homeowners because the royalties compensated for the smell and the spattering.

In the twenties black gold spouted in far greater volume at Montebello, Huntington Beach, Santa Fe Springs, Signal Hill, Baldwin Hills, Venice, El Segundo, Dominguez, and Wilmington. Los Angeles had a surfeit comparable to one of the Arab states today. The local market was far overshot and storage facilities were limited. Wellhead prices dropped. The Panama Canal, just opened, offered an outlet. Tankers shuttled from Los Angeles harbor to the east coast with bargain-priced crude for the eastern refineries. A small fraction of the profit remained in Los Angeles.

There were those who worried that a prime resource of the West was being plundered for the economic overlord of Wall Street and the industrialized Northeast. But with such good things going in the orange trade, moviemaking, the tourists who kept pouring in, and the steady stream of new residents, many of them palpably rich, Angelenos had few complaints.

A Motor Trip in 1910

JACKSON A. GRAVES

Jackson A. Graves came to Los Angeles to practice law in 1875. Convinced, by his own account, that he could not become a "great lawyer," he devoted himself to the more lucrative phases of civil practice, particularly the perfecting of Mexican and Spanish land titles. By easy transition he shifted to banking and became president of the Farmers and Merchants Bank of Los Angeles. Motoring became one of his avocations.

On June 7, 1910, at 7 a.m., Mrs Graves and myself, with Miss Ruth Stevenson, our son Francis and Dr. A. L. Macleish, left our home at Alhambra in a six-cylinder Franklin, with Harry Graves at the wheel, for an extended trip through Northern California.

It was a cool, cloudy morning. We never saw the sun until we reached Saugus. We were soon over the Newhall grade. ... At Newhall we took on gasoline. As we passed Saugus a passenger train, northbound, pulled out. We went through Mint Canyon, the train to the right of us. When we reached Acton we were astonished to see this train just coming into the station. Palmdale was passed by us at 10:45 a.m. We were then about one hundred yards ahead of the train, which was at Acton when we left there. We were not running fast, but we kept going. Between Acton and Palmdale at times the train was ahead of us. Then when it would strike a stiff grade it would fall behind. The train crew and passengers were all watching us, making signs of exultation whenever the train was ahead. They kept silent when we were in the lead. The train stopped at Alpine, which gave us a clear lead to Palmdale. Here we left the railroad, going west, it north. The engineer saluted us and the passengers waved their hats, and the impromptu race was off.

Autos and Movies and Oil

When we got to Fairmont a gale was blowing from the northwest, a scorching desert wind, which burned our faces and dried our nostrils. The further we went the stronger it blew. Our top and glass front were up, and with throttle wide open it was impossible to run better than fifteen miles an hour, although the road was excellent.

We had promised ourselves an easy first day's run, and that we would stop at Lebec the first night, but we reached that place at 1 p.m., and concluded to go on to Bakersfield where we arrived at 4:45 p.m. It was then so hot and the hotels were so crowded, that the place did not look at all inviting. I had read a few days before of the refurnishing of a hotel at Tulare. We concluded to go to it. Left Bakersfield at 5 p.m., and, while the roads were bad, reached Tulare at 8:10 p.m., having traveled 235 miles in eleven and one-half hours. We were not unduly fatigued, and after getting a cup of tea and a bite to eat at a restaurant, the hotel dining room being closed, we retired in good clean beds and airy rooms, and slept soundly until 7:30 next morning.

During the previous afternoon, as we came out of the Tejon Canyon, the smell of crude oil was very distinct. The wind was blowing strongly from the west. After getting beyond a point of hills west of us, we could see the oil derricks and smoke from drilling rigs at Maricopa, many miles away, with a field glass. The smell of crude oil came with the wind that distance, probably from the Lake View gusher. For full ten miles we were in the path of the odor from these oil wells. The smell of oil was by no means unpleasant. . . .

[On then to Fresno and eastward 52 miles to a construction camp for the San Joaquin Light and Power Company.] The company is employing over eleven hundred men in building a new dam, putting in power plants and clearing timber from reservoir site. Some five hundred men were being cared for at this camp. The arrangements for feeding this large number of persons were excellent. The kitchen was manned by a large force of clean, intelligent young Chinamen. . . .

After seeing the excellent manner in which the Chinamen handled this army of hungry laborers, I could not help reflecting on the utter absurdity of closing our doors to the Chinese. The exclusion act should be amended at once allowing 100,000 Chinamen a year, for several years, to be admitted to the country. . . . They would willingly perform services which white people will not perform for love or money. . . .

A Motor Trip in 1910

[Via Pacheco Pass to Gilroy], which we reached at 6:45 p.m. Stopping there was out of the question. We made San Jose, thirty miles distant, over perfect roads, in forty-five minutes.

Our transmission brake was in need of repairs and oil pump was not working satisfactorialy. We spent a few hours next morning having them repaired. Left San Jose at 11:45 a.m., for San Francisco, by way of Oakland. . . .

On the Oakland Mole three men in a machine ran abreast of us. They all seemed to be intoxicated. The driver, holding his wheel with his left hand, waved his right hand at us. Just then his machine veered into the fence separating the driveway from the railroad tracks. He ripped off boards, tore off his fenders, smashed his lamps, knocked out spokes of his front wheel and sprung an axle, besides suffering other minor injuries. We hastened out of the way fearing that he might run into us. We had to wait at the Ferry. Before it started the trio appeared, with a much battered machine. They were in high spirits and evidently thought the accident a great joke.

[Ferrying across to Sausalito, they went by Point Reyes, Tomales, and Valley Ford to the Russion River.] Ten miles out of Tocaloma we had ascended a hill about a mile long, with patches here and there, two hundred yards in extent, as steep as our Newhall grade, with a loose broken roadbed, which made it hard work for our machine. Beyond Jenner we got just such another hill, only worse. . . . At 6 p.m. reached Point Arena, one hundred and four miles from Tocaloma. This was as tough a drive as an auto, loaded as we were, ever made.

Point Arena is a one street town. This street has been oiled but is now badly out of repair and full of chuck holes. The town has three or more hotels, a livery stable, a few business houses and plenty of saloons. We ask ourselves why Southern California progresses, why it looks better, cleaner, more attractive to the eye than much of Northern California. From several trips which I have made through the state in an automobile, I have come to the conclusion that the saloons make the difference.

For the best part of two days we had been toiling along the bluffs overlooking a bleak, barren, repulsive yet entrancing ocean beach, upon which the surf beat mercilessly. . . .

We went through Inglenook, Westport, Hardy, and many other

251

shipping ports, many of them without wharves. Biding their time, between wind and tide, the lumber schooners run as close to shore as they dare to. Each vessel is anchored from the seaward side by numerous heavy cables. Another cable is stretched from the deck to the top of a cliff. Lying there, rolling in the choppy sea, each vessel's upbound freight is discharged in slings over the shore cable. In the same manner, a cargo of lumber or railroad ties is passed back to her. . . .

Beyond Modyville . . . an old bridge tumbled down with us. . . . We blocked up the rear wheels, worked a bridge timber, upon which the fly-wheel of our machine rested, out of the way, and the machine pulled herself out on her own power. Some people, who had assembled on hearing the crash when the bridge fell, warned us of three other bridges. We passed them safely by getting out of the auto and pulling it over with a rope.

Near Garberville we ran out of gasoline. A dwelling was near by. We found a lady there from whom we got two gallons of coal oil (the Franklin will run on coal oil). . . .

We ran into our first grove of giant redwoods. There were trees in this grove from fifty to one hundred feet in circumference. . . . We took off our hats and wandered about speechless. . . . We thought that it would be a crime to cut or mar one of these giant trees, yet they will surely be destroyed. Shortly after passing Dyersville we came to where the mills were already working on just such timber. . . .

On June 13th . . . the spring which was injured when the bridge broke down, succumbed. We took off the upper half of the spring, reversed it, set the broken end under a bolt passed through the eye of the lower half, held same in place with a clip, securely bolted in place with a flat monkey wrench also held in place by the same clip, over the broken spring, so that the end could not fly up or get sideways. Thus mended, this spring carried us safely six hundred and thirty miles, until we got to San Francisco and had it repaired. . . .

Monday I spent with officers of the Sacramento Valley Sugar Company, in which I am interested, and with Major Driffill of Oxnard in looking over the beet fields of the company on each side of the Sacramento River. . . .

We left Woodland . . . and caught the 9:30 boat at Vallejo, sixty-three miles away, for San Francisco. . . . [Two days later] fifty miles from Pismo, a little south of Los Olivos, trouble developed. A gear made of compressed rawhide, set upon the end of the cam shaft, wore out, and we were out of the running. By telephoning from a neighboring farmhouse, we got a team to tow our machine back to Los Olivos. Fortunately, Mr. M. S. Chapman, of Altadena, was stopping at the "Alamo Pintado" Inn. He heard of our trouble and very kindly came in his machine and conveyed our party to the Inn. We wired for a new gear but it did not reach us until Tuesday night.

It is a pleasure for the traveler to know that at the end of a day's run from Los Angeles there is so comfortable a stopping place as the Alamo. Mr. Mattie, who conducts it, is worthy of the greatest praise. . . . By one o'clock Wednesday our car was adjusted. . . .

The drive through the Gaviota Pass was dusty. The road from this side of the Pass to Santa Barbara has been much improved during the past year. We had a very pleasant run to Shepard's Inn. . . . As we could not get breakfast there until seven o'clock in the morning, we got up at the unusual hour of 3:30 a.m., and by 4 a.m., under a bright moon, and with our lamps lit, we started upon the last leg of our journey. . . .

We were away just four weeks. We traveled 2,275 miles over all sorts of roads, and our average running time for the entire trip was better than nineteen miles an hour. . . . Traveling in an automobile is certainly the way to see the country.

Jackson A. Graves, *California Memories* (Los Angeles, 1930), 167–183.

Enter the Moviemakers
REMI NADEAU

Environmental analysis, scientifically applied, would have identified the Los Angeles area as the ideal location for moving picture making. As Remi Nadeau tells, the coming of the moviemakers was far less by design and much more casual. From this hilarious start-up came the industry that, over the next two generations, was Los Angeles' most glamorous.

Toward the end of 1907 two somewhat desperate-looking individuals got off the train in Los Angeles carrying a motion-picture camera. One was Francis Boggs, director for the Selig Company. The other was Thomas Persons, who served as cameraman and all the other specialties requisite to a movie outfit. All, that is, except the actors. In Chicago they had already filmed a good part of a one-reel (twelve-minute) version of *The Count of Monte Cristo*. But winter had descended on Lake Michigan and they had come to California in search of the sun. Since it was too expensive to bring the cast out west, they simply recruited new actors in Los Angeles for the remaining scenes. This might be slightly confusing to audiences, but no matter. In 1907 the movies were such a novelty that you could sell anything on film.

And so the happy pioneers—for they were the first movie-makers in California—went down to Santa Monica Bay for the big outdoor scene of the picture. With them was a Los Angeles actor who may or may not have borne a resemblance to the leading character in the Chicago scenes. With them also was a luxuriant wig for the hero to wear as he emerged from the water after escaping from prison. Persons set up his camera on the beach; the hero waded into the water and submerged, wig and all; presumably Boggs shouted the 1907 equivalent of "Action!"

Just as the actor rose from the depths he was smacked from behind by a large wave and sent to the bottom. To the terror of the two men on shore, he stayed down. What was worse, the wig was serenely drifting out to sea.

"Hey!" cried Persons. "I put up a ten-dollar deposit on that wig."

Both men splashed into the surf and swam for the hairpiece. While they were out there they also rescued the actor.

254

Soon after this Boggs and Persons shipped the final scenes of *The Count of Monte Cristo* back to Chicago. While it was being released for the delight and puzzlement of moviegoers, they rented the roof of a building in downtown Los Angeles and started filming a one-reel version of *Carmen*—without benefit of a senorita or a bull. Like the generations of movie producers who would follow them, they at least thought big.

With this simple and unaffected entrance the cinema came to Los Angeles—and Los Angeles has never been the same since. The invasion was not sudden; the first companies spent only the winter months, without thought of shifting their seat of operations from New York City.

In the early 1900s the art of the motion picture was in its infancy—in fact, it could hardly be dignified with the term "art." Since Thomas A. Edison had invented it in 1889, the picture-that-moves had been little more than an adult toy. People had paid a nickel to see one-reel shows which in the earlier days did not even tell a story. The usual procedure was to conceive and film a show in one day and print it the next. As Adolph Zukor later wrote.

"The demand was ahead of the supply; anything could be sold and nobody took the business seriously."

There is a tradition that the pictures came to Los Angeles because the Edison motion-picture trust held such a tight grip on the use of cameras that bootleg operators wanted to be near the safety of the Mexican border. Available evidence indicates that only one company came to California primarily for this reason. Most of the pioneer companies to operate in Los Angeles—Selig, Kalem, Essanay, and Biograph—were themselves members of the trust. The overriding reason for the migration of the moviemakers was the same reason that was attracting normal Americans—sunshine. Artificial lighting had not yet achieved the intensity required for interior shots, and cameramen had to rely on the sun. Indoor scenes were shot against three walls and an open ceiling. When the sun went behind a cloud, shooting stopped; the actors, who became known as "sun worshippers," would gather round to look at the sky through pieces of dark film, all the while expounding weather prophecies. The stage was so exposed that on a cold day many a love scene or sedate drawing-room episode was filmed complete with chattering teeth, goose-pimples, and steamy breath.

Such inconveniences were supposedly minimized by the California sun. Florida might have beckoned the movies, but there was little variety to the Florida landscape. In California you could shoot pirates on a South Sea beach, Foreign Legionnaires marching across Sahara sands, Hannibal crossing the Alps. And westerns! Without mountains, how could you cut 'em off at the pass?

And so the moviemakers trekked into Los Angeles. It was one of the few things that happened to southern California spontaneously. No booster program drew this industry—except the general campaign that advertised the climate. Not even the imaginative boosters could foresee the magical growth of Hollywood.

Consequently, the first movie people often got a chilly reception. Working on budgets measured in the hundreds of dollars, they became the world's foremost opportunists. Wherever a crowd gathered for an accident, a parade, or a fire, the cameramen came running up for a shot. More than once they faked their own accident in order to draw a crowd. When fire broke out at one studio they changed the script of the movie they were shooting to include a fire-fighting episode, and two rival companies came rushing up to use the flames as a background. Front yards and even buildings were invaded by these cheerful trespassers, who shot first and asked permission if they were caught. One woman had to pour a tubful of scalding water on her annoyers before they would vacate her front lawn. As often as not a proprietor would arrive to make a protest, only to have himself filmed in the act and his angry gesturing incorporated in the story.

Needless to say, these madmen were soon the bane of local police. At one of the Vanderbilt Cup automobile races in Santa Monica the grandstanders were horrified to see a wild car go dashing by dragging a body behind. The attending policemen leaped forward to halt the runaway, only to be sent flying in all directions. A delighted movie crew, which had set the whole episode in motion with the runaway car, packed up its equipment and escaped with some magnificent footage. Two of Mack Sennett's men attracted a huge crowd by doing stunts on a structure high above a downtown street. While the cameraman got the whole action, a fire truck, a police wagon, and an ambulance careened to the scene. At the proper moment the performers tossed a dummy into the crowd, snatched their camera, and beat a retreat before the cops could catch them.

But events were already stirring that would make the movies welcome. By about 1910 the novelty of the flickers had worn thin; nickelodeon customers would no longer pay to have their intelligence insulted. Box-office receipts were diving and some exhibitors were ready to quit. As a last resort the moviemakers thought of an expedient that would help them through many a subsequent crisis —better pictures. Stories began to be plotted with some attention to plausibility. A few hungry stage actors and actresses were induced to risk their reputations by appearing, sometimes under assumed names, in motion pictures. Some directors began to toy with the idea that a story like *Monte Cristo* or *Carmen* might be told better in two reels, or twenty-four minutes. This might mean spending an entire week on a production instead of one or two days; but the movie people were still thinking big. It began to look as though the movies might be something more than a toy, in which case the industry might turn out to be a valuable asset to ambitious Los Angeles.

One of the earliest protagonists of the new school was Thomas H. Ince, a young director who came to Los Angeles late in 1911. At that time a wild West show, complete with horses, trick riders, and a long string of covered wagons, was wintering near Santa Monica. When Ince saw this magnificent caravan the epic movie was born. At the unheard-of rate of $2,100 a week he hired the show for the whole winter. Without benefit of script, he began shooting the first picture, making up the story as he went along.

The western was not a new idea, but before Tom Ince most of them had been made on Long Island by people who had never been west of Hoboken. Establishing himself at Inceville, five miles north of Santa Monica, Tom built a sprawling studio complete with authentic Sioux Indians, buffalo, and cowboys who found they could make more money riding for the camera than punching cattle. Ince was the first to exploit the fact that the western setting contained in superlative degree all the elements of dramatic form—action, conflict, emotion, suspense. He was above all a realist, turning out tight little stories that were hard-hitting and believable. He was such a realist that when an actor friend named Bill Hart arrived at Inceville in 1914 and wanted to make westerns, Ince was discouraging. "Bill," he sighed, "it's a damn shame, but you're too late. This country has been flooded with Western pictures. . . . They are a drug on the market."

But Tom himself had helped to make the western immortal. At Hart's insistence, the two made more horse operas—and sold them. A Westerner who could speak to the Sioux extras in their own language, Hart also was a fanatical realist. When he made his horse fall at the feet of the cameraman, he did his own riding without benefit of a double. And when he slugged it out in a fist fight with a heavy, it was a real brawl with no punch-pulling. Under Ince's direction Bill Hart became the idol of every boy in the United States and Europe who was big enough to hold up a toy pistol and holler "Bang!" After nearly half a century and countless predictions that "westerns are through," the horse opera is still the best-established form in screen repertoire.

Hard on the heels of Tom Ince came a different kind of storyteller, Mack Sennett. Having just formed the Keystone Comedies with two New York partners, Sennett arrived in Los Angeles in January, 1912, to take over the Edendale studio near Glendale. Among those with him were Ford Sterling and Mabel Normand, two pioneers in the business of putting laughs on film. Within half an hour this irrepressible crew had thrown Los Angeles into new confusion. A Shriners' convention was in town, and the costumed potentates were at that very moment parading down Main Street to the tune of the horn and drum. On the sidelines a faithful Los Angeles crowd was cheering as they passed.

"We got us a spectacle, kids," whooped Mack Sennett, always the opportunist. "Look at that crowd scene—all free!"

Swiftly the Sennett troupe jumped into action. One of them ran into a department store and bought a large baby-sized doll. Mabel Normand put on a shawl, took the doll, and ran up to the files of marching Shriners while Sennett's cameraman cranked away. Run-

258

ning beside them, she held out the doll and pleaded for the father to show himself. The reaction was splendid. The hapless Shriners shrank from her in horror. But one of them stepped out of line to offer help.

"Move in, Ford," urged the relentless Sennett.

Ford Sterling, clad in a huge overcoat, dashed up and got into an arm-flailing argument with the poor Shriner. Several Los Angeles policemen, complete in round-shaped helmets and brass-buttoned uniforms, descended on Ford. He naturally insulted them and ran off —past the camera, of course. They gave angry chase, billy clubs in the air.

Grabbing their camera, the Sennett gang sped immediately for the new studio. There they took some more shots to round out the first Keystone Comedy. As for the Los Angeles policemen, they never caught up with their quarry but were soon immortalized on film.

"God bless the police!" Sennett later wrote. "They were the first Keystone Cops."

With this entrance Sennett entrenched himself at his Edendale studio and proceeded to proclaim himself the "King of Comedy." Slapstick, from the prat-fall to the swift kick, had long been a staple of vaudeville and burlesque. But Sennett's merry madcaps added new dimension with the auto chase, the cliff hang, and not least, the custard pie. Sennett's comedies may have been short on motivation but nobody ever accused them of dullness. He shot his pictures at a rapid rate—140 the first year—and they flickered before audiences at the same breathless pace. Life at the Keystone Studios was a succession of emergencies. One moment Sennett would hear of a news event—a fire, a balloon ascension, a bicycle race—and the next moment his crew was bouncing madly over a California highway, making up a story as they headed for the scene.

Providing the fabric for this framework was the world's greatest collection of slapstick artists—Ford Sterling, Roscoe ("Fatty") Arbuckle, Slim Summerville, Charlie Murray, Chester Conklin, Ben Turpin, Harry Langdon, Charlie Chase, and the incomparable Mabel Normand. There was nothing subtle about these clowns; wounded human dignity was their stock comedy situation, and a pie-in-the-face the quickest way of achieving it. But they made a nation laugh, launched such immortals of mirth as Charlie Chaplin and Harold Lloyd, and opened an era of celluloid buffoonery that must ever be called the Golden Age of Comedy.

Remi Nadeau, *Los Angeles from Mission to Modern City* (New York: Longmans, Green & Company, 1960), 204–210.

"The Crime of the Century"
GRACE HEILMAN STIMSON

As early as 1859 Los Angeles had a local of the typographical union. Over the next five decades many other stalwart unionists labored here. Yet no other American city, as Gordon Watkins has observed, "has presented so able an array of militant, uncompromising opponents of unionism and as fervent a championship of the open shop." In 1910 election of a prolabor mayor seemed probable, but the bombing of the Times Building, here described, reversed all that and kept organized labor under a cloud not dispelled until federal intervention with the Wagner Act in 1935. Rounding out her meticulously fair monograph on fifty years of labor history in Los Angeles, Grace Heilman Stimson describes the McNamara trial, the confession arranged by Lincoln Steffens, Judge Bordwell's unexpectedly harsh sentences, and the emergence of Los Angeles as the foremost champion of the open shop.

On the morning of October 1, 1910, a slim, four-page issue of the Los Angeles *Times*, printed in antiquated type, gave mute evidence of the catastrophe announced in a bold headline, "Unionist Bombs Wreck The Times." Some hours previously, at 1 a.m., an explosion had occurred in Ink Alley, a passageway separating the stereotyping and press rooms of the *Times* building at First Street and Broadway. The initial blast blew out the first floor wall on one side of the building, and caused tons of ink stored in the alley to explode. Within seconds the entire three-story structure was on fire, and the hundred or more employees at work inside were making frantic efforts to escape. The firemen and equipment hastily summoned to the scene could make no headway against the rapidly spreading flames, and when some hours later the fire had spent itself, only a skeleton of the building remained. Total property damage was assessed at slightly over half a million dollars, though more than half of this loss was recovered through insurance and salvage. . . .

The difficulty of identifying the bodies found in the ashes led to an initial estimate that twenty-one persons had lost their lives in the explosion and fire; the number was later corrected to twenty. The *Times* memorialized the victims in the following inscription on a monument dedicated in November, 1911:

"This imposing pile, reared by the Los Angeles Times, stands here to perpetuate the names, the virtues and the memories of those Honored Dead who in life toiled in the ranks of the journal which they served so long and so well, and who fell at their posts in the Times Building on the awful morning of October 1, 1910—victims of conspiracy, dynamite and fire: The Crime of the Century."

No summary of the meaning imputed by the *Times* to its "Crime of the Century" could have been more apt than these words from the dedicatory oration of the Reverend Dr. Robert L. Burdette: "Above your dust, oh, sacred dead, we consecrate this monument. We dedicate it to the cause for which you died. To free labor for free men; to the unfettered hand; to the unshackled mind; to the free soul."

Underneath the public display of emotionalism, however, lay an opportunity to extract benefit from the catastrophe; to fasten the deed on unionists would not only enhance the righteousness of the *Times'* battle for industrial freedom but also discredit the cause of organized labor. Harrison Gray Otis, proprietor of the *Times*, was en route home from Mexico at the time of the disaster. Arriving on the afternoon of October 1, he immediately reaffirmed his newspaper's accusation of union responsibility. So serious a charge did not go unchallenged by local unionists. Denying all prior knowledge of and any responsibility for the explosion, they placed the blame on faulty gas fixtures and inadequate escape facilities in the building. For some weeks previous, *Times* employees had complained of gas leakages; because of this Ben Robinson of the Typographical Union, during his membership on the Board of Fire Commissioners, had fruitlessly requested an investigation. Several employees reported that the odor of gas was particularly strong on the night of the explosion. Although some extremists went so far as to charge that Otis had blown up his own plant in order to "frame" organized labor, most local unionists accepted and proclaimed the gas theory. Thus at the very start the conflicting accusations of dynamite and gas were clearly delineated. . . .

Even labor leaders who hesitated to place direct responsibility upon Otis found indications that the *Times* proprietor was well prepared for the disaster. Since 1901 he had made no substantial improvements in the old building, evidently a fire trap with a faulty gas system, but instead had drawn up complete plans for a new structure. Furthermore, Otis had built and fully equipped an auxiliary plant for any emergency. Even more curious, according to an investigatory committee of the California State Federation of Labor, was the fact that despite the quickness of the flames the *Times* had lost no valuable records and no executive personnel in the conflagration. With a speculative eye on such coincidences, labor unionists could not help wondering whether Otis had himself had a guilty hand in the destruction of life and property on the morning of October 1. A national Socialist paper gave more forthright expression to this notion. Pointing out that antiunion forces would gain far more than organized labor from an outrage fraudulently attributed to union members, it asked: "Was this a huge conspiracy against union labor in Los Angeles? General Otis admits that he 'expected' the calamity. What led him to expect it and are his own hands clean?"

Although Otis' direct implication in the disaster was usually more obliquely suggested than this, his moral responsibility for goading unionists into violence—if organized labor were indeed guilty—was openly proclaimed by observers both friendly and neutral to labor unions. . . . These opinions represented the school of thought which, while tacitly assuming labor's guilt, suggested that the *Times* proprietor must accept a share of the responsibility. At the other extreme were journalistic expressions like that of Alfred Holman, editor of the San Francisco *Argonaut*, who conceded no extenuating circumstances to lessen the blame on organized labor: "The world will understand . . . that this incident represents the spirit and criminal aggression of labor unionism as we have it on the Pacific Coast. . . ."

An investigatory committee of experts in the fields of mining, engineering, chemistry, and high explosives was appointed by Mayor Alexander on October 1. On October 8 it reported that detonation of nitroglycerin or a product of nitroglycerin, placed in a passageway on the street floor, had caused destruction of the *Times* building. This was enough for the newspaper management, which declared that even if the perpetrators, "lashed into a frenzy of bitter hatred by the vicious utterances of designing, unscrupulous union leaders," were never caught, the tragedy would be a blight on organized labor until the end of time. The report of the coroner's jury, submitted much later, established incineration as the cause of death, and agreed with the mayor's committee in imputing the fire to a dynamite explosion. . . .

Rapid progress was made in the tripartite investigation of the *Times* disaster by Detective Samuel Browne of the district attorney's office, Earl Rogers for the Merchants and Manufacturers' Association, and William Burns for the mayor of Los Angeles. . . . The clue which served as the starting point of the investigation was the unusually strong 80 per cent dynamite found in the unexploded Zeehandelaar bomb [he was the president of M. and M.]. It was stamped with the name of the Giant Powder Works . . . and had been made to special order. This made indentification of the purchasers simple. . . . Much of the investigation had centered in San Francisco, where the three conspirators had made their preparations for the Los Angeles explosion. This gave rise to the supposition that northern labor leaders, particularly Tveitmoe and Anton Johannsen, were implicated in the plot. . . .

A special grand jury of nineteen members, charged with ascertaining the cause of the *Times* disaster and returning indictments against identifiable culprits, commenced its deliberations on October

263

27, 1910. Although proceedings were secret, it was learned that 174 witnesses, including a considerable number from San Francisco, were subpoenaed. Tveitmoe and Johannsen were among those who testified. Because of his investigations in San Francisco and his preliminary talks with witnesses, Earl Rogers was appointed as special prosecutor before the grand jury. The granting of official status to a representative of an organization opposed to unionism stirred the anger of organized labor. . . . On January 5, 1911, after twenty-five days of investigation, the grand jury returned twenty-three indictments. . . .

Burns believed that to implicate John McNamara, a lawyer and high union official, he would have to extract a confession from one of the suspects. He therefore decided, in April, 1911, after some six months of one of the most exciting and dramatic manhunts in American history, to close the net on McManigal and James McNamara in the hope of obtaining the needed confession from McManigal. . . . At Detroit, with police officers from both Detroit and Chicago, Burns' son Raymond arrested McManigal and McNamara ten minutes after they had checked in under their assumed names at the Oxford Hotel. . . . Their luggage contained six clock batteries like those used in the unexploded bombs in Peoria and Los Angeles, as well as three guns, one equipped with a silencer. The prisoners, on being told they were wanted for a recent bank robbery in Chicago, for which they had alibis, waived extradition and voluntarily accompanied the police to Chicago. . . . Upon arrival at their destination, the prisoners were taken to the home of Chicago Police Sergeant William H. Reed for questioning. The maneuver was part of Burns' plan to keep the arrests secret until he could extract a confession from McManigal and take John McNamara into custody.

Burns took upon himself the task of getting a confession from McManigal . . . Burns pointed out to McManigal that he could hardly expect the same support from the union that his fellow prisoner (the brother of a top official) would get; . . . that under the conspiracy laws McManigal was as guilty of the *Times* explosion as the two McNamaras. . . .

In the presence of Burns, a member of the Chicago police force, and a police stenographer, McManigal dictated and signed his confession, . . . a complete and detailed account of the bombings. . . .

With McManigal's confession, Burns was ready to proceed against John McNamara. The necessary papers for extradition of the three men arrived at Indianapolis on April 21, and were signed by the Governor of Indiana. On the 22d, Burns, accompanied by representatives of the Indianapolis police, . . . walked in on a meeting of the executive board of iron workers' union. . . . McNamara was immediately rushed to police court, [which] granted the requisition for extradition. The prisoner was then hustled into an automobile and within half an hour of his apprehension was on his way out of Indianapolis in the custody of Burns operatives and a police officer representing the state of California. . . . That afternoon James McNamara and McManigal had been turned over to two Los Angeles police officers, who took them to Joliet, Illinois. That night the party boarded a special car on a Santa Fe train bound for Los Angeles. John McNamara was placed on the same train at Dodge City, Kansas, and the three prisoners arrived in Los Angeles on April 26 and were lodged in the county jail.

Grace Heilman Stimson, *Rise of the Labor Movement in Los Angeles* (Berkeley and Los Angeles: University of California Press, 1955), 366–389.

"Casey Jones Was an Angeleno"

JOE HILL

On trial in Utah in 1914 on a murder charge, the proof of which was sketchy and the historians' jury is still out, Joe Hill spent almost another two years behind bars before facing a firing squad. He improved that time by writing dozens more of his parodies on gospel and popular songs—sometimes wryly humorous, sometimes caustic, and usually preaching One Big Union. His case became a cause celèbre for unions and the workingman, which is how he saw it as typified by his parting telegram, "Don't waste any time in mourning. Organize."

Autos and Movies and Oil

His song writing began at Los Angeles Harbor in 1910 or 1911 where as a dedicated Wobbly (Industrial Workers of the World) he was trying to organize the dock workers. "Long-haired Preachers," in which "In the sweet bye and bye" comes out "You'll eat pie, in the sky," is Joe Hill at his best. Second only in enduring popularity is what he did to "Casey Jones," converting that folk hero into "The Union Scab." During a shopworkers' strike at San Pedro in 1911, engineers continued to operate Southern Pacific trains. With "Casey Jones—the Union Scab," as Barrie Stavis has observed, "Joe Hill's song writing career was launched. The song helped to hold the strikers together. It was sung by men on the picket line and by those who were clubbed and thrown into jail. It was printed on colored cards, about the size of a playing card, and sold, the proceeds going to the strike fund. Overnight the song became famous. Migratory laborers carried it on their lips as they moved across the nation; sailors carried it across the ocean."

From prison in 1915 Joe wrote, "By the way, I got a letter from Swasey in NY and he told me that 'Casey Jones' made quite a hit in London and 'Casey Jones,' he was an Angeleno you know, and I never expected he would leave Los Angeles at all."

Casey Jones—the Union Scab

The Workers on the S.P. line to strike sent out a call;
But Casey Jones, the engineer, he wouldn't strike at all;
His boiler it was leaking, and its drivers on the bum,
And his engine and its bearings, they were all out of plumb.

Casey Jones kept his junk pile running;
Casey Jones was working double time;
Casey Jones got a wooden medal,
For being good and faithful on the S.P. line.

The Workers said to Casey: "Won't you help us with this strike?"
But Casey said: "Let me alone, you'd better take a hike."
Then someone put a bunch of railroad ties across the track,
And Casey hit the bottom with an awful crack.

"Casey Jones Was an Angeleno"

Casey Jones hit the river bottom;
Casey Jones broke his blessed spine,
Casey Jones was an Angelino,
He took a trip to heaven on the S.P. line.

When Casey Jones got up to heaven to the Pearly Gate,
He said: "I'm Casey Jones, the guy that pulled the S. P. freight."
"You're just the man," said Peter, "our musicians went on strike;
You can get a job a-scabbing any time you like."

Casey Jones got up to heaven;
Casey Jones was doing mighty fine;
Casey Jones went scabbing on the angels,
Just like he did to workers on the S.P. line.

The angels got together, and they said it wasn't fair,
For Casey Jones to go around a-scabbing everywhere.
The Angels Union No. 23, they sure were there,
And they promptly fired Casey down the Golden Stair.

Casey Jones went to Hell a-flying.
"Casey Jones," the Devil said, "Oh, fine;
Casey Jones, get busy shoveling sulpher—
That's what you get for scabbing on the S.P. line."

Two decades later, in a haunting ballad for another generation, Earl Robinson and Alfred Hayes paid tribute to the inspired lyricist of the IWW, partially quoted below.

> I dreamed I saw Joe Hill last night
> Alive as you and me.
> Says I, "But Joe, you're ten years dead."
> "I never died," says he.
> "I never died," says he.
>
> "In Salt Lake, Joe, by God," says I,
> Him standing by my bed,
> "They framed you on a murder charge."
> Says Joe, "But I ain't dead."
> Says Joe, "But I ain't dead."
>
> "The copper bosses killed you, Joe,
> They shot you, Joe," says I.
> "Takes more than guns to kill a man,"
> Says Joe, "I didn't die."
> Says Joe, "I didn't die."

267

And standing there as big as life
And smiling with his eyes,
Joe says, "What they forgot to kill
Went on to organize,
Went on to organize."

"Casey Jones—the Union Scab," *I.W.W. Songbook*, 4th ed., Earl Robinson and Alfred Hayes, "Joe Hill" (1938).

The Chaparral

FRANCIS M. FULTZ

The chaparral is the least understood part of the Los Angeles environment. Periodically there are reminders of how serious a fire it can fuel and of the flood hazard that follows the fire. The Forest Service is considering an experiment of clearing the brush and planting to grass, and there are those who argue for controlled burns. An exasperated water engineer once advocated blacktopping all these foothills so that the total rainfall would be available below. Naturalist Francis M. Fultz, with loving understanding of this type of forest and how it functions, would certainly have rejected the switch to grass or blacktop. As to burns, while admitting that they are part of Nature's elfin forest management, he would have warned that controlling is easier said than done.

The fame of California's Giant-Forest has spread around the world; but who, outside of a few botanists and those most interested in the conservation of our land, knows of the wonders of the Elfin-Wood? Yet this dwarf forest of the Southwest is really the more marvelous of the two. . . .

In territorial extension it rivals the giant-forests. It covers almost all of the mountainous regions of the southern half of California, extends far into Old Mexico and invades to some extent Nevada and Arizona. It is in the Golden State, however, that it reaches its highest degree of perfection.

Tourists, visitors, and newcomers to the region see the foothills and mountains covered with a low, scrubby, woody growth and they immediately get the idea that Nature has treated Southern California very shabbily in the matter of forests. To them the chaparral is just so much brush cumbering the ground. In its stead, to their way of thinking, there should be a forest of sizable trees that are fit for lumber, shingles, cross-ties, fence posts, telephone poles and fuel. When they try to invade the chaparral, and are repulsed by the dense, tough and spiny growth, they are not only confirmed in their first unfavorable opinion, but they add to it the conviction that the elfin-wood is a positive curse, and that the land would be far better off without it.

But Dame Nature knew her business when she developed the chaparral. Without it the mountains of the Southwest would be stark pinnacles and naked ridges, the foothills barren, rocky slopes, and the valleys nothing but beds of cobble-stones and gravel. The growing season on the Southwest Coast is the short, cool, wet winter; the resting period is the long, hot, arid summer. Forest trees are not constituted to do their growing during three or four months of winter rains, and then rest through eight or nine months of absolute drought; the shrubs of the chaparral are. Pines, spruces, firs and cedars need some soil, or at least some deposits of rock-waste, in which to spread their root-systems; a rock-crevice is all that many of the chaparral shrubs demand.

The wealth of Southern California lies in the mountains; not in the gold and other minerals which may be hidden there, but in the water stored away from the winter rains and snows. And the mountains would be very poor reservoirs, indeed, if it were not for the blanket of elfin-tree growth which keeps the rain from running off as it falls, holds the covering of soil and rock waste in place, and prevents an enormous amount of evaporation. How defenseless the mountains are without their coat of chaparral against the elements, and how much of the rainfall they let run away which they should store up, we just now have the opportunity of seeing vividly illustrated in the Pacoima and

Big Tejunga region, and in the Big Dalton and San Dimas section, where a few years ago fire swept away every vestige of vegetation. . . .

To those who have only a casual acquaintance with the chaparral, its various shrubs have little individuality. It is all brush. They may recognize the fact that the shrubs are not all alike, yet the distinctions between them are hazy. But to one who frequents the trails of the southern mountains, and who familiarizes himself with what is found along them, there is as distinctive a make-up to the Elfin-Wood as there is to the forest of giant trees. He notes as he passes that here is a manzanita, there a buckthorn, and yonder a greasewood; and he does it just as commonly and in the same manner-of-fact way as a traveler in the East notes the hickory, the elm, the maple, and the oak; or as the woodsman of the North the fir, the spruce, the cedar, and the pine. When a person puts himself resolutely to the task, learning to know the various shrubs of the chaparral is no more difficult than learning to know the trees of the forests of larger growth—except, perhaps, that it takes more time, because the number of species in the chaparral is much the greater.

Winter is the growing period of the chaparral . . . for there is no growth without a supply of moisture. In Southern California the moisture comes only in the winter time. Then the supply is copious; but the season is short, and heat—another essential of rapid and luxuriant growth—lacking. So the growth of the chaparral shrubs is slow. The result is dwarfed stature and a general toughness and hardness of wood. Shrubs of twenty-five years or more may not have a greater diameter than two or three inches and a height of five or six feet.

The chaparral is mostly evergreen, yet there is a great change of color with the passing from the period of rest to the growing season. Throughout the summer and autumn months, the foothills and mountains are of a brown, lifeless tone; but with the first rains of winter they "grow green in a night," as it were, and literally sparkle with new life. When the rains quit in the spring—usually by March, or April at the latest—the hue of verdant green begins to fade at once. The change is not so sudden, nor so marked as that at the beginning of the growing season, but it is fully as rapid as the change from summer to autumn colors in the deciduous forests of the East. . . .

The Chaparral

Nearly the whole area of the chaparral belt lies within national forests. The old Spanish and Mexican land grants—which are mostly now cut up into small holdings—often included areas of chaparral along the lower parts of the foothills. But the Dons never ran the lines of their grants so as to include any of the undesirable brush that could possibly be avoided. Chaparral made poor pasture land. And, as a rule, they made haste to get rid of whatever may have fallen to their lot, by burning. Later when the homesteader was looking for desirable land it never appealed very strongly to him. So when our government at last began to establish forest reserves it found most of the chaparral still in its possession. And Uncle Sam, in the interest of land-conservation, promptly drew the boundaries of his national forests so as to include it all [except, it should be noted, the Santa Monica Mountains]. . . .

Fire protection is the one urgent need of the chaparral. It is spared the danger of the lumberman's ax, on account of its size; and is not in jeopardy of the pioneer's mattock, because of its position; but it is doubly exposed to that greatest of all forest foes, fire. It burns like a torch of fat. Its evergreen leaves not only burn as readily as do pine needles, but the denseness of the cover furnishes a continuous, unbroken sheet of fuel, in which for long distances there is no break of any sort where the flames may be brought to a stop. Then, too, the long, hot summer period dries out the twigs and desiccates the grasses, flowers and weeds, until finally the thicketed slopes are as inflammable as a match. Let a fire once get started on a thickly set chaparral slope and there is no stopping it until it reaches the ridge above. It furnishes conflagrations which light up the region for leagues around, and which make the very world seem on fire. . . .

A burned-over chaparral slope is as desolate looking a region as a fire-swept forest of pines. It has one advantage, however: it is more apt to recover, and requires a much shorter time in doing it. In fact, its "come-back" is often so rapid as to appear only a little less than a miracle. Then, too, Nature seems to take pains to hide the fire scars, even while she is getting ready for another growth of chaparral. She calls forth a troop of phacelias or other wild flowers to occupy the ground, or festoons the charred and blackened skeletons which the fire has left with garlands of wild morning-glories.

271

But however much Nature may thus beautify the burned and blackened earth, she loses no time in covering it again with chaparral. Some of the new growth comes from the old roots which have successfully resisted the fire; some from the seeds that were buried deeply enough to survive the heat; and some from fresh seeds carried in by birds and small mammals. A few seeds, such as those of the clematis and mountain mahogany, are brought in by the wind. Often by three of four years the new growth is making a respectable showing, and within fifteen or twenty years the chaparral may have fully come into its own again. In thus making haste to "rechaparral" a ravished slope it is as if Nature knew there were urgent need for no delay. And she does. One season of torrential rains may sweep away from an unprotected mountain side the results of a century's growth of chaparral. If the soil and rock waste are to be held in place, there must be a new forest-covering at once. . . .

In number of species the Elfin-Wood far surpasses the giant forests of the North or the hardwood forests of the East. There are about 150 different species of the chaparral. As in every forest, some species are dominant, some fairly well represented, and some of only casual occurrence. Of the dominant type of chaparral species there are about twenty; and to these belong nine-tenths of all the growth. Of secondary species there are about sixty. The remainder, as forest-cover, may be regarded as unimportant.

In local distribution, the Elfin-Wood mimics the forests of greater stature. Each species pre-empts those areas which by position and soil are most favorable to its growth and less hospitable to other species. So it happens that we often find a solid stand of manzanita, or of ceanothus, or of greasewood, or of some other species. Again, where the conditions seem to invite all alike, we run across a mixed growth of several species. Occasionally there are stretches where the growth is sparse, and sometimes noticeably dwarfed. Some patches of the mountain side—especially higher altitudes—seem so inhospitable that only the manzanitas, those sturdy gnomes of the chaparral, pluck up courage enough to invade them.

Francis M. Fultz, *The Elfin Forest of California* (Los Angeles: Times Mirror Press, 1923), 21–39.

The Belled Doe

ROBINSON JEFFERS

Once he chose Carmel for his home, Robinson Jeffers, the man and his poetry, became inseparable from the rugged Big Sur country. But Los Angeles claims him during the important years of his youth as an undergraduate at Occidental College and in graduate school at the University of Southern California. There he met Una Call Kuster, who became his wife.

Of these years Lawrence Clark Powell, his biographer, wrote: "His love of poetry and nature deepened. . . . He had a passion for birds, winds, sunsets, long solitary walks, and trips afoot or on horseback alone into the mountains. . . . During the summer vacations he lived at Hermosa Beach on Redondo Bay . . . he roamed the wharves and hobnobbed with long-shoremen unloading fragrant Oregon pine from coasting schooners, or drank with them at night in the waterfront saloons. There were fishing-boats too, with ill-smelling cargoes; and in the south the Palos Verdes, the great hills which rise from sea-cliffs to high domes, stood away to Point Firmin and San Pedro Bay."

Californians, Jeffers's second publication, long out of print, Powell characterizes as "a volume of tender maturity and apprenticeship." Some of its poems bear witness to the sojourn here, in particular The Belled Doe, a tale of the chaparral.

           —A waterfall
Hung never wavering from the mountain wall,
So windless was the vale: a thread of fleece
Much longer than the tallest cedar trees,
Or the dark-tufted beauty of any fir,
The waterfall appeared; calm whisperer
Of music all night long and all the day.

273

Autos and Movies and Oil

Below that precipice the plowland lay,
Crossed by the brook; the lowly vine-grown house
Was under broad twin oaks, but orchard boughs
Heavy with ripening apples folded it.

I have never seen a more immured retreat;
The unbroken hills all round were deeply grown
With ancient forest: one tall peak alone—
San Gabriel's—was far visible above
The girdling heights. It was a place to love;
And in my memory perhaps appears
Yet lovelier than it was: for many years
Are vanished since the kindly man who tilled
In the deep valley that enchanted field,
Told me in homelier, fewer and better words
Than I can use, this tale:

                    —The fledgling birds
Are flown before we know it (he said); and then
It does no good to wish them home again.
You'd never think, to see us living here,
Us two alone together, year on year,
We'd had six girls and boys; and every one
Grew up here, and the last of them is gone.
O, they write often:—all but Charles; for he
Has lived too long somewhere beyond the sea,
And maybe has forgotten us. The last
Was Barbara; three years and more are past
Since she was here. For now having a home
And babies of her own, she cannot come
To visit us so often as before.

But we are sorry that we hear no more
Her tame doe in the mountains. Barbara
Was just eighteen when out Dark Canyon way,
At foot of Sister Elsie Peak, I found
A little orphan fawn on the black ground
Under a fernbrake lying. The mother doe
Had been shot by some scoundrel—(for you know
That does are guarded by the forest law)—
And on the low leaves of the ferns I saw
A trail of darkened blood. The fawn was lying
Half-starved, and made a pitiful faint crying
When I came near; and struggled once to rise,
But could not; and it watched me with wild eyes.

274

The Belled Doe

I carried it, so light it was and weak,
To a ranch over on Tujunga Creek,
Where they had Jerseys pastured, and it soon
Learned to take milk in driblets from a spoon.
And though I had to leave it there, in ten
Or eleven days I went for it again
And brought it home. Our Barbara loved it so
That when it grew to be a sleek young doe,
And pined for freedom, round its throat I hung
A small brass cow-bell with a noisy tongue
To warn the hunters off. It used to roam
The mountains all night long, and yet would come
Home to our cabin often; and it played
With Barbara like a tame lamb unafraid.
I had to fence the garden-patch, and yet
Never could keep it out.

                    One evening late,
When in the summer heat we'd left our door
Wide open, it stepped in, as oft before
Jingling its bell. But in the shade without
I saw another one that moved about
Just on the edge of light.

                    The doe had brought
Her mate avisiting; but quick as thought
When we'd have looked at him the stag was gone.
Then the doe came less often. Very soon
Barbara too had found her mate; and we
Were left here quite alone. I used to see
Sometimes in the early morning Barbara's doe
Along the brookside; but it seemed to know
That Barbara was gone. Its bell would sound;
It would not come; but with a leap and bound
Be off into the forest. Lonely men
Have heard its bell above Pacoima glen;
And summer campers where the West Fork runs
Into San Gabriel saw it once.
But in the chaparral of Strawberry Peak
It was both seen and heard; and where the creek
Drops down through Devil's Canyon. Bob Devore,
The ranger, was on duty there, before
He went to Foxbrook Flats, and brought us word
In passing. But the pretty sound was heard

No more after a year; we could not tell
Whether the thong had broken and the bell
Been lost among the mountains; or astray
Our daughter's pet had wandered far away.
—We hope it did not come to any harm.

Thus he made end of speech.

                                        Upon his farm
Below the mountain-peak and lofty trees
There breathed, I thought, an air of the innocent peace
That does appear forgotten; but is not
All perished, in a world thus vexed and hot,
And full of stabs unlooked for, and fierce toil.

Robinson Jeffers, *Californians* (New York: Macmillan Company, 1916), 133–138.

The Real Estate Boom
of the Twenties
W. W. ROBINSON

*W. W. Robinson was the erudite but jovial expert on Califor-
nia as real estate. His writings were numerous, ranging from
the authoritative* Land in California *to a multitude of pamphlets and essays in the scholarly and more popular journals.
Here he writes of an extravaganza, part of which he witnessed
in person.*

In 1849 sailors abandoned their ships in San Francisco Bay to rush to
the California gold fields. In 1922 and 1923 white-collar clerks in

The Real Estate Boom

Los Angeles Title Insurance and Trust Company

Traffic congestion, 1925

southern California everywhere deserted good office jobs to become real estate salesmen. . . .

Between 1920 and 1924 at least one hundred thousand people a year poured into Los Angeles alone. A real estate and building boom was inevitable and the joyous antics of the Eighties were duplicated in a milder way, with new features added. Building permits rose from $28 million in 1919 to $121 million in 1922. In 1923 the grand total was $200 million, exceeded only by the permits of New York and Chicago. The newcomers were home-seekers, hence the abnormal demand for real estate. Prices rose, quick profits developed and speculators were happy.

In two years fourteen hundred new tracts were opened in Los Angeles County. Salesmanship became a fine art. Rows of tiny flags waving before every piece of acreage gave southern California a red, yellow and gala appearance. Advertising was as fantastic as in the Eighties.

One dealer announced in the Los Angeles Times of June 17, 1923: "$850 profit now. This is the best real estate investment offered today! We are *not* subdividers; we are manufacturers and are starting erection of a Two Million-Dollar Worsted Plant. With our plant staked out we find some fine business frontage that we don't need. It's on Central Avenue and 108th Street."

In Carthay Center, lots were sold on the strength of their being fourteen minutes from Pershing Square, the heart of Los Angeles, by *subway*. That subway is still a lovely dream.

Beach clubs, golf clubs, trout clubs, lake clubs, saltwater swimming clubs, artists clubs, all with fine club houses, extensive equipment and grounds were organized daily. Full page ads in the papers, with pictures of handsome structures, did the trick. . . .

Beverly Wood, five minutes north of the Beverly Hills Hotel, the "Switzerland of Los Angeles," was offered as a refreshingly cool retreat when "heat blankets Los Angeles," with homesites at $2,000 to $4,000.

In hundreds of tracts oil rights were sold with each lot. Dummy leases were recorded and fractional royalty interests went with every parcel of land. . . .

The motion picture colony at Hollywood was drawn upon to furnish color and entertainment at tract "openings," in addition to bands, barbecues and lot lotteries. Miss India Hughes, star of "The Common Law," presented a free "garden homesite" at Longacres on the afternoon of June 10, 1923, under the auspices of the promoters. Longacres was twenty-five minutes from Hollywood and the half-acre lots were $575. Jack Hoxie and his cowboys helped to "open" the townsite of Whitley, where streets were paved with seven and a half inches of concrete asphalt. . . . On Sunday afternoons Palos Verdes Estates gave free programs of music, Spanish dancing, stunt flying, athletic contests, aquaplaning, and yacht racing. . . .

The most fun for observer or speculator during the period that began in 1921 was to take a free bus ride and listen to the broker-spieler. It was not hard to take such a trip; in fact, it was very hard not to, for solicitors, with tickets in extended hands, flocked the streets. Agents scoured the southland for prospective passengers. A beautiful trip and a free lunch were the inducements. Here are bits, verbatim, from a travelogue delivered as late as July, 1929, during a ride that started every morning on Wilshire Boulevard:

"To the left is the site of the new Southern California Athletic and Country Club, which sold in 1916 for $12,500 and is now worth $700,000.

"The big white house across the street was moved across the city intact from Figueroa Street. The people never even moved from the house; they held a party there during the moving. . . .

"On the left you enter Fremont Place. . . . No. 56 is the former home of Mary Pickford. . . . The big house with the palms; they are Hawaiian palms and were brought over here at enormous cost. . . .

"The large white school on the corner is the Marlborough School for Girls. Eight years ago this was so far out in the country that they refused to deliver milk there. . . .

"This now brings us to the Wilshire Country Club. Memberships in this club cost $5,000. Solicitors became obnoxious during the summer of 1921, trying to sell memberships at $100 each. . . .

"In the distance you will see the large sign of Hollywoodland. Above this sign, on the top of the hill, Mack Sennett is building this beautiful home at a cost of over one million dollars. . . .

"At Vine and Sunset you will see the location of the old Paramount Studios. They have moved to San Fernando Valley because of the profit they can take. They purchased two blocks for $250,000 and now are selling one for $6,000,000. . . .

"And now here we are. . . . Follow my advice and buy one, or ten, of these lots, regardless of the sacrifice it might mean. Ten thousand banks may close, stocks may smash, bonds may shrink to little or nothing, but this tract and Los Angeles real estate stand like the Rock of Gibraltar for safety, certainty and profit. Don't be satsified with six per cent on your money. Don't be satisfied with twelve per cent. Buy property like this and keep it, and as sure as the world moves it will pay you one hundred per cent to one thousand per cent."

W. W. Robinson, "The Southern California Real Estate Boom of the Twenties," *Southern California Quarterly*, 24 (1942), 25–30.

The House that God Built

AIMEE SEMPLE MCPHERSON

Besides being a public relations man's dream, Aimee Semple McPherson filled several other rolls. She had a place in the remarkably broad theological panorama. She headed a noteworthy welfare program. She ministered to the social needs of thousands whose lives otherwise would have been dreary. She employed visual aids and dramatization long before they came in style among educators. And she was advance agent for later-model women libbers.

All this time the Lord had continued to assure me that He would provide for me a little home for the children. He spoke to other people throughout the city on the same lines insomuch that they were calling me up on the telephone with the word that God had been showing them that the little children should have a home and place to go to school.

One Sunday night when the place was packed to the doors with people, a young lady sprang to her feet saying,

"The Lord shows me that I am to give a lot to Mrs. McPherson. I have four lots of land and do not need them all. I am not called to preach the Gospel, while she is, and by giving the land that the little ones may have a home and she may be free to come and go in the Lord's work, I will share in her reward." A brother sprang to his feet, saying:

"Yes, and I will help dig the cellar." Others chimed in with: "Yes, I will help lay the foundation," "I will do the lathing," "I will do the plastering," "I will furnish the dining room" and so it went on until even the little canary bird was promised.

A lady promised rose bushes. Now the canary and the rose bushes touched my heart and caused me to shout more than all else, for small as the incidents may seem, I could see God, for the canary and the rose bushes were the two things the children had asked for beyond all else. The Heavenly Father had not forgotten.

When all was arranged a day of dedication and earth-turning was set, and after singing and prayer the saints formed a long line and marched round the lot single file, asking the Lord for the needed means with which to erect the little home.

Away back yonder, when out of the will of God, how I had struggled to get a little rented flat furnished, and what misery I had gone through, but now God is Himself planning a home which would be our own, a home given and built by the saints, where every tap of the hammer drove nails of love into the building and into our hearts. Perhaps none of my readers who have always had a home for their little ones, a pillow of their own at night, could enter in with me into this wonderful joy in their behalf.

Brother Blake was a builder by trade, and he undertook to oversee the erection of the little home. Soon the brothers were digging the cellar and doing the work either entirely free or at a very low figure. One brother who offered his services was tested by the enemy, who said to him:

"Now you know you should be working somewhere where you could earn a good day's pay to take home to the wife and family."

He knew God had spoken to him, however, and toiled away at the foundation. On his way home one night it began to rain, and right at his feet lay fifteen dollars. God had richly paid him for his two days' labor. Hallelujah!

This is just one instance out of many where God has blessed every undertaking about this little home. It was a wonderful thing, also, that the lot of land, just on the suburbs of Los Angeles, while away from the influence of the city, should be just across the street from a fine school. Let everybody that reads say "Glory." We ourselves are so full of thankfulness and praise we can cry with David,

"Oh, where, my soul, shall I begin to praise the name of Jesus?"

Just three months from the date the lot was donated, the "little gray home in the west" was finished and ourselves and babies in it. Each blow of the hammer, each smoothing of the trowel, was done by Spirit-filled brethren who shouted and sang as they worked, whilst consecrated sisters cooked for them and sang in the garage which was erected first. What a little haven of rest it has been, that little home, a gift from the Father of Love.

Aimee Semple McPherson, *This is That* (Los Angeles: Bridal Call Publishing House, 1921), 187–189.

Across the Generation Gap
RALPH S. BUNCHE

From John Adams Junior High School and Jefferson High School, Ralph Bunche went on to UCLA, graduating in 1927. He found his career in the Department of State and the United Nations working for brotherhood and peace. Among many honors, he was awarded the Spingarn Medal by the NAACP and the highest of all distinctions, the Nobel Peace Prize. He is UCLA's most prestigious alumnus.

At about the time of his graduation from college, Bunche was invited to speak to an adult audience on a subject of his choice. He decided to present the thoughts of the "young fry" on certain crucial contemporary problems. Much of what he said would have fitted a white-to-white confrontation of the generations; part bore down much harder on what he recognized as Negro problems. He was speaking some forty years before "black" displaced "Negro" in our usage. Also, he felt perfectly comfortable reinforcing his points with dialect stories about an "old Negro" or a "darkey."

John Adams and Jefferson schools now are deeply segregated, but in his day they reflected the overall community. It is, therefore, more striking that the issue he most stressed was that all Negroes must stand against the insult of the "For Colored Only" swimming pool. Give in on that, he warned, and no telling how far the virus of segregation would spread.

282

Across the Generation Gap

The older and the younger generations of our race are quite estranged. They live, so to speak, in worlds apart. They lead different lives, think differently upon differing issues and are far too often arraigned against one another. But the good of our kind demands universal unity.

I sincerely hope that the general opinion of the younger Negro as held by the older folk isn't that generally expressed in the customary barbershop ballyhooing. I rarely ever step into my barbershop but what I hear some "old timer" ranting and raving about the evils of the modern-day society. He invariably disparages the young Negro; calls him wild, criminal, evil, everything but good. And without fail he ends up with the sinister prophecy that the young Negro of today is dancing and "motoring" his way straight to hell. You all know the type, and the future of the race is indeed a dark and ominous one, if we are to accept his ranting as gospel. But I'm not so inclined. . . .

In taking up some of our more immediate problems, it is no doubt appropriate to dwell briefly upon one which is most timely at present, namely politics. Politics have played quite an important role in the history of our people. It was politics intermingled with economic motives which led to our enslavement. And it certainly was politics plus the same economic motives and a certain degree of philanthropic decent-mindedness in the North, which led to our liberation.

I don't wish to detract from the glory of that most glorious of men, Abe Lincoln; no man ever stood for the right more staunchly than he. But had it not been for this great game of politics and its attendant virtues or vices, however we may regard them, Abe Lincoln could never have convinced the North and held them to his course.

Due to the very nature of the circumstances surrounding its emancipation, the Negro Race became almost solidly Republican in its party affiliation. And this position it has, and largely continues to maintain to the present day. Whenever a block of Negro votes is to be found, there is a block of Republican votes. And this irrespective of the merits or demerits of the party candidate. If he is a Republican, he is good; if he is anything else, he is unworthy of consideration.

Such an attitude has had its advantages in the past—likewise its disadvantages. But I believe such a policy has fulfilled its mission and is no longer called for today.

Autos and Movies and Oil

I think I can truthfully sound a warning to you that the New Negro isn't thinking in terms of Republican or Democrat any longer; he is thinking in terms of men and merits!

The young Negro will no longer support a candidate merely because he signs his name John So & So, Republican. We don't intend to follow in the rut of single-track Republicanism or anything elseism. We are interested not so much in knowing the candidate's party affiliation, as in knowing what he has done and what he is likely to do and, more important, what are the probabilities of his benefitting the Race?

The young Negro voter is becoming emancipated from the chains of traditional blind party allegiance just as surely as our forbears were freed of the more obvious but no more restricting bonds of physical servitude.

The young voting Negro today might well be likened to the Texas colored man who had been in a virtual state of slavery to his Southern white "boss." But by dint of careful saving he was able to take a short trip to Los Angeles and partake of the freedom and grandeur of the Southland and, more particularly, the pure liberty-inspiring atmosphere of our own Central Avenue.

Needless to relate, the Texas colored man returned home truant and rebellious. He didn't try to regain his old job—oh no. But his Southern master finally came to him and said: "Sam, you'd better come on back on the job. We've just killed a new batch of hogs, and I've got some mighty fine hog-jowls for you."

But Sam just shook his kinky head wisely and, with a superior air, told the white man, "Uh uh boss. You ain't talkin' to me, no suh. I've been to Los Angeles and I don' want yo' old hog-jowls, cuz I'm eatin' High on up on de hog now!"

And so it is with the rising voter. He's kicking off the shackles, voting for men, not parties or traditions. He's looking a "little Higher" than mere party ties.

Then to dwell a bit upon an ever-vital question among our group —that of racial discrimination and segregation.

Whatever may be the attitude of you older people toward this dastardly practice of insolently slapping the Race in the face, I can tell in all sincerity that there is a violently smouldering fire of indignation among those of us who are younger in years and who have not yet become inured to such insults. And I sincerely offer the prayer that we never shall become so.

I hope that the future generations of our Race rise as one to combat this vicious habit at every opportunity until it is completely broken down.

I want to tell you that when I think of such outrageous atrocities as this latest swimming pool incident, which has been perpetrated upon Los Angeles Negroes, my blood boils. And when I see my people so foolhardy as to patronize such a place, and thus give it their sanction, my disgust is trebled. Any Los Angeles Negro who would go bathing in that dirty hole with that sign, "For Colored Only," gawking down at him in insolent mockery of his Race, is either a fool or a traitor to his kind.

It is true we have made a rather feeble protest against it. But why stop with that because of a slight set-back? Must we go on passively like lambs in the fold and accept such conditions, which can only be the forerunner of greater discriminations in the future? Or should we not rise in a body to fight such an absurd action in a state which guarantees freedom and equality to all alike?

If we have a segregated swimming pool—segregated in the ultimate sense of the word, too, for that pool is for colored and colored only; no white people are admitted, though there are white residents in the neighborhood who desire to make use of this so-called "public utility." If we accept this can't you see that we will only too soon have separate, inferior schools, parks, and who knows, perhaps Jim Crow cars forced upon us?

I think I speak sanely when I say that if it costs the Negroes of Los Angeles a cold million dollars to overcome this menace, the money should be willingly contributed, for it would certainly be well spent. If we don't combat such segregation to the bitter end, we can draw only one conclusion—that the Los Angeles Negro is cowed, that he lacks racial pride and racial consciousness.

My ideal type of Negro is that type personified in the story of the old Southern darkey who owned a small bit of land on which was planted sugar cane. It happened that soon after the great Teddy Roosevelt had returned from his famous big-game hunting trip, he and a small party were making a short trip through the South by motor. The party by chance stopped momentarily close by the old darkey's abbreviated plantation. Roosevelt was fond of sugar cane, and spying the choice stalks growing upon the old Negro's land, with characteristic impetuosity, strode over and broke off several stalks.

The old man had been watching every move and, seeing the President's actions, ran over and began to remonstrate excitedly about the theft. A member of the President's party immediately interceded, explaining to the old Negro in awe-inspiring tones that the accused one was "the great Teddy Roosevelt."

The old Negro looked upon the interceder with a look of scornful disdain, and replied, "Huh! White man, I don't care if he's Booker T. Washington, he can't steal *my* sugar cane."

To that old man, Booker T. Washington, his fellow Race-man, personified the greatest of all men. I only wish that the great men of our race, and there are a goodly number of them, were better known by our people. If they were, I am sure that racial pride and integrity would be at a much higher level.

This leads to the final topic to be discussed, which perhaps is to our Race the most vital of all at the present time. Whatever progress we may make in the future, whatever forward steps may be taken toward the breaking down of this infernal inferiority complex which besets so many of our kind; whatever success we may have in convincing the other races of our absolute equality in every line of endeavor, must come through the medium of ever-increasing education. Education, to the Negro, is the keynote for his advancement. Education is the panacea for his ills.

Young Negroes must attain higher education in increasingly larger numbers. Else we need not hope to compete successfully with other peoples. We must meet their standards or be left in the rut. And heaven knows we've been in the rut long enough already.

I'm sure that the returns will far exceed our fondest hopes. All we younger folks ask of you is to give us a little cooperative encouragement—just a little better than a fighting chance—and we'll guarantee you achievements which will compel the other races to afford the Negro that respect which is his due and birthright!

We have youth; we have racial pride; we have indomitable will and boundless optimism for the future. We can't help but come out on top of the heap!

True, we have certain modern ways and mannerisms which some of you can't quite reconcile with what you term "decency." But times change, you know. Short skirts, bobbed hair, dancing the Charleston, all find accord in the conventions of today. So don't disparage us too much for our modernism. We are merely the children of our age just as you were in your youth.

All we ask is for you to lend us a helping hand. Jump on the bandwagon with us, and we'll assure you that by the time we've had the advantage of a few more years experience, .we'll make you all proud of the young Negro.

He'll make his mark in the world today, just as you have made yours; and then he'll go you one better!

Manuscript, Ralph Bunche Papers, UCLA Library.

Millionaires' Retreat
MORROW MAYO

Soon Pasadena would have to share its laurels, if not its wealth, with Flintridge and San Marino, subsumed of course under Greater Pasadena, and with Beverly Hills, Bel Air, Brentwood, and other palisaded preserves. But in the teens and twenties, Orange Grove Avenue was Millionaires' Row and Pasadena was the universally understood symbol for the gilt-edged well-to-do, dispersed somewhat more widely though they were.

The Chamber of Commerce, as I have said, objects to Pasadena's being called "the millionaire town." The plutocrats, on the other hand,

287

In the twenties the Los Angeles oil strikes characteristically overran residential areas platted and at least partly built up. The Signal Hill oil field, particularly in the foreground, shows oil wells and houses in close association.

object to its being called anything else. Aside from their own domestic servants and commercial attachés, these retired men of great wealth do not want any working people in the town. The working classes, they point out with unimpeachable logic, can go to San Pedro, or, better still, to hell. They know by experience that whenever working people congregate near them, social unrest inevitably follows. Naturally, a retired underwear-manufacturer has seen enough of such monkey business in his active years of sweating women and children. Now, as peace reigns and his arteries harden and the Angel of Death begins to flash a coy eye at him, he does not want to hear any more about that.

These vigilant old men—these amiable old rogues—are surely not babes in the woods when it comes to strategy. They join the Pasadena Chamber of Commerce for the unique purpose of keeping commerce out of the town. It is a charming idea. And, however selfish their motives, however personal their interest, however incongruous their position, it seems to me that they perform a real service. For the active Babbitts of Pasadena, like business men everywhere, are natural vandals. Tomorrow, if it were possible, they would convert Busch Sunken Gardens into a site for a glue-manufacturing plant, and chop down every unprogressive, obstructing tree in order to display their exquisite advertising signs. They have endeavored to improve and Americanize the town for years, and only a moss-backed, city-planning commission, composed of retired millionaires, has prevented it.

Thus it is dog eat dog. Many are the fights in the Chamber of Commerce between the practising, red-blooded go-getters who yell: "We must have more payrolls": and the retired, nature-loving millionaries who shout back apoplectically: "When the smoke-stacks come, we go!" As a result, there is much surreptitious activity on the part of the business men to get "desirable industry" quietly: many secret, solemn conferences and much plain and fancy double-crossing all around. It is interesting to note that some of the most violent beauty-lovers are retired manufacturers from such centers of culture and loveliness as Brockton, Massachusetts, East St. Louis, Scranton, Pennsylvania, and Bluefields, West Virginia. The spectacle is a sort of *reductio ad absurdum* of something; I confess that I do not know exactly what.

The town glides along from day to day, tranquil, sunshiny, warm, friendly, complacent, and rich. The Los Angeles patriots go into hysterics at the mere mention of the word "radical," but the Pasadena plutocrats are more tolerant of this strange species. Pasadena is probably the only town in the country where Mr. Upton Sinclair could live for years without creating a ripple on the surface. Mr. Sinclair, alas, was never taken seriously. He was simply dismissed with a vague, cordial wave of the hand, as one might say to a lunatic: "Sure, sure, that's right, Napoleon." Mr. Roger Baldwin, of the American Civil Liberties Union, was permitted to speak in Pasadena in spite of the American Legion and the Better America Federation. He arrived in a Hispano-Suiza piloted by the Socialistic croix-de-guerre owner, Crane Gartz, which, in itself, was enough to insure a hearing. Pasadena police have ousted Los Angeles "open-shop" bands bodily from the town's annual Tournament of Roses parades. This small metropolis, indeed, is a paradox. The richest city in America, it is also one of the friendliest to organized Labor, a friendliness which goes back to the days of the McNamara case. The files of the Los Angeles *Citizen* disclose that during those hectic days the labor organ received most of its advertising from Pasadena merchants.

Mainly responsible for this state of affairs is Charles H. Prisk, editor and owner of the Pasadena *Star-News*. In an article in the *American Mercury* a few years ago on the California literati, George W. West referred to this journal as "an oasis in the desert." After years of easy but persistent pressure Mr. Prisk has gradually created a spirit of live-and-let-live in the community. The *Star-News* has long been the envy and wonder of newspaper publishers on the Pacific coast. Its policy of giving all sides in a controversy an "even break" is often termed spineless by persons whose idea of courage is to suppress the opposition.

Mr. Prisk is a modest, genial, dignified, mild-mannered man, a former president of the town's Rotary Club. Thirty years ago, just out of Stanford, a cantankerous young man from the wilds of Grass Valley, he went to Pasadena and started a paper. A short time after he arrived, the political boss of the town went to his office and tried to dictate to the young editor. The conference ended in a knock-down, drag-out fight between the two. They rolled over the floor. The battle finally ended in the traditional manner, after noses were bloodied, glasses broken, and furniture wrecked, when "Kid" Prisk threw his opponent bodily through the front door, glass and all.

Many times since then the man has had occasion to show his courage, his generosity, and his intelligence. He had one fight with Labor and won, but since he was not vindictive, he was willing to shake hands after the fight. Today not only is his paper, in an open-shop paradise, run mechanically by union labor; the heads of the mechanical departments are officials of national and international unions. Mr. Prisk is the despair of all the Los Angeles Red-baiters and Labor-haters; he is full of humor and common decency, and hence among most of the capitalists of southern California he stands out like a redwood in a growth of stunted pine.

Morrow Mayo, *Los Angeles* (New York: Alfred A. Knopf, 1933), 215–218.

A Time of Catastrophe

"The Depression did make a temporary dip in growth, but there was too much going on for it really to stop the boom and then, of course, the Los Angeles Chamber of Commerce did not permit such disloyalty."

David Gebhard and Harriette von Breton

John Palmer

Watts Towers

8

A Time of Catastrophe

In 1928 Los Angeles, through its Department of Water and Power, shouldered the blame for a horrendous disaster. For water storage and for generating electricity, along its aqueduct from Owens River, the city had built a dam 172 feet high in San Francisquito Canyon. The footing on one side was on a formation that slickened and weakened when soaked, and just before midnight on March 12, 1928, the dam failed and all the water rushed out. Its course to the ocean was away from the city, down the Santa Clara River to its mouth midway between Oxnard and Ventura. More than 400 persons were killed. The city accepted full responsibility and made what restitution it could for property damaged or destroyed.

Five years later almost to the day another disaster struck, again a few miles off center from the city. An earthquake, measuring 6 on the Richter scale, occurred on the Newport-Inglewood fault, with substantial damage in Los Angeles and more severe destruction in Compton and still worse in Long Beach, by which name this earthquake is known. The San Francisquito tragedy is called manmade and the Long Beach earthquake is attributed to nature. Significantly, however, the casualties and the property damage occurred as manmade "improvements" came tumbling down. In Gabrielino times this earthquake probably would have caused no material damage.

In 1934 and 1938 the Los Angeles basin experienced horrendous floods, two of the worst on record. Each came from a storm that dropped as much as 10 inches of rain at various measuring stations in the city and two to three times that much at certain stations in the mountain part of the watershed.

These buffetings were in keeping with a more general malaise, the Great Depression. On Black Friday in 1929, when the stock market collapsed, most Angelenos were not directly affected, but before long

293

there was a slackening in business and a decline in employment. As in earlier panics or hard times, Los Angeles was late in feeling the impact, which encouraged continued migration in this direction. Throughout the Depression people kept on coming, preferring, some said, to starve in comfort. Later it seemed that the depression was worse in California, our production being slanted to such an extent to optional goods such as oranges and lettuce, moving pictures, and vacation services.

After a time, Los Angeles tried to pull in the welcome mat. Its police department sent patrols to intercept indigents at the state line and turn them back. Also Los Angeles urged federal officials to identify Mexican aliens and repatriate them for the duration of the depression. More Mexicans departed Los Angeles than any other city.

Sinclair's EPIC campaign, the Townsend Plan, and the Utopian Society offered panaceas. Another homegrown crusade christened Ham and Eggs commanded the attention of politicians and recurrently threatened to become an initiative proposition.

The imprint of the depression shows in several of the selections that follow, but there was a positive side too. Population growth continued notwithstanding. Foundations were laid for flourishing businesses as, for instances, in drugs and berries. In the thirties, with civic encouragement, the Los Angeles railroads banded together and built Union Station, one of the most attractive in its genre. Also, the willingness of Los Angeles to contract for most of the hydroelectric power that would be available made it possible to go ahead with construction of Boulder Dam. The task was so formidable that a consortium of six companies was needed. The cost of the dam was double that of the aqueduct from Owens Valley.

Four decades later, from the perspective of another depression more baffling because surpluses as well as shortages set off more rounds of price increases, temptation arose to see the plight of the thirties as less contrived and therefore more legitimate. Thus David Gebhard and Harriette Von Breton, concerned primarily with the city's architectural contours, could call that decade a "golden age" because of the balance between the pressures and the potential of what technology and society could achieve.

Reviewing the Gebhard-Von Breton book, Robert Kirsch, literary critic of the Los Angeles Times, agreed that in the thirties Los Angeles was spacious and uncluttered, suffused with "lemon sunshine and postcard blue" as caught in the aerial views and streetscapes, and un-marred by crowds or polluted air. "Life was good"; you could drive along "with the scent of eucalyptus in your nostrils." Even those who did not have cars could live in garden-centered courts on palm-lined streets. We could "wander in Fern Dell" or "take the Red Cars to the beaches." We had been released "to the friendly open spaces. Los Angeles then had planners and architects, notably Richard Neutra, who sought and caught at least a gleam of the future. Noting that much that survives from that era still works, Kirsch concludes, "Who knows? We lived through a golden age without really knowing it." Memory that actually recalls the thirties will remind that want and frustration were real.

The Failure of San Francisquito Dam

CHARLES OUTLAND

In his book Man-Made Disaster, *Charles F. Outland analyzes the remote-control discovery of the power outage and pin-pointing of the disaster at San Francisquito. Besides following the crest as it hurtled down the canyon and on down the Santa Clara, Outland credits those who warned and rescued, and those who handled the city's program of recompensation. He also identifies the fundamental mistake that led to the dam's failure, which in lives lost, between 400 and 450, was second only to the San Francisco Earthquake and Fire of 1906.*

A Time of Catastrophe

Monday, March 12, 1928, 11:25 p.m.

The lights of Powerhouse No. 2 gleamed brilliantly in San Fran-cisquito's crisp night air; only the whine of the generators disturbed the primitive stillness. An automobile came slowly up the mountain road and disappeared around the horseshoe bend in the canyon. Dean Keagy, warehouseman for Bureau of Power and Light at Powerhouse No. 1. would soon be home.

Three people were chatting light-heartedly as they sat in the car in front of Harley Berry's house near the lower powerhouse. Mrs. Berry was endeavoring to entice her friends, Katherine Span and Elmer Steen, to come in for coffee and sandwiches. Earlier the trio had driv-en to Newhall, where the car had been filled with gas and serviced. Miss Span watched with casual interest as three figures emerged from the powerhouse and walked across the bridge over the canal. The two-hundred-watt lamp that lighted the way cast eerie shadows of the men coming off duty.

It was getting late, too late to accept the invitation of Mrs. Berry. Miss Span laughingly settled the question by stating she would get coffee for Steen and herself when they reached the upper power-house.

It was quiet as the couple drove up the grade past the dam, un-naturally so. No light was visible anywhere; not a car was in sight, and there was an absolute calm to the air. Miss Span was impressed with the canyon's behavior.

"It is quite spooky tonight, terribly quiet," she remarked to her companion.

Far down the canyon a lone motorcyclist, Ace Hopewell, was fol-lowing the road taken earlier by Miss Span and Steen. Hopewell, a Bureau of Power and Light carpenter, lived in the construction camp at Powerhouse No. 1. The motorcycle with sidecar was handled cau-tiously as the driver negotiated the twisting canyon road. From time to time the lone headlight would reveal details of the creek bed, as it overshot the road on a particularly sharp curve. After passing Powerhouse No. 2, the concrete lining of the canal replaced the creek bottom; but Hopewell saw nothing of extraordinary interest. Slowly he climbed the grade past the dam. The cyclist noted there were no lights on the structure. Only the high, dull glow cast by a moon hidden behind the hills, and car lights far up the canyon, broke the monotonous blackness.

A mile beyond the dam Hopewell stopped suddenly. Above the roar of the motor he had heard something ominous. Landslides were frequent on this stretch of the road, and that had sounded like rocks rolling down the mountain. He dismounted and smoked a cigarette, surveying the steep hillsides above. The motor was idling, but from the distance there still came the faint sounds that had first alerted him. Obviously the slide, if one, was behind him. Hopewell remounted the motorcycle and continued his journey.

March 12, 11:57½ p.m.

Fifty miles to the south people who had not gone to bed saw the lights of Los Angeles flicker momentarily. The Bureau of Power and Light operators at Receiving Stations "A" and "B" noted a sharp drop in voltage for two seconds. Neither man could know that the trouble was miles away in San Francisquito Canyon, or that they had witnessed the first faint signals of disaster.

At the Saugus substation of the Southern California Edison Company, however, this first manifestation of southern California's greatest tragedy was anything but faint. With dramatic suddenness the Edison transmission line to Lancaster shorted out, blowing up an oil switch in the line and bringing the resident personnel to emergency duty. A lineman was dispatched up San Francisquito Canyon to search for the cause of the trouble.

Midnight

Atop the mountain above Powerhouse No. 2 surge-chamber attendant, E. H. Thomas, was awakened by his mother, "I think there's been an earthquake." They waited for a second shock, and looked at each other expectantly as the windows began to rattle. The vibrations became stronger; the windows rattled louder; and now the whole house was trembling. This was a strange earthquake. Suddenly the lights dipped to a dull glow, remained for a second or two, and then went out. Something was wrong at the powerhouse! Thomas dressed and started for the penstocks, where he could make his way down to the floor of the canyon.

Below, in the canyon, Ray Rising was awakened by a roar that brought back memories of his former home in Minnesota. Tornado! Jumping from bed, he ran to the front door. Moments later a wall of water as high as a ten story building loomed up in the night, and Rising knew only that he was fighting for his life. He became the first of hundreds to experience the hell of this surging monster with its deadly cargo of debris, uprooted trees, sickening mud for its victims to swallow, and miles of entangling wire. A rooftop came floating out of the night, and Rising with a supreme effort climbed aboard. In the twisting, narrow canyon his impromptu raft was thrown against the mountain; and Rising jumped to safety. He began calling his wife and children, but no answer ever came. At dawn Ray Rising met the only other survivors from twenty-eight workmen and their families living at Powerhouse No. 2, Mrs. Curtis and her two year old son.

Tuesday, March 13, 12:02½ a.m.

It has taken the liquid avalanche five minutes to travel the mile and one-half from the ruptured dam to Powerhouse No. 2. This was not the express train speed portrayed by pulp writers, but the generated destructive horsepower is impossible to visualize. With a depth varying from 100 to 140 feet for the first few miles, nothing could withstand the violence of the flood wave. Huge pieces of the dam, some weighing ten thousand tons, were washed one-half mile or more down the canyon.

Powerhouse No. 2 was a sturdy concrete building 65 feet high, but the water was 120 feet above the floor. The massive structure was crushed as easily as an eggshell.

Tuesday, March 13, 12:05 a.m.

In the canyon above the fast-draining reservoir, a bewildered operator watched the board at Powerhouse No. 1. Henry (Ray) Silvey had gone on duty at 11:00 p.m. after his regular days off, time spent in Santa Paula with relatives and friends. Returning home, he had passed the dam at nine o'clock. Silvey had talked with the lower powerhouse at 11:47, checking the load and exchanging good-

298

natured banter with operator Lou Burns. At midnight Silvey had again called the Powerhouse No. 2 operator only to discover that the phone lines were dead.

The original trouble encountered on the Edison lines at 11:57½ had shown momentarily on Silvey's board. In the parlance of the business, "we got a nibble or fish bite. Everything was clear and there was no indication of any trouble, and according to our time, at 12:02½ it went down in a heap, everything went black. Power was all gone."

H. S. Tate was working on the floor, but there was nothing to do. "We did not have any load and there was a ground on the system and we could not pick up any kilowatts." Tate went up to the board and stood watching as the operator went through the routine emergency procedures.

"Did you ever see anything like that?" Silvey asked.

"No."

"I never did either. It has me stumped."

Silver phoned Chief Operator Spainhower and highline patrolman Lindstrum and told them of the trouble. . . .

Shortly after four o'clock the flood reached the Saticoy Bridge and swiftly rose to a point where the flooring was submerged. Miraculously the old structure stood the pounding, although a portion of the south approach was undermined and threatened to wash out. For days this one-way road would be the only route open to emergency traffic from Los Angeles.

The speed of the water had decreased from its original 18 miles-per-hour to a mere 6.3 miles-per-hour, with a corresponding lessening of the destructive force; but it was still dangerous and an awesome sight. Somewhere on its journey the flood had picked up tons of baled hay to add to its collection of debris, and hundreds of these tightly wrapped bundles of fodder were bobbing and sinking as they floated past. By now the flood waters of St. Francis Reservoir could be analyzed as 50% water, 25% mud, and 25% miscellaneous trash.

Four miles downstream from Saticoy the ancient Montalvo Bridge crossed the Santa Clara and carried the traffic of Highway 101. Its

299

narrow wooden spans had been the first "dry" crossing of the river, having been dedicated in 1898. A short distance beyond stood the heavy railroad bridge of the Southern Pacific's Coast Line. The railroad had received warning of the disaster several hours earlier, and all trains were being held at Montalvo or Ventura on the north, and Oxnard on the south.

Highway Patrolman Ken Murphy stood guard on the north side of the river turning back traffic as the flood approached. Only an impatient Pickwick Stage driver was giving Murphy any trouble, as he sought permission to cross while there was still time. Murphy took a dim view of such foolhardiness, and a few words were exchanged. While the argument was in progress, the floodwaters rolled over the bridge and washed out two hundred feet of the approach. The chagrined bus driver stood staring at the void that would have swallowed his human cargo if a determined patrolman had not intervened.

Now the debris began to pile up against the supports of the railroad bridge, forcing the relentless water to shoot high in the air as it sought room to move through. On the Oxnard side of the river a section of track gave way and disappeared, but the sturdy bridge withstood the rapidly diminishing force. In the flatlands near tidewater its speed had been reduced to a mere five miles-per-hour, but the water had spread out to a width of over two miles. Vineyard Avenue at "Simon Cohen's Corner" felt the dampness, while at another point it lapped Gonzales Road. The city of Oxnard was safe, but the water came close enough to justify the evacuation set in motion three hours earlier by Eddie Hearne.

As the first grey light of a new day broke over the Santa Clara Valley, hundreds of Venturans gathered on the hills to watch the last of the great drama. In the words of Roy Pinkerton, editor of the Ventura County *Star:* "At daybreak, from our Ventura hillside house we saw the stream, filled with trees, houses, and debris, pour in a great arc over the Montalvo bridge. In the ocean, it formed a wide grey stripe stretching out to the channel islands."

George F. Outland, *Man-Made Disaster: The Story of St. Francis Dam* (Glendale: Arthur H. Clark Company, 1963), 9, 75–78, 128–130.

The Long Beach Earthquake
LA REE CAUGHEY

San Franciscans are sufficiently reconciled to their earthquake, though defensively calling it The Fire, to allow voluminous publication on it. On southern California's most damaging quake very little has been written.

The shock of the Long Beach earthquake caused people thirty or so miles away from its center, as we were, momentarily to blank out. Some could not account for strange experiences and behavior. A friend told that he had seen the quake coming like a land wave rolling toward him across a field. Another was unshakable in her remembrance of a shower of lights falling as from a large Fourth of July sparkler.

We were about to have supper when we felt the impact and undulation. John and the children, Nancy, age 3½, and 7-month-old Ariel, were in the breakfast nook, which was playpenned off from the kitchen where I had just turned from the stove holding a pot of soup. We remember snatching up the girls and rushing outside. We remember the swinging telephone lines and the quiet except for the howling of neighborhood dogs. To this day, forty-two years later, something else I remember. In that first shuddering instant, as I had moved toward the children, the floor surged up and took the soup pot from my hands. When we came back in, I was not surprised to see it sitting in the middle of the floor.

Anyone who lives in California is exposed to folklore about earthquakes. A muggy, breezeless afternoon will be spoken of as earthquake weather. Those who have had the experience and lived through it will agree that the moment of truth when the earth shakes is a gone feeling.

A Time of Catastrophe

At 6.3 on the logarithmic scale the Long Beach earthquake was of far less magnitude than San Francisco's, which rated 8.3, and its force was dampened by reason of the center being offshore. Even so, the damage was extensive. Hardest hit were Long Beach and Compton, but damage extended throughout the Los Angeles basin. The property loss was an estimated $50 million; exchanged from depression dollars into today's, that figure would be many times greater. And it snuffed out 120 lives.

By great good fortune this quake of March 10, 1933, held off until 5:54 in the afternoon. Had it come during school hours there could have been thousands killed, the toll of children unbearable.

The San Francisco earthquake underlined the need for fire-fighting equipment that would not become the first casualty of another such disaster. The Long Beach earthquake was an object lesson proving how not to build in earthquake country.

Historical Collections, Security Pacific National Bank

Earthquake damage in Compton

Hundreds of brick chimneys were snapped off at the roofline because the reinforcing rods had not been carried from the foundation all the way to the top. Many two- and three-story hotels and rooming houses stood, so far as the interior walls and floors were concerned, but were rudely exposed because the outer walls crumbled and fell away. Brick veneer and stone cornices came cascading down from business blocks. Churches disintegrated when walls buckled and their roofs caved in.

Los Angeles school board member Robert Docter remembers that on that afternoon he was playing in the backyard of his aunt's home at 23d and Avalon in Long Beach. "I saw the sky go gray," he says, "and I heard a rumble and roar. I felt the ground move beneath me, and the old frame house and the palm trees in front of it leaped through the air and I was thrown to the ground."

The most alarming damage was to school buildings. Some, such as Long Beach Polytechnic and John Muir High, were complete losses. In West Los Angeles, where we lived, the auditorium of University High School, though it did not collapse, was so severely damaged that it had to be rebuilt.

School buildings, according to geologist William Putnam, were exceptionally vulnerable because of poor construction and faults in the design currently favored. He writes, "Wide spans were used for classroom floors in multistory buildings and at the same time outer walls were weakened through the extensive use of large windows."

Many of the lessons learned were promptly carried over into building codes. The legislature in 1935, in perhaps the most rigorous code in the nation, adopted the Field Act, which specified construction standards for school buildings and other public accommodations. The standards do not call for the buildings to be absolutely earthquake proof but substantially earthquake resistant. Unfortunately the law was not retroactive. It applied only to new construction.

The legislature also set 1975 as the deadline after which school buildings judged earthquake hazardous were no longer to be used. Its timetable could hardly be called scientific. The cutoff year may well have been drawn at random from a hat or chosen for convenience as the time when most of the pre-1933 buildings would be worn out.

In the fairly severe Sylmar quake in 1971, which came at 6:01 in

303

the morning on February 9, the school children again were lucky. After studying the extensive damage done, the County Earthquake Commission warned that the children should be taken out of unsafe school buildings at once "even if they have to go to school in tents." But astoundingly, a year later 738 earthquake hazardous classrooms were still in use in Los Angeles.

As 1975 approached and it became apparent that some school districts would not meet the deadline, the legislature, playing God again, extended the grace period to 1977. The flaw in this generosity is that earthquakes come not by the legislature's calendar but by Nature's time clock. In 1975 there were school districts, Los Angeles included, still playing Russian roulette with the lives and limbs of thousands on thousands of children by assigning them to hazard duty in unsafe school buildings protected only by the legislative fiat that no earthquake before July 1, 1977, would count.

I, Governor of California, and How I Ended Poverty

Upton Sinclair

Upton Sinclair's EPIC campaign in 1934 is a textbook example of breaking all the rules in the politician's Baedeker. True, there have been recent experiments in running against the establishment, spurning big contributions, relying instead on grass-roots dimes and quarters, and facing up to the hardest issues. Once in a blue moon such a campaign has succeeded.

A wispy little man, a recluse, a supposedly impractical idealist, and worse yet an inveterate writer, Sinclair seemed an implausible candidate. But his writing style, lucid and to the point, translated into magnetic speech, and his criticisms of the power structure rang true. He rushed on to tell how he would end poverty in California by getting workers onto land where they could farm cooperatively, making similar use of idle factories, and distributing the products where needed.

In the twenties such a plan would have been hooted down as un-American. In the midst of the stark tragedy of the depression, the collective approach had much more appeal, and it was the only positive program offered Californians. On a tide of enthusiastic support, Sinclair handily won the nomination for governor. He might have been elected except for the most scurrilous campaign ever waged in California. As Judson A. Grenier puts it, "He was denounced by press and film as an atheist, anarchist, Bolshevist, social fascist, free-love advocate—all of which he was not." Cartoonists drew him as a wild man. He was charged with profiteering on his campaign pamphlet and the EPIC News and with advocating "statesmates" to help couples in a childless marriage—again untrue. He was berated for Elmer Gantry though that was a book by Sinclair Lewis. Hollywood perjured itself in a fake newsreel purporting to show freeloading bums coming to get in on the EPIC handouts. Fear was pervasive; our next-door neighbor climaxed an argument with "Do you want your daughters raped!" At the time they were five and two.

FDR studiously withheld his blessing. The Democratic party sat tight. The media of the day—newspapers, radio, and pulpit—issued stern warnings. The voters turned thumbs down.

But Sinclair had, in effect, run interference for Dr. Francis Townsend's narrower old-age pension plan and, indirectly, for social security, unemployment insurance, medicare, and welfare payments, a program that by the seventies involved much more statism than was in the mechanisms of EPIC.

Sinclair, meanwhile, had turned the other cheek. He wrote another book, straightforwardly entitled I, Candidate for Governor, and How I Got Licked.

A Time of Catastrophe

In *The Industrial Republic*, published in 1907, I predicted that the Democratic party would be the instrument through which the needed changes would be brought about in America. I declared that the Democratic president who performed this service would "write his name in our history beside the names of Washington and Lincoln."

I have watched with satisfaction a new birth of the Democratic principle under the leadership of Franklin D. Roosevelt. He has barely got started on his journey, but he is headed in the right direction, towards government control of business and industry—and I am shoving! When Democrats invite me to join their party and become their candidate in California, my hesitations are not political, but personal. I have to explain them, in order that you may understand the sort of man you are dealing with, and what he has to offer.

The thirty-nine writing years of my life have been interrupted many times by what in our family are known as "crusades." A "crusade" to save the American people from being fed poisoned meat; a "crusade" against slavery in the steel mills, and one against child labor, and one on behalf of woman's suffrage; a "crusade" for the women and children of the Colorado coal-mines, who had been shot and burned to death by Rockefeller gunmen; a "crusade" to support America's cause in the World War; a "crusade" to defend civil liberty in Southern California—so through a long list. Each of these episodes took its toll of time, money, and health. On the last-named occasion I made so bold as to attempt to read the Constitution of the United States in public, while standing on private property with the written consent of the owner; for which offense I was arrested, and kidnapped by the Los Angeles police and held incommunicado for eighteen hours—a most unpleasant experience to myself and a harrowing one for my wife. Of late, being no longer so young, I have said to myself, "No more of this!" I have said to my wife, with solemn vows: "From now on I am a writer of books. For the rest of my days I am going to avoid every other claim upon my time and strength." I devised form letters declining to make speeches, to attend congresses and conventions, to do all the many things which people all over the world ask of me.

And now here comes a letter proposing that I shall incur the risk of being elected Governor of California!

There are persons who would welcome such a danger. There are men who like to go into crowds and be stared at and photographed; who like to eat banquets and make after-dinner speeches; who like to stand on platforms and be hurrahed and have the limelight turned upon them. They would find it thrilling to ride about town in a big limousine, with a chauffeur in uniform and half a dozen motorcycle policemen blowing sirens. They would esteem it the triumph of a lifetime to be able to write, "I, John Jones, Governor of California."

All I can answer is what I like: to get up early in the morning and go into my garden with a high wall around it, and see the new sunshine on the wet grass, and on the scarlet hibiscus flowers and the pink oleanders and the purple and golden lilies; to stroll around in an old dressing-gown, with my mind full of my next chapter, and then presently bring a typewriter out into the sunshine, and sit there and pick away for three or four hours. After I have had a bit of lunch, I like to sit in the sunshine again—that is what I came to California for—and read my mail and answer it, and then dig in the garden an hour or two, or else take a walk, and after supper read the magazines or a good book until ten o'clock, and go to sleep with my thoughts on the chapter I am going to write next morning. Once a week I enjoy meeting a few friends, or perhaps going to a show—this is enough of "public life" for me.

By living that way most of the time, I have managed to write forty-seven books, some hundreds of magazine articles, and tens of thousands of letters. . . .

And now it is proposed that I shall drop this routine of life, and go out as a political organizer and campaigner! Travel around making speeches, and saying the same things over and over! Start writing articles, manifestoes, and appeals! Set up a list of district organizers! Have the telephone ringing all day, and visitors calling when I want to think—how well I know it, from many experiences!

This new "crusade" would be the longest of all. I should have to give fourteen months to organizing and campaigning, and then, if I were elected, I should have to devote four years to a hard and complex practical job. I should have to face all kinds of slander and misrepresentation, perhaps betrayal, perhaps destruction by the cruel and wicked forces which rule our world today. If I were to put my hand to this red-hot plow it would be goodbye to any thought of writing books for five years, possibly forever. It would mean goodbye to peace, rest, health, happiness—possibly forever!

And yet, . . . it is not so easy to hold yourself to the job of writing when you hear the thunder of this battle all around you. It is not so easy to enjoy the sunshine and the hibiscus flowers and the oleanders and the lilies, when you know that millions of your fellow-citizens are suffering from hunger. When your doorbell rings and before you stands a trembling wretch who knows that he has no business to disturb you, but is driven to brave your annoyance to beg a bite of bread or a chance to earn a quarter!

"Look!" says the voice which wakes me in the middle of the night and keeps me awake. "Here in this Golden State are most of the natural sources of wealth. Here is a land ready to produce almost everything which humans need. Here are machines of production, marvellous creations of human ingenuity. Here are roads for distributing, the finest on the whole earth. Here are factories, farms, homes—everything to make people comfortable and secure. Yet a strange paralysis has fallen upon this land. Here are fruits rotting on the ground, and vegetables being dumped into the bays because there is no market for them. Here are thousands of people wandering homeless, and thousands of homes which no one is allowed to occupy. Here are a million people who want work and are not allowed to work. Here are another million being taxed out of homes and farms to provide the money to feed those starving ones, who would be glad to earn their food but are not allowed to!"

I find myself asking a question: What will a monkey do when he has too many cocoanuts? Will he starve to death? Will he let his baby monkeys grow up to be malformed and stunted, because he has gathered too many cocoanuts? What is this madness which has fallen upon the people of my home State, that they starve because they have produced too much food, and go in rags because they have woven too much cloth, and sleep under bridges and in alley-ways because they have built too many houses? Here we boast the finest school system in the world, here at any rate we have the most costly buildings and the most highly paid staff of teachers—and yet we have not been able to teach our people as much sense as the monkeys in the jungle!

The men who have made this condition are a little band of "insiders," the masters of our chain banks, railroads, and public service corporations. In my book, *The Goose-Step*, written ten years ago, I described them as "the Black Hand of California." Ever since the World War they have maintained a terrorist organization known as "The Better American Federation," by means of which they have excluded from public life in this State every man and woman who is not their servant. . . .

These men have the mentality of birds of prey. They are exploiters, to whom men and women are commodities; they are gamblers, so fixed in habit that they cannot find recreation save in trying to win one another's money. Their idea of meeting this depression is to sit tight and wait for the storm to blow over. That this means hundreds of thousands of our people sentenced to slow extermination troubles the masters not at all. So long as the masses submit, they despise them; and when they revolt, they send the police with machine-guns and poison gas.

By their system of subsidizing political parties, these "booted and spurred" ones have had the naming of all our governors. In the eighteen years that I have lived in this State, they have given us half a dozen such officials, of whom I find myself able to recollect the last names of three and the complete name of one; but I cannot recall a single word that any one of these men ever spoke, or any action they took that helped the mass of our people. I have seen corruption rampant in politics, in business, and in the dealings between the two, and I have felt the helplessness of a man in the presence of a forest fire, an avalanche, a tornado. . . .

There is nothing novel about the idea of taking possession of one of the old parties and using it to serve the people. In Wisconsin the elder LaFollette took the republican party away from the old gang. Hiram Johnson did it in California, Norris did it in Nebraska. Woodrow Wilson took the Democratic party of New Jersey out of the hands of boodlers, and Franklin D. Roosevelt is very earnestly trying to make the Democratic party of the nation into a party of the public welfare. Why cannot the same thing be done by the Democrats of California?

Agreeing upon this idea of a Democrat, I place myself at your service. I am willing, but not anxious. If you can find anyone else who will serve the cause better, I will be pleased. Unfortunately, however, I do not know of any person prominent in your party in California who has pledged himself to this cause. That is the reason I have been called, and assuredly it is the only reason I am responding.

I propose a campaign slogan, brief and simple:

END POVERTY IN CALIFORNIA!

I do not put that forward as a means of catching votes, but as a solemn pledge which I make before the people of this State.

I say there is no excuse for poverty in a civilized and wealthy State like ours. I say that we can and should see to it that all men and women of our State who are willing to work should have work suited to their capacities, and should be paid a wage that will enable them to maintain a decent home and an American standard of living. I say that every old person should be provided for in comfort, and likewise every orphaned child and every person who is sick or incapacitated. I repeat that this can be done, and that I know how to do it. If I take up the job I will stick until it is finished, and there will be no delay and no shilly-shallying. There will be action, and continuous action, until the last man, woman, and child has these fundamental economic rights. Again I say:

END POVERTY IN CALIFORNIA!

Just how do I mean to do it? It is your right to ask, and my duty to answer. Some of my friends, who think they know about politics, advise me that it is not wise to talk too much. They say, make general statements, and not too strong. They point out that Franklin D. Roosevelt was mild in his promises; if he had announced during his campaign what he was going to do after his inauguration, he would never have been elected. All I can say is that I have to act according to my nature, and it is too late to begin changing on my fifty-fifth birthday. My life's study has been to say what I mean.

I put my proposition in the form of a history. In the pages that follow you will find a record of public events in California, beginning August, 1933, and ending December, 1938, [that is, through the campaign to come and a four-year term as governor]. First, I portray events, and then I put down my pen and try to make them happen. You who read this history have to decide what part you will play in it;

whether you will be among the Jeffersons, the Washingtons, and the Franklins of this new American revolution, or whether you will be among those whom I cannot name, because history has not preserved their names, but lumps them as "tories" and "royalists."

So far as I know, this is the first time an historian has set out to make his history true. It will be something for the rest of the world to watch, and you, citizens of California, may be conscious of the fact that forty nations as well as forty centuries are looking down upon you. There are forty-seven other States in this Union, each of which has the job of ending poverty, and will be interested to learn how it can be done. There are some among us who preach that the job cannot be done except by violence and class terror. But I assert that there is a peaceful way, an orderly way, a democratic way—and that this is the American way.

Upton Sinclair, *I, Governor of California, and How I Ended Poverty* (1933), 2–8.

The Miracle of the Boysenberry
ROGER HOLMES AND PAUL BAILEY

Knott's Berry Farm is the bucolic showplace of southern California. Walter and Cordelia Knott, loyally assisted by their four children, built it on the boysenberry, the roadside stand, Cordelia's pies and jams and chicken dinners, a collage of western color (stagecoach, ghost town, and cable cars), and a lush garden setting. All proved marvelously popular. A new ride has been added, an educational tour with soundtrack past the stations of the Knott family history—delayed for a time because of a three million dollar fire in this new annex to the Farm. Here is Horatio Alger at his best, a model of rectitude, an arch conservative, and most modest about it all.

311

A Time of Catastrophe

Japanese truck gardens at Palos Verdes

Jim Preston had been getting a good price for all the berries he could grow, so he had every reason to believe the crop from the additional twenty acres of land, which later was to be the Berry Farm, would add substantially to his earnings. As for Walter Knott, he had sunk every dollar he possessed into soil preparation, equipment, root stock and living expenses long before the vines brought forth their first fruits. . . .

Walter had learned from his previous farming experiences that growing alone was not enough to make a farmer successful; one had to market the products raised, and insofar as possible, control the market. Jim had always been strictly a producer, leaving the selling and distributing to others.

While Jim looked on indulgently, Walter set up a little roadside stand. To sell berries and garden produce to passing motorists one must, Walter reasoned, create attention. . . . What Walter felt was really needed, however, was an improved product—a berry that would put them ahead of all roadside competitors.

The Miracle of the Boysenberry

His search was rewarded one day by a newspaper article which told of the new and wonderful "Youngberries," a cross between dewberries and loganberries, being grown around Citronelle. The article described them as larger than other bush berries, not difficult to raise and having a fine flavor. With such a berry could not one set the standard and perhaps get something above the present deflated price? It took a little time to discover that Citronelle was in Alabama. But with the bold impulsiveness of a man with an idea, Walter ordered enough starts of the new berry for half an acre. . . .

In 1927 the berry farm was surrounded by an oil boom. Land in the vicinity had risen sharply to $1500 an acre. But by then Walter and Jim had sampled what could be done in berries, and had definitely decided to remain in agriculture. The landlord, however, with good reason, thought it wiser to sell his twenty acres for $1500 cash per acre than to lease it to them for $50 an acre per year. It was a logical decision on his part, but it forced Preston and Knott to either buy the land at the inflated rate, or abandon all they had worked so hard to establish. Jim decided to withdraw from the partnership; Walter clung to the berry patch. . . .

The owner agreed to sell ten acres for no down payment, provided Walter would accept an interest rate at seven per cent on the whole unpaid balance. Without legal help of any kind, the owner and Walter drew up and signed a contract. The interest on the ten acres was $105 per acre per year—more than twice as much as the rent had been. But the Berry Farm remained a living thing.

During these years of struggle, a time during which their last child, Marion, was born, the Knotts lived in a tiny cottage one-fourth mile from the acreage. Walter had paid $8 a month rental for these modest and crowded quarters. The little money Walter now had he put into a building consisting of living quarters in the rear and a berry stand facing the road. New hope was infused into the family by a combination of debt peril and the fact that at last they stood alone, and as owners.

The tireless and thrifty Cordelia now began making jams, preserves and luscious berry pies to sell along with fresh berries from the stand. "I'm not going into the restaurant business," she warned. It was rugged work, but business kept getting better and better. Cordelia had a knack with customers, and they came back repeatedly for her pies

313

and preserves along with the berries she so neatly arrayed on the stand. The youngsters daily helped pick the fruit, which dwarfed in size and quality that of their competitors. Virginia and Russell can remember flagging down the motorists with immense stalks of rhubarb which grew in the garden area of the little farm. By toil, and the closest family teamwork, the Knotts began to see a path out of their wilderness of debt.

Nevertheless, for two years Walter could pay only the interest on their land. The oil craze subsided, property began declining in price, and then came the great depression of 1929. Land prices in Buena Park tumbled to new lows. Walter still wanted to farm a full twenty acres as before, so he priced some land adjoining them on the north. It could now be had, at depression prices, for $350 an acre. He agreed to buy it. Unfortunately, immediately after this second bold step, the price of berries followed the price of land in its downward tumble.

The original ten acres, of course, were still not paid for. In fact, he still owed the full $1500 an acre on the balance. Everyone advised and even urged him to abandon his first purchase and move onto the new and more fortunate acquirement. . . . After pondering the right and wrong of the matter, he turned his stubborn ear to the "good" advice. . . .

One day a Mr. George M. Darrow of the U.S. Department of Agriculture paid the Knotts a visit. Darrow was head of the Bureau of Plant Industry at the experimental station, Bettsville, Maryland, and he came to Walter, as the most important berry man in Orange County, for advice and help in a problem. A number of years previous a Mr. Coolidge had written of a strange new berry—enormous in size —which they had tried out for a "Mr. Boysen" of Orange County. . . . "I figured," Mr. Darrow explained, "that you, being in Orange County, would most certainly know of this Mr. Boysen, whoever he is. At the time he contacted Mr. Coolidge, Boysen lived in your county."

Walter was at a complete loss as to who Mr. Boysen might be. He had never heard of the man, but the facts obviously deserved a thorough search. Anaheim, second largest city in Orange County, was only five miles distant, and it would be as good a place as any for them to start. As the automobile sped them on what was to prove an amazing quest, Mr. Darrow told all he knew of the will-of-the-wisp discovery.

"Coolidge's record shows that Boysen somehow crossed a logan-berry, blackberry and raspberry," Darrow said. "Out of that wedding of strains, apparently, came a giant. But the giant is gone—and so is Mr. Boysen."

In Anaheim the men made many inquiries; they searched in the telephone directory. The only Boysen they could find was a Rudolph Boysen, Anaheim city park superintendent. They telephoned him. He *was* the man. Yes, he'd grown such a berry, but it was so long ago he'd almost forgotten about it. Yes, he was the man who had given the start to Coolidge.

"Do you have any growing now?" Darrow asked excitedly.

Boysen shook his head, and the government man looked as though he had been clubbed. "Did you plant any *anywhere?*" he asked.

"I had six plants growing along a ditch bank at an orange grove I once owned," Rudolph said. "But I sold the place."

"Would you mind taking us there?" Walter asked, grasping at a straw.

"Of course not," Rudolph said. "The people shouldn't mind letting us on the place. But I doubt. . . ."

"Let's go," urged Walter, thoroughly alive to the search.

And through this casual chain of circumstances and its equally casual conversation came the berry discovery of the ages.

The new owner had no objection to the three men searching for anything so oddly ridiculous as a berry vine. He had never dug around that weed-grown area at the side of his grove. If they could find any berry vines there, they were welcome to them.

They found the berry vines all right—weed matted, and all but dead from neglect.

Boysen and Darrow, with the ready consent of the property owner, were willing and anxious that such an experienced berry man as Walter Knott take over the six tragically forgotten plants. In the fall, when the vines had died back, Walter moved them to Buena Park, and nursed this wonderful strain with tender care. It took three years, from 1933 through 1936, to multiply these six plants into production status. But these same six plants became the predecessors of the now universally popular boysenberry—named, of course, in honor of its modest discoverer, Rudolph Boysen.

When Walter finally got these giant berries into production (very limited production at first) he discovered that as few as twenty-five berries filled a standard half-pound basket. The berries, retailed through the Knott stand, returned, in spite of the depression, $1737.50 per acre the very first year of their full production. The demand was enormous. Everyone wanted them. Root-stock of the new and wonderful fruit could be sold to nurseries, berry men and backyard farmers as fast as the earth could yield them. By 1940 boysenberries, principally through pioneering efforts and faith of Walter Knott, had become a staple on the national market. . . .

While all this was taking place, America wallowed through its most horrible depression. Knott's Berry Farm itself could never have survived had it not been for the toil and teamwork of every member of the family, coupled with the sagacity of a quiet man of deep faith. It seems unbelievable that any project so burdened with debt could have kept itself alive through the universal bank failure, and bankruptcy of small farmers everywhere. Many a farmer less harassed and burdened had given up for the more sure paycheck of the W.P.A. Through these years Walter and Cordelia did not give up, but they found it difficult going, indeed.

One thing Walter had noticed was the increased volume of automobile traffic past their roadside stand in Buena Park. The highway was not the main traffic artery for Pacific Coast southbound travel, but it apparently had become an important one principally to Pasadena residents who found it the shortest route to the yacht harbors at Newport and Balboa.

These fine cars loaded with his opulent neighbors to the north had become constant stoppers at the Knott Berry Farm to purchase baskets of giant boysenberries and to sample and carry home Cordelia's jams, preserves and tender-crusted berry pies. . . .

The revenue from the berry stand had been the one thing essential to their survival. Cordelia's jams and jellies had bolstered the income of the fresh berries and vegetable sales. In order to further increase this desperately needed revenue Cordelia had next started serving light lunches, such as hot rolls, coffee and berry pie. These things, with Walter's berry farming, kept the venture afloat through the lean times. And then had come the fateful year of 1934.

316

"I want you to understand one thing for sure," Cordelia again reiterated one evening, "we're *not* going into the restaurant business."

"Lordamighty, no," Walter agreed, sitting down wearily in the living room chair. "It's tough enough without that."

"But I *have* decided to try serving a chicken dinner—along with the snacks. Maybe the dinners will go; maybe they won't."

Walter looked quizzically at his wife. "Thought you said—"

"Just an experiment. And only for a little while. Might help us to pick up financially a bit. Tomorrow I'm going to try it."

Neither Cordelia nor Walter had the least inkling of where this casual idea was destined to lead them.

Roger Holmes and Paul Bailey, *Fabulous Farmer: The Story of Walter Knott and His Berry Farm* (Los Angeles: Westernlore Publishers, 1941), 95–109.

Simon Rodia
ANDREW F. ROLLE

Asked to pick the most beautiful and magical spot in California, historian Page Smith chose Watts Towers. "Besides the beauty of the towers themselves," he said, "they symbolize for me the dreams and hopes of generations of immigrants coming to the United States. It seems clear that Rodia's impulse was both touching and tragic. He wished to transport to his new home some of the grace and beauty and some of the capacity to celebrate life that was so characteristic of his native land."

Columnist Jack Smith reports he overheard a visitor say to a child looking up at the highest tower: "They tried to knock it down but they couldn't." He called it a wonderful irony when the towers were put to a ten-thousand-pound pull test that "the testing rig buckled; the towers stood."

317

A Time of Catastrophe

These bizarre artistic creations, ninety-nine, ninety-seven, and fifty-five feet high, were fashioned out of bits of glass, tile, artifacts (such as corncobs), and old boots garnered from near-by junk heaps. Rodia had come to America from his native Italy at about the age of ten. He had virtually no education and was reputedly a widower when he showed up in southern California. Without scaffolding, Rodia built the first of the towers in 1921 on a piece of property he had purchased along East 107th Street. Five years later, when Los Angeles annexed the town of Watts, Rodia became involved in a conflict with the city's Department of Building and Safety. Because he had no building permit, and because the towers were considered unsafe, demolition and condemnation hearings dragged on for years. Meanwhile, Rodia, who said he wanted to build something really big, went on with thirty-three years of erecting and defending a "gigantic fantasy of concrete, steel and rubble." The tallest tower is almost ten stories high.

Sam Rodia, as he came to be called, was a persistent, indeed obstinate, laborer. He fought off anything that interrupted construction of his towers. For years neighbors heard him singing Italian arias at the top of his voice while he worked. Fastened to a scaffolding by a window-washer's belt, he gripped a pail of cement and a burlap pouch filled with broken tile and sea shells. Sam paid local children a penny or more for bits of tile, bottles, or castoff crockery. What he could not use he buried in his back yard, as he did his 1927 Hudson touring car. "I'm worried to death to get this work done before I leave," he once confided to a bystander, "but I'm a happy man." Another observer recalled that "everyone thought he was crazy" as he sang away in his beloved towers.

During the World War II blackouts, Rodia was ordered to take down the gay lights with which he had decorated his towers. As the war years passed, he grew more tense and quarreled increasingly with some of his neighbors. Children tormented the aging eccentric, throwing rubble over his seven-foot-high property walls. They also stole apricots from his precious tree, although he was generous in giving them its fruit as well as cookies. There was recurring trouble with city authorities who questioned the safety of the towers. Rodia proudly reassured critics that his filigreed lacework of chicken wire, steel rods and cemented bathroom tiles would withstand any earthquake. Sam was also plagued by curiosity seekers who asked him the same questions over and over and who resented his refusal to allow them to take his photograph. He no longer seemed pleased to see friends from the Temple Bethel Pentecostal Church on Washington Avenue or to provide them with bed sheets to cover newly baptized converts. The days of drinking "Dago Red" in the gazebo of his garden lay behind.

In 1954, at the age of eighty-one, Rodia tired of his project, deeded the towers to Louis Sauceda, gave away his furniture and household effects, and left Los Angeles for the northern California town of Martinez. Publicity and public bickering over whether the towers were structurally sound left him so embittered that he never returned to Los Angeles. Rodia, who died in 1965, apparently felt misunderstood and rejected by the society for which he had performed a labor of love. For four years, during which time the towers were left unattended, the white sea shells that ringed Rodia's "boat of Marco Polo" were smashed by vandals. Many of the plates that the old man had imbedded in his structures were broken in a ridiculous search to find rumored hidden treasure. . . .

Rodia's towers were ultimately declared a monument to be protected by the Los Angeles Cultural Heritage Board.

Andrew F. Rolle, *The Immigrant Upraised* (Norman: University of Oklahoma Press, 1968), 285–287.

Introducing the
Cut-Rate Drug Store
DAVID E. ALBERT

The cut-rate drug store may or may not be one of California's contributions to civilization. For Los Angeles, at least, David

A Time of Catastrophe

E. Albert, benefiting from observation of the method in a cigar-selling chain, opened the first such store. An immigrant from Russia, a bellhop at the Del Monte near Monterey, and then a tobacco salesman, he found his real niche in the drug business. His memoirs are cast as a long letter to his grandson.

At that time, there was only one drug chain outfit here. It occupied the best and most expensive locations in the business district. All drug stores were getting full retail price for everything. On special advertised sales days, you could buy a dollar item, like a well-known mouth wash, at the very low(!) reduced price of 97 cents. All this is leading up to one memorable Monday morning when I made my regular call on The Brothers.

The older one of the two was on deck and he said to me, "You are too smart to be a tobacco peddler all your life. Why don't you come in with us and you will be a partner, in business for yourself." . . . I told him how appreciative I was of his confidence in me and that I would like nothing better than to be associated with him, but not in the tobacco business, thank you.

"What business do you want to go into?" he asked.

"The drug business," I replied.

"Oh," he said. "I didn't know you were a druggist."

I then explained to him that I was not but, from a study of the drug industry, I had decided that the retail drug field was very sick and needed a shot of The Brothers' methods to revive it. I gave him a summary of conditions in the industry as I had observed them.

Next morning I stopped again at The Brothers for my daily order and was greeted with a "Hello, there. I got a drug store for you. Come with me and I'll show you." He took me to a location next to a very busy market. It was a store in an old building in the old section of Los Angeles. When I looked at it my heart sank. This store was about 14 feet front by 70 deep. The rear 50 feet was a near-beer and corned-beef joint. The front 20 feet had a cigar stand on one side and a malted milk stand on the other. . . . The Chief must have seen the bafflement and disappointment on my face. . . .

I told him I had no money to invest and he said, "We don't need your money, we have plenty. You can draw the same weekly salary you did on your salesman job and you will have a half interest in this store. . . ."

The orthodox drug store of those days was a sort of hush-hush business. Every bit of merchandise was under glass. To get at it you had to open glass showcases. All the wall fixtures were cabinets with glass doors, which had to be opened to serve a customer with a tube of toothpaste or a tin of aspirin, and then closed again. Drug store windows of that time looked like narrow display cases, about eighteen inches deep, and the displays were mostly on the order of cardboard lithographs in colors, depicting girls with "toothy" smiles holding a toothbrush or a tube of toothpaste, or whatever product it was intended to show. . . .

When the workmen were finished with the installation of our "cloak and suit" window, the Chief and I, with hammer and saw, made our own interior fixtures. These were merely shelving against the walls on each side and counters in front of them. . . . We didn't even stain the boards. . . .

In the meantime, I had engaged one druggist. We needed only one registered pharmacist because our hours were from 9 a.m. to 6 p.m. and we were closed on Sundays. I also hired two salesgirls. The prevailing wages for that type of help in those days in department and syndicate stores was about $12.00 per week. I started them at $18.00 and thought I was a philanthropist. The Chief reprimanded me, and suggested our minimum for salesgirls should be $22.00 per week, plus commissions on profitable merchandise, to be paid monthly.

But back again to our wonderful show windows. We made wooden steps, starting from the bottom to the top of the windows, and we put real merchandise in our displays, not cardboard picture cutouts, not empty dummies, but the real goods. If it was a popular brand of toothpaste, or face cream, or proprietary medicine, or mouth wash, we put in not two or three of each, or a dozen of each, but we piled in a gross or two . . . always giving the impression of heavy stocks, of lots of merchandise and indicating that we were doing a big business. This is exactly the effect it had on the public. There was always a big crowd around our windows, on the sidewalk and in the fifteen-foot long lobby. No one ever saw cloak and suit windows used to display drug store merchandise before nor the big price tags on each item.

The prices! They were stunning, astounding, unheard of and unbelievable. Every standard, advertised and popular item known to every man or woman who ever entered a drug store, was here in sight at a cut price of 21 per cent. Every item for which the buying public had paid a dollar for years, was to be had for 79 cents; every 50 cent item was 39 cents and every 25 cent item was 19 cents, and all other items in proportion.

Inside the store, there were massive displays on the counters, and the shelves were bulging with more merchandise, all in open displays that you could see with your eyes and touch with your hands. Many, indeed, felt it necessary to touch these goods, examine the labels and so on, to make sure they weren't phony or fake at those prices.

We unveiled our windows at 10 a.m. and by noon we had to call in two police officers to keep people in line. Of course, it took knowledge of the psychology of the buying public, coupled with vision and confidence, for which I give my associates full credit. They had had more experience than I, but I was learning fast. . . .

We do not claim that it took any master-minding to launch this enterprise. . . . It looked so easy that The Brothers opened three or four more stores on their own account—in which I had no financial interest—and they were equally successful. Being by that time more familiar with drug buying, I did a supply job for their other stores. . . .

At the end of the first year, the operations of this one store showed a clear net profit of nearly $50,000, and half of it was mine, more money than I had ever had in my life. . . .

The Brothers came to me one day and in a few words advised me that, inasmuch as I was doing a swell job for their other stores in which I had no stake, they had decided to make me a partner in the entire operation.

Little did I realize what lay before me. There was an ominous cloud hanging over us which was soon to break into a raging storm. After all, we were the little fellows and when the drug industry came awake to what we were doing we had huge aggregations of capital to fight.

Executives from wholesale houses and the one or two old line outmoded chain stores, with their gestapo-like investigators, watched our operations personally. They visited our stores, saw the crowds of customers, saw our cash registers get hot from constant ringing and, strangely enough, stood around waiting for us to go broke. They were sure of this. They insisted that what we were doing couldn't be done, but we grew stronger as time went by. At last, they realized we were prospering and decided on drastic methods to throttle us. Suddenly, without warning, our sources of supply began to dry up. The grapevine had got busy.

This underground spread the message in all directions, to wholesalers, jobbers, manufacturers and manufacturers' agents, that no one must sell to The Brothers. Trade journals condemned us. We were devils with horns. Everybody in the trade hated us, but the buying public loved us.

It was my job to see that our stores had merchandise. I canvassed every small jobber and sub-jobber in the country, to whom our large volume buying and ready cash really meant something. These were sources of supply which were too far from the battleground on the West Coast. They did not belong to monopolistic associations and, therefore, did not care to whom they sold as long as it was for cash.

We had to pay double freight charges. We paid high prices, and it took a lot of doing, but there was still enough profit in the drug business. We greatly increased and enlarged our promotions of sundry merchandise, . . . which we could buy in open markets. . . . We continued to open other stores out of earnings. . . .

To combat this combination of wholesalers and manufacturers arrayed against us, I got up a fine assembly of private label products. I bought mineral oil, cod liver oil, open formula antiseptics and mouth washes in bulk. I was buying 5-grain aspirin tablets in ten million lots. All these I bottled under our own labels, which we registered in the U.S. Patent Office . . . and sold at a much lower price than the advertised brands. We were making great inroads on these latter. Customers began to ask for preparations by our own coined names. . . .

I decided to go east and see all the manufacturers, not for the purpose of buying anything from them, but to sell them something. I wanted to sell them The Brothers. I wanted them to know at first hand, and not from hearsay, what we were doing and why. . . . I wanted to tell them that their practice of interfering with free com-

merce was economically unsound and would be productive of undesirable results eventually. . . .

I picked the best-known pharmaceutical firm on which to call first.
. . . There was no trouble about getting an interview. . . . The adverse
publicity we had been given by the trade journals had sufficiently
aroused everybody's curiosity to see me, horns, tail, and all. . . .

The vice-president in charge of sales . . . looked at me with about
the same degree of cordiality as I had evinced for the fat lice which I
had ejected from the seams of my clothes when I was a young boy in
Russia. . . .

I wanted at first to arouse his attention by deliberately making him
angry. . . .

Me.: "Mr. V.P., do you know the viscosity of your mineral oil?"

V.P.: "This is a question our laboratory technicians can answer
better than I can."

Me: "Do you happen to know the specific gravity of your mineral
oil?"

V.P.: "The answer is the same."

Me.: "Do you know your source of supply of your mineral oil?"

V.P.: "That is within the province of our purchasing department to
answer."

Me: "I am not a chemist but I can tell you that the viscosity and
specific gravity of your mineral oil is such and such, and you buy it
from the Standard Oil Company. I am buying the same oil from the
same company. I probably pay a little more than you do per barrel. I
am bottling it myself. I give the specifications on my label and, as I
can't use your trade name, I label it 'Universal Mineral Oil.' You demand a dollar a pint for your oil from the consumer. I sell mine for 49
cents a pint, and make a very good profit. The same is true of your
cod liver oil at $1.25 a pint. I import the same quality, bottle it and sell
it for 69 cents a pint.

"You enjoy a big distribution of your toothpaste at 50 cents a
tube," I continued. "I sell as good a toothpaste twice the size of yours
at 29 cents a tube and give our clerks 5 cents commission on each
tube. Of course, they sell three times the quantity of our private label
toothpaste, as against yours. Five-grain aspirin is, after all, just five-
grain aspirin under any label so long as it is U.S.P. and, at 19 cents for

a bottle of 100 tablets, we have practically killed the demand in our stores for your aspirin at 75 cents per hundred. How long do you think this can go on without a marked effect on the sale of your products? We have no patent on our type of drug store operation. Already drug stores like ours are opening up all over the country and it should give you something to think about."

. . . When all the evidence was in and I was wobbly from exhaustion, he gave me the verdict. . . .

"From now on you are on our list of direct buyers. You may draw your supplies from our warehouses in your city and, if you will give me a list of manufacturers on whom you intend to call, I will give you letters of recommendation to each one and will do all I can to help you open accounts with them. . . ."

The V.P. was good as his word. Today, the regular price of their mineral oil is 59 cents the pint instead of a dollar, and their other products have been proportionately reduced. Other manufacturers followed suit, resulting in savings of millions of dollars to the buying public all over the country. . . .

Five years after my retirement in 1940, the Chief also decided to retire and our company was bought by a large national drug chain at an attractive figure; our employees who held shares in our firm received about 10 times the amount they originally paid for them.

David E. Albert, *Dear Grandson* (Philadelphia: Olivier, Maney & Co., 1950), 154–177.

Building Boulder Dam
FRANK WATERS

The first gigantic project of the Bureau of Reclamation was the harnessing of the Colorado. Truly multipurpose, this program involved flood control, stabilization that improved navigation, several times as much power as generated at Niagara Falls, and capture for domestic, industrial, and agricultural use of a vast amount of water that was wasting into the Gulf of California.

Supplementary works such as the All-American Canal, the Metropolitan Aqueduct, and the transmission lines would run the cost to an astronomical sum. The keystone of the entire undertaking would be Boulder Dam, contracted and constructed in the depth of the depression. In its magnitude and in its circumstances the task was forbidding. Its completion was the great forward step of the decade.

A consortium of western builders did the job. They gambled that the Colorado would not have a near-record flood before the diversion tunnels were opened and the dam interposed. Their managerial and engineering skills met all challenges, and their cost estimate proved accurate. Los Angeles and environs provided a major impetus and placed a firm order for electric power sufficient to underwrite the financing.

Boulder Dam is the Great Pyramid of the American Desert, the Ninth Symphony of our day, and the key to the future of the whole Colorado River basin.

No other single piece of man's handiwork in this vast wilderness hinterland has epitomized so well during its construction all the strange and complex ramifications of our American Way—all its democratic faults and virtues, the political interlocking of local, state and federal governments, the meshed and rival economies of public and private enterprise, the conflicting needs of urban, agrarian and industrial groups. Finished, it stands in its desert gorge like a fabulous, unearthly dream. A visual symphony written in steel and concrete —the terms of our mathematical and machine-age culture—it is inexpressibly beautiful of line and texture, magnificently original, strong, simple and majestic as the greatest works of art of all time and all peoples, and as eloquently expressive of our own as anything ever achieved. Yet wholly utilitarian and built to endure, it is the greatest single work yet undertaken to control a natural resource dominating an area of nearly a quarter million square miles.

Boulder Dam, the biggest dam on the face of the earth and the first major work in the Colorado River Project. Already the blue chips were down. The United States Reclamation Service had finished the specifications. Government lawyers had condemned 150,000 acres above the site. The secretary of the interior had planned the route of the little construction railway running from Las Vegas, Nevada, and on July 7, 1930, the traditional silver spike had been driven.

It was now nearly eight months later, and in two days bids for the construction of the dam were due. Yet no one knew if there was a man or company in the country big enough to ask for the job.

No one but a small group of men in the St. Francis Hospital, San Francisco. They were gathered about the deathbed of an old man of seventy-two. A muffled knock on the door broke the silence. Into the room came a younger man of forty-eight wheeling a strange contraption. The eyes of the old man lighted up as it was placed beside his bed. It was a scale model of Boulder Dam. The younger man had made it just as he was to construct it fullsize later. He knew it. All the others felt it in his voice as carefully now he went over its every detail. At last he was finished. For a moment there was silence. The old man on his deathbed waved his hand in approval.

"One last thing," another spoke up. "What'll we add to the cost for profit?"

"Profit? Twenty-five per cent! Tidy up the estimates and get the bid in."

"Right!" Quietly the men shook hands and left. W. H. Wattis sank back content into his pillows.

Wattis and his brother, E. O. Wattis, were Mormons and contractors. They helped build the old Colorado Midland Railroad through the mountains from Colorado Springs to Ogden. They founded the Utah Construction Company which built the Hetch Hetchy dam that impounded water for San Francisco. They determined to build Boulder Dam.

Because the project was too big for the Utah Construction Company, they appealed to Morrison-Knudsen Company of Boise, Idaho. Frank T. Crowe of this firm had just finished building the Guernsey dam in Wyoming and the Deadwood dam in Idaho. Prior to that he had been general superintendent of the United States Bureau of Reclamation and in 1919 had made one of its first rough estimates of Boulder Dam.

Boulder Dam, they figured, would cost from 40 to 50 million dollars. At least 5 million working capital would be needed to start it. The Wattis brothers offered to put up one million and Morrison-Knudsen agreed to chip in $500,000. Together they approached the J. F. Shea Company of Los Angeles, which agreed to ante $500,000 and suggested that the Pacific Bridge Company of Portland be called in. This company was famous for its underwater work. It had driven the piers for the first bridge across the Willamette River at Portland, and working with Shea had laid the water line across the Mokelumne River. It too agreed to put up $500,000. The fifth company picked was MacDonald and Kahn of San Francisco, builders of the Mark Hopkins Hotel of San Francisco and other large office buildings. They added another million dollars, but the total was still $1,500,000 short.

Meanwhile another group of men had become just as interested in the biggest dam in the world. W. D. Bechtel of San Francisco and his son S. D. Bechtel, Henry J. Kaiser of Oakland, and John Dearborn of Warren Brothers in Cambridge, Massachusetts. Obviously the two groups could not be rivals; the dam was bigger than both of them. Accordingly the Bechtel, Kaiser and Warren firms teamed up with the preceding five firms as the sixth company, adding the remaining $1,500,000 split between them.

For the new combine Kahn suggested the appropriate name of Six Companies, Inc., called after the famous tribunal to which the Chinese tongs in San Francisco had submitted their differences in preference to warring with hatchet men.

Approved in Wattis's hospital room, the last preliminaries were then agreed upon. Next night Crowe made up the final bid of $48,890,000 from three separate estimates. The following day, March 4, 1931, it was submitted.

There were only two other bids on Boulder Dam. One was $5,000,000 and the other $10,000,000 higher; the Six Companies' bid was taken. Wattis and Morrison had hit the nail on the head in figuring the minimum working capital that would be required. For the surety companies, which first demanded $8,000,000 for underwriting the job, now agreed to accept the $5,000,000. And on April 20, 1931, the Six Companies received notice to begin. . . .

Swirling westward out of Grand Cañon and gorged with its cutting silt, the Colorado makes a sudden turn due southward to form the boundary between Nevada and Arizona. Its channel is a series of deep, steep-walled cañons. Not far below the turn is Black Cañon, dark and forbidding as its name. The stark black and purple rock cliffs on each side rise a quarter of a mile high from the water's edge. Beyond these the tawny desert stretches away unbroken save for a rough dirt road straggling toward the west. It terminates near the upper end of a cañon at a break in the rock wall. Here a tent is pitched. In it is camped an old couple making coffee for some booted visitors whose motorboat is drawn up on the sandy bank near by.

This was Black Cañon when I saw it early in 1930. We got into the boat and pushed off. Instantly the current grabbed it and sucked us deep into the cañon. On the westward wall appeared some white bench marks one of the engineers had painted the week before.

"How far above the waterline do you figure the lowest one is?" he asked as we rushed past.

"Five feet! Twenty-five!"

It was the 100-foot mark, and it designated the site of Boulder Dam. Immediately we turned about and began to fight our way back upriver. The trip down from the landing had taken about ten minutes. The return trip took almost a half hour.

Nothing, certainly no statistics, could portray as did this short, casual ride the entire problem of building Boulder Dam: bridging sheer, unbroken cañon walls so high that they distorted perspective; the lack of even a sand bar for initial footage; the desolate desert on each side without housing or transportation facilities; and greatest of all, the terrific current of the silt-choked river. . . .

Soon "5,000 men in a 4,000 foot cañon" were at work on the dam. First the sheer rock walls had to be cleared over 2,000 feet high of loose rock and boulders. Work began at the top as "cherry pickers" carrying jack-hammer drills and dynamite were let down with ropes. This was one of the most dangerous tasks of the entire job. A miscalculation of distance and a man would drop a quarter mile into the river; of time, and he would be blown to bits by his own charge of explosive. Above these was the terrific desert heat reflected from the narrow cañon walls, which dehydrated the hard-laboring workers quickly. They were soon required to carry water bags at all times—and to empty them regularly. Owing to all such precautionary measures taken, only 110 men were killed during the entire construction.

Once the walls were cleaned and safe to work under, a spectacular job began. The bottom of the river bed had to be bared as well, and kept clean and dry during the whole period of construction—and bedrock lay under the rushing red river and 200 feet of sand. To divert the river, two by-pass tunnels were cut through the cañon walls on each side. Each of the four was a mile long, 50 feet in diameter and lined with 3 feet of concrete. These alone required 1,200 men one year to build, riding air-drill carriages into the tunnels and blasting their way with dynamite.

Work progressed at tremendous speed, day and night, without cessation. At the end of the first year Six Companies was in the clear. The men were ahead of schedule, had got back all their working capital and made a million dollars in profits.

On November 13, 1932, the by-pass tunnels were done. The Colorado began flowing through the cliffs, forsaking the channel it had been cutting for perhaps 15,000,000 years.

One midnight, soon after, I stood on the bed of the river. The vast chasm seemed a slit through earth and time alike. The rank smell of Mesozoic ooze and primeval muck filled the air. Thousands of pale lights, like newly lit stars, shone on the heights of the cliffs. Down below grunted and growled prehistoric monsters—great brute dinosaurs with massive bellies, with long necks like the brontosaurus, and with armored hides thick as those of the stegosaurus. They were steam shovels and cranes feeding on the muck, a ton at a gulp. In a steady file other monsters rumbled down, stopping just long enough to shift gears while their bodies were filled with a single avalanche, then racing backward without turning around. From the walls above shot beams of searchlights, playing over this vast subterranean arena. They revealed puny pygmies scurrying like ants from wall to wall; mahouts, naked to the waist, riding the heads of their mounts, standing with one foot on the running board and peering over the tops of the cabs while driving with one hand. and all this incessant, monstrous activity took place in silence, in jungle heat, and as if in the crepuscular darkness of a world taking shape before the dawn of man.

Meanwhile the largest concrete-mixing plant in the world had been built high on the Nevada wall. Its daily output was equivalent to a stream of concrete 20 feet wide, nearly 1 foot deep and 1 mile long, and it was to flow steadily for 2½ years. On June 6, 1933, it began flowing: replacing nearly 6,500,000 cubic yards of excavated rock and sand with 3,250,000 cubic yards of concrete—more than the United States Bureau of Reclamation had used in the past quarter of a century. Into it dipped the first steel bucket, scooping up 16 tons. Swiftly it was carried across the gorge on cables and then let down to dump its contents in the frames. Pouring had begun.

At first the structure looked little like a dam; more like a vast jumble of wooden boxes filled with concrete. There was reason for such a design. Had the dam been built solid, 125 years would have been required for it to cool by itself, and under the great stresses of expansion it would have cracked and split apart. Hence to cool it an ammonia refrigerator plant was built. From it 662 miles of tubing were run between and through these immense blocks, carrying water just above freezing to maintain the rate of cooling at the right temperature.

Swiftly these water-cooled boxes heaped higher across the gorge. The wooden frames were removed. There it stood: a huge, rough, pyramidal block of concrete 660 feet thick at the bottom and 45 feet thick at the top, 1,282 feet long at its crest between the canon walls, and 727 feet high—over half again as high as Washington Monument. But still honeycombed with narrow passages, galleries and ducts. One walked through the base of the dam, the length of three city blocks, or rode a small elevator to its crest, the height of a 60-story skyscraper. A labyrinth of cold passages; the dark interior of a great pyramid; the heart of a stone mountain; the depths of a mine—it was all of these. Then the tubing was removed, the corridors were pumped full of concrete, and the dam was sealed to resist the 45,000-pound-per-square-foot water pressure on its base.

Inside both the Nevada and Arizona walls of the cañon the diversion works were now finished. . . . Finally at the bottom of the dam was built the world's largest powerhouse to date. U-shaped, each of its two wings was a city block long and high as a 20-story building. In it were to be installed two generators of 40,000 kilovolt-ampere capacity—as large as any in the world—and fifteen of 82,500 kilovolt-ampere capacity, run by two small turbines of 55,000 horsepower and fifteen large turbines of 115,000 horsepower each. From here across the desert to Los Angeles, 250 miles away, began to march the great steel Martian towers carrying high-voltage transmission lines to supply 3,000,000 people with power.

In May, 1935, one year ahead of schedule, Boulder Dam was completed. An unequaled engineering achievement, it had been constructed in exactly 4 years and 354 days.

The by-pass tunnels were now plugged, and the Colorado began backing up against the dam. In March, 1936, the government took over Boulder, and on September 11th, President Franklin D. Roosevelt pushed a golden key starting the first generator. It was not too soon. Hitler was preparing to march through Europe, beginning World War II. The United States was to become involved, and the West Coast to need every ounce of power available for building bombers, tanks, guns and ships. Hence Boulder's ultimate capacity of 1,835,000 horsepower, originally planned to be reached in forty years, was to be attained in five in order to meet the national emergency.

Frank Waters, *The Colorado* (New York: Rinehart, 1946), 337–350.

Raymond Chandler's Los Angeles
PHILIP DURHAM

Undoubtedly most readers of Raymond Chandler are intent on coming through the maze with Philip Marlowe and discovering who done it. His detective stories also are acclaimed as extraordinarily vivid capsule descriptions of Los Angeles as it was in the thirties, forties, and fifties. "No one in our time,"

Raymond Chandler's Los Angeles

according to Christopher Isherwood, better captures "the personality and feeling of the city." In his biography of Chandler, Philip Durham discusses this portraiture by Marlowe as recorded by Chandler.

When Raymond Chandler had originally gone to Los Angeles to live he had thought of the city as an exciting place, and when he began to write about it in 1933 it was still full of interest and the challenge of humanity. Through the years the detective-hero Philip Marlow—by seeing beyond the brightly colored façade and by going down the mean streets in the rear—had brought Los Angeles to the attention of the world. Perhaps it was only Marlowe's city but it had reality. . . .

A few years ago a story was told of an English girl arriving in Los Angeles for the first time. She was picked up at the railway station by her host who drove her through downtown Los Angeles on the way to his home in Westwood Village. The English girl made no comment as she observed the civic buildings and the streets filled with more automobiles than the sidewalks were with pedestrians. But suddenly she shouted, "Wilshire Boulevard!" The host, unable to account for so much enthusiasm over Wilshire, looked to the girl for an explanation. Wilshire, the visitor said, was one of the most frequently traveled streets in Raymond Chandler's stories, and now that she was on it she was oriented and was at home in the city. . . .

When Raymond Chandler deserted Los Angeles for a small beach town in 1946, it was the signal for Philip Marlowe to turn against the big city that had once been so challenging. In *The Little Sister* (1949) he was to grumble his way west on Sunset Boulevard while being swallowed up by "race-track drivers who were pushing their mounts hard to get nowhere and do nothing." As drivers honked at him, yelled at him, and cut in on him, he began talking to himself: "I used to like this town. A long time ago. There were trees along Wilshire Boulevard. Beverly Hills was a country town. Westwood was bare hills and lots offering at eleven hundred dollars and no takers. Hollywood was a bunch of frame houses on the interurban line. Los Angeles was just a big dry sunny place with ugly homes and no style, but good-hearted and peaceful." But now the homey attractiveness had gone, having given way to pansy decorators, Lesbian dress designers, riffraff of a "big hard-boiled city with no more personality than a paper cup"—a city without the "individual bony structure" a real city must have.

In the old days Marlowe had driven along that same Sunset Boulevard on a "crisp morning with just enough snap in the air to make life seem simple and sweet." On the way back down the coast from Malibu, he had driven on a highway washed clean by the rain; on his left were low rolling hills of yellow-white sand terraced with pink moss"; on his right the gulls were wheeling and swooping over something in the surf. Marlowe was on his way into the city to do his bit for the betterment of society, and willingly. . . .

As Marlowe moved back and forth across the city, its suburbs, and adjacent towns, his reaction to each area depended largely on his relationship to, or feeling about, a section of humanity. The fact that the hero appeared really to care about the people and their plights, to be sensitive to each little detail of their lives and surrounding, provided an intimacy between the reader and the city.

On the eastern edge of Los Angeles was Pasadena where, during the early years of the twentieth century, there came the retired couples from the middle west to build a "wealthy close-mouthed provincial town." A house typical of the kind they lived in was the one in the Oak Knoll section, "a big solid cool-looking house with burgundy brick walls, a terra cotta tile roof, and a white stone trim." The front downstairs windows were leaded, and the upstairs windows were of the "cottage type and had a lot of rococo imitation stonework trimming around them." From the house "a half acre or so of fine green lawn drifted in a gentle slope down to the street, passing on the way an enormous deodar around which it flowed like a cool green tide around a rock." Marlowe, always one to note the kinds of flowers and the trees that went with a house and its inhabitants, pointed out three white acacias "that were worth seeing." It was a nice cool day for Pasadena, in that pre-smog era, but there "was a heavy scent of summer on the morning and everything that grew was perfectly still in the breathless air. . . ."

Immediately to the east of Pasadena, in Chandler's day, began the orange-grove country. From the highway one saw the "fat straight rows of orange trees spin by." Even at night in a heavy rain, the "drenched darkness" could not hide the "flawless lines of the orange trees wheeling away like endless spokes into the night."

Continuing along the highway with Marlowe, one traveled the long slope south of San Dimas, over the ridge, and down into Pomona—the ultimate end of the fog belt, "and the beginning of that semi-desert region where the sun is as light and dry as old sherry in the morning, as hot as a blast furnace at noon, and drops like an angry brick at nightfall." Only a few miles beyond Pomona was Ontario where Marlowe turned north in order to travel along Euclid and its "five miles of the finest grevillea trees in the world. . . ."

Coming out of his office onto Sunset Boulevard, Marlowe was on one of the city's oldest and longest thoroughfairs. In the old days Sunset had been a wagon road that started down at the pueblo and wandered gently west by northwest along the "solid, uneven, comfortable line of the foothills" for twenty-two miles to the sea. Today, following the same route, the detective headed west, curved through the Strip, drove by the antique shop, the "windows full of point lace and ancient pewter," the nightclubs, a "drive-in lunch which somehow didn't belong," speeded up a bit along the "cool quiet of Beverly Hills where the bridle path divides the boulevard," noticed the University on his left as he went by, soon skirted the huge green polo field, and a few minutes later turned right into the foothills.

In the foothills along Sunset Boulevard were thousands of homes or mansions in which the rich lived, one of Marlowe's most formidable antagonists. With a few exceptions—old General Sternwood or the tough, gutty movie queen Mavis Weld—the rich symbolized much of the city's evil. They cut themselves off from the people by living behind twelve-foot walls with a "special brand of sunshine, very quiet, put up in noiseproof containers just for the upper classes." If the outsider could get inside he could see two or more late-model Buicks, one or two limousines, and at least one canary-yellow convertible looking about "as inconspicuous as a privy on a front lawn."

It if were the Grayle estate, one would look beyond the parking space to a sunken garden with a fountain at each of the four corners. The entrance would be barred by a wrought-iron gate with a flying Cupid in the middle. There would be a pool with stone water lilies in it and a big stone bullfrog sitting on one of the leaves. Off to one side there would be a wild garden with a sundial in the corner near an angle of wall that was built to look like a ruin. The house would not be much—smaller than Buckingham Palace and with fewer windows than the Chrysler Building. . . .

On another day Marlowe went into the old, lost, shabby area of Bunker Hill, to deal with the poor and lonely. The day here was just as depressing as the one with the rich, but the private eye was more sympathetic and less cynical. In Bunker Hill there remained a few signs to show that it was once the choice residential part of Los Angeles, mainly the old Gothic mansions with full corner bay windows with spindle turrets. And rising from Hill Street there still operated the funny little funicular railway called Angels Flight on which the old people rode up the steep embankment, people too worn out to climb the steps carrying their bread and potatoes. The old mansions were shabby apartment houses, on whose front porches old men sat staring at nothing, "old men with faces like lost battles." From out of these dilapidated mansions came "women who should be young but have faces like stale beer. . . ."

Whether Chandler was pleased with his city or disgusted with it, he never failed to portray it with a detailed kind of descriptive intimacy. In the spring there were those clear, bright "summer mornings," when the hills were green and the snow could be seen on the high mountains. In the autumn a Santa Ana wind came down off the desert through the mountain passes, making the skin itch, the nerves jump, and the inside of the nostrils feel tight and drawn. In summer Marlowe frequently noticed "a touch of that peculiar tomcat smell that eucalyptus trees give off in warm weather." The mornings were all "blue and gold" with the birds in the ornamental trees "crazy with song after the rain." At evening the detective looked up from the city streets as "darkness prowls slowly on the hills."

Philip Durham, *Down These Mean Streets a Man Must Go: Raymond Chandler's Knight* (Chapel Hill: University of North Carolina Press, 1963), 49–59.

The White Wing as Artist
MATT WEINSTOCK

*Matt Weinstock was a most unpretentious columnist, which
may be part of the explanation of the warm memories of him
that persist. Leaving world affairs and national crises to others,
he made his beat the local scene, beginning on the street hard
by the office of the* Daily News.

When old timers get together and cry in their beer over the days that
used to be in Los Angeles, they invariably think of Morris Schlocker,
though many of them don't know him by name.

Morris Schlocker painted no picture, designed no bridge, founded
no memorial. He was, in fact, only a street sweeper. But in his way, he
was an artist.

Schlocker was no ordinary man with a broom, giving whatever
street he was assigned a lick and a promise. Cleanliness and crafts-
manship and civic pride were inborn in him. An immaculate gutter
was his badge of honor.

When he went to work for the city in 1912 he was given a tryout at
the Plaza, the sleepy square near the civic center where Los Angeles
had its origin. He was provided with a broom and a scraper, a dust-
pan type of receptacle on wheels. It was small but adequate, for Los
Angeles was cleaner then despite the presence of an occasional horse.

Schlocker made good immediately and was given a beat on Broadway. His inherent neatness and willingness to work hard to achieve it
won him attention by his superiors and he remained on this busy
thoroughfare for twelve years. But Broadway was in a sense his apprenticeship, during which he was developing a technique and a personality.

His real opportunity came in 1924, when he was transferred to
Spring Street—first from First Street to Third Street, later from First to
Seventh. To the ordinary sweeper, one street is like another—always

337

dirty and needing cleaning. To Schlocker, Spring Street soon became home grounds. Whereas Broadway, with its big stores and theaters and teeming crowds represented the throbbing pulse of downtown Los Angeles, Spring Street, one block away, represented nostalgia and gayety and achievement with its financial section and restaurants and old attorneys who had grown up with the city.

By this time, Schlocker's scraper had been replaced by a wheelcart, a garbage can type of receptacle mounted on high, thin "wagon wheels," with two smaller rollers in front to keep it balanced.

Schlocker's cart looked like the carts all the hand sweepers in the city pushed in front of them in their work, but it wasn't. His cart was named Betsy and she was a very special girl indeed, sometimes frivolous, sometimes affectionate, sometimes frankly mischievous.

With seeming unconcern, Schlocker would push her hard away from him while he did a little broom work in a gutter. He would look up, discover she had rolled farther than he intended, and shaking his head like a disapproving parent, call softly, "Whoa, Betsy, whoa!" The cart, as if heeding him, would come to an instant halt. Other times when he pushed her, Betsy would understand that he meant for her to stop fifteen feet away and turn slightly to the right or left so she would be in a position to receive the refuse he was sweeping toward her. On such occasions, she executed a dainty swirl in turning right or left, then stopped.

Betsy's best trick was to roll away from Schlocker at his touch, stop momentarily fifteen feet away and then, as he called, in gentle, affectionate reproof, "Whoa, Baby, come back now!" to roll back contritely to where he stood, patiently waiting.

It was like a triumphal adagio performance and the office girls in the stock exchange section peeked out of their windows to see it. Motorists, traffic policemen and passers-by gawked in amazement and in time dubbed Schlocker the unofficial Mayor of Spring Street.

All sorts of rumors gained currency. One was that Schlocker controlled his cart with a hidden magnet. Another was that he had some sort of concealed gyroscope in it. Another was that he had placed some counter-balancing springs under it. Schlocker merely smiled enigmatically. It was a secret between him and Betsy. After all, does a magician reveal his tricks? Does an artist impart, even to his admirers, what took him years of constant work to achieve?

Schlocker was a street sweeper. He performed his job well, so well he was rated one of the best white wings on the force. But his affair with Betsy was a personal matter, not to be discussed in public. It was an added fillip to his work. Perhaps Joseph Conrad explained it when he wrote, in *The Mirror of the Sea:* "Efficiency of a practically flawless kind may be reached naturally in the struggle for bread. But there is something beyond—a higher point, a subtle and unmistakeable touch of love and pride beyond mere skill; almost an inspiration which gives to all work that finish which is almost art—which *is* art."

Schlocker remained on the Spring Street beat for twenty years, until he was honorably retired by the city in 1944 at the age of seventy, after thirty-two years as a street sweeper. He lives quietly on South Olive Street but occasionally he goes downtown to see old friends in the bureau of street maintenance. Even without his visored cap and white coat, he is recognized by strangers as the former Mayor of Spring Street. If they get him talking, he will contrast conditions when he patrolled downtown L.A. with conditions today and express disapproval of the present. He used to get up at 4 a.m. and go to work and he received $100 a month. I wouldn't do the job now for $100 a day," he says.

As for the secret of Betsy, he explains simply, "I just kept her oiled and I took good care of her and I knew what she would do."

Matt Weinstock, *Muscatel at Noon* (New York: William Morrow and Company, 1951), 120–123.

What Makes Sammy Run?
BUDD SCHULBERG

For another decade at least Hollywood would be the acknowl-edged center of the motion picture industry. It should not be assumed that Budd Schulberg's novel is a complete history of this remarkable art and business. His Sammy, nevertheless, is

typecast to represent the uninhibited ruthless self-aggrandiz-
ing that this volatile and amorphous industry invited. The se-
lection here presented consists of the first few and the last two
pages of the novel, introducing this embodiment of ambition
and soliloquizing on his career. It should be read with aware-
ness that the intervening pages carry the character develop-
ment and the illumination of this part of the history of Los
Angeles.

The first time I saw him he couldn't have been much more than sixteen years old, a little ferret of a kid, sharp and quick. Sammy Glick.
Used to run copy for me. Always ran. Always looked thirsty.

"Good morning, Mr. Manheim," he said to me the first time we
met, "I'm the new office boy, but I ain't going to be an office boy
long."

"Don't say ain't," I said, "or you'll be an office boy forever."

"Thanks, Mr. Manheim," he said, "that's why I took this job, so I
can be around writers and learn all about grammar and how to act
right."

Nine out of ten times I wouldn't have even looked up, but there
was something about the kid's voice that got me. It must have been
charged with a couple of thousand volts.

"So you're a pretty smart little feller," I said.

"Oh, I keep my ears and eyes open," he said.

"You don't do a bad job with your mouth either," I said.

"I wondered if newspapermen always wisecrack the way they do in
the movies," he said.

"Get the hell out of here," I answered.

He raced out, too quickly, a little ferret. Smart kid, I thought. Smart
little yid. He made me uneasy. That sharp, neat, eager little face. I
watched the thin, wiry body dart around the corner in high gear. It
made me uncomfortable. I guess I've always been afraid of people
who can be agile without grace.

The boss told me Sammy was getting a three-week tryout. But
Sammy did more running around that office in those three weeks than

Paavo Nurmi did in his whole career. Every time I handed him a page of copy, he ran off with it as if his life depended on it. I can still see Sammy racing between the desks, his tie flying, wild-eyed, desperate.

After the second trip he would come back to me panting, like a frantic puppy retrieving a ball. I never saw a guy work so hard for twelve bucks a week in my life. You had to hand it to him. He might not have been the most lovable little child in the world, but you knew he must have something. I used to stop right in the middle of a sentence and watch him go.

"Hey, kid, take it easy."

That was like cautioning Niagara to fall more slowly.

"You said rush, Mr. Manheim."

"I didn't ask you to drop dead on us."

"I don't drop dead very easy, Mr. Manheim."

"Like your job, Sammy?"

"It's a damn good job—this year."

"What do you mean—this year?"

"If I still have it next year, it'll stink."

He looked so tense and serious I almost laughed in his face. I liked him. Maybe he was a little too fresh, but he was quite a boy.

"I'll keep my ear to the ground for you, kid. Maybe in a couple of years I'll have a chance to slip you in as a cub reporter."

That was the first time he ever scared me. Here I was going out of my way to be nice to him and he answered me with a look that was almost contemptuous.

"Thanks, Mr. Manheim," he said, "but don't do me any favors. I know this newspaper racket. Couple of years at cub reporter? Twenty bucks. Then another stretch as district man. Thirty-five. And finally you're a great big reporter and get forty-five for the rest of your life. No, thanks."

I just stood there looking at him, staggered. Then . . .

"Hey, boy!" And he's off again, breaking the indoor record for the hundred-yard dash.

Well, I guess he knew what he was doing. The world was a race to Sammy. He was running against time. Sometimes I used to sit at the bar at Bleeck's, stare at the reflection in my highball glass and say, "Al, I don't give a goddam if you never move your ass off this seat

341

again. If you never write another line. I default. If it's a race, you can scratch my name right now. Al Manheim does not choose to run."
And then it would start running through my head: What makes Sammy run? *What makes Sammy run?* I would take another drink, and ask one of the bartenders:

"Say, Henry, what makes Sammy run?"

"What the hell are you talking about, Al?"

"I'm talking about Sammy Glick, that's who I'm talking about. What makes Sammy run?"

"You're drunk, Al. Your teeth are swimming."

"Goddam it, don't try to get out of it! That's an important question. Now, Henry, as man to man, What makes Sammy run?"

Henry wiped his sweaty forehead with his sleeve. "Jesus, Al, how the hell should I know?"

"But I've got to know. (I was yelling by this time.) Don't you see, but it's the answer to everything."

But Henry didn't seem to see.

"Mr. Manheim, you're nuts," he said sympathetically.

"It's driving me nuts," I said. "I guess it's something for Karl Marx or Einstein or a Big Brain; it's too deep for me."

"For Chri'sake, Al," Henry pleaded, "you better have another drink."

I guess I took Henry's advice, because this time I got back to the office with an awful load on. I had to bat out my column on what seemed like six typewriters at the same time. And strangely enough that's how I had my first run in with Sammy Glick.

Next morning a tornado twisted through the office. It began in the office of O'Brien the managing editor and it headed straight for the desk of the drama editor, which was me.

"Why in hell don't you look what you're doing, Manheim?" O'Brien yelled.

The best I could do on the spur of the moment was:

"What's eating you?"

"Nothing's eating me," he screamed. "But I know what's eating you—maggots—in your brain. Maybe you didn't read your column over before you filed it last night?"

As a matter of fact I hadn't even been able to *see* my column. And at best I was always on the Milquetoast side. So I simply asked meekly, "Why, was something wrong with it?"

"Nothing much," he sneered in that terrible voice managing editors always manage to cultivate. "Just one slight omission. You left all the verbs out of the last paragraph. If it hadn't been for that kid Sammy Glick it would have run the way you wrote it."

"What's Sammy Glick got to do with it?" I demanded, getting sore.

"Everything," said the managing editor. "He read it on his way down to the desk. . . ."

"Glick read it?" I shouted.

"Shut up," he said. "He read it on his way to the desk, and when he saw that last paragraph he sat right down and re-wrote it himself. And damn well, too."

"That's fine," I said. "He's a great kid. I'll have to thank him."

"I thanked him in the only language he understands," the editor said, "with a pair for the Sharkey-Carnera scrap. And in *your name.*"

A few minutes later I came face to face with that good samaritan Samuel Glick himself.

"Nice work, Sammy," I said.

"Oh, that's all right, old man," he said.

It was the first time he had ever called me anything but Mr. Manheim.

"Listen, wise guy," I said, "if you found something wrong with my stuff, why didn't you come and tell me? You always know where I am."

"Sure I did," he said, "but I didn't think we had time."

"But you just had time to show it to the managing editor first," I said. "Smart boy."

"Gee, Mr. Manheim," he said, "I'm sorry. I just wanted to help you."

"You helped me," I said. "The way Flit helps flies."

Ever since Sammy started working four or five months back he had done a fairly conscientious job of sucking around me. He hardly ever let a day go by without telling me how much he liked my column, and of course I'd be flattered and give him pointers here and there on his grammar, or what to read, or sometimes I'd slip him a couple of tickets for a show and we'd talk it over and I'd find myself listening to him give out with Glick on the Theater. Anyway, he had played me for a good thing and always treated me with as much respect as a fresh kid like that could, but right here, as I watched that face, I actually felt I could see it change. The city editor hadn't hung a medal on his chest but he had put a glint in Sammy's eye. You could see he was so gaga about his success that he didn't care how sore I was. That was the beginning.

"Don't you think it's dangerous to drop so many verbs?" he asked. "You might hit somebody down below."

"Listen," I said, "tell me one thing. How the hell can you read when you're running so fast?"

"That's how I learned to read," he cracked, "while I was running so fast. Errands."

It made me sore. He was probably right. Somebody called him and he spun around and started running. What makes Sammy run? I pondered, looking after him, what makes Sammy run?

***

He walked me to the door and then he left the door open and walked me to my car. He could not bear to be alone. He put one foot on the running board and leaned through the window.

"Before you go," he said, "forget everything I told you tonight. I don't know what the hell got into me for a minute. What the hell have I got to kick about? I feel great. I got the world by the balls. Keep in touch with me, sweetheart."

There in the silence I could almost hear the motor in him beginning to pick up speed again.

As I drove off I saw him standing outside on his palatial stone steps, under his giant eucalyptus trees, looking out over his hundred yards of landscaping that terraced down to the wall that surrounded his property. He was a lonely little figure in the shadows of Glickfair, the terrible little conqueror, the poor little guy, staring after my car as it drove out through the main gates, waiting for Sheik to bring the girls and the laughter.

I drove back slowly, heavy with the exhaustion I always felt after

344

being with Sammy too long. I thought of him wandering alone through all his brightly lit rooms. Not only tonight, but all the nights of his life. No matter where he would ever be, at banquets, at gala house parties, in crowded night clubs, in big poker games, at intimate dinners, he would still be wandering alone through all his brightly lit rooms. He would still have to send out frantic S.O.S.s to Sheik, that virile eunuch: Help! Help! I'm lonely. I'm nervous. I'm friendless. I'm desperate. Bring girls, bring Scotch, bring laughs. Bring a pause in the day's occupation, the quick sponge for the sweaty marathoner, the recreational pause that is brief and vulgar and titillating and quickly forgotten, like a dirty joke.

I thought how, unconsciously, I had been waiting for justice suddenly to rise up and smite him in all its vengeance, secretly hoping to be around when Sammy got what was coming to him; only I had expected something conclusive and fatal and now I realized that *what was coming to him* was not a sudden pay-off but a process, a disease he had caught in the epidemic that swept over his birthplace like plague; a cancer that was slowly eating him away, the symptoms developing and intensifying: success, loneliness, fear. Fear of all the bright young men, the newer, fresher Sammy Glicks that would spring up to harass him, to threaten him and finally to overtake him.

I thought of all the things I might have told him. You never had the first idea of give-and-take, the social intercourse. It had to be all you, all the way. You had to make individualism the most frightening ism of all. You act as if the world is just a blindfold free-for-all. Only the first time you get it in the belly you holler brotherhood. But you can't have your brothers and eat them too. You're alone, pal, all alone. That's the way you wanted it, that's the way you learned it. Sing it, Sammy, sing it deep and sad, all alone and feeling blue, all alone in crowded theaters, company conventions, all alone with twenty of Gladys' girls tying themselves into lewd knots for you. All alone in sickness and in health, for better or for worse, with power and with Harringtons till death parts you from your only friend, your worst enemy, yourself.

But what good are words when not even experience will regenerate. It was too late to hate him or change him. Sammy's will had stiffened. It had been free for an instant at birth, poised bird-free in the doctor's hand that moment in the beginning before it began to be formed to the life-molds, the terrible hungers of body and brain, the imposed wants, the traditional oppressions and persecutions, until at last Sammy's will had curled in on itself, like an ingrown hair festering, spreading infection.

Now Sammy's career meteored through my mind in all its destructive brilliance, his blitzkrieg against his fellow men. My mind skipped from conquest to conquest, like the scrapbook on his exploits I had been keeping ever since that memorable birthday party at the Algonquin. It was a terrifying and wonderful document, the record of where Sammy ran, and if you looked behind the picture and between the lines you might even discover what made him run. And some day I would like to see it published, as a blueprint of a way of life that was paying dividends in America in the first half of the twentieth century.

Budd Schulberg, *What Makes Sammy Run?* (New York: Random House, 1941), 3–8, 301–303.

The First Freeway
H. MARSHALL GOODWIN, JR.

To a later generation the Pasadena Freeway was anathema for its curvature, its narrowness, its lack of turnouts, its awkward on and off ramps, its underengineered speed. But to the generation of drivers for which it was for some time California's only freeway, it was a delight and a thrill and a thing of beauty. H. Marshall Goodwin, Jr., is the prime authority on California's freeways.

The Pasadena Freeway, connecting downtown Los Angeles with Pasadena, follows the bed of an intermittent stream which flows from the San Gabriel Mountains to the Los Angeles River and long served

Adam C. Vroman

Arroyo Seco before the freeway

as a natural transportation route. In 1895 T. D. Allen of Pasadena surveyed the Arroyo for a highway and two years later Horace Dobbins purchased a right of way from Green Street in Pasadena to Raymond Hill along what is now Arroyo Parkway, with the intention of building a bicycle speedway, but never completed it.

In 1911 the Los Angeles City Park Commission proposed the

purchase of the Arroyo for a park and planned a winding road through it which would connect with Elysian Park via a bridge across the Los Angeles River. No action was taken until 1922 when Los Angeles and South Pasadena began the purchase of park land in the Arroyo. At the same time the Los Angeles City Traffic Commission completed plans for major highway routes in the county including a dual roadway separated by the Arroyo Seco channel. Angelenos approved the proposal in 1924, preliminary surveys were made in 1928 and the project authorized in 1931 as a way "to aid the unemployment situation."

Once work commenced several businessmen from Highland Park, including C. R. and Jesse W. Ivers of Ivers' Department Store, petitioned the Los Angeles City Council to stop the work. They argued that the lands had been acquired for a park by local assessment and thus could not be used for a highway, but in reality they feared the diversion of traffic from North Figueroa to the new road would reduce their business. When the city stopped construction, letters poured in supporting the project as a way to provide jobs, and work soon recommenced.

The delay proved beneficial; by September, 1934, the Board of Park Commissioners had expanded their proposal to include a 40-foot pleasure roadway separated by a 6-foot planted divider from a 24-foot frontage road. The revised plan stimulated renewed opposition from Highland Park's business community which favored a narrow road with frequent intersections to prevent any traffic diversion.

Early in 1934 J. W. C. Hinshaw of the Pasadena Realty Board, anxious to see that the new road benefited Pasadena, proposed that the highway continue eastward from the Arroyo through South Pasadena and then northward along South Broadway (now Arroyo Parkway) rather than northward through the Arroyo to Devil's Gate Dam. He showed the plan to Pasadena City Councilman William Dunkerly, Pasadena Planning Commissioner Harrison R. Baker, and Los Angeles County Planner Earl J. Esse. By presenting Hinshaw's plan as the Los Angeles Regional Planning Commission's proposal, they persuaded the South Pasadena City Council and the Pasadena Board of Directors to adopt on the same day resolutions in favor of the route "provided it is constructed in such a manner as to make possible a

reasonably continuous flow of traffic into and out of the cities of
South Pasadena, Pasadena and Los Angeles on a right-of-way of major width (100' or over 76' of free roadway) and provided further that
the city of South Pasadena (or Pasadena) be not called upon to finance
the project from any special assessment district and provided also that
all details and engineering treatment shall be subject to approval of
the City Council."

The cities then began applying for county, state and federal funds.
In January, 1935, the State Emergency Relief Administration appro-
priated $20,000 for surveying the route and in March the County
Planning Commission applied for $1,324,000 in federal aid for the
Arroyo Seco Freeway.

In the meantime Pasadena's freeway boosters approached Assemblywoman Eleanor Miller who then introduced a measure to include
the proposed route in the state highway system. Because of opposition to increasing the mileage in the state highway system the measure
failed to obtain approval until Los Angeles County agreed to assume
responsibility for the Pear Blossom Highway from Palmdale to Cajon
Pass.

The State Division of Highways then developed plans for a depressed, limited access highway through South Pasadena. Many
residents who had expected the route to pass through the community
on the existing Grevelia Street quickly organized in opposition. They
objected on the grounds that the proposed freeway "would definitely
segregate a substantial part of the City of South Pasadena from the
remainder thereof, destroy valuable property and property rights,
create many dead end streets and would be of no local benefit or advantage. . . ." Opponents referred to the route as the "big ditch," an
"eyesore," and a "menace to life and limb." The controversy became
heated and was injected into the 1936 South Pasadena City Council
election which the supporters of the parkway won.

On March 24, 1936, the Pasadena Board of Directors passed a
resolution favoring the proposed route as "the safest and shortest between Pasadena and Los Angeles . . . [and] the least expensive." A
few days later the Los Angeles City Council approved the parkway
plan, and on April 4, the state Highway Commission sanctioned the
route.

A Time of Catastrophe

Despite various obstructionist tactics by freeway opponents, the State Division of Highways awarded the first contract for the Parkway on March 9, 1938, and ground breaking ceremonies took place on March 21 at Arroyo Drive and Sterling Place. Tournament of Roses Queen Cheryl Walker moved the first shovel of dirt on the freeway when she pulled the lever on a steam shovel. Hinshaw, Baker, Dunkerly, Assemblywoman Miller and others received recognition for their efforts in support of the project.

On January 4, 1939, the first section of the Arroyo Seco Parkway opened, providing "a rather tantalizing glimpse of what the road will be like when completed." The Los Angeles *Times* declared, "it demonstrates what a six-lane center divided highway can do to promote speed with safety."

In compliance with their promises to local citizens, the Division of Highways and the park departments of the three cities jointly undertook beautification of the freeway with the WPA providing the funds. The object was to beautify and at the same time prevent erosion. Some ten thousand plants were used in the landscaping of the entire freeway, among which were ceanothus or wild lilac, fremontia with its golden yellow blossoms, catalina cherry and the holly leafed cherry, both used for their rich green foliage, matilija poppies, California holly, barberry, wild roses, purple and blue sage, bush snapdragons, manzanita, fuchsias, elderberry, and others, all planned to provide coloring for the parkway throughout the year. To reduce headlight glare, shrubs were planted in the center island. As a result of the landscaping, the Pasadena Freeway was long considered the most beautiful in the state.

Because of the rapid rate of speed permitted by the freeway, a fence was erected to prevent pedestrians and animals from attempting to cross the parkway. To provide additional safety, sodium vapor lights were installed at all exits and entrances.

On July 20, 1940, a 3.7 mile section from Avenue 40 to Orange Grove Avenue was opened to traffic, and on November 1 an additional mile was opened. On November 11, the 4.7 mile route through Highland Park was formally dedicated. Then on December 20, the remaining section was opened to traffic.

The completed Parkway cost $5,048,487.46, not including the

original expenditures of South Pasadena and Los Angeles for the park lands or the money spent by Los Angeles in grading the roadway prior to its inclusion in the state highway system. The WPA provided $1,394,364.73 of the total; the Public Works Administration supplied $472,315.63. South Pasadena appropriated $644.16 out of city funds and $77,049.40 from its share of the ¼-cent gasoline tax; Los Angeles spent $113,584.14 of its city funds and $40,000 of the ¼-cent gasoline tax funds, and the state provided $2,614,547.72 from the 1½ cent gasoline tax funds. Of this amount, $1,588,300 went for bridges, and $4-5,000 for right-of-way costs, an extremely low figure because much of the parkway went through city park lands.

In dedicating the parkway Governor Culbert L. Olson wondered what sort of road Mr. T. D. Allen had in mind when he made the first survey 45 years earlier. The repeated delays in construction had proven beneficial, for with the passage of time the road had expanded from a narrow winding park road to a six lane, divided highway with complete elimination of grade crossings. In his dedication speech Los Angeles Mayor Fletcher Bowron referred to "the traffic dead, the thousands whose lives have been snuffed out on congested highways, streets and grade crossings . . . , the solemn and mute evidence that we must have the greater safety of freeways and broad divided highways without grade crossings."

Basically the freeway was a victory for the developers. By providing faster access, the parkway encouraged residential and business expansion in Pasadena and South Pasadena. Instead of hurting business along by-passed North Figueroa, the Freeway, by removing through traffic made the stores more accessible, and the Ivers later reported increased sales. Subsequent studies of freeways have shown that depressed freeways like the "big gulch" through South Pasadena create less noise and visual pollution and have a more favorable impact on property values than do elevated or at grade routes. Despite design inadequacies—narrow lanes and dividers, sharp curves, lack of shoulders and lack of merging space at on ramps—the Pasadena Freeway has long had one of the lowest accident and death rates of any freeway in the state, fully justifying Mayor Bowron's comment.

An amplified account is found in H. Marshall Goodwin, Jr., "From Dry Gulch to Freeway," *Southern California Quarterly*, 47 (1965), 73–102.

A Time of Catastrophe

"When I Return from a Trip to the East"

CAREY MCWILLIAMS

*In the thirties and forties Carey McWilliams was the foremost
commentator on California, its achievements and its problems.
Then, to the relief of the reactionaries, he left to take over the
editorship of the* Nation, *without, however, ceasing to be a
Californian. The reverie that follows closes his* Southern California Country: An Island on the Land, *which was published
in 1946 but accumulates impressions built up in the twenties
and thirties as well as the war years.*

As one of the newcomers who came to Southern California in the
great influx of the 'twenties, I have become as devoted to the region as
a native son. When I first arrived in Los Angeles, I hated, as so many
other people have hated, the big, sprawling, deformed character of the
place. I loathed the crowds of dull and stupid people that milled
around the downtown sections dawdling and staring, poking and
pointing, like villagers visiting a city for the first time. I found nothing
about Los Angeles to like and a great many things to detest. Without
benefit of chart or guide or compass, I had to discover the charm of
the city and the region for myself (one reason, doubtless, why I like it
so much today). In those days, I did not know California, and, not
knowing California, it was impossible for me to sense the strategic importance of Southern California, its difference, its uniqueness. More
important, perhaps, was the fact that I had then seen little of America
and hence could not appreciate this curious western amalgam of all
America, of all the states, of all the peoples and cultures of America.

My feeling about this weirdly inflated village in which I had come
to make my home (haunted by memories of a boyhood spent in the
beautiful mountain parks, the timber-line country, of northwestern

Max Yavno

Migrant labor camp at Ventura Boulevard and Moorpark

Colorado), suddenly changed after I had lived in Los Angeles for seven long years of exile. I have never been able to discover any apparent reason for this swift and startling conversion, but I do associate it with a particular occasion. I had spent an extremely active evening in Hollywood and had been deposited toward morning, by some kind soul, in a room at the Biltmore Hotel. Emerging next day from the hotel into the painfully bright sunlight, I started the rocky pilgrimage through Pershing Square to my office in a state of miserable decrepitude. In front of the hotel newsboys were shouting the headlines of the hour: an awful trunk-murder had just been committed; the district attorney had been indicted for bribery; Aimee Semple McPherson had once again stood the town on its ear by some spectacular caper; a University of Southern California football star had been caught robbing a bank; a love-mart had been discovered in the Los Feliz Hills; a motion-picture producer had just wired the Egyptian government a fancy offer for permission to illuminate the pyramids to advertise a forthcoming production; and, in the intervals between these revelations, there was news about another prophet, fresh from the desert, who had predicted the doom of the city, a prediction for

353

which I was morbidly grateful. In the center of the park, a little self-conscious of my evening clothes, I stopped to watch a typical Pershing Square divertissement: an aged and frowsy blonde, skirts held high above her knees, cheered by a crowd of grimacing and leering old goats, was singing a gospel hymn as she danced gaily around the fountain. Then it suddenly occurred to me that, in all the world, there neither was nor would there ever be another place like this City of the Angels. Here the American people were erupting, like lava from a volcano; here, indeed, was the place for me—a ringside seat at the circus.

Nowadays when I return from a trip to the East, I can hardly wait for the train to make the final swift descent through Cajon Pass to the floor of the plain at San Bernardino where it begins to pick up speed for the race through the orange groves to Los Angeles. Long before the descent has been made, I begin to dream of Point Sal—a favorite spot for me—where one looks down from a height of a thousand feet to the curving shoreline that stretches toward Point Conception and westward out across the forever cool blue waters of the Pacific. I dream, too, of beautiful Santa Ynez Valley and of the hills back of Santa Barbara; of Smiley Heights in Redlands and San Timeteo Canyon; of the spread of lights from Mt. Wilson on a clear cold December night or the harbor lights of San Pedro seen from the Palos Verdes Hills; of the many times I have made the drive from San Jacinto over the hills to Palm Springs, I think of a thousand and one afternoons and evenings spent in exploring Southern California from "the foothills to the sea"; from Bunker Hill and Central Avenue in Los Angeles through the foothill homes and gardens from Montecito to San Diego. I close my eyes and I see Olive Hill, crowned with the perennially charming house that Frank Lloyd Wright did for Aline Barnsdale, with its colonnade of eucalyptus trees, and the pugnacious signs, around the rim of the hill, in which Miss Barnsdale warns the British to free India as she once warned California to free Tom Mooney.

But most often I think of the first crisp days of fall after the "hot spell" which invariably ends the long summer. I think of the view from a favorite arroyo in the late afternoon, the east slope still bathed in sunlight, the far slope already full of dark shade and lengthening shadows. A cool breeze, as always at this time of day, gently ascends the arroyo. At the head of the arroyo, one can look back across the plains, out over miles of homes and trees, and hear the faraway hum of traffic on the highways and see the golden light filtering through the mist-laden air. And then I think of the sudden descent of night, when the sun catapults into the ocean—of the "sad red splendid sunsets," of the starless night skies, mysteriously vivid and luminous, full of a quick and radiant animation; and I think of the soft-silent muffled slap of the waters along the coast, far above Malibu, on nights of thick wet fog and spray and the smell of the sea. . . .

It is then that I realize that this land deserves something better, in the way of inhabitants, than the swamis, the realtors, the motion-picture tycoons, the fakirs, the fat widows, the nondescript clerks, the bewildered ex-farmers, the corrupt pension-plan schemers, the tight-fisted "empire builders," and all the other curious migratory creatures who have flocked here from the far corners of the earth. For this strip of coast, this tiny region, seems to be looking westward across the Pacific, waiting for the future that one can somehow sense, and feel, and see. Here America will build its great city of the Pacific, the most fantastic city in the world. For the American West coast, as Mr. Grafton has said, "is destined to be the world's metropolis." Nowadays one can see that the Spaniards were right after all and that we, in our technological conceit, were wrong. For with its planes whirling out over the Pacific toward China and India, California is, indeed, "at the right hand of the Indies," and, in Southern California, it does have a Terrestrial Paradise, an Amazon Island, abounding in gold and certainly "infested with many griffins."

Carey McWilliams, *Southern California Country* (New York: Duell, Sloan & Pearce, 1946), 375–378.

Adjusting to War and to Peace

"In eastern cities gasoline rationing was just an incident. The average Angeleno, however, was as dependent on his car as an Eskimo on his snowshoes, the full gasoline tank was a more compelling symbol than the full dinner pail had ever been, and to qualify for a B ration book was an achievement supreme."

J. C.

Max Yavno

Hollywood premiere

9

Adjusting to War and to Peace

World War II, at a conservative estimate, was the biggest thing that ever happened to Los Angeles. Earlier wars had seemed remote: the war for independence from Spain, fought in southern Mexico; the war against Mexico, with only incidental fighting here; the Civil War, on which Angelenos were divided; World War I, with all the fighting far away. But in World War II the people of Los Angeles were directly involved.

When the fighting erupted in Europe in 1939, Los Angeles received large orders for planes and other military gear. After Pearl Harbor plunged the United States into two wars, in Europe and in the Pacific, munitions orders were tremendously increased. The federal government paid for much of the expansion in plants, footing two-thirds of the bill in the aircraft industry and nine-tenths of the cost in shipbuilding. By 1945 aircraft contracts in Los Angeles had passed 7 billion dollars and for ships 1.7 billion.

Employment in the county's aircraft plants rose from 20,000 in 1939 to 243,000 in 1943. Los Angeles had the workers to fit these new assignments. In addition, many prospective war workers poured in and many women joined the work force.

With ordinary construction activities curtailed or shut down, and rationing required for food and gasoline, Los Angeles was pinched and crowded. People queued up for groceries and everything else. They played what came to be understood as the charade of civil defense, engaging in airplane spotting and a long range of other actions, down to the stockpiling of sand and water to counter incendiary bombs. Defense plants were camouflaged and barrage balloons floated reassuringly. Los Angeles was so much involved in munition-making that it was a logical target for attack, but very shortly the strategists were aware that Japan had neither the intention nor the capacity to strike. Meanwhile, the people of Los Angeles, though less wedded to their automobiles than would be true a generation later, made do with severely rationed driving so that tires would last for the duration.

The selections that follow touch some of these points. California's first freeway would certainly have been copied and recopied except for the military priorities. Pacifism and respect for certain guaranteed freedoms were set aside for the duration. Women and minorities had access to new roles, but local opinion sanctioned the much-to-be regretted incarceration of everyone of Japanese descent. Soldiers and sailors on leave are principally blamed for the zoot-suit riots, yet the weight of the police came down heavily against the pachucos.

Los Angeles emerged from the war years with tremendous capital available for investment. It emerged with vastly improved technical skills and a much larger work force. Partly because of an accumulation of shortages in housing, schools, telephones, sewers, automobiles, and much else, substitutes for war work materialized. There were new problems—smog of course heading the list. Opportunities arose to strengthen the economy by greatly expanding familiar enterprises, such as the garment industry and the care and entertaining of tourists. To the astonishment of many professional planners an array of new industries and undertakings made spectacular contribution to postwar prosperity.

Johnny Got His Gun
DALTON TRUMBO

In the thirties and forties Dalton Trumbo was a highly successful screenwriter. Summoned before the House Un-American Activities Committee, he was an uncooperative witness for whom there was no protection in the First Amendment. He went to jail and as one of the Hollywood Ten was blacklisted. Sub rosa, he kept on writing for much less compensation than he formerly earned. One of his scripts, smug-

*gled in under an assumed name, won an Oscar. Eventually the
climate changed somewhat, the blacklist lost some of its rigor,
and he was permitted to come out into the open and pick up
the fragments of his career.*

*Johnny Got His Gun, written in 1938 and published just as
World War II broke out, may well be the most powerful anti-
war novel ever written. Its narrator is the ultimate among dis-
abled veterans. At one point he says, "If I had arms I could
move I could push I could widen the walls I could throw back
the covers I could get into a bigger place. If I had a voice I
could yell and holler for help I could talk to myself and be
some company to myself. If I had legs I could run I could get
away I could come out into the open where there is air where
there is room where I'm not in a hole and smothering. But I
haven't got any of these things I can't do any of these things
so you must help me."*

*Written with a tension that never relaxes, Johnny Got His
Gun is impossible to scissor. The preface that Trumbo wrote
for the ninth printing twenty years later is a life history of the
book, and more. Between the lines it casts light on Los
Angeles, the author's home, in the period of the almost unan-
imously supported World War II and gives some hints on
stresses in the postwar years.*

World War I began like a summer festival—all billowing skirts and
golden epaulets. Millions upon millions cheered from the sidewalks
while plumed imperial highnesses, serenities, field marshals and other
such fools paraded through the capital cities of Europe at the head of
their shining legions.

It was a season of generosity; a time for boasts, bands, poems,
songs, innocent prayers. It was an August made palpitant and breathless by the pre-nuptial nights of young gentlemen-officers and the
girls they left permanently behind them. One of the Highland regi-
ments went over the top in its first battle behind forty kilted bag-
pipers, skirling away for all they were worth—at machine guns.

Nine million corpses later, when the bands stopped and the serenities started running, the wail of bagpipes would never again sound
quite the same. It was the last of the romantic wars; and *Johnny Got*

His Gun was probably the last novel written about it before an entirely different affair called World War II got under way.

The book has a weird political history. Written in 1938 when pacifism was anathema to the American left and most of the center, it went to the printers in the spring of 1939 and was published on September third—ten days after the Nazi-Soviet pact, two days after the start of World War II.

Shortly thereafter, on the recommendation of Mr. Joseph Wharton Lippincott (who felt it would stimulate sales), serial rights were sold to *The Daily Worker* of New York City. For months thereafter the book was a rally point for the left.

After Pearl Harbor its subject matter seemed as inappropriate to the times as the shriek of bagpipes. Mr. Paul Blanshard, speaking of army censorship in *The Right to Read* (1955) says, "A few pro-Axis foreign-language magazines had been banned, as well as three books, including Dalton Trumbo's *Johnny Get Your Gun*, produced during the period of the Hitler-Stalin pact."

Since Mr. Blanshard fell into what I hope was unconscious error both as to the period of the book's "production" and the title under which it was "produced," I can't place too much faith in his story of its suppression. Certainly I was not informed of it; I received a number of letters from service men overseas who had read it through Army libraries; and, in 1945, I myself ran across a copy in Okinawa while fighting was still in progress.

If, however, it had been banned and I had known about it, I doubt that I should have protested very loudly. There are times when it may be needful for certain private rights to give way to the requirements of a larger public good. I know that's a dangerous thought, and I shouldn't wish to carry it too far, but World War II was *not* a romantic war.

As the conflict deepened, and *Johnny* went out of print altogether, its unavailability became a civil liberties issue with the extreme American right. Peace organizations and "Mothers" groups from all over the country showered me with fiercely sympathetic letters denouncing Jews, Communists, New Dealers and international bankers, who had suppressed my novel to intimidate millions of true Americans who demanded an immediate negotiated peace.

Johnny Got His Gun

My correspondents, a number of whom used elegant stationery and sported tidewater addresses, maintained a network of communications that extended to the detention camps of pro-Nazi internees. They pushed the price of the book above six dollars for a used copy, which displeased me for a number of reasons, one of them fiscal. They proposed a national rally for peace-now, with me as cheer leader; they promised (and delivered) a letter campaign to pressure the publisher for a fresh edition.

Nothing could have convinced me so quickly that *Johnny* was exactly the sort of book that shouldn't be reprinted until the war was at an end. The publishers agreed. At the insistence of friends who felt my correspondents' efforts could adversely affect the war effort, I foolishly reported their activities to the F.B.I. But when a beautifully matched pair of investigators arrived at my house, their interest lay not in the letters but in me. I have the feeling that it still does, and it serves me right.

After 1945, those two or three new editions which appeared found favor with the general left, and apparently were completely ignored by everybody else, including all those passionate war-time mothers. It was out of print again during the Korean War, at which time I purchased the plates rather than have them sold to the Government for conversion into munitions. And there the story ends, or begins.

Reading it once more after so many years, I've had to resist a nervous itch to touch it up here, to change it there, to clarify, correct, elaborate, cut. After all, the book is twenty years younger than I, and I have changed so much, and it hasn't. Or has it?

Is it possible for anything to resist change, even a mere commodity that can be bought, buried, banned, damned, praised, or ignored for all the wrong reasons? Probably not. *Johnny* held a different meaning for three different wars. Its present meaning is what each reader conceives it to be, and each reader is gloriously different from every other reader, and each is also changing.

I've let it remain as it was to see what it is.

Dalton Trumbo

Los Angeles, March 25, 1959

Dalton Trumbo, *Johnny Got His Gun* (9th printing; New York: Lyle Stuart, 1950), 1–7.

The Great Los Angeles Air Raid

Jack Smith

For months the Pearl Harbor syndrome had strong hold on the people of Los Angeles. Amateur strategists all, we reasoned that the Japanese bombers were to be expected any night. Psychologically we were ready for the alert when, in due course, it came, and for the brave counterattack.

The Great Los Angeles Air Raid occurred on the night of Feb. 26, 1942. It began at 2:25 A.M. when the U.S. Army announced the approach of hostile aircraft and the city's air raid warning system went into effect for the first time in World War II.

Suddenly the night was rent by sirens. Searchlights began to sweep the sky. Minutes later gun crews at emplacements along the coastline began pumping the first 1,433 rounds of ack-ack into the moonlight.

Thousands of volunteer air raid wardens tumbled from their beds and grabbed their boots and helmets. Citizens awakened to the screech of sirens and, heedless of the blackout warning, began snapping on their lights. Policemen turned to. Reporters rushed into the streets.

The din continued unabated for two hours. Finally the guns fell silent. The enemy, evidently, had been routed. Los Angeles began to taste the exhilaration of its first military victory.

The *Times* was on the streets at daylight with a dramatic account of that gaudy night: "Roaring out of a brilliant moonlit western sky, foreign aircraft flying both in large formation and singly flew over Southern California early today and drew heavy barrages of anti-aircraft fire—the first ever to sound over United States continental soil against an enemy invader."

But the second paragraph was rather a letdown: "No bombs were reported dropped." However, the account went on, "At 5 A.M. the police reported that an airplane had been shot down near 185th St.

and Vermont Ave. Details were not available. . . ." (Neither, as it turned out later, was the airplane.)

Though no bombs had been dropped, the city had not escaped its baptism of fire without casualties, including five fatalities. So many cars were dashing back and forth in the blackout that three persons were killed in automobile collisions. Two others died of heart attacks.

A radio announcer named Stokey, hurrying to get to his post in the dark, suffered a deep laceration over his right eye when he ran into an awning. A policeman named Larker, seeing a light on in a Hollywood store, kicked in the window and suffered a half-inch laceration on his right leg. A *Times* reporter, hurrying from his Inglewood home to the nearby police station, underestimated the height of a curbing and jolted his backbone.

The toll was particularly high among air raid wardens, who were said to have acted with valor throughout. In Pasadena a warden named Hoffman fell from a 5-foot wall while looking into a lighted apartment and fractured a leg. Another named Barber jumped a 3-foot fence in Hollywood to reach a house that had a light on and sprained his right ankle. A warden named Campbell fell down his own front stairs and broke his left arm.

There was also scattered structural damage. Several roofs were holed by ack-ack projectiles which had failed to explode in the sky, but worked fine as soon as they struck ground, demolishing a room here, a patio there, and in one case blowing out the tire of a parked automobile.

Exultation turned to outrage the next day when the secretary of the Navy said there had been no enemy planes at all. It was just a case of "jitters." The Army, being thus accused of shooting up an empty sky, was outraged. Los Angeles authorities were outraged, especially the sheriff, who had valiantly helped the FBI round up numerous Japanese nurserymen and gardeners who were supposedly caught in the act of signaling the enemy planes.

At length the secretary of war came up with a face-saving theory. There had been no enemy military planes, but it was believed there had been 15 "commercial" planes flown by "enemy agents." Though no one believed this romantic fancy, most agreed with the secretary of war that "It is better to be too alert than not alert enough."

No . . . , there was no aircraft carrier. There were no Zeros. There were no bombs. There was no raid.

But it was a glorious night, if only a dream.

Los Angeles *Times*, April 8, 1975.

Why It Happened Here
ROGER DANIELS

The wartime removal of all persons of Japanese ancestry from the West Coast was a federal action sanctioned by highest authority; the President gave prior consent and the Supreme Court, after reviewing in Hirabayashi *and again in* Korematsu *and* Endo, *left standing. As Roger Daniels details, public opinion in Los Angeles was vigorously fanned. Mayor Fletcher Bowron, Governor Culbert Olson, and Attorney General Earl Warren pushed hard for removal. Of these dignitaries, only Mayor Bowron publicly recanted. Los Angeles contributed the largest contingent of the men, women, and children concentrated in these camps.*

Writing in *Harper's* Magazine in September, 1945, constitutional law specialist Eugene V. Rostow unhesitatingly characterized the evacuation and incarceration of the West Coast Japanese as "our worst wartime mistake." Two decades of scholarship have merely rung the changes on that indictment. Professor A. Russell Buchanan writing on World War II in the authoritative New American Nation Series argued that it was "the most widespread disregard of personal rights since . . . slavery." Most educated persons today would echo these sentiments; in addition, most Americans seem to have changed their

366

basic attitudes toward the Japanese. This dramatic change of image is perhaps best reflected in a pair of Gallup polls which asked a cross-section of Americans to characterize Japanese. In 1942, the image was negative: the five most frequently mentioned adjectives were "treacherous," "sly," "cruel," "warlike" and "hard-working." In 1961 the same question drew a quite positive set of adjectives: "hard-working" moved to the top, followed by "artistic," "intelligent" and "progressive," and a residual "sly" ranking fifth.

With this highly favorable image, in part at least a result of the magnificent and well-publicized performance of Japanese-American troops during the war plus a reaction against wartime excesses, it is almost impossible for the generations that have come to maturity since the war to comprehend how it was possible for such an undemocratic act to occur in this country under the most liberal government it had ever known. When one tries to explain to students that it was one of the most popular wartime acts, many react with stunned disbelief. . . .

To convey something of the feeling of the weeks after Pearl Harbor in Los Angeles: much of the material presented will be drawn from the pages of the Los Angeles *Times*. The result would be much the same had almost any other California newspaper been used: the *Times* was not especially prejudiced against Japanese (by 1941 California standards that is) and was more moderate than many papers. The predominant feeling that one gets from reading the press of that period is one of near hysteria. Hawaii, which had actually been attacked, was relatively calm. California, thousands of miles from the scene of operations, was nervous and trigger happy. The paranoid style in California life is not as recent as some would have us believe. A thousand movies and stories and reminiscences have recorded the solemn mood with which the nation reacted on that "day of infamy" in 1941. Yet, at Gilmore Field, the *Times* informs us, "Eighteen thousand spectators at the Hollywood Bears-Columbus Bulldogs football game . . . jumped to their feet and cheered wildly when the public address system announced that a state of war existed between Japan and the United States."

In its first editorial reaction, the *Times* announced that California was a "zone of danger": and invoked the ancient vigilante tradition of the state by calling for "alert, keen-eyed civilians [who could be] of yeoman service in cooperating with the military and . . . civilian authorities against spies, saboteurs and fifth columnists. We have thousands of Japanese here. . . . Some, perhaps many, are . . . good Americans. What the rest may be we do not know, nor can we take a chance in the light of yesterday's demonstration that treachery and double-dealing are major Japanese weapons."

Day after day, throughout December, January, February, and March, the *Times* and the rest of the California press spewed forth racial venom against the Japanese. The term "Jap," of course, was standard usage. Japanese were also "Nips," "yellow men," "mad dogs" and "yellow vermin," to name only a few of the choicer epithets. . . .

While the press was throwing fuel on the fires of racial animosity, other faggots were contributed by politicians, federal officials, and, above all, the military. The Governor of California, Culbert L. Olson, a liberal Democrat, had insisted, before Pearl Harbor, that Japanese Americans should enjoy all their rights and privileges even if war with Japan came, and correctly pointed out that equal protection under the law was a "basic tenet" of American government. But Olson's constitutional scruples were a casualty of Pearl Harbor: on December 8, the Governor told the press that he was thinking of ordering all Japanese, alien and citizen, to observe house arrest "to avoid riot and disturbance. . . ."

The Federal Department of Justice . . . announced the sealing off of the Mexican and Canadian borders to "all persons of Japanese ancestry, whether citizen or alien." Thus by December 8, 1941, that branch of the federal government particularly charged with protecting the rights of our citizens was willing to single out one ethnic group for invidious treatment. . . .

Even more damaging were the mendacious statements of Frank Knox, Roosevelt's Secretary of the Navy. On December 15, in a story that made front pages all over the country, Secretary Knox, returning from a quick inspection of the damage at Pearl Harbor, spoke of "treachery" there and insisted that much of the disaster was caused by "the most effective fifth column work that's come out of the war, except in Norway. . . ." The Japanese population of Hawaii—and indirectly all Japanese Americans—were made the scapegoats. . . .

Why It Happened Here

By mid-January [General John L. De Witt] was telling the War Department that any raid on the West Coast would be accompanied by "a violent outburst of coordinated and controlled sabotage." On January 24 he added: "The fact that nothing has happened so far is more or less ominous in that I feel that in view of the fact that we have had no sporadic attempts at sabotage there is control being exercised and when we have it it will be on a mass basis. . . ."

On January 27 De Witt met with Governor Olson of California and told Washington afterwards that "the best people in California" wanted all the Japanese out. Two days later De Witt saw Attorney General Earl Warren, a Republican who was then preparing his campaign that would defeat Olson in November. Warren, the General told Washington, was in thorough agreement with the Governor that the Japanese population should be removed from the coastal areas. . . .

On February 6, Provost Marshal General [Allen W.] Guillon and [Major Karl R.] Bendetsen rejected De Witt's California-oriented suggestions about resettlement within the state—in the words of the key Provost Marshal memorandum on the subject because it contained "too much of the spirit of Rotary" and ignored "the necessary cold-bloodedness of war. . . ."

The conflict at the Cabinet level [between the Secretary of War and the Attorney General] necessitated an appeal to the Commander-in-Chief, whose final approval would have been needed in any event. On Wednesday, February 11, 1942—the real day of infamy as far as the Constitution was concerned—Henry L. Stimson and John J. McCloy sent Franklin D. Roosevelt a brief memorandum that listed four alternatives. . . .

President Roosevelt refused to choose. After a brief telephone call the decision making power was passed to two men who had never been elected to any office. "We have *carte blanche* to do what we want as far as the President is concerned," McCloy telephoned Bendetsen at the Presidio. According to the Assistant Secretary, Roosevelt's only qualification was "Be as reasonable as you can."

Why did Roosevelt do it? . . . Roosevelt was concerned, first of all, with winning the war, and secondly with unity at home, so that he, unlike Wilson, could win the peace with the advice and consent of the Senate. He could read the congressional signs well and knew that

369

cracking down on the Japanese Americans would be popular both on Capitol Hill and with the nation at large. And the last thing he wanted was rift with the establishment Republicans such as Stimson and McCloy. So do what you think you have to do to win the war, he told the civilian spokesmen for the military. And one can imagine him on the phone in the great Oval office where so much of our history has been made, that leonine head lifting up and with the politican's charm and equivocation, saying, "Be as reasonable as you can."

From an address by Roger Daniels in a symposium in Los Angeles on the twenty-fifth anniversary of the relocation. For additional details see Roger Daniels and Spencer C. Olin, Jr., *Racism in California* (New York: The Macmillan Company, 1972), 167–176.

Impact of Relocation
S. J. OKI AND THE MINIDOKA *IRRIGATOR*

Much has been written about the experience of Los Angeles and other West Coast Japanese who were clapped into seclusion during World War II. The range extends from the formidable volumes by a team of sociologists from Berkeley to camera studies by Ansel Adams and Dorothea Lange, reminiscent testimony by those who ran the camps and some of the people who were in them, and historical novels. The following are two contemporary comments from the camps, one in correspondence, the other an editorial in a camp newspaper.

Why? Why?

Objectively, and on the whole, life in a relocation center is not unbearable. There are dust-storms and mud. Housing is inadequate, with families of six living in single rooms in many cases. Food is

Clem Albers

Los Angeles child being sent to concentration camp

below the standard set for prisoners of war. In some of the camps hospitals are at times understaffed and supplies meager, as in many ordinary communities. . . .

What is not so bearable lies much deeper than the physical make-up of a center. It is seen in the face of Mr. Yokida, 65, a Montebello farmer. It is seen in the face of Mrs. Wata, 50, a grocer's widow from Long Beach. It is seen in the face of little John Zendo, 9, son of an Oakland restaurant owner. It is seen in the face of Mary Uchido, former sophomore from UCLA and the daughter of a Little Tokyo merchant. It is seen in the face of Sus Tana, young kibei who had been an employee in a vegetable stand in Hollywood.

Their faces look bewildered as they stare at the barbed-wire fences and sentry towers that surround the camp. Their eyes ask: Why? Why? What is all this?

Kats Ento, serious-looking ex-farmer from Norwalk, has made up his mind. He says: "I am an American citizen. I was born and brought up in California. I have never been outside the United States, and I don't know Japan or what Japan stands for. But because my parents weren't considerate enough to give me blue eyes, reddish hair, and a high nose, I am here, in camp, interned without the formality of a charge, to say nothing of a trial. Does the Constitution say that only white men are created equal? Put me down as disloyal, if you will, but I'm going where I won't have to live the rest of my life on the wrong side of the tracks just because my face is yellow. Keep me in camp for the duration. I will find my future in the Orient. . . ."

Mr. Yokida, technically an enemy alien after forty years' continuous residence in California, appears tired. "For forty years I worked in central and southern California. I can remember when Los Angeles was only a small town compared to San Francisco. This country never gave me citizenship, but I never went back to Japan and I have no interests there. The evacuation has worked a hardship on me and my family, but I suppose in time of war you have to stand for a lot of hardships. . . ."

"I have a son in the army," says Mrs. Wata. "Besides, my daughter has volunteered to join the WAACS. I am an alien, and being an alien I have nothing to say about evacuation or having to live in camp, although it would have been so nice to have spent the last winter in Long Beach. It was so cold here, and the stove in my apartment never gave out enough heat. I do wish, though, that they would let my children go back to California on furloughs. They have so many friends out there, and they miss them."

John Zendo, 9, is always talking about his friends, too, says his mother. "He was a pretty popular boy in the neighborhood," she smiles reminiscently as she speaks. "He talks about them all the time, and asks me when we can go back to them. . . ."

"I keep on thinking about Los Angeles and the people I know," says Mary Uchido. My girl friend writes me and tells me all about the changes that have taken place since evacuation. How the Little Tokyo has been left unoccupied, how some of our Chinese and Korean friends are working in airplane factories, things like that. But I don't want to go back there any more, except perhaps for a visit. . . . Maybe I will try to get a domestic job or something, because I can't possibly hope to continue my education. I would join the WAACS if they would put us in an ordinary unit instead of an all-Japanese unit."

Sus Tana, 32, is a volunteer for the special Japanese-American combat team. He smiles broadly and seems jolly, but his dark eyebrows betray an uneasiness which is concealed somewhat behind his sunburned forehead. "I am a kibei and a Young Democrat. I lived and worked in Los Angeles nine years after my return from Japan. I never made over a hundred dollars a month, mostly seventy-five to eighty, and I could never save enough money to buy anything. So when evacuation came, I had nothing to lose. I do miss my friends among the Young Democrats, though. They were such a fine bunch. You forgot you were a Jap when you were with them; you were just an American fighting for the President and the New Deal. I do wish I could be back there now. Maybe I could get a defense job and do what I can. But I am glad that we are going to have a combat unit. Maybe I can show the reactionaries in California that a Japanese-American can be just as good a soldier as any American—if not better."

—as reported by S. J. Oki.

Two Trains

The train that came from Tule [with Japanese-Americans who were to be allowed to stay in the United States] met at a junction the train going to Tule [with evacuees classified as "disloyal" and to be sent to Japan]. The occupants looked at each other, but no conversation was possible. They were patterned from the same genus, skin and hair color. Many of them were Japanese-Americans. They shared typical American lives, knew the love for slang, coke and hamburgers. The Issei nursed the earth, they did their bit in the making of the United States into one of the greatest industrial nations in the world. They lived, loved, and laughed in the cosmopolitanism that is America.

But yet a Himalayan wall of psychological difference placed the groups in two tragically distinctive categories.

One group, a tragic picture of lost faith, had bowed to the desire to walk down a metropolitan street and see faces with the same structure and color; they had swayed to a longing to walk through life free of prejudiced glances. But all of them had left their lives strewn in memorable bits around the country they loved. In the rusting plow in the barn back on the Coast, in the baby willow planted on the river bank, in the carved initials on the drug store counter at Bills, in the basketball championship trophy displayed at the High with the lone Japanese name inscribed on it, in the waving apple orchard in the dip of the valley. . . .

The other group chose to go back to that drug store counter, to urge on once more the plow, to add another name to the trophy, to nurse the willow to be a stalwart bulwark. They heard and answered defiantly the challenge in every doubting look of other Americans. They chose to fight to extinguish the ugly red light of discrimination. They chose to fight until democracy was real.

—note in the *Minidoka Irrigator.*

Reproduced in Carey McWilliams, *Prejudice* (Boston: Little, Brown and Company, 1944), 211–214, 219.

One Big Assembly Line
DONALD W. DOUGLAS

Along with a multitude of other contributions to the war effort, Los Angeles was the major arsenal turning out the needed aircraft. The local share would have been even greater had the government not thought it essential to decentralize plants and contracts. Looking back at the first anniversary of Pearl Harbor, the president of one of the southern California companies tells how it was done. The essence was cooperative pooling of trade secrets, machine time, administration, and brains—all shored up by cost-plus contracts.

*For the duration, and in some instances much longer,
women held jobs long considered men's work.*

Scarcely more than a year after Japan's sneak attack on Pearl Harbor, our Commander-in-Chief will have the weapon he first demanded to heap vengeance on our Axis enemies; an armada of 60,000 warplanes. Next year, I am confident, this fleet will be augmented by 125,000 additional planes rolling in uninterrupted streams from the assembly lines of the country's aircraft factories. This will be the greatest single striking force any nation has ever assembled.

Putting this first 60,000-plane armada in the air—more than our industry had built since the Wright brothers first flew; more than all the Axis factories turned out this year—rates as one of the prodigious feats of history. It has been possible only because of the ability of free enterprise to submerge private interests in the emergency and voluntarily function as a single industry.

Let me take you backstage for a glimpse of how democracy functions when it is behind the eight ball. The presidents of eight aircraft companies located in Southern California—Consolidated, Douglas,

Lockheed, North American, Northrop, Ryan, Vega and Vultee—and frequently a spokesman for the Boeing Aircraft Company of Seattle, are seated around a big table in an office in Los Angeles. We are all rugged individualists and keen rivals. Prior to the war, we had almost nothing to do with each other, and this zealous competitive spirit swept down through the ranks of our thousands of employees.

Around the table, we discovered that the sudden plunge into all-out warfare had given us much in common. We had to black out our plants, protect them from sabotage, train women to replace thousands of our men whom the Army and Navy wanted, develop new sources of supplies, find ways of turning out planes as they had never been produced before. Working around the clock, our factories were building 64 per cent of the warplanes manufactured in this country. Straining every resource, we had managed to step up the combined industry production to 1,800 planes a month for the Army, the Navy, and for our allies.

That seemed a phenomenal output, until the President called for 185,000 planes in two years. . . . We concluded then and there that the only way to deliver this fabulous fleet on time was to pool everything we had—materials, machines, man power and know-how. We set up a corporation which we called Aircraft War Production Council, Inc., and through it we made available to each factory every engineering and aerodynamics study any of our technicians had made. Some of these were costly research jobs that represented years of work. One that I know about ran over a million dollars. For the duration, it became available to anyone in the industry at no expense. We no longer had trade secrets from one another. . . . When the dictators are finally bombed off this earth, we shall become rugged individualists and rivals again. But until then, we are an army of hundreds of thousands of aircraft workers with one aim only—victory.

The Council itself is merely the nerve center of a voluntary aircraft pool. . . . It is on the assembly lines that you see democracy at work. Since Pearl Harbor our output of planes has been stepped up tremendously. The man-hours and woman-hours on the planes have increased only half that of the plane output. This is due to industry teamwork . . . in each of the plants to work out the routine for this "borrowing over the back fence."

Before we knew it, the men in rival plants, who never knew each other before Pearl Harbor, were on first-name terms. Mike Craemer, factory manager of Vega at Burbank, was phoning Paul Buckner, factory manager of Northrop at El Segundo, 25 miles away, and saying, "Paul, we're up against it for five sets of landing-gear forgings to keep the Flying Fortress line moving. Can you lend us some?" And Buckner was answering, "Sure, Mike, send your truck over." Or Lockheed's materiel manager, Harry Taylor, was rushing 300,000 pounds of sheet metal to Vultee and Boeing in a single day to keep the hydropresses stamping.

The layman looks at a Flying Fortress and sees one sleek, stream-lined machine. An aircraft builder looks at the same Flying Fortress and sees 110,000 separate parts, welded and riveted together by thousands of men and women, most of whom never saw the inside of a bomber until less than a year ago. The 110,000 parts flow together in continuous streams, which have to join at the right moment somewhere along the assembly line. . . . If anything interrupts that flow to assembly lines, it means loss of hours or days that can never be regained. . . .

Once several much-needed planes were held on the ground for lack of cotter pins. At the North American factory a fleet of fighters were ready for shipment except for the motor-cooling fluid, which failed to arrive on time. Another plant supplied the fluid and the fighters caught a ship scheduled for a crucial battle area. The bombers with which Jimmy Doolittle and his crew lambasted Tokio were off the assembly line on schedule only because the North American factory was able to borrow some special fuel-line valves from another plant.

Almost as important is the borrowing of machine time. . . . At Northrop the hydropress that shapes the empennage parts for Flying Fortresses broke down one day. It looked like a two weeks' delay on the assembly line while the press was undergoing repair. The factory manager called other plants. North American's press was ahead of schedule, so it took over the Northrop job for the emergency. . . . Before long Consolidated was on the spot. A press quit when their assembly line critically needed wing ribs stamped for Liberator bombers. That afternoon they loaded their dies and materials into trucks, sped them to the Douglas Long Beach plant 100 miles away. Over-night, the hydropress night crew stamped enough wing ribs to keep the Liberator line moving, and the parts were back in San Diego by sunrise. That's the kind of teamwork that will crack the dictatorships.

Equally important in the Council's speed-up of plane building is the pooling of know-how. As individualists and competitors, each company has forged ahead in special fields. Consolidated developed a treatment of sheet-aluminum alloy to make it harder and stronger. Lockheed was out in front in sheet-metal forming. Control surfaces and high-altitude tests were Douglas specialties. North American had developed steel-alloy substitutes for aluminum. And so on. Since these trade secrets have been pooled, they have saved months in carrying the war to our enemies. North American, for instance, was instructed by the Army to build a special plane with wing brakes. Their designers had never worked on that type of wing flap. Vultee's had. Everything Vultee knew was delivered promptly to North American's engineers. I heard J. H. Kindelberger, North American's president, say that the Vultee know-how saved his company six months of expensive research. That was six months gained on Hitler.

Like every other industry, aircraft is facing the problem of finding substitutes, not only for alluminum alloys, rubber fittings, and other common materials, but now substitutes for substitutes. This calls for costly studies by technical brains that are too few to go around. By dividing the work and ending duplication, the industry is making its research brains go five or six times as far and fast, the sooner to outfight the Axis in the air.

Donald W. Douglas, *Los Angeles Times Magazine*, December 13, 1942, 4–6.

War on the Zoot-Suiters

JOHN D. WEAVER

A hundred years after John Bidwell, John D. Weaver, by his own account, "crossed the plains in a covered Chevrolet to homestead in the Hollywood hills." He has written informedly on such diverse subjects as Lenny Bruce, Earl Warren, the

378

War on the Zoot-Suiters

Brownsville Raid, and Los Angeles. The cruel vendetta mounted unofficially and officially in the early forties against the pachucos or zoot suiters, precursors of the Chicanos, was protested but not prevented.

"Race does not lie in the language but exclusively in the blood," wrote Adolf Hitler, and, in the summer of 1942, his Berlin radio station was happy to quote similar sentiments expressed in a report prepared by the Los Angeles County sheriff's office, setting forth the official explanation of juvenile delinquency in the Mexican-American barrios.

"The Caucasian, especially the Anglo-Saxon, when engaged in fighting, particularly among youths, resorts to fisticuffs and may at times kick each other, which is considered unsportive; but this Mexican element considers all that to be a sign of weakness, and all he knows and feels is a desire to use a knife or some lethal weapon. In other words, his desire is to kill, or at least let blood. . . . When there is added to *this inborn characteristic* that has come down through the ages, the use of liquor, then we certainly have crimes of violence" (emphasis added).

Violence, in short, was presumed to be in the liquor-heated blood of these brown-skinned youngsters whose forebears had founded the pueblo which now excluded them from so many public parks and pools, theaters, dance halls and restaurants, but not from selective service.

"We are Americans for the draft, but Mexicans for jobs and the police," young men complained.

This generation of Mexican-American Angelenos had sprung from the Depression years, when the city's Spanish-speaking shops and cafes were drifting away from the Plaza, inching south as far as Third and Fourth Streets, engulfing ten-cent stores and movie houses along the way.

"Being strangers to an urban environment," Carey McWilliams points out in *North From Mexico* (1948), "the first generation tended to respect the boundaries of the Mexican communities. But the second generation was lured far beyond these boundaries into the downtown shopping districts, to the beaches, and above all, to the 'glamor' of Hollywood. It was this generation of Mexicans, the *pachuco* generation, that first came to the general notice and attention of the Anglo-American population."

The *pachuco* adopted as his uniform the "drape-shape" or, as it was called outside the *barrios*, the "zoot-suit." To the police, inflamed by the sight of the pleated, peg-topped, high-waisted trousers and the long, loose, wide-shouldered coats, the bizarre costume identified young gangsters who, from time to time, had to be rounded up and worked over.

In August, 1942, when the body of young José Díaz was found in the vicinity of an abandoned gravel pit near Slauson and Atlantic Boulevards (a local newspaperman dubbed it "The Sleepy Lagoon"), police arrested twenty-four young Mexican-Americans, including two who had signed up with the United States Navy. On January 12, 1943, twelve of the defendants were found guilty of murder and five of assault. The evidence against them was so flimsy that their convictions were overturned by the District Court of Appeal, but not before eight of the young men had served nearly two years in San Quentin. . . .

In the meantime, while the Sleepy Lagoon youngsters were still behind bars, trouble had broken out in Venice between *pachucos* in "drapes" and some teenage Anglos reinforced by sailors spoiling for a fight. "The only thing we could do to break it up," a police officer later recalled, "was to arrest the Mexican kids." Inflammatory reports in the local press helped make an explosion inevitable.

It was sparked on the night of Thursday, June 3, 1943, after eleven sailors walking along the 1700 block of North Main Street were set upon by what they described as a gang of zoot-suiters. Next evening some two hundred sailors took over a fleet of taxicabs (how they found the cabs remains a mystery) and invaded the east side *barrios*, leaving four youths lying on blood-stained pavements. Nine sailors were arrested, but no charges were ever brought against them.

The Army and the Marine Corps joined the Navy in the following night's assault. Arms linked, the servicemen stormed the downtown streets four abreast. Civil and military authorities obligingly looked the other way, but when some young Mexican-Americans gathered on a street corner, they were promptly packed off to jail. On Sunday, June 6, sailors beat up eight *barrio* teenagers and wrecked a bar on Indiana Street. The police made forty-four arrests. All were Mexican-American and all had been badly mauled.

On Monday night, a mob of several thousand servicemen and civilians swarmed over the Central City, halting street cars and breaking into theaters, dragging *pachucos* out into the streets, stripping them naked and beating them senseless. It was a Mexican version of the Chinese Massacre of 1871, and it lost little in the translation. Local authorities, then as earlier, not only made no serious effort to stop the bloodletting, some even joined in the evening's sport. . . .

"Most of the citizens of the city have been delighted with what has been going on," beamed the *Eagle Rock Advertiser*, echoing the pueblo's vigilante past, and County Supervisor Roger Jessup might well have been draped across the Bella Union bar in the 1850's knocking back a shot of rye with Major Horace Bell when he delivered himself of the opinion, "All that is needed to end lawlessness is more of the same action."

John D. Weaver, *L.A.: El Pueblo Grande* (Los Angeles: Ward Ritchie Press, 1973), 102–105.

Smog Settles Over Los Angeles
JOHN ANSON FORD

The five supervisors who rule the seven million residents of Los Angeles County have been identified as the greatest potentates this side of the Arab states. The gentlest and most durable of them all was John Anson Ford. Here he describes the onset of smog, another Los Angeles first, and the early steps taken to deal with what, thirty or so years later, Art Seidenbaum would call "that great brown bag in the sky."

Port of Call for the Ark   Paul Conrad

On December 7, 1941, the attack on Pearl Harbor galvanized the nation into action. Los Angeles in a few short months became industrialized on a scale that the most optimistic members of the Chamber of Commerce had once assumed would take many years. Smoke, microscopic dust, nauseating gases, and chemical fumes of various hues poured forth from thousands of newly built plants, and nobody gave the question of pure air a thought. Men had only one feverish purpose—to win the war.

But one day—September 8, 1943—a daylight dim-out caused by smog occurred. It was so devastating that air pollution could no longer be ignored by local officials. The Los Angeles *Times*, which was destined to become the chief champion of air-pollution control, declared: "Thousands of eyes smarted. Many wept, sneezed and coughed. Throughout the downtown area and into the foothills the fumes spread their irritation."

Thus a problem that had been in the making ever since the acceleration of industrial growth came to an unhappy climax. Air pollution was the most baffling, the most unprecedented, and the most widely distributed affliction ever to harass the county. The deleterious dust and gases were something that no man or beast could escape. On days like that dark September 8 the population shrilly demanded relief.

Sooner or later every section of the county except the desert area north of the mountain range suffered from smog attacks. But Pasadena and the foothill communities most frequently experienced suffocating blights. Particularly in the autumn and early winter, balmy cloudless days were made dark and disagreeably pungent by an ominous gray and yellowing overcast, originating in the vicinity of the oil refineries and large industrial plants lying between downtown Los Angeles and the ocean. By early afternoon temperatures in the city and countryside would rise higher than on the seashore, and the smog-laden air would begin drifting slowly toward the foothills. There the mountain range served as a barrier, causing the polluted air to concentrate in a pall that at times endangered health and not infrequently sent asthmatics to the hospital.

It was no wonder that Pasadena citizens were aroused to an unprecedented pitch of indignation. One doubts if even the crisis produced by World War II so stirred the population. It was not a one-day crisis that faced Los Angeles County but recurring crises; they came day after day during hot, dry months and not for one year or season but at various intervals for more than a decade. . . .

Little by little the public gained a better understanding of the smog problem and the reasons why Los Angeles County was so acutely afflicted. The much-praised, balmy, sunny climate with no rainfall for eight to ten months was one factor. In these long rainless periods the unwashed air carried increasing quantities of dust and gases. For weeks at a time there would be no strong winds such as replaced the foul air of Chicago, Pittsburgh, and St. Louis—each of which suffered from coal smoke and industrial fumes but had the benefit of summer rains as well as heavy air currents. There being practically no coal burned in southern California, except at the Kaiser steel plant in San Bernardino County, the problem was very different from that of eastern cities. Months of scientific research, with chemical tests made in many instances by instruments built by the district's own staff, pointed to the great oil refineries in southern California and the millions of automobiles as major sources of pollution.

It was one thing to recognize the peculiar geographic and climatic conditions that produced smog, but it was quite another matter to be specific as to the sources and remedies. In point of fact more than ten years were consumed in identifying the many pollutants that were poisoning southern California air. No one community could solve the problem. In the middle forties the officials of the various cities as well as the county supervisors and health authorities finally realized that some kind of county-wide control was necessary to grapple with the evil. Assemblyman A. I. Stewart, whose district included Pasadena, introduced a bill that gave the county supervisors full authority to abate the smog nuisance. Every one of the thirty-four assemblymen in the county joined in supporting this unprecedented measure that became law. This responsibility, which the supervisors many times were to wish they could escape, made them the object of repeated attacks. Suffering even more from public indignation were the head of the newly authorized Air Pollution Control District and his staff. This group consisted of scientists and engineers who, despite top-level technical training, were almost as new to the Los Angeles air-pollution problem as were the elected officials.

The Western Oil and Gas Association, representing the major petroleum interests in California, was very apprehensive about the county's APCD. Its powerful lobby in Sacramento had strategically avoided head-on opposition to Assemblyman Stewart's "smog bill," but at each forward step toward county control it made its opposition felt, particularly in the earlier years. The organized petroleum interests feared any type of regulation. They were influential in setting up an agency known as the Southern California Air Pollution Foundation, whose first president and managing director was brought from New York at a salary of $50,000 a year. But in spite of the foundation's public propaganda, often intended to embarrass or discredit the APCD, the latter continued in determined fashion to formulate rules and regulations to curtail the production of pollutants. After hotly debated hearings, required by state statute, the supervisors enacted these provisions into law.

Industry-wide inspections were conducted constantly, and hundreds of industrial firms, including refineries, were compelled to modify their procedures. Among those who early defied the county were the financially powerful metal industries. Nevertheless, the APCD was successful in ordering the installation of electrical precipitators on open-hearth steel furnaces and the full-scale collection of contaminants from gray iron cupolas by means of bag-houses. A heavy fine was levied against the operators of a dry kiln who had defied the control district. Thousands of orchard heaters, used in below-freezing weather to prevent frost damage to citrus fruit, were condemned because they filled the countryside with black smoke. After a stubborn fight the orchardists abandoned their old heaters and installed new models that made no smoke. Real estate subdividers were among those who objected to a prohibition of outdoor burning because they were uprooting trees by the thousands every week and openly burning them, preparatory to converting the land into building lots. They were compelled to stop this practice.

One of the most bitter fights of all centered around the banning of backyard incinerators. This battle raged for many weeks, with disgruntled housewives eagerly joining the makers of incinerators in accusing the supervisors of stupidity and chicanery. Apartment-house owners whose facilities included incinerators for consuming their tenants' refuse charged the county with near confiscation.

The most discouraging aspect of the whole smog situation was that the supervisors could never prove that the enactment of any one of these restrictions, or all of them put together, was eliminating smog. At times long periods of blue unpolluted sky seemed to indicate that relief had come at last; then would follow periods of dense, eye-smarting smog that overnight shattered the public's hopes and put in jeopardy the public life of every elected official.

Louis C. McCabe, chief of the coal branch of the United States

Bureau of Mines, was called from Washington as the first director of the Los Angeles County Air Pollution Control District. In his short stay with the county he accomplished many important changes. He was of the opinion that sulphur derivatives released into the air by the refineries were major contributors to the pollution problem. . . . The Hancock Chemical Company built and put into operation a million-dollar sulphur-recovery plant. Its product consisted of tons on tons of pure liquid sulphur, which cooled to a bright yellow solid and was sold at a gratifying profit. For a moment, so to speak, the supervisors thought they had finally discovered the smog cure and likewise a source of income for the oil companies, which had been treating the sulphur as a valueless by-product. But as the months passed, the officials and the public with smarting eyes found that smog was still with them.

Actually the APCD accomplished a great deal, but to the average citizen tangible results seemed negligible. Meteorological stations at several points in the county furnished valuable hour-by-hour data not only upon changes in temperature, humidity, and air current but upon the chemical nature and quantity of impurities in the air. The district had been compelled to design and build many of its own instruments to serve its scientific needs. Analyses showed the deleterious changes in organic compounds that resulted from their exposure to sunlight in the presence of oxides of nitrogen. It was discovered that these otherwise harmless substances were undergoing a reaction in the atmosphere from which were generated the specific compounds that reduced visibility, streaked and damaged growing vegetation, cracked the sidewalls of rubber tires, and caused the ubiquitous eye-irritation aspects of smog attacks. Also born from the reaction was the toxic ozone, which later was designated as a "trigger" for the county's smog-alert program.

The refineries submitted sometimes reluctantly to regulations promulgated by the district's engineers and enforcement officers. . . . The director of the privately financed Air Pollution Foundation eventually returned to New York, and the organization he headed was no longer the source of headlines. It passed out of existence in 1960.

During these years of uncertainty, automobiles and trucks were accused with increasing frequency of being the major cause of baneful air contamination. . . . But for a considerable period after the Air Pollution Control District was in operation, the automobile manufacturers did not take seriously the public mutterings that automobile exhaust gases were a major source of contamination. The cheap low-grade fuel used by the buses made them particularly objectionable to both motorists and pedestrians. Again and again the findings of the county's research scientists pointed to motorcars as the source of an even greater quantity of pollution. By the end of 1960 three million motor vehicles were registered in Los Angeles County. With these cars consuming from one to ten gallons of gasoline per day, .the volume of exhaust fumes discharged into the county's tranquil atmosphere in twenty-four hours was enormous. These facts, when repeatedly brought to public attention, gradually shifted the object of the citizens' protests from industrial plants to passenger cars, while buses and trucks continued to be criticized violently.

With apparent reluctance and with a little condescension, the Detroit motorcar manufacturers sent committees to Los Angeles to confer with the county authorities. At luncheon conferences the county supervisors were assured that the car makers were "working hard on this difficult problem" but so far had not come up with a muffler or exhaust that satisfactorily met the need. Three or four years might be required, they said, before new cars could be equipped with such devices even after they were perfected. When "three or four" years had passed with no antismog results, the supervisors became convinced that legal prohibition would have to replace persuasion in dealing with the car manufacturers.

This tardiness in getting results from the motorcar engineers and the growing realization that smog control had proven to be a regional rather than a county problem caused the Los Angeles supervisors to seek state-wide legislation. Governor Edmund G. Brown proved very co-operative, and, after a series of conferences with southern California officials and business interests, he sponsored air-pollution legislation that was enacted in January 1959. The newly created state commission was endowed with control over all internal-combustion vehicles in the state, while control over stationary installations of all kinds was left to local regulation. The inauguration of full motor-vehicle control was contingent on the perfection of two or more types of apparatus that would eliminate at least four fifths of the undesirable emissions. Before such devices received state certification, they had to pass extensive scientific tests and meet a low-cost requirement. It was anticipated that by 1964 or 1965 all motor vehicles in California would be equipped with satisfactory exhaust apparatus, the installation of which was looked upon as the major step in eliminating smog.

John Anson Ford, *Thirty Explosive Years in Los Angeles* (San Marino: Huntington Library, 1961), 120–127.

Scotching Restrictive Covenants

LOREN MILLER

In 1948 in Shelley v. Kraemer *and* Hurd v. Hodge *the Supreme Court ruled that enforcement of restrictive covenants against selling residential properties to Negroes was violative of the 14th Amendment and the Civil Rights Act of 1866. A Los Angeles case,* Barrows v. Jackson *(1953), closed the last loophole by ruling out damage suits against the seller of a property covered by restrictive covenant. Loren Miller participated as counsel in that case.*

After a long review of constitutional history and Supreme Court decisions, Chief Justice Fred Vinson pronounced the ultimate judgment [in *Shelley*]:

"We hold that in granting judicial enforcement of the restrictive agreements in these cases, the States have denied [Negroes] the equal protection of the laws and that, therefore, the action of the state courts cannot stand." Judicial enforcement of racially restrictive covenants

388

by state courts had come to an end, but the Court was careful to say that its decision did not preclude voluntary compliance with a covenant if the signers chose to do so. Covenants were not void; they were unenforcible. . . .

After the decisions in the *Shelley* and *Hurd* cases, those who had exerted their giant's strength so long and so effectively in judicial enforcement of covenants cast around for means of evading the restraint placed on them. The Los Angeles Realty Board and the California Real Estate Association proposed a constitutional amendment to restore the old order, but more realistic proponents hit upon the idea that indirect enforcement could be achieved through damage suits by signers of the covenants against other signers who sold restricted property to Negroes. Missouri and Oklahoma courts upheld the validity of damage suits; Michigan and District of Columbia courts disagreed. The issue was settled by a case that went from California to the Supreme Court: *Barrows v. Jackson*, decided in 1953.

Leola Jackson signed a racially restrictive convenant in 1944, covering real property in Los Angeles. Among the co-signers of the agreement were Olive Barrows and M. M. O'Gara and an owner who later sold to Richard Pikaar. After the decision in the *Shelley* case, Mrs. Jackson sold her property to Negroes, and Mrs. Barrows, Mr. O'Gara, and Mr. Pikaar sued her for some $16,000 in damages for violation of the agreement. California courts held that a damage suit could not be entertained and dismissed the action, saying in effect that the damage suit was only an indirect attempt to enforce the racially restrictive agreement and that enforcement could no more be had through indirection than through the direct device of injunction which had been forbidden in the *Shelley* case. It placed its decision squarely on the proposition that indirect enforcement would deny equal protection of the laws to Mrs. Jackson.

Mrs. Barrows' Supreme Court lawyers found a flaw, or what they thought was a flaw, in that reasoning. They agreed that the Negro buyer of Mrs. Jackson's property could not be sued, either for an injunction or for damages, and that he could continue to occupy the property. The constitutional right protected in the *Shelley* case, they said, was a Negro's constitutional right to "acquire, own, enjoy and dispose of" property without discriminatory action on the part of the

389

state. But, they insisted, Mrs. Jackson was a white woman who could not excuse her violation of her contract by claiming protection of the constitutional right of a Negro to buy or rent property whenever he could find a seller or landlord willing to sell or rent to him. She had signed the agreement; she must abide by it or respond in damages, they concluded.

Justice Minton wrote the opinion for the eight-to-one majority upholding the California courts. "To compel [Mrs. Jackson] to respond in damages would be for the State to punish her for her failure to perform her covenant to discriminate against non-Caucasians in the use of her property," he said. "The result of that sanction by the State would be to encourage the use of restrictive covenants. To that extent, the State would put its sanction behind the covenants. If the State may thus punish [Mrs. Jackson] for her failure to carry out the covenant, she is coerced to use her property in a discriminatory manner, which in essence is the purpose of the covenant. Thus, it becomes not [her] voluntary choice but the State's choice that she observe the covenant or suffer damages."

Would the state action in allowing damages deprive anyone of his constitutional rights? Yes, answered Justice Minton: "If a state court awards damages for breach of a restrictive covenant, a prospective seller of restricted land will either refuse to sell to non-Caucasions or will . . . require a higher price to meet the damages. . . . Solely because of their race, non-Caucasians will be unable to purchase, own, and enjoy property on the same terms as Caucasians," he insisted.

There was one final question because of the Court's long-standing rule that "one may not claim standing in this Court to vindicate the constitutional rights of some third party." But, said Justice Minton, there are exceptions to every rule, and this case presented a "unique situation." He was of opinion that "under the peculiar circumstances of this case, we believe the reasons which underlie our denying standing to raise another's rights, which is only a rule of practice, are outweighed by the need to protect the fundamental rights which would be denied by permitting the damage action to be maintained." Mrs. Jackson could assert the constitutional rights of Negro buyers to excuse her violation of the agreement. . . .

The *Barrows* case marked the end of litigation over racially restrictive covenants. The issue of judicial enforcement had been settled: signers of covenants could not enforce them by injunctive proceedings, and they could not collect damages from a person who violated his agreement not to sell to a non-Caucasian.

Loren Miller, *The Petitioners: The Story of the Supreme Court of the United States and the Negro.* (New York: Pantheon Books, 1966), 325–328.

The Garment Industry
CAREY MCWILLIAMS

With every increase in its population Los Angeles could count on proportionate growth in lines tied to the locale—the construction industry, retailing, baking, printing. By the forties some of its output was also selling much better nationally. With some rub off from the motion picture industry and more from the willingness of Southern Californians to dress more informally, Los Angeles garment makers expanded rapidly.

Today [1949] Los Angeles ranks second only to New York as a garment-making center. Almost two-thirds of the state's garment-making industry is concentrated in Los Angeles where a thousand or so manufacturers, mostly small operators, are engaged in the industry. Between 1936 and 1944, the industry showed a 475 per cent increase in volume of production. Nowadays some 3,000 apparel buyers troop into Los Angeles each year to place orders for spring and summer garments, primarily sportswear, whereas a decade ago most of these buyers would have gone to New York. By 1944 the Los Angeles garment industry employed 35,000 workers, turned out a

391

product worth $265,000,000, and was selling 85 per cent of its prod-
ucts *east* of the Rockies. How is one to account for this phenomenal
increase?

The word "sportswear" is the key. The impress of California
styling in clothes first became noticeable about thirty years ago, and,
primarily in connection with sportswear. Novel conditions of living, reflecting climatic differences, created a compulsion to invent
something new and different in the way of clothing. California
manufacturers began to meet this need by designing new types of
sportswear which, being better adapted to local conditions than the
standardized products offered by eastern manufacturers, promptly
found a market. Certain of these products gradually began to move
eastward, carrying the California label, and, here and there, small
shops were opened in eastern cities for the sale of "California
Sportswear." In a rather insidious manner, the word "California"
became associated in the public mind with the word "sportswear."
The success of these new designs in California cannot be fully explained merely by noting that they were better adapted to local conditions. The *willingness* of the Californians to try them was also a
factor. California *is* different from Iowa, and this difference means
that it is possible to dress differently without being regarded as a
"crank" or "freak." This willingness to experiment, to try something
new, has also served as a stimulus to the designers.

When California sportswear first began to invade the eastern
markets, New York manufacturers made the mistake of assuming
that it would not "catch on" as a national fashion fad. This is the mistake that the nation has so consistently made about California, and it
is one of California's secret trade weapons. Never make the mistake of
assuming that what works in California will not work elsewhere for
the exact opposite is nearer the truth. Los Angeles garment manufacturers, being aware of this trade secret, were able to avoid direct competition with eastern manufacturers by concentrating on sportswear.
By concentrating on bold, original designs in women's casual clothes,
they not only took possession of a largely non-competitive niche in
the market, but initiated a trend toward casualness in clothes which is
now nation-wide. What started out as a California "fad" has become
a nation-wide fashion.

To understand the underlying cultural dynamic, however, a further finesse must be noted. Garment design in New York is not primarily geared to need but is largely determined by more or less accidental appraisals of what is or might become fashionable. In New York, as one manufacturer has noted, a good design may be something "picked out of the air or picked up in Paris." California designs, on the contrary, are based on need. This is not to say that California designers are smarter than New York designers, but it does imply that California has a compulsive environment. "Anything and everything" simply will not work in California; design must be based on function and need. This is what the Los Angeles designers mean when they say that California manufacturers are "less traditional, less conventional," than eastern manufacturers. The fact is that they *had* to be less traditional in order to gain a foothold in the local market; the lack of conventionality is not studied or invented—it is born of necessity. And a nice paradox is involved here. For "what works" in California is likely to succeed elsewhere precisely because it was designed to meet a specific need. Seymour Graff, head of the California Apparel Creators, has summarized the history of garment-making in this statement: "We were originally small manufacturers in an area where styling had to be 'different' if we were to exist."

Carey McWilliams, *California the Great Exception* (New York: A. A. Wyn, 1949), 218–220.

From War Profits
to Peace Profits

EARL POMEROY

In his book-length essay on the six states west of the Rockies, heavily weighted toward the twentieth century, Earl Pomeroy includes a discerning look at how Los Angeles readjusted its

393

industrial sights from wartime demands to peacetime opportunities, to the discomfiture of those who had been prophesying a sharp recession.

At the end of the war, in 1945, the Pacific slope could point to substantial increases in industrial capacity and to new uses for it. . . . Yet much of this basis for economic growth was evident only later.

The San Francisco *Chronicle*, surveying the prospects in 1943, found them mixed. Ten or fifteen years would see the end of petroleum in California. Electric power was in the wrong places—Nevada, Arizona, and the Northwest—rather than where the people were. "If the Columbia River would only flow through Los Angeles county," the *Chronicle* commented, "you could give Detroit and Pittsburgh back to the Indians." The aluminum and magnesium industries faced problems of climate and long hauls. Most of the shipyards were sure to go. The commercial airlines planned to expand their operations, but designing and producing large cargo and passenger planes might take as long as four years; the aircraft industry expected two years of reconversion, unemployment, and confusion. In Los Angeles, chief producer of aircraft, there was confusion over whether the region ought to attract basic industries, which the Chamber of Commerce promoted but the mayor feared would make the land of sunshine into a "smoky Monongahela Valley. . . ."

As the war ended, two years later, industrial employment declined with military orders, and manufactures on the coast expected it to decline still further after conversion to peacetime production—to less than half the volume of 1943. . . . Unemployment did rise sharply in the six months after the war . . . but then it declined rapidly. By September, 1946, employment was close to what it had been at the time of the Japanese surrender a year before. . . .

For all the speed and—compared to expectations—the ease of the change from war to peace in the West, the new economy was much more than a larger version of the old. A major factor in the success of its demobilization was that it did not, in fact, fully demobilize. Production of aircraft, which two years after the war still was the larg-

est single industry . . . depended principally on military requirements. Even when total military spending declined, the West's share
increased, particularly in California. . . . By 1962 the Los Angeles
Times estimated that one out of three workers in the area of Los
Angeles and Long Beach depended on a defense industry. . . .

Economists who surveyed the prospects of Los Angeles at the end
of the war learned by 1950 that in their most optimistic predictions
they had badly underestimated the growth of both state and county.
. . . Only New York had as high a percentage of workers in distribution and in the service trades as California; the two states were similar
in their commercial and financial leadership, in the tourist industry, in
levels of income. Los Angeles, which had dreamed of being a Western
Miami or Palm Beach, dominated a metropolitan area only slightly
behind Chicago and its neighbors in numbers and congestion. . . .

Los Angeles had been a long time establishing confidence in a solid
economic base of its own apart from the savings of newcomers,
"retired elderly people, whose health has broken down, and who have
come here to live on their incomes," according to Upton Sinclair, who
called the area "a parasite upon the great industrial centers of other
parts of America." The success of its first major industry, the production of motion pictures, which was fairly clear by the time Jesse L.
Lasky, Samuel Goldwyn, and Cecil B. DeMille produced *The Squaw
Man* in 1914, reinforced impressions of an economic facade or gigantic stage set.

But the completion of the Los Angeles Aqueduct and the arrival of
natural gas from the San Joaquin Valley in 1913 already had con-
tributed to more orthodox industrial development. By the time of the
discoveries of oil in 1920–22 at Huntington Beach, Signal Hill, Santa
Fe Springs, and Torrance, which made Los Angeles the center of both
producing and refining, other industries were immigrating in force.
Whether because of fuels and raw materials or, as the Los Angeles
Times insisted, because of the open shop, by 1923 the port of Los
Angeles handled more tonnage than San Francisco; in 1925 Los
Angeles had almost as many factory workers as San Francisco and
Portland combined. It was easy to miss what was happening in
an area where cultural community lagged behind economic integra-
tion. . . . The promoters themselves had absorbed much of the

rhetoric of the entertainment and tourist industries, describing (to quote from a publication of a firm of financial representatives and advisers in 1923) Los Angeles as "the home of monster industries" in "a valley still retaining the romantic charm of the Spanish occupation . . . quiet streets, mirroring the splendors of Rome and the glories of Greece."

After the war the change was inescapable, though much of the new research-based electronic economy took shape in plants as clean and almost as quiet as the ubiquitous Western college campuses: southern California's smog may have been the price of progress, but apparently came more from the automobile exhaust than directly from factories. By 1950 a fourth of the jobs were in manufacturing, more than in San Francisco or Seattle. Between 1945 and 1955, capital expenditures on plants and equipment in the Los Angeles area exceeded six billion dollars, and the rate of growth more than doubled in the second half of the decade.

Although defense industries still were prominent, the economy of southern California no longer seemed to depend on airplanes, entertainment, or oranges. Motion pictures, television, and radio accounted for only 3 percent of employment in Los Angeles in 1950, and expansion in the clothing trades, steel, and assorted industries serving the Western market tended to make even severe fluctuations in missile contracts less than decisive. Surveying postwar changes in 1956, the Bank of America pointed out that California was no longer a peripheral economy, supplying a few specialties to the national market in return for most of its manufactured goods: it covered its own needs and more.

Earl Pomeroy, *The Pacific Slope* (New York: Alfred Knopf, 1965), 299–307.

Megalopolis

"Smile, Los Angeles, you're the center of the world. Sooner or later it had to happen. After all, who's got a better climate? Or an easier life-style? Just look at our population. By the mid-1970's we'll be the biggest city in the world. Where are all the new trends in music and art coming from? Where are all the athletic teams moving? Look at all the big companies building L.A. offices. We deserve to be the center of the world."

—TWA ad, November 4, 1969

Los Angeles Convention and Visitors Bureau

Inner city

10

Megalopolis

Los Angeles' growth came to its prodigious climax in the forties, fifties, and sixties. All earlier generations cumulatively brought the metropolitan population to almost five million by 1940. The war and postwar generation added that many more, plus a large floating population of visitors, tourists, and conventioners. This growth fed and was fed by an unparalleled flourishing of the economy throughout this period.

The construction industry, diverted or demobilized during the war, entered on an extravaganza. Housing needs had accumulated. Single-family house building resumed, but the volume was in covering fields with acre after acre of tract housing. Later the trend shifted to multi-story apartments and still later to high-rise housing and condominiums. Park La Brea had been the first major complex; soon high-rise apartments marched out Wilshire and popped up on the Hollywood Strip, at the beaches, and in other unexpected places.

Prime growth in commercial structures first emphasized shopping centers, well scattered. Much of the air- and space-age industry located in modest quarters near the airport or the old plane-building plants. Later the banks, oil companies, and hotel chains raised skyscrapers at Century City and Bunker Hill, in clusters along Wilshire, and downtown.

The public school system for years needed a new school building every week. UCLA crowded its campus with medical school plant, classroom and laboratory buildings, and parking structures. At Northridge, Dominguez, and Long Beach, the State University system outfitted entirely new campuses. USC, Cal Tech, and others in the private sector invested in their share of new buildings. City, county, state, and federal governments carried through major building programs at the Civic Center and outstations.

Megalopolis

The largest pouring of concrete, by courtesy of the State Highway Commission and federal funding, was in the freeways. Along with that a comparable acreage was paved over for street parking and parking lots.

This generation also saw revolutions in transportation. The passenger train reached its zenith in the diesel-powered streamliners, five a day to Chicago and five more to San Francisco, St. Louis, New Orleans, and San Diego. Jets and widebodied planes made Los Angeles Airport one of the busiest. State and interstate freeways beckoned autos, campers, and trucks. Los Angeles, more than any other city, became so enamoured of its local freeway network that it allowed all other forms of local transport to wither away. The jets even more thoroughly drove out the streamliners and the ocean liners—except for the *Queen Mary* as a forlorn reminder at the Port of Long Beach, and Union Station as a retired architectural gem.

An industrial changeover almost comparable took place, giving emphasis to electronics and computers and to highly sophisticated air, space, and weaponry programs. These developments brought a societal change. The companies recruited thousands of scientists and engineers to work on research and design, production and testing, and selling and servicing. Local professional schools developed laboratories and research center personnel supportive to these industries directly and by training in the relevant fields. The Los Angeles area came to have an extraordinary concentration of scientists and engineers.

The area also drew a large influx of far less skilled workers and their families. In the war years and for a time thereafter on-the-job training sufficed for much of the work that was to be done. Even after employment became more difficult to find, migration continued. Dramatically, in this generation, east Los Angeles, within and beyond the city limits, came to have the largest Mexican community (or barrio) north of Mexico City, and south central Los Angeles, within and beyond the city limits, the largest number of blacks other than in New York and Chicago.

Cultural enrichment visibly accompanied this prospering. The most impressive evidences may have been in the proliferation of spectator sports as represented by Dodger Stadium, the Sports Arena, and the Forum, and participatory recreation in sailing, surfing, fishing, skiing, camping, and tennis. The regional resources in painting and sculpture gained encouragements in the art row on La Cienega, the sculpture garden at UCLA, the Pasadena and Getty museums, and the new County Art Museum on Wilshire which in 1975 unveiled its own sculpture garden. Thanks to private funding that owed much to the initiative of Dorothy Chandler, music at its best gained an incomparably better setting at the Chandler Pavilion and the two other auditoriums of the Music Center, along with the Art Museum now affectionately known as the Pyramids of Los Angeles.

Much that went on in the United States in the fifties was conditioned by the Cold War. Throughout America the sixties were a time of ferment. Students demanded that college administrators and faculties show relevance. Women claimed long overdue equal rights. Negroes sought protection under rights legislated a century earlier, and Chicanos, Indians, and other minorities objected to discriminations. Unease over the war in Vietnam mounted and became the prime issue in the presidential selection in 1968.

In varying degree all these movements surfaced in Los Angeles. Los Angeles sent freedom riders to Mississippi, saw the issue of school segregation come out into the open, experienced the largest race riot and, at Century Park, a mammoth confrontation between peace demonstrators and the police. The wrestling with these problems carried over into the seventies.

Supersubdivider
REMI NADEAU

Assembly-line construction symbolizes the postwar housing boom. Suburban Lakewood is a monumental example. Inside the city limits Westchester came into being almost as suddenly, as did several new subdivisions in San Fernando Valley. The stress at this stage was on single-family residences.

401

Young couples stood in line at tract offices to buy homes before the foundations were laid.

Biggest operator by far was Louis H. Boyar, who had started as a developer in 1939 with $700 in borrowed capital. Through FHA guarantees he secured huge loans covering most of the development costs, and then built enormous tracts with comparatively little personal investment. His greatest promotion was Lakewood Park, which he launched by purchasing 3,375 acres of farm land for $8.8 million in 1950. Here, with the help of professional city planners, he laid out a community of 17,000 homes for a population of 70,000 —the biggest single-ownership development in the nation and twice as big as the famed Levittown of Long Island, New York.

While the farmers were harvesting the last crop from the land, Boyar's construction crews were starting to lay 133 miles of paved streets. Small teams of specialists moved down one side of each street with fantastic new machinery. Great power diggers gouged out a foundation trench for a house in fifteen minutes. Lumber arrived pre-cut for each home. Conveyer belts carried shingles to the roofs. Carpenters used automatic nailing machines and powered door-hanging machines. Expediters with radio cars moved from one home to another looking for bottlenecks. On some days as many as 100 new homes were started; 10,000 were finished in the first two years. Mass construction was matched by mass sales; by late 1950 the volume reached 107 sales in a single hour.

Lakewood was only the most spectacular project in a real estate boom that burst over the entire Los Angeles area. Neighboring Orange County, which had been largely an agricultural region before the war, suddenly became the fastest growing county in the nation. Since the war the population has quadrupled to 710,000 people—the vast rows of orange trees giving way to rows of tract homes. Along the Sierra Madre foothills more communities blossomed; the homes replaced the orange groves so swiftly that for the first time in decades Los Angeles lost its place as the number one agricultural county in the nation, and relinquished to Florida the leadership in the citrus industry.

While this was a blow to Angeleno boosters, the fact was that Los Angeles had outgrown its pastoral age at last. With the pressure of population still rising, the land was too valuable for farming. Los

Angeles was no longer a garden city, but an urban city in the traditional eastern sense—with all the problems of urban congestion. . . . In all, the tract boom was a conspicuous tribute to the explosive vitality of Los Angeles business. It provided comfortable homes by the tens of thousands at reasonable prices and low terms. It solved a desperate housing shortage. It gave employment to thousands at a time when Los Angeles heavy industry had retrenched. . . .

Nowhere was southern California's growth more spectacular than in San Fernando Valley, which was chiefly responsible for the growth of the city of Los Angeles from 1.5 million just before the war to 2.5 million by [1960]. As late as 1944, when about 170,000 valley people lived in an area the size of Chicago, grass was growing in the streets and there was an annual appropriation from the gas tax fund to remove it. The area was chiefly agricultural, with a few scattered towns serving as market centers for the farmers.

As the war ended in 1945 valley land prices began to rise. By 1946 the tract home craze was fairly launched. In the longest uninterrupted real estate boom in the city's history San Fernando Valley's population [by 1960] multiplied five times, to 850,000.

Such an overwhelming inpouring of people was bound to create shortages. The telephone company found itself more than a year behind in filling orders for new subscribers. The valley's sewer lines were so overloaded that many developers in the west end were forced to use cesspools; for a time, in one section where the earth was unsuited for cesspools, the effluent ran down the streets. By 1953 some 38,000 city school children were on half-day sessions due to the classroom shortage—most of them in San Fernando Valley. Evidence of overcrowding was everywhere. Ex-GI's who had vowed never to stand in line again found themselves queuing up for everything from the grocery counter to the parking lot. During one holiday rush a valley supermarket became so crowded that an employee was stationed at the door to bar customers—admitting one person at a time for every one leaving.

The valley's growth might have been less painful had the Los Angeles authorities been alert to their responsibilities. Though valleyites made themselves a nuisance at city hall demanding the simple necessities, the city refused to accept the valley as anything but a rural community. Most of the other sections of Los Angeles had long since

403

had their curbings, storm drains, sewers, and sidewalks; but the City Council continued to allocate public works money so that each councilman could go back to his district with a piece of the pie. When the issue of giving a baseball stadium site to the Dodgers came before the voters, most of the opposition came from the valley; its people were not so much opposed to the idea of the gift as to the expenditure of several million dollars in city funds for access streets and allied improvements which were more desperately needed in the valley. On a rainy day in 1958 so many children could not reach school because of flooded streets that two thirds of the valleys public schools (sixty-four) were closed; no public schools were closed in the rest of the city.

The valley's worst single difficulty is its inadequate street system; except for the widening of a few arteries, it is substantially the same as it was before the war. In essence, a community the size of San Francisco is trying to make out with country roads. Equally difficult is the problem of commuters in getting out of the valley in the rush hour. Only two arteries lead out of this vast area to the industrial centers of Los Angeles and these are jammed bumper to bumper. Public transportation is wholly inadequate; in the early fifties the last Pacific Electric rail lines were abandoned and their place was taken by buses, which added to the street congestion. It requires twice as long to commute from the valley to downtown Los Angeles by bus as by auto. Reaching many other areas of the city by bus is a practical impossibility.

Remi Nadeau, *Los Angeles from Mission to Modern City* (New York: Longmans, Green, and Company, 1961), 275–279.

The Sign-Up

ABRAHAM POLONSKY

Los Angeles, more than the average in the United States, went into hysterics over the threat of communism within the nation. Los Angeles practiced McCarthyism before the name of the Senator from Wisconsin was attached to this method of

404

The Sign-Up

character assassination. Abraham Polonsky's A Season of Fear *looks not at the screening of policy makers or to those who might influence American minds, as was attributed to Holly-wood. Its protagonist is a journeyman employee in a strictly mechanical municipal operation.*

All day long the light had become hotter and more crystalline and now from the Water and Power building where the men had been sitting for hours the city moved into absolute focus under the blazing sun. Each thing stood in its own unique and marvelous dimension. It was a delight just to look, to have human eyes and see.

For these water engineers the world was divided in two: above, an oasis lavish with green, and below, the eternal desert in which hollow pipes endlessly branching formed two great veins, one going to the high Sierra snows and the other to a hot and muddy river. Sorenson, the chief engineer and general manager of the water department, had planned and built the great system and Charles Hare had driven the last two-hundred-and-thirty-mile aqueduct to the Colorado River. It was their system, it was their work, and more profoundly their idea. They knew it all from the first drip of melting ice to the mapped millions of flowering arterial capillaries that lay in the waste beneath the city.

As usual when he was irritated, Sorenson fanned himself. He never felt the heat any more, being so old, he said, and dried up, his eyes perpetually crinkled against the memory of the inland suns. He fanned himself with his yellow envelope. On Hare's desk there was another which glowed in the sunlight glancing off the pigeon guano on the concrete cornices of the building.

"Well, Charles," Sorenson asked, "what do you think?" His voice was dry and monotonous, strongly accented like the ordinary talk of the plains.

"I don't know, Chief. On hot days like this I don't think. It's every man for himself."

The chief engineer put the yellow envelope to his lips and whistled. "Anyhow," he seemed to be saying goodby to the city, to be putting it away in memory now that it would never be actual again, "anyhow, it's a good view."

Sorenson wrinkled his nose with distaste. "I know the type." He seemed to smell a leaking drain. "Antiques, a shelf full of odd herbs, dirt, and diarrhea." Sorenson got up and moved restlessly about the room. "I don't get it," he said. "I just don't get it. I mean I'm a Protestant. My mind belongs to God and me and no one, theological, political, economical, has the right to ask me what's in it. I have a basic and fundamental morality. You have. We could never violate it."

Charley grinned uncomfortable within this intimacy. He joked about it. "Well, Chief, the truth is I never had to. I never had to cheat at school. I knew the answers. I liked my work. I fell in love and married young and did my job and voted. You know how it is. I did what I had to do and no one ever asked me to do anything I would really consider wrong. That's life for most people."

"What about the time you were offered a bribe to put the pipe through ten miles on the other side of Great Flats?"

Charley laughed. "All they offered was money."

Sorenson's face crinkled with a fond smile. "How naive we both are!"

"Naive?"

"Innocent. We think morality is a question of majority vote."

"Well," Charley said slowly, estimating it, "morality is something that people have together, isn't it?"

"Yes," Sorenson replied, "That's when it's comfortable and right. But just you wait until it's right and uncomfortable."

The door swung open with a rush and Commissioner O'Brien's soft wet laugh came in like a dog's tongue. "Up, men," he called. "To the gas chamber!" He reversed in his track, yellow envelope in hand, and each man took his yellow envelope and followed.

In the calm, cold corridor faced with marble and as wide as a city street they joined the division heads, each of whom was tailed by his assistants, technicians, clerical staff, until a long lumpy line like an intestine wound through the corridor past the banked elevators to a small office near the fire stairs. Here behind a temporary desk sat a notary public. She was a middle-aged woman from the mayor's office and wore heavy glasses on her amiable face. As she took each signature she checked the names against the civil service registry and counterchecked it from a secret list compiled by the attorney general's office.

The Sign-Up

Counting faces, Commissioner O'Brien looked down the great line which hummed with conversation and the break in routine. "Well," he said to Sorenson, "it looks like we're all here and accounted for, patriots all."

Hare looked vaguely over their heads to the familiar, famous view. Above the flat gridiron of boulevards and streets, above the mountains, above the far yellow hills pinned to earth with oil derricks, a cloud slightly flattened at the bottom floated immense and motionless in the bright sky. There was no smoke and there was no wind. A ledge from the story above cut the direct sun from his eyes and he seemed to float out into a fine and constant light which had no source but glowed, so it appeared, from an infinite number of grains of air delicately tinted in pink and dazzling blue.

Hare slouched on the line, his eyes half closed against the window, hearing the separate conversations behind him as separate waves make surf. He was a big, easy muscled man who liked lots of room, a house and yard with size, collars not too tight, a big roomy car, a roomy life. He was uncomfortable now and disliked standing in line. He never did when he could help it. He wouldn't shop in stores where you had to take tickets and wait your turn. When he saw a queue before a movie house he didn't try to go in. He sent away for his license plates by mail. For him there was something peculiar about a line and being in it. A line violated his adulthood, his independence. It changed a man from an American and the abundant life to a European and the parsimonious one where there never was enough of anything and all existence was a waiting. Although like many Americans he had been ticketed and fingerprinted and listed during the various wars and government jobs, he deliberately carried in his wallet only the essential driving license and never less than one hundred dollars in cash.

O'Brien said, "Charley, do you have a brother?"

"No." Curiously Hare observed the innocent fatness of the Commissioner's head that was really shrewd and nimble in the brain. "Why?"

"Well, there was a man in here a few weeks ago, from one of the state security boards, I'll be damned if I know which, I get so many, and he was asking about a brother of yours."

"I have no brother."

"It must be some other Hare, then."

"What did he want to know?"

"We never got around to it."

Sorenson said, "They're around all the time now. It's a way to live."

O'Brien laughed again in his fat wet way. He always laughed his way in and out of conversations, meetings, crises, and small talk, and no one could tell which was which in his mind. "All right, all right. We're in the water business. The hell with it."

Down the corridor the general hum gave way to a single voice raised in suppressed anger. "Well, do something then. Do something. Everybody says we *ought*, but no one *does*."

Hare turned as did everyone else and there in the center of the line a knot of arguing men had suddenly bulged out, a sudden swell of figures, a spasm, undigested and indigestible.

There was the heavy silence of all the others now listening and the little group as quickly straightened out and lost themselves in the line again, and yet there was an unusual movement there, an obstacle. Everyone felt it even though there was no more talk, and the marble corridor magnified the wait and the quiet.

A thin little man with a shock of golden hair above a pointed face stepped from the line. He looked more like a bright child than a man, and he wore a blue shirt with rolled up sleeves and an open collar. The yellow envelope was in his hand. He stood away from the line, outside all the others, and the line felt it as he did. Automatically the line drew closer together, protecting itself with anonymity while this little man waited outside of it. Someone reached a hand out to pull the little man back and a voice said, "Come back. We were only kidding." The man in the blue shirt continued to hesitate. The yellow envelope was bright against the dark blue and then it disappeared as the man turned and began to move away. He went rapidly, almost trotting. He hurried down the length of the line and never stopped until he disappeared into one of the many rooms.

Like pale sequins the faces were all turned the same way and all caught the light the same way.

"Who's that?" Commissioner O'Brien asked sharply.

The chief and his assistant exchanged embarrassed looks but

they didn't answer. From the anonymous line the reply came, "Al Hamner."

The faces all waited for the Commissioner to say something else but all he did was turn away, and in a rush the voices began, humming and buzzing. Without even intending to, the people on the line straightened out the kinks and bends and slowly the line became more unified, the shortest distance between the door to the notary and the very last man. He stood as close to the man in front of him as he could so no one would think he was not part of the line.

The line began to move.

Charles Hare signed that he was loyal, that he was not now nor had he ever been a Communist, that he did not belong to any organization which had as its aim the overthrow of the government by force and violence or the teaching or advocacy of the same.

His one idea as he smiled and exchanged a little joke with the notary was to get away from the line. He hurried back to his office and busied himself for a half hour with some work. He tried to put all of it from his mind, the line, little Al Hamner walking off, the questions about a nonexistent brother, yet nevertheless he felt oppressed with something alien, as if among the thousands of kisses which are love, one was different, the beginning of the end, suspicions, agonies, betrayal.

Abraham Polonsky, *A Season of Fear* (New York: Cameron Associates, 1956), 9–14.

Hyperion to a Satyr
ALDOUS HUXLEY

After making Los Angeles his home, or at least his home away from England, Aldous Huxley occasionally chose local subject matter. His "Ozymandios" is a historical and philosophical es-

Megalopolis

say on the utopian colony at Llano del Rio in Antelope Valley.
His biographical novel, After Many a Summer, *in its attention*
to the cultural setting is a commentary on Los Angeles and one
of its distant suburbs. For the essay here quoted, Huxley
found his inspiration in an improbable facility.

A few months before the outbreak of the Second World War I took a
walk with Thomas Mann on a beach some fifteen or twenty miles
southwest of Los Angeles. Between the breakers and the highway
stretched a broad belt of sand, smooth, gently sloping and (blissful
surprise!) void of all life but that of the pelicans and godwits. Gone
was the congestion of Santa Monica and Venice. Hardly a house was
to be seen; there were no children, no promenading loincloths and
brassières, not a single sun-bather was practicing his strange obsessive
cult. Miraculously, we were alone. Talking of Shakespeare and the
musical glasses, the great man and I strolled ahead. The ladies followed. It was they, more observant than their all too literary spouses,
who first remarked the truly astounding phenomenon. "Wait," they
called, "wait!" And when they had come up with us, they silently
pointed. At our feet, and as far as the eye could reach in all directions,
the sand was covered with small whitish objects, like dead caterpillars.
Recognition dawned. The dead caterpillars were made of rubber and
had once been contraceptives of the kind so eloquently characterized
by Mantegazza as *"una tela di ragno contro l'infezione, una corrazza
contro il piacere."*

> Continuous as the stars that shine
> and twinkle in milky way,
> They stretched in never-ending line
> Along the margin of a bay:
> Ten thousand saw I at a glance . . .

Ten thousand? But we were in California, not the Lake District. The
scale was American, the figures astronomical. Ten million saw I at a
glance. Ten million emblems and mementoes of Modern Love.

> O bitter barren woman! what's the name,
> The name, the name, the new name thou hast won?

And the old name, the name of the bitter fertile woman—what was that? These are questions that can only be asked and talked about, never answered in any but the most broadly misleading way. Generalizing about Woman is like indicting a Nation—an amusing pastime, but very unlikely to be productive either of truth or utility.

Meanwhile, there was another, a simpler and more concrete question: How on earth had these objects got here, and why in such orgiastic profusion? Still speculating, we resumed our walk. A moment later our noses gave us the unpleasant answer. Offshore from this noble beach was the outfall through which Los Angeles discharged, raw and untreated, the contents of its sewers. The emblems of modern love and the other things had come in with the spring tide. Hence that miraculous solitude. We turned and made all speed towards the parked car.

Since that memorable walk was taken, fifteen years have passed. Inland from the beach, three or four large cities have leapt into existence. The bean fields and Japanese truck gardens of those ancient days are now covered with houses, drugstores, supermarkets, drive-in theaters, junior colleges, jet-plane factories, laundromats, six-lane highways. But instead of being, as one would expect, even more thickly constellated with Malthusian flotsam and unspeakable jetsam, the sands are now clean, the quarantine has been lifted. Children dig, well-basted sun-bathers slowly brown, there is splashing and shouting in the surf. A happy consummation—but one has seen this sort of thing before. The novelty lies, not in the pleasantly commonplace end—people enjoying themselves—but in the fantastically ingenious means whereby that end has been brought about.

Forty feet above the beach, in a seventy-five-acre oasis scooped out of the sand dunes, stands one of the marvels of modern technology, the Hyperion Activated Sludge Plant. . . .

An underground river rushes into Hyperion. Its purity of 99.7 per cent exceeds that of Ivory Soap. But two hundred million gallons are a lot of water; and the three thousandth part of that daily quota represents a formidable quantity of muck. But happily the ratio between muck and muckrakers remains constant. As the faecal tonnage rises, so does the population of aerobic and anaerobic bacteria. Busier than bees and infinitely more numerous, they work unceasing-

411

ly on our behalf. First to attack the problem are the aerobes. The chemical revolution begins in a series of huge shallow pools, whose surface is perpetually foamy with the suds of Surf, Tide, Dreft and all the other monosyllables that have come to take the place of soap. For the sanitary engineers, these new detergents are a major problem. Soap turns very easily into something else; but the monosyllables remain intractably themselves, frothing so violently that it has become necessary to spray the surface of the aerobes' pools with overhead sprinklers. Only in this way can the suds be prevented from rising like the foam on a mug of beer and being blown about the countryside. And this is not the only price that must be paid for easier dishwashing. The detergents are greedy for oxygen. Mechanically and chemically, they prevent the aerobes from getting all the air they require. Enormous compressors must be kept working night and day to supply the needs of the suffocating bacteria. A cubic foot of compressed air to every cubic foot of sludgy liquid. What will happen when Zoom, Bang and Whiz come to replace the relatively mild monosyllables of today, nobody, in the sanitation business, cares to speculate.

When, with the assistance of the compressors, the aerobes have done all they are capable of doing, the sludge, now thickly concentrated, is pumped into the Digestion System. To the superficial glance, the Digestion System looks remarkably like eighteen very large Etruscan mausoleums. In fact it consists of a battery of cylindrical tanks, each more than a hundred feet in diameter and sunk fifty feet into the ground. Within these huge cylinders steam pipes maintain a cherishing heat of ninety-five degrees—the temperature at which the anaerobes are able to do their work with maximum efficiency. From something hideous and pestilential the sludge is gradually transformed by these most faithful of allies into sweetness and light—light in the form of methane, which fuels nine supercharged Diesel engines, each of seventeen hundred horsepower, and sweetness in the form of an odorless solid which, when dried, pelleted and sacked, sells to farmers at ten dollars a ton. The exhaust of the Diesels raises the steam which heats the Digestion System, and their power is geared together to electric generators or centrifugal blowers. The electricity works the pumps and the machinery of the fertilizer plant, the blowers supply the aerobes with oxygen. Nothing is wasted. Even the emblems of modern love contribute their quota of hydrocarbons to the finished products, gaseous and solid. And meanwhile another torrent, this time about 99.95 per cent pure, rushes down through the submarine outfall and mingles, a mile offshore, with the Pacific. The problem of keeping a great city clean without polluting a river or fouling the beaches, and without robbing the soil of its fertility, has been triumphantly solved.

Aldous Huxley, *Tomorrow and Tomorrow and Tomorrow* (New York: Harper & Bros., 1956), 149–151, 163–165.

A Revolution under the Ribs
LAWRENCE LIPTON

In Venice West in the fifties Lawrence Lipton was in the midst of a rejection of the currently accepted ethic of America. The beats, for whom he became the guru, confounded the squares by the totality of their alienation. As Lipton puts it, "We felt that it was not we but the times that were out of joint." The philosophy and life-style that he describes have bearing but not complete flow-through to the student revolution of the sixties, the hippie communes, the drug culture, and the street people of the Haight-Ashbury district in San Francisco.

That the typical member of the beat generation does not regard himself as a citizen in the usual meaning of that term is clear from all my observations and interviews. He does not value his right to vote, although he would be opposed to any move to take it away from those who do. His attitude toward the ballot is simply that it is usually meaningless; it does not present such vital issues as war and peace to

413

the voter nor give him any voice in—or control over—such important matters as wages, prices, rents, and only the most indirect and ineffective control over taxation. His choices at the polls are limited by such tricky devices as conventions, gerrymandering, legal restrictions on party representation on the ballot, to say nothing of boss rule, back room deals and big campaign contributions. Elections are rigged, he will tell you, and the whole political game is a shuck.

He does not have to spend a dime for a newspaper or waste reading time in order to document his thesis that politics is a social lie. All he has to do is glance at the headlines as he passes the newsstand. Or listen to any five-minute summary of the news on the radio. Or—the plainest giveaway of all—look at the face and listen to the voice of any office-seeking politician on television. As for national conventions on television, the spectacle is too much for even the squares to take. They tuned out by the millions on the last convention broadcasts.

A beatnik busted for smoking pot could entertain you for hours about the lawbreaking of the lawmakers. And the law enforcers. For an apolitical he often displays a surprising knowledge of the above-the-law, around-the-law and against-the-law activities of policemen and politicians.

All the vital decisions, he will tell you, are beyond the control of the electorate, so why go to the polls? The decision makers and the taste makers are nonelective and nonappointive. They elect themselves and their ballot is the dollar. Moneytheism is not only a religion but a form of *Realpolitik*. The moves of power politicians, once covert, are now open. Even the businessman in politics no longer feels constrained to mask his motives or his methods. More and more the show goes on the boards without props and without disguises.

The voter has no control over the uses to which atomic energy is being put by the businessman and the politician. Cold wars are launched without declaration and are well under way in the Pentagon and the State Department before he is told that they are even contemplated. The war machine is fed billions without any by-your-leave on the ballot. He is presented with a choice between a general with a folksy grin and a governor with an egghead vocabulary. Voting becomes a mass ritual, but an empty one without any art or healing in it. It was once a kind of popular revel at least, a saturnalia on a low and vulgar level, with whisky for a libation and broken bottles in place of phallic ikons. But even that is now forbiddden, thanks to the prohibitionists who have made Election Day their last stand and only national triumph.

The voter, the beat generation will tell you, does not have any control even over the air he breathes. What's good for General Motors is proving to be poisonous for the American air. And what's good for the defense industries, and is conned up to look good in the employment statistics, is proving poisonous to the atmosphere of the whole globe. "Have you had your Strontium 90 today?" is a greeting you will hear any morning among the beat.

The list of shucks that the disaffiliate can reel off for you would take many pages to repeat here. A few, on which there is more or less unanimous agreement, will have to suffice.

First in order is the shuck of war, hot or cold, and the "defense" industries that are maintained to feed and perpetuate it, which the beat call Murder, Incorporated.

A close second is the shuck of "business ethics" and the morality of the businessman, the wide profit margin between his pretensions and his practices. Even the youngest among the beat generation are thoroughly familiar with the call girl sell, for instance, the bedroom bribery by which the businessmen bribe (and blackmail) buyers to the tune of millions of dollars. The older ones among the beat have not forgotten the cost-plus racket on defense contracts that created bulging bank accounts for the new war millionaires while the boys were fighting a battle of another kind of bulge in the Ardennes and planting Old Glory on a hilltop on Iwo Jima.

Another widely recognized shuck is the "Our" shuck. *Our* national safety . . . *our* natural resources . . . *our* railroads . . . *our* security . . . *our* national honor . . . *our* foreign trade . . . *our* annual income . . . *our* representative in Congress . . . *our* side of the iron curtain. . . . It's *ours* when it's our sweat and blood they want, but it's theirs when it comes to the profits, the beat will tell you.

They did not need Philip Wylie to tell them about the shuck of Momism—or Popism, either. Academicism was an open book to them long before it became a theme for faculty exposés in novels and what's-wrong-with-our-educational-system articles in magazines.

415

All of these shucks, and many more, are known to millions. The difference between the beatnik and the square is that the beatnik *acts* on his knowledge and tries to avoid the avoidable contagions.

"Cynical" is a word that the sensation-mongering newspaper and magazine writers like to tag onto their stories about the beat generation. If the beatnik lives in a state of voluntary poverty, he isn't being sincere about it—how can anybody turn down a buck?—so he must be cynical. If he turns his back on the installment-slavery of Madison Avenue's "engineered public consent" and phony "customer demand" propaganda, and tries to do without kitchen machinery and keep off the car-a-year pay-and-trade-in treadmill, he isn't being sincere about it. How *can* he be? He must be cynical, just trying to put on a show of superiority by sneering at all the things that make life really worth living and which he secretly yearns for but hasn't got the get-up-and-go to acquire for himself. That is the "party line" and you will find some form of it in all the mass circulation magazines and newspapers whenever they refer to the subject.

Another gambit of the mass circulation media is: They just don't like to work. Out of perhaps a hundred beatniks there may be one, usually an artist, who is so ridden by the Muse that he is utterly unfit for any steady job and tries to make it any way he can without having to punch a time clock. The other ninety-nine are not artists. They chose "the life" because they like it better than what Squaresville has to offer. They work, full time or part time, but without any of that good old stick-to-itivness and never-watch-the-clock devotion that was the slogan of the boomtime twenties—and ended for the go-getters in breadlines and apple-peddling. The beatnik of today who adopts the dedicated poverty is simply honoring the old Polish proverb: He who sleeps on the floor has no fear of falling out of bed.

In a society geared to the production of murderous hardware and commodities with built-in obsolescence for minimum use at maximum prices on an artificially stimulated mass consumption basis, poverty by choice is subversive and probably a sin against Jesus Christ who was, according to Bruce Barton, the first Great Salesman. It makes monkeys out of the soft-soap-sell radio newscasters and commentators who slip so glibly from the horror tales of the mushroom cloud and death on the freeways into the fairy tales of

Success by hair oil and Beauty by mud pack, thrill points, homogenized beauty cream or whatever the latest shuck happens to be. It is no wonder, then, that simple-living beatniks come in for vicious tongue-lashings by hucksters posing as reporters and pundits.

It is the voice of Business speaking. Business has its song of Prosperity Unlimited to sing while it picks your pockets, and the razzberry obligato of the holy barbarians and their dedicated poverty is a jarring note.

The editorials and the ads and the speechmakers keep telling youth that the world is his, the future is his, and in the next breath cries out with alarm that "the other side" is plotting to blow up the world with hydrogen bombs. The holy barbarian's answer to all this can be summed up in the remark of Itchy Dave Gelden when he dropped in one day with an evangelist leaflet that some "christer" had shoved into his hand, announcing that the world was coming to an end—

> "*Whose* world is coming to an end?"
> Not the holy barbarian's.

Lawrence Lipton, *The Holy Barbarians* (New York: Julian Messner, 1959), 306–309.

A Plea for Abolition of the Death Penalty

EDMUND G. (PAT) BROWN

When he was sworn in in 1959, Governor Edmund G. Brown inherited a score of capital punishment cases to review, among them one from Los Angeles that had become a cause célèbre. On a charge of forcing a girl to move from one car to another and thereby violating the state's "Little Lindbergh" antikidnapping statute, Caryl Chessman had been given a death sentence. Because of irregularities as to the transcript and other

417

deficiencies that hampered appeal, he spent ten years on Death Row. There was substantial evidence that this man, who had never taken a life, was rehabilitated and could safely be returned to society. That same year the American Civil Liberties Union of Southern California identified the death penalty as having become a "cruel and unusual punishment" violative of the Eighth Amendment as it must be construed in the twentieth century. In the seventies the State Supreme Court agreed and executions ceased in California.

Governor Brown carefully inspected the record of every man on Death Row. Because Chessman had earlier convictions, his sentence could not be commuted without consent of the State Supreme Court. Brown inquired informally if that consent would be given and was told emphatically that it would not. He was not willing to force the issue on the court publicly and in May 1960 Chessman was executed. Two months earlier, Brown sent this reasoned and impassioned recommendation to the legislature:

As an act of public conscience from the experience of over a decade and a half in law enforcement work, I ask the Legislature to abolish the death penalty in California. There are powerful and compelling reasons why this should be done. It is not based on maudlin sympathy for the criminal and depraved. And although I believe the death penalty constitutes an affront to human dignity and brutalizes and degrades society, I do not merely for these reasons urge this course for our State.

I have reached this momentous resolution after 16 years of careful, intimate and personal experience with the application of the death penalty in this State. This experience embraces seven years as District Attorney of San Francisco, eight years as Attorney General of this State, and now 14 months as Governor. I have had a day-to-day, first-hand familiarity with crime and punishment surpassed by very few.

Society has both the right and moral duty to protect itself against its enemies. This natural and prehistoric axiom has never successfully been refuted. If by ordered death, society is really protected and our homes and institutions guarded, then even the most extreme of all penalties can be justified.

But the naked, simple fact is that the death penalty has been a gross failure. Beyond its horror and incivility, it has neither protected the innocent nor deterred the wicked. The recurrent spectacle of publicly sanctioned killing has cheapened human life and dignity without the redeeming grace which comes from justice meted out swiftly, evenly, humanely.

The death penalty is invoked too randomly, too irregularly, too unpredictably, and too tardily to be defended as an effective example warning away wrong-doers.

In California, for example, in 1955, there were 417 homicides. But only 52 defendants were convicted of first degree murder. And only 8, or 2%, were in fact sentenced to death. There can be no meaningful exemplary value in a punishment the incidence of which is but one to 50.

Nor is the death penalty to be explained as society's ultimate weapon of desperation against the unregenerate and perverse. The study of executions over a 15-year period produces the startling facts that of 110 condemned cases, 49% of those executed had never suffered a prior felony conviction; that 75% of them came from families which had been broken by divorce, separation or otherwise when the condemned was still in his teens.

Again I say, that if this most drastic of sanctions could be said substantially to serve the ends of legal justice by adding to our safety and security, it would deserve some greater place in our respect. But no available data from any place or time that I have been able to find from research over many years gives support to the grand argument that the presence or absence of the death penalty exerts any substantial effect upon the incidence of homicide.

Specifically, the death penalty has been abolished in nine states (Minnesota, Wisconsin, Michigan, Rhode Island, North Dakota, Maine, Alaska and Hawaii) and in 30 foreign countries (Sweden, Belgium, Norway, Italy, Western Germany, Puerto Rico, Austria and 22 others).

In none of these states had the homicide rate increased, and indeed, in comparison with other states their rates seem somewhat lower. And these rates are lower not because of the death penalty but because of particular social organization, composition of population, economic and political conditions.

I have attached to this document a map of the United States in which the various states are shaded to indicate their murder rate over a 10-year period from 1948 through 1957, compiled by the California Department of Corrections. It shows graphically that the states without capital punishment along with several others which do retain the death penalty have the least incidence of homicides. And in striking contrast, 12 southern states, all zealously applying the death penalty, have the highest homicide rate.

This last fact points up the most glaring weakness of all, and that is that, no matter how efficient and fair the death penalty may seem in theory, in actual practice in California as elsewhere it is primarily inflicted upon the weak, the poor, the ignorant, and against racial minorities. In California, and in the Nation as a whole, the overwhelming majority of those executed are psychotic or near-psychotic, alcoholic, mentally defective, or otherwise demonstrably mentally unstable. In the experience of former Wardens Lewis Lawes of Sing Sing and Clinton P. Duffy of San Quentin, seldom are those with funds or prestige convicted of capital offenses, and even more seldom are they executed.

As shocking as may be the statistics in our deep South where the most extensive use of the death penalty is made against the most defenseless and downtrodden of the population, the Negroes, let it be remembered too that in California, in the 15-year period ending in 1953, covering 110 executions, 30% were of Mexicans and Negroes, more than double the combined population percentages of these two groups at the time. Indeed, only last year, 1959, out of 48 executions in the United States, 21 only were whites, while 27 were Negroes. I believe you will find [these figures] compelling evidence of the gross unfairness and social injustice which has characterized the application of the death penalty.

And finally, I bring to your attention the lessons I have learned here, in California, in 16 years of public service, but especially since I became Governor. Last January I inaugurated the practice of personally conducting executive clemency hearings in every death case upon request. Every such case is carefully investigated and comes to me complete with transcripts, investigative reports, and up-to-date psychological, neuropsychiatric, and sociological evaluations.

These are all hard cases to review and consider. There have been 19 of them these past 14 months. They present a dreary procession of sordid, senseless violence, perpetrated by the wandering outcasts of the state. Not a single one of these 19 accomplished a pittance of material gain. Nine of the 19 suffered obvious and deep mental imbalance. In the only three cases where actual murder was entertained by conscious design, sickness of mind was clinically established to have existed for many years. All of them were products of the hinterlands of social, economic, and educational disadvantage.

Six of these I have commuted to life imprisonment without possibility of parole. Eight of them we have given unto the executioner: miserable, bewildered sacrifices. We have taken their lives. But I have seen in the files and transcripts, in the books which we have now closed upon them, that who they were and what they were played just as big a part in their ultimate condemnation as what they did. And I saw also that, but for just the slightest twist of circumstances, these 19 might have received a term of years as did the other 98% of those who killed.

I have studied their cases and I know that not a single execution has ever halted the sale of a single gun or restrained a moment's blind rage.

And in these cases, too, there looms always the ugly chance that innocent men may be condemned, however careful are our courts and juries. Our judicial system gives us pride, but tempered by the realization that mankind is subject to error.

And this to me has been no idle fear. Within six months after I became Governor there came to me the duty to pardon a man who had, despite the care of court and counsel of his choice, been convicted of the willful slaying of his wife.

This man, John Henry Fry by name, admittedly under the influence of alcohol at the time of the crime, stood convicted by the force of circumstances which he could not explain. Happily, he was not executed. And last June 16th we pardoned him for that which he had never done.

421

Megalopolis

Here, but for the grace of God, there might now be on our hands the blood of a man, poor, ignorant, friendless—and innocent.

I issue this call for consideration of the death penalty as a matter of conviction and conscience.

I believe the entire history of our civilization is a struggle to bring about a greater measure of humanity, compassion and dignity among us. I believe those qualities will be the greater when the action proposed here is achieved—and not just for the wretches whose execution is changed to life imprisonment, but for each of us.

Governor Edmund G. Brown, Message to the Legislature, March 2, 1960.

H₂O'Malley, or, Let 'em Drink Beer

JIM MURRAY

So long as big league schedules were based on overnight hops by train, Los Angeles clearly was out-of-bounds and frustrated in its ambition to become the sports capital of the world. With the increased speed and range of airplane flights, a welcome change came. The Cleveland Rams led the way, followed by the Milwaukee Lakers, incongruous name and all. The highest inducements by far were dangled before Walter O'Malley and his Brooklyn Dodgers. Part of the deal was a free homestead in Chavez Ravine on land condemned and cleared for public housing, on which the voters later reneged. The Dodgers came. Pending construction of their stadium and mammoth parking lot, they improvised for a few seasons in front of a 75-foot screen in the Coliseum. Jim Murray's H₂O'Malley commemorates the official opening of Dodger Stadium.

422

H₂O'Malley

Max Yavno

Chavez Ravine before the Dodgers

I first heard about the great Chavez Ravine water shortage from my secretary, Vi Stevens. Vi was helpless from laughter. "You've got lots of mail," she said. "From people who say they can't get a drink of water in Dodger Stadium." She added laughing, "There's not a drink-

423

ing fountain in the place! Did you ever hear of such a boo-boo in your life?!"

I waited till the peals of laughter subsided. "Vi," I told her, "there are lots of boo-boos in O'Malley Stadium, but lack of drinking fountains ain't one of them. It's the oldest carnie trick in the game.."

I lit a cigarette. "You see, Vi," I went on, like the Ancient Mariner, "years ago a movie exhibitor found a long line at his drinking fountain in the lobby. He asked one of the customers why. 'It's the popcorn, the fellow told him. 'Popcorn! What popcorn?' the exhibitor shouted. 'The popcorn we got in the Greek Candy Kitchen next door,' the fellow shrugged. 'Makes you thirsty.'

"Well, you know what happened. The exhibitor thereupon put in his own popcorn. Then he shut off the water fountain to a trickle you'd be lucky to brush your teeth with. It's known in the trade as putting in 'Coca-Cola plumbing.'

"The Greek Candy Kitchen went out of business, but the Greeks got even by building candy kitchens with theaters attached. The next thing they did was make lousier movies because it is well established that the lousier movies are, the hungrier customers get. They improved the strain of popcorn, the better theater chains bought their own hybrid cornfields, but they didn't give a hoot what kind of schlock they put on the screen.

"Now, O'Malley has the same kind of 'out.' If the team gets lousier, the crowds will get smaller. But they'll eat and drink more. The day the Giants beat them, 19-8, in Chavez will be the day all records will fall. They'll need a stomach pump for every second person. In the meantime, he can't guarantee they'll be hungry, but he can be damn sure they're thirsty. Either that, or they'll start seeing mirages—like the Angels winning the pennant.

"O'Malley has pointed out repeatedly that concession revenues are frequently the difference between a profit and loss season. Many an All-Star shortstop has been paid for on a million bags of popcorn. And I shudder to think how many cans of beer it took to get Frank Howard.

"For some reason, people eat their fool heads off when they go to ball games, sad movies, or funerals, or anything else they enjoy— like a guy getting stuck in a cave. The psychologists can explain it.

H₂O'Malley

O'Malley is just channeling this wholesome morbidity into money. It's just good old American know-how, after all. I mean, supplying water fountains is just an extension of the damn welfare state, isn't it?"

Vi was impressed. So was I, to tell the truth. I mean, I didn't think I had it in me.

I even got a kick out of the Dodgers' explanation which was also in the finest American tradition. Why, there were a couple hundred water faucets in the powder rooms, they said defensively. Of course, not everybody likes hot water. And those paper towels leak. You can, to be sure, drink direct from the tap. All you have to do is hang by your heels from the water pipes like a sloth. This way, you get more exercise than the left-fielder.

The Dodgers might also have pointed out there is plenty of water under the ground, too, if the patrons would only take the trouble to drill for it.

The biggest danger, as I see it, is that O'Malley may have unwittingly furnished Arizona with a powerful argument in its water fight with California. If it can be shown that over 2½ million Californians subsisted without water during the 1962 pennant chase, it can be argued that they don't need the Colorado River as much as they need a pipeline from Anheuser-Busch.

"Let 'em drink beer" may some day rival "54-40 or Fight" as a slogan for a cold war over boundary rights.

The City Council is loudly threatening to get into the act. I don't know what they can do except send a mercy fleet of Sparkletts trucks into the Ravine with Red Cross flags on them so O'Malley won't shoot them down—or charge them for parking.

But they like to point out that the Coliseum had 150 drinking fountains. On the other hand, you have to remember the Coliseum didn't have anything stronger than water. At least, not legally, it didn't. The Ravine has everything but the chaser. But then, O'Malley is Irish—or half so—and you all know the old story about the Irishman who went in and ordered a double whiskey and when asked if he wanted water on the side, roared, "When I want to take a bath, I'll let you know." When someone asked O'Malley if he was going to put water in Chavez, he probably thought they meant showers.

425

Clearly, he never reckoned on the Lace Curtain Set. Next thing you know they'll be wanting tea.

Los Angeles *Times*, April 19, 1962.

Nobody Was Listening
ELIZABETH POE

Writing immediately after that sultry night of August 11, 1965, when the Watts Riot erupted, the author gets to the root causes and the warning signs that most Angelenos had missed.

For the past ten years, Watts has been the chief port of entry for Negroes coming to California. More Negroes have migrated to California since 1950 than to any other state in the country. Since 1940 the Negro population of New York City has increased nearly two and one half times. In Philadelphia, Negroes have doubled in number; in Detroit the Negro population has more than tripled. But the Negro population of Los Angeles County has exploded since 1940, increasing eight times, from 75,000 to 600,000.

When they reached Los Angeles, the migrating Negroes quickly learned that though they might have left the land of repression, they had not necessarily entered the land of freedom and jobs. Only 20,000 Negroes in Los Angeles have been able to find housing outside the steaming ghetto in the central slum city, and most of these are living in smaller ghettos developed in a few outlying areas like Pacoima and Santa Monica. If the present trend continues, the ghetto that burst into flames last month will stretch from Los Angeles City Hall west to Torrance in the next twenty years.

There are fewer Negro suburban dwellers in the Los Angeles area than in any major southern city in the United States. In Los Angeles 3.1 per cent of the Negroes live in the suburbs; in Atlanta, 8.5 per cent; in New Orleans, 14.1 per cent; Memphis, 13.3 per cent; and Houston, 10.3 per cent. Los Angeles looks no better in comparison with northern cities.

Most of the migrants to Los Angeles come from the ill-educated south and southwest, from what sociologists call "rurban" areas— small towns with a population of 2,000 to 3,000. When they arrive, most of them settle in the central section of Los Angeles where the expanding ghetto is characterized by almost completely segregated schools. At present there are 58 almost all-Negro elementary schools in Los Angeles as well as 10 almost all-black high schools and junior high schools. . . .

Even within this ghetto where problems have multiplied daily for the past ten years, housing is gradually becoming hard to find, and is deteriorating at a rapid rate because of the high population density. Landlords made four-family units out of two-family homes and rented them without limitation on the number of children allowed. New four- to ten-family apartment houses went up completely surrounded with concrete—not a tree or bush in sight. City departments responsible for zoning regulations relaxed standards because the residents were apathetic, always hoping they could move into a better neighborhood and therefore not inspired to improve the one they were in. As the ghetto crept outward, city services declined. Parkways grew up in untrimmed grass; streets were not cleaned; the community drifted downward.

Though nearly a million dwelling units have been built in Los Angeles County since 1940, no more than 1.4 per cent of these new houses are available to minority groups.

Unemployment in the Watts area at present is more than double the national average. Most of the new migrants are unskilled as well as unschooled. Before the riots, 20 percent of Watts was receiving welfare aid, as compared with 5 percent of the rest of the county.

As soon as the dimensions of the great migration became apparent six to seven years ago, predictions of an outbreak like last month's disaster began to appear in the public statements of social workers, Negro leaders, and civil rights workers.

Los Angeles Times

Interlude in the Watts Riot

Five years ago Negro leaders were complaining of lack of planning among social agencies to meet the social problems of the new Negro population. Nothing was being done, they said, to help these migrants orient themselves to urban living because the social agencies in existence were not tackling the problem. Most Negroes moved to Los Angeles with a built-in southern fear of law-enforcement officers. When one of their number was arrested or questioned by a policeman, they gathered around him in support and posed a threatening situation for the officer. There has been no community planning here to help migrants gain respect for law enforcement or to learn their own responsibility to the community in regard to supporting law enforcement. The migrants think of the law only in terms of fear. Five years ago it was clear that teen-age gang activity was increasing. These gangs were self-organized, unattached to any adult authority or community agency, and delinquent-oriented.

The gathering anguish over these steadily-developing problems began to produce sporadic outbreaks of violence in Los Angeles more than five years ago. Two hundred Negro teen-agers and young adults rioted in Compton, near Watts, in 1961. On Memorial Day of that year, another group of youngsters battled police in Griffith Park, taking over the merry-go-round with the cry that they were freedom riders. By the summer of 1963, when Negroes took to the streets all over the United States, Los Angeles Negroes, or at least the organized portion of them, called for a meeting with the white leaders of the city to present grievances. Dr. Christopher L. Taylor, a dentist who was then chairman of the Los Angeles chapter of the National Association for the Advancement of Colored People, was among the speakers who issued a warning to the assembled Negroes, social workers, and a few business men at the Statler Hotel. "We are already suspect with many elements in our community because we are taking the course of conference first instead of action now," he said. "If we cannot together work out our immediate achievable goals, the techniques of direct action will prevail out of sheer frustration and desperation. Direct action based on frustration and desperation, and the fear that is the inevitable reaction, are not the kind of emotions easily controlled."

That afternoon Norman B. Houston, insurance company executive who now heads the Los Angeles NAACP chapter, asked management, organized labor and government to work together for merit employment in the recruitment, selection, training, promotion and job assignment of Negroes and Mexican-Americans. Since that summer there has been considerable opening of employment opportunities by business in Los Angeles, but the grassroot problem of employment of the mass of Los Angeles Negroes has remained unsolved. . . .

Dr. H. H. Brookins, pastor of the most prestigious church in the Negro community, asked for a strong, comprehensive fair housing ordinance. Since then the voters of California have repealed in a general election the state fair housing law which might have opened the ghetto gates a little.

That same afternoon Mrs. Marnesba Tackett, a worker for the improvement of schools in the Negro ghetto, demanded integration of the city's segregated schools. Since then more schools have become all-Negro, and the Board of Education has bought property to build a new high school that will be all-Negro. (It is to be named after a Negro author.) . . . The Board of Education has taken the position that it is not obligated by law to do anything about its growing number of ghetto schools. . . .

Finally, on that hot afternoon when nobody was listening, Thomas G. Neusom, a Los Angeles attorney, brought up a fourth issue—the one that was not only the trigger but probably a basic cause of the Watts riot along with unemployment, bad housing, and bad education. "We are not at this time going to labor with statistics or individual complaints; we say to you that Negroes do not receive equal treatment at the hands of law enforcement officers in the City of Los Angeles and the County of Los Angeles. . . . This is a potential powder keg which men of good will acting in good will, acting in good faith, should seek to resolve before our city is involved in dangerous incident."

The police and the people of the ghetto are set on a collision course by many factors over which neither has much control. Crime inevitably flows from a chaotic, depressed area of hopeless lives. And whatever the normal police behavior is, Negroes were manhandled during the riots. The question arises, were rioters killed who need not have been? Police Chief William H. Parker made his attitude plain: "We're on top and they're on the bottom." They behaved, he added, "like monkeys in a zoo." At this writing, large numbers of the 3,000 Negroes arrested had been released without charges.

When liberals concerned with the problems of the Negro community look back at years of hard, dedicated work to improve conditions, all their efforts seem remote and unreal in the aftermath of the week of violence. Even if Proposition 14 hadn't repealed the fair housing law, it is unlikely that the bitterly disappointed people of Watts would feel any different. Whether they have the right to buy or rent a home where they please is of course academic for them. The dead and injured rioters and looters had no hope of ever buying their way out of Watts. They knew that the city slum is no longer an in-

cubator for the middle class, but a prison. They were jobless, hope-
lessly alienated, and tired of waiting.

Why did it happen in Los Angeles, where almost nobody expected
an uprising on such a scale? Why haven't southern cities experienced
riots like this one? Perhaps because disappointment becomes unbearable when expectation is high.

Elizabeth Poe, "Watts," *Frontier* (September, 1965), 5–7.

La Ley—The Law
RUBEN SALAZAR

*Reporter and occasionally feature writer for the Los Angeles
Times, Ruben Salazar succeeded remarkably well as a bridge-
builder between the Chicanos and the rank and file Angelenos.
In August, 1970, while covering a police-Chicano confrontation in East Los Angeles, he was killed by a gas shell fired into
a bar. "La Ley" summarizes testimony earlier that year at a
hearing of the U.S. Commission on Civil Rights.*

Justice is the most important word in race relations. Yet too many
Mexican Americans in the Southwest feel with David Sánchez, Los
Angeles Brown Beret leader, that "to Anglos justice means 'just us.'"

La Ley or the Law, as Mexican Americanos call the administration
of justice, takes forms that Anglos—and even Negroes—never have to
experience. A Mexican American, though a third-generation American, for instance, may have to prove with documents that he is an
American citizen at border crossings, while a blue-eyed blond German
immigrant, for example, can cross by merely saying "American."

Besides the usual complaints made by racial minorities about police
brutality and harassment, Mexican Americans have an added prob-

lem: sometimes they literally cannot communicate with the police. A commission report told of a young Mexican American who, while trying to quell a potentially explosive situation, was arrested because the police officers, who did not understand Spanish, thought that he was trying to incite the crowd to riot. . . .

One of the many reasons a Mexican American cannot relate well to *la Ley* is that he doesn't see many of his own in positions of authority serving on agencies which administer justice. The 1960 census indicated that Mexican Americans represent about 12 percent of the Southwest's population. In 1968, only 7.4 percent of the total uniformed personnel in law-enforcement agencies in the Southwest were Mexican Americans, according to those agencies answering a commission questionnaire.

As for policy-making positions, the commission learned in its survey that only ten law-enforcement agencies are headed by Mexican Americans and eight of these are in communities of less than ten thousand in population.

A commission study of the grand-jury system of twenty-two California counties concluded that discrimination against Mexican Americans in juror selection is "as severe—sometimes more severe—as discrimination against Negroes in grand juries in the South."

In east Los Angeles, which is the largest single urban Mexican American community in the United States, "friction between law enforcement and the Mexican American community" is on the increase, according to a psychiatric social worker, Armando Morales. . . .

One of the reasons for this increasing friction, Morales told the commission, was that "gradually the Mexican American community is becoming much more aggressive as to its social demands, its social needs. It is becoming more active. And at the same time, law enforcement is becoming more suppressive, hence creating that much more friction between the two." Morales also contended that police aggressive behavior seems to be condoned by high-level government.

Morales charged "indifference and apathy to the justice and needs of the Mexican American" by the federal government. He said his council investigated twenty-five cases of alleged police brutality, five of which were submitted for consideration to the FBI. The FBI referred them to the U.S. Department of Justice, which in turn ignored the matter, according to Morales.

The Reverend John P. Luce, rector of the Epiphany Parish in east Los Angeles, agreed with Morales that communication between Mexican Americans and the Los Angeles police had broken down and said he feared "we are on a collision course in Los Angeles" along the lines of a "police-barrio confrontation." Reverend Luce charged that the Los Angeles police and sheriff departments "refuse to talk with militant and political leaders with whom they might disagree, with young people, with a whole variety of activist people who want change."

The Anglo clergyman told the commission that the indictment of thirteen Mexican American leaders in the March 1968 East Los Angeles High School walkouts has led to the strong feeling that "the [Los Angeles] district attorney has singled out the Mexican community because he thought they were weaker than some other communities" but that he "miscalculated on this point, because the Mexican is organizing even that much more."

A commission staff report said that "one of the most common complaints throughout the Southwest was that Anglo juvenile offenders are released to the custody of their parents and no charges are brought, while Mexican American youths are charged with offenses, held in custody, and sent to a reformatory."

The commission's report further stated that it is felt throughout the Southwest that "the most serious police harassment involves interference with attempts by Mexican Americans to organize themselves in order to assert their collective power."

Ruben Salazar, *Strangers in One's Land* (Washington: U.S. Civil Rights Commission, 1970).

Home is a Freeway

WILLIAM BRONSON

Anecdotes abound about Angelenos who shave, fix their hair, apply makeup, eat, read, dictate letters, or plug in an instruc-

tional cassette as they tool along in the rush-hour freeway traffic.

William Bronson's interview with the Farriers, embellished with snapshots of them in their motor home and with a map showing their daily commuting circuit, appeared in Cry California, *a publication of California Tomorrow, an organization dedicated to saving the environment. The placement suggested something other than eulogy of the neatly combined solution of housing and commuting, but the piece also can be read as testament to adjustment to this great fact of life in modern Los Angeles.*

HOW DID YOU COME TO LIVE IN A MOTOR HOME?

Well, I guess I should start at the beginning. When I first came down from Seattle in 1960 looking for a job, I went to work for Lockheed as a tool crib attendant. I met Marilee—I call her Lee—through friends, and before the year was up, we were married. Since Lee was working, we figured it would be cheaper to own than rent, so we bought a house out in Tujunga. We borrowed the down payment from her father and paid it back at $100 a month. By the middle of 1962, I had it paid off.

Lee and I really enjoy the out-of-doors, and as soon as we paid off the loan, we bought a used camper on contract and kept it for about a year. We'd gotten into the habit of making high payments, so toward the end of 1963, we began looking at motor homes. We did quite a bit of figuring, and even though the initial cost was high—it ran a little over $10,000—we decided to buy a new one since we had sufficient income and we could get good use out of it.

At that time, our house payments were $128, and the motor home payments would be $192. When it came time to sell the camper, I was lucky to get as much for it as I still owed, so I had to borrow the $3,000 for the down payment from a loan company on a second mortgage. They took 12% for a loan fee, incidentally, and charged 10% interest on the $3,000, but the monthly payment was only $45.

Altogether with taxes, licenses, and insurance, the payments on the first and second mortgages and the motor home came to about $415 a month. By that time, I'd gotten a new job with one of the airlines at a higher rate, and Lee and I were making almost $10,000 a year gross, and although $415 in basic payments is a lot of money, we were able to swing it by spending very little on clothing or recreation and entertainment, other than travel. Even though the going was a little rough occasionally, we could look forward to owning our motor home outright in four years and being able to do a lot of travelling in the meantime.

Then something happened that we hadn't counted on, and it threw our finances into a tailspin. In June of 1964, Lee discovered she was going to have a baby.

The first thing I did was get a night job working in a parking lot downtown. This was tough on both of us. I hardly saw Lee at all. The doctor made Lee quit her job four months before she was due, so that by the time the baby came, I had fallen behind on payments so badly that the second mortgage holder threatened to foreclose. We had sold our old '56 Ford and I was using the motor home to commute to and from work in.

Without going into all the details, it became clear to us that we had the choice between keeping the motor home or our house, and although we wouldn't have decided the way we did if everything had been equal, we had no choice but to give up our house and keep the motor home for one very simple reason. Just like when you buy a new car, the first year's depreciation is a big chunk of the price you pay. If I had given up the motor home, I would have lost all the money I had borrowed to pay for it. Fortunately, we got enough for the house to make up back payments and avoid foreclosure, so my credit rating hasn't been damaged too badly. That is something you have to worry about these days.

We could have stayed with Lee's mother, but living with in-laws just doesn't work out very well. And to tell the truth, living in a motor home isn't all that difficult.

WOULD YOU DESCRIBE A TYPICAL DAY DURING THE WORK WEEK?

Sure. The weekdays have settled down to a very smooth routine. At about 7 o'clock in the morning, Lee gets up, changes and feeds the baby, fixes my lunch, starts the run from downtown on the

Hollywood Freeway, and doesn't waken me until we pass the Cahuenga off-ramp. When we get to the plant, we eat a light breakfast and then she takes the Golden State and San Bernardino Freeways back to her mother's place in El Monte, leaves the baby, and then goes to her half-day job in a small department store in West Covina. When she's through with her shift at 3 o'clock, she goes back to her mother's, picks up the baby, and prepares our dinner. Then she reversed her tracks to Burbank to pick me up. On the way to down-town L.A., I warm up the dinner, and by the time we get to the parking lot where we spend the night, dinner's ready and we eat together. I go to work at 6:30 and work to 2:30 in the morning. The lot where I work is about four blocks from the lot where we have arrangements to park. Fortunately, I can sleep part of the time on the job, or I wouldn't be able to make it. When the shift ends, I walk back to our motor home, go to bed, and then the next morning, it's off to Burbank again, and one day is just the same as the next.

All together, it's about 128 miles of driving a day, which happens to work out to about 10 gallons of gas a day. If you figure 22 working days, that means we spend about $75 a month on gas for commuting which really isn't so bad. We spend more than that, of course, because we go to the beach or the mountains or the desert every weekend.

HOW DO YOU TAKE CARE OF THINGS LIKE BATHING, LAUNDRY, AND STORAGE?

Well, that's really quite simple. I have time to shower and dress between the time Lee wakes me and the time when we arrive at the plant. Lee showers at her mother's when she gets there in the morn-ing, and she either bathes the baby in our sink or at her mother's.

One of the first things you learn living in a motor home is to carry an absolute minimum of baggage of one sort or another with you. As soon as you let it become cluttered, you feel trapped. We store most of our clothes at Lee's mother's place, and long ago we sold all of our furniture and appliances. It's really quite a relief to travel as lightly as we do.

Lee's mother does the baby's diapers every day, but we don't feel we can ask her to do more than that. So Lee goes to the laundromat on Tuesday and Friday and she manages very nicely. She goes to the bank once a week to make our deposit and we keep a post office box right next to where Lee works. We have to avoid imposing as much as possible on her mother, but as you can see, life would be a lot more difficult for us if she didn't live in the area.

ISN'T IT A LOT MORE EXPENSIVE TO LIVE ON THE FREEWAYS AS YOU DO THAN TO LIVE IN A HOUSE?

No. Our payments are $192 and it averages out a little under $200 a month additional for gasoline, tires, routine maintenance, insurance and registration fees. I worked this all out for my own satisfaction, and it's actually a lot cheaper than owning a house *and* driving a car, even if the car is all paid for.

LIFE MUST BE SOMEWHAT DIFFERENT FOR YOU DESPITE THE FACT THAT YOU'VE GOT IT DOWN TO A FAIRLY PAT ROUTINE

Oh, yes. For one thing, you don't have any neighbors, but since we both have friends at work, we really don't miss having them too much. Actually, we had a few neighbors in Tujunga we were happy to leave behind.

Another point is that although we didn't notice it in the beginning, we've really begun to feel that the freeways, particularly the Hollywood Freeway, which is a beautiful road, belong to us. It's not the same feeling you get about a house and a lot, of course, but it's definitely a sense of ownership.

And then, every so often something very funny will happen. For instance, whenever there is a tie-up on the freeway that lasts more than half an hour, one or more people will leave their cars and come up to ask to use our bathroom, and of course you really can't turn a person down.

WELL, THAT BRINGS UP ANOTHER POINT. HOW DO YOU MANAGE TO KEEP YOUR UNIT SERVICED?

Well, to begin with, Lee picks up water twice a day. I use up almost a full tank with my shower and she needs another tankful to take care of washing dishes, hands and faces, and so on. We drain the toilet tank whenever it's necessary. Frankly, we use the toilet as little as possible, because it's kind of a pain in the neck. For heating and cooking we get a new 20-pound bottle as often as twice a week when it's cold. In summer we can get three weeks out of a bottle. Since we can carry 40 gallons of gasoline, Lee only has to fill up about twice a week. We give all our gasoline trade to one station in exchange for our night parking space.

WHAT DO YOU PLAN TO DO WHEN YOU'VE PAID OFF THE MOTOR HOME?

We've thought a lot about that. With the baby growing up, we obviously can't live all our lives on the road, and we've considered a number of possibilities. We'll have this paid off before Christmas of 1967, and we have pretty well decided to buy a 40-foot Chinese junk, with a diesel engine, and berth it at Marina Del Rey, you know, just south of Venice. The style we have our eye on has three staterooms, a galley and what they call a saloon, which is really a living room. I must say that although things have worked out all right, it will be good to have our home in one place again.

[In 1966, following the appearance of this interview, reporters descended on the author to learn more about the Farriers. The author insisted that they and their routine were a hoax. At least one reporter went away not quite convinced. The freeways themselves seemed to call for just such use. "I suspect," said Neil Morgan, "that people like the Farriers are driving about Los Angeles today."]

William Bronson, "Home Is a Freeway," *Cry California* (Summer 1966), 8–13.

Farewell to California's "Loyalty" Oath
JOHN CAUGHEY

In the postwar decades California was a favorite hunting-ground of the House Un-American Activities Committee, its Senate equivalents, and the legislature's imitation. California also used all the popular devices to expose Communist party

Farewell to California's "Loyalty" Oath

members, fellow travelers, and dupes. The method most relied on was the test oath or oath of denial. In proportion to the real menace a tremendous amount of overkill was applied, but no more than popular opinion through the fifties and well into the sixties vigorously supported. "The Sign-Up" suggests the impact. "Farewell" comments on the rise and fall of the state's cornerstone "loyalty" oath. Los Angeles provided the largest number of swearers and also the case that turned out to be terminal.

On December 21, 1967, the wire services reported the death of California's misnamed loyalty oath—in reality an oath of denial of disloyalty. Since 1950 that oath had been required of every nonalien on the regular or casual payroll of the state or any of its subdivisions or agencies. The scope was such that millions, literally millions, of executions of the oath had been recorded. Among the signatories were every public school teacher and every professor in the state university, the state colleges, and the junior colleges.

The obituary, coming as it did on the fourth day before Christmas, was almost lost in the visions of sugarplums, the ads, and the hurly-burly of last minute shopping. But to the alert it meant that Santa Claus was on the way and already as far south as the State Building in San Francisco, or, more accurately, that the Wise Men were there with a gift many had been yearning for for seventeen years. The tidings were that the California Supreme Court, in a six-to-one division, had held invalid the second paragraph of Section 3, Article XX, of the state constitution as violative of First Amendment rights. The objectionable language read:

And I do further swear (or affirm) that I do not advocate, nor am I a member of any party or organization, political or otherwise, that now advocates the overthrow of the Government of the United States or of the State of California by force or violence or other unlawful means; that within the five years immediately preceding the taking of this oath (or affirmation) I have not been a member of any party or organization, political or otherwise, that advocated the overthrow of the Government of the United States or of the State of California by force or violence or other unlawful means except as follows: (If no affiliations, write in the words "No Exceptions") and that during such time as I hold the office of (name of office) I will not advocate nor become a member of any party or organization, political or otherwise, that advocates the overthrow of the Government of the United States or of the State of California by force or violence or by other unlawful means.

439

By eliminating this paragraph the court struck the language of disclaimer and denial which the people had written into the state constitution by amendment in 1952. That language in turn had incorporated the gist of the Levering oath voted by the legislature in 1950.

The decision signaled a return to the positive. Remaining in use would be a forward-looking pledge such as had served the state from 1849 through 1949 and which now could emerge from its long encrustation of negativism.

The court was affirming a ruling made a few months earlier in Judge Robert Kenny's trial court that the disclaimer paragraph was unconstitutional.

California's confidence in its machinery of justice is tempered to this extent: The state imposes a sixty-day cooling-off period before it becomes mandatory to cease and desist from unconstitutional behavior. A strict constructionist might have held, therefore, that on January 7, when the legislature assembled, new members should swear the old oath, the whole oath, the unconstitutional second paragraph as well as the valid first paragraph. The legislature's legal advisor held that it would suffice if the two presiding officers performed this symbolic act. The honor fell thus to Speaker Jesse M. Unruh and President of the Senate Hugh Burns to be the principals in the last official curtsy to the Levering oath.

Elsewhere up and down the stratification of public employment the word spread that the improper second paragraph was to be deleted and that only the first paragraph in its pristine positiveness was to be sworn to. In time, new simplified forms would be provided; in the meantime, the old forms should be used up. That is a graceless and unsightly way to carry out the solemn act of dedicating one's self to faithful performance. Yet, since the trial court and the State Supreme Court ruled on the basis of a taxpayer's action protesting wrongful use of public funds, the token element of economizing may be appropriate.

California's test oath was enacted before Senator Joseph McCarthy seized leadership in the clamor against alleged Communists in government. The oath had more indebtedness to Martin Dies' Committee on Un-American Activities, Jack B. Tenney's "Little Dies" committee,

440

the 1947 Los Angeles security check, the interrogation of the Hollywood Ten, and the University of California test oath of 1949.

Under the principle of divide and compel, the university oath should have had easy sailing because it bore on only a few thousand persons. But resistance was vigorous and highly vocal. The university oath was challenged as a blow to academic and intellectual freedom, contrary to explicit constitutional provisions, and discriminatory in that it singled out a small minority among the citizenry.

Governor Earl Warren, reacting to the last of these arguments, arranged to have Assemblyman Harold Levering introduce a measure requiring all civil defense workers to subscribe to a similar though not identical oath. The category of civil defense workers technically included all state employees and the later presumably embraced university personnel. The legislature responded with gusto. Two years later, popular vote incorporated the oath of denial into the constitution.

That same autumn, 1952, on one decision day the California Supreme Court out-Solomoned itself by upsetting the university oath and upholding the Levering oath. In an eloquent dissent to the decision on the Levering oath, Justice Jesse Carter rebuked the court for a fundamental inconsistency as well as for misreading, as he saw it, the constitution. But in voiding the university oath the court had not ruled on discrimination against a small class on the public payroll. It chose rather the technical point that the legislature earlier had preempted the field and that the regents in setting up an oath requirement were unauthorized interlopers.

In the early 1950's the frustrations of the Korean War, the proddings of McCarthy, the Hiss and Rosenberg convictions, and the uncertainties of the temperature controls on the Cold War made for unease. The climate of opinion supported additional legislation. The Luckel Act demanded that state employees respond to legislative and other governmental questioners. The Dilworth Act instructed school districts to probe into membership records. Still another measure required affidavits of non-communism from churches and veterans as a condition for tax exemption. An initiative measure, which among other matters would have required a suspect to prove that he was not a Communist, surprisingly failed of adoption, but the legislature, county and city governments, and boards of education adopted many such rules and regulations. The mood extended to social events where those assembled made the exhilarating gesture of a mass swearing of the oath. The university regents, midway in their controversy with the nonsigning professors, had set this example.

From the outset some Californians disapproved of the test oath and all its attachments. Organizing a Committee to Repeal the Levering Oath, they used such channels as were open to them. The chances for repeal seemed slim. A. L. Wirin, counsel for the American Civil Liberties Union of Southern California, failed to get a hearing in a suit protesting the oath as a condition of getting a license as notary public. He also tried to bring the oath requirement to trial when a lecture fee was held up. On that occasion the school district managed to find other funds from which to pay the fee and the suit became moot.

A test case on the church and veterans oath requirement reached the Supreme Court of the United States in 1958 and that law fell. Several years later the requirement of a noncommunist affidavit from any organization wishing to use a public auditorium met a similar rebuff. As of the late 1950s a committee of the legislature held hearings on the utility of the test oath requirements. In particular it considered fencing in the oath by limiting the requirement to a very few high officials, but no such enactment resulted.

Meanwhile, oaths by the hundreds of thousands were executed and filed as condition for steady or the most incidental employment by the state or any of its agencies or subdivisions. No one who would not sign was hired or paid. A screening process operated, though opinion differed on who was screened out—Communists or the non-Communists who objected to the inquisition.

Under the Dilworth Act or in other contexts a few persons who signed the oath were put under questioning and, not answering, were fired for disobedience or recalcitrance. A major talking point for the oath was that dishonest signatures would open the door for prosecution for perjury. To the best of my knowledge, in the entire life-span of the Levering oath not one person was tried and convicted on such a charge.

A dozen years went by. Then the Supreme Court of the United States began to withdraw much of the support it had given to disclaimer oaths and related interrogations. The court moved away from the position that mere membership was equivalent to knowing association with an organization's aims and methods. In *Elfbrandt* v. *Russell*, the case of an Arizona schoolteacher, it stated that the crux of the problem was not knowledge or ignorance of the unlawful purpose of an organization but whether a person participated in unlawful activities.

In *Keyishian* v. *Board of Regents* the Supreme Court, on that same basis, toppled the major part of New York's Feinberg Act. The court had ruled similarly with regard to oaths required by Florida and Washington. In November, 1967, it voided Maryland's oath. Meanwhile, courts in New Hampshire, Oregon, Colorado, Georgia, and Idaho invalidated comparable oath requirements.

Although this news penetrated to California, the Committee for Repeal of the Levering Oath experienced no rash of new members and no discernible optimism that the California electorate could soon be persuaded to amend this oath out of the constitution.

Relief came by quite a different route. Taxpayer Robert Vogel went to court in Los Angeles asking a summary judgment to stop expenditure of public funds for administering and enforcing the oath requirement. The complaint went to the cost of the printing, the paper it was printed on, the time of the notaries, and the filing and record keeping.

What a commentary that a matter of such importance and emotion should die of a tap on the head! One wonders if the court would have moved to the same result on the leverage of a refusal to sign by a space scientist, a candidate for the bar, or a teacher.

The dissenting opinion by Justice Marshall F. McComb capably reviews much past law, parts of which are only three or four years out of date. It ends on a note of judicial abdication: "In my opinion," Justice McComb says, "the judiciary should not disregard the law as laid down by the citizens of California, directly or through their representatives in the state Legislature."

The majority opinion by Justice Raymond E. Peters is terse and emphatic. It ends on a note that may stir regret, a footnote listing contentions of plaintiff or friends of the court on which the court now could say it was unnecessary to express an opinion. These were:

that the oath is vague,
that it constitutes an improper prior restraint on the exercise of First Amendment
    freedoms,
that it improperly shifts the burden of proof of loyalty,
that it constitutes a bill of attainder,
that the absence of a provision for a hearing results in a denial of due process of law,
that the oath invades a field pre-empted by federal law,
and that the oath results in a violation of the privilege against self-incrimination.

To a layman it would appear that a decision based on such a package of fundamentals would have been even more of a landmark. But to say that, no doubt, is an ungracious way of thanking the court for terminating the seventeen-year bar sinister of the Levering oath.

Pacific Historical Review, XXXVIII (May 1969), 123–126.

Overview
NEIL MORGAN

Will Robinson made the point that getting to know Los Angeles at ground level was almost hopeless because the city stretches endlessly in all directions. He recommended inspecting it from the freeways. Not as a driver, because coping with the competing and even the cooperating traffic requires constant attention. But as passenger, he insisted, one could see what this spread-out metropolis really consists of and how it functions. Neil Morgan has gone him one better, finding a viewpoint more impressionistic but reassuring.

Direct commuter flights between San Francisco and San Diego pass over Los Angeles at altitudes of about twenty thousand feet, setting off a variety of impressions among passengers. Remembering slow dreary hours in Los Angeles traffic, I always feel an elation in crossing this congested metropolis at five or six hundred miles an hour. It is seventy miles from north to south across the Los Angeles metropolitan area as it is described by the Census Bureau. At ground level this is a bewildering expanse of coastal plain with mile after mile of squat skyline rising no higher than the long rows of palm trees that line many of its streets. There are ugly patches of derricks and rocker pumps, some of them covered over and soundproofed, some landscaped but many of them blatantly creating an oilscape. Factories and subdivisions, equally faceless, sprout up from the pastures and bean fields and orange groves. The location of the city is improbable. In a setting with inadequate water, it is insulated from the interior by high mountains. Unlike San Francisco, it is without a natural harbor or a fertile back country.

Yet looking down from twenty thousand feet, especially if it is night and offshore breezes have cleared the air of smog and given this vast seaside saucer a chance to look its electric best, I am always stunned at the appearance of orderliness. Within sight are a hundred or more separate municipalities run together in an almost unbroken grid of lights. Great hunks of the city are drab and others are ugly, but darkness and altitude mask these flaws. What one sees is the most expansive urban area of America, spilling over into five counties and nine thousand square miles at elevations ranging from sea level up to more than ten thousand feet. The brightly lighted freeways circle and bisect the metropolis in a plausible pattern.

Los Angeles spreads along a coastal plain in a southerly arc that begins where the Santa Monica Mountains rise out of the sea. After twenty miles or so the coast turns almost due east and Los Angeles turns with it past its man-made harbor, on beyond Long Beach and the coast of Orange county, where the dazzle of lights begins to fade into a dimmer patchwork of coastal towns. Off to the north as the jet crosses the center of Los Angeles is the dark strip that marks the ridge of the Santa Monica Mountains, setting apart the million people who live on the other side in San Fernando Valley, the geographical center of California population. To the north and east, beyond other mountains, lie the deserts.

I am content when I fly high over Los Angeles at such moments,

Megalopolis

for I feel I can give up worrying about it. When I am poking around at ground level by day, I am always eager to get where I am going and be off the streets. The air may be acrid with smog or not, but there is still not much to see. Los Angeles does not communicate the physical sense of excitement that many cities do. I have immense respect for Los Angeles, more than a little concern, and sometimes even a trace of affection; but the affection always passes quickly, for I can seldom define it—only, perhaps, at twenty thousand feet, from where Los Angeles seems to be all one place.

Neil Morgan, *The California Syndrome* (Englewood Cliffs, N.J.: Prentice-Hall, Inc., 1969), 235–236.

City Limits or New Horizons

"As the great undersea tectonic plates move away from spreading centers, an ill-fated slice of the Far West, including Baja California and the section of California west of the San Andreas Fault, will secede from the lower 48 and head toward Alaska. In 10 million years Los Angeles will be opposite San Francisco, and in 60 million years Los Angeles will begin a slow but disastrous descent into the Aleutian Trench."

—Anonymous

The Santa Monicas block urban sprawl—at least for the time being

11

City Limits or New Horizons

By the late sixties urban sprawl had blurred the lines that technically bounded the City of Los Angeles. By then the major problems and issues related to Greater Los Angeles—the metropolitan area. There were still limits, and when the Los Angeles Angels moved to a stadium in Anaheim that seemed out of bounds. But on most matters the larger outlook prevailed.

The Santa Monica Mountains, long seen mainly as a barrier between West Los Angeles and the Valley, were discovered as a potential urban park and air conditioner. The flow of housing up the canyons and slopes changed the running fires in the chaparral into an urban problem. The need for more energy involved Los Angeles in the despoiling of Black Mesa and the Four Corners in Navajo country. Smog from the city spread to Ventura and San Diego and flowed over the passes to Victorville and Palm Springs.

With the exception of the school board's stubborn insistence on segregated schools, no branch of government imposed any enforcement of discrimination by race or ethnic classification. Tensions remained both in the black and Chicano communities. Social criticism and analysis filtered through their traditional outlets, but from Los Angeles there emanated a much more pervasive expression in the medium of prime-time television entertainment, threaded with dramatized social criticism.

In its scheduled events Los Angeles could claim to be the sports capital of the world. Its energetic citizens also engaged year-round in participatory play from surfing to skiing. Los Angeles exhibited large purchasing power for books and the arts, encouraged writers and artists, offered some publishing outlets, and much more in the way of showcasing art. In its Music Center which houses the Philharmonic Orchestra, its art galleries, its theaters, its libraries, its universities, Los

449

Angeles met the standard tests for a civilized community. It also could see itself humorously, as its cartoonists and columnists demonstrated.

Earlier, catchwords such as oasis, sun, orange groves, Hollywood, auto, and sprawl had been offered as the essence of Los Angeles. Now it was Freeway City—a strange result because the freeway originally was to be an intercity link, supplemented later as a bypass around cities. Los Angeles by its generous dimensions subverted the freeway into the channel for the bulk of its within-the-city movement. Although Reyner Banham is by no means the first to notice this takeover, his is a special tribute to the average citizen of Los Angeles as a virtuoso in the art of driving the freeways.

The Mountains and the Megalopolis
JOSEPH E. BROWN

Pressed to nominate a landmark, "something spectacular, strikingly impressive in size, undeniably beautiful, dignified and enduring," that would be to Los Angeles what the Eifel Tower, Statue of Liberty, and Golden Gate Bridge are to their cities, Art Seidenbaum considered the possibilities, manmade or to be made. "Why not," he asked, "that most rare of land- marks—the land itself? Why not the Santa Monica Mountains as a public park?"

"Nothing in these dense days," he continued, "could be more spectacular and striking than 200,000 empty acres in the middle of a megalop. Remember, we have something naturally unique here—a mountain range running east and west to shape two mammoth basins. The Santa Monicas aren't the Andes but they punctuate our town better than any building. Flying home on a clear day, I'd know Los Angeles anywhere."

Carrying out that suggestion would fulfill the hopes of Councilman Marvin Braude, long the guardian of these mountains.

Mountains and the Megalopolis

On a balmy spring morning a lizard, in retreat from the sun's increasing heat, slithers beneath a sumac bush. Not far away, a young gray fox pauses to slake his thirst at a small stream, flanked by graceful laurels and willows standing motionless on this breathless, windless day. Then he scurries up a ridge toward a sandstone peak. To the southwest, beyond the shoreline at the mountains' feet, beyond sight or hearing of either lizard of fox but surveyed by a flock of terns, three California gray whales lumber northward. Their destination, the Arctic; their annual migration to the Baja California calving grounds fulfilled once again.

There is much more in these Santa Monica mountains, along this seashore—hidden valleys, steep cliffs, submarine canyons, placid ponds, and shady groves. Companions of the fox: bobcat, coyote, ground squirrel, deer. Waterbirds and shorebirds. And an archeological treasure: more than 600 Indian sites dating back nearly 7,000 years identified so far, possibly only a tenth of the number still awaiting discovery.

The Santa Monica Mountains, running roughly east-west parallel to the meandering Pacific shoreline, rise abruptly out of the agricultural Oxnard plain in the west, and in the east the range buries its feet beneath the asphalt of freeways and the concrete and glass of highrises almost at the heart of downtown Los Angeles. To the north lies the sprawl of the heavily populated San Fernando Valley, but to the south the range adjoins one of the most outstanding marine areas left between Santa Barbara and San Clemente, containing an extremely rich marine biota, kelp beds, and a spectacular stretch of sand beaches and rocky headlands. Together, mountains and shore contribute to Los Angeles' physical identity, provide a clear airshed for smog-contaminated inland cities, offer recreational alternatives to overused Southern California beaches, and support a surprising variety of plant and animal species.

One would hesitate to equate these mountains with some of California's other natural wonders—Lake Tahoe, for example, or Yosemite, or the giant redwoods. Yet to the ten million residents of the Los Angeles megalopolis, the 46-mile long, 10-mile wide, 220,000-acre Santa Monica mountain range and its neighboring shoreline are far more important. For Los Angeles has less public lands and parks than any other American city, including New York. Worse, open space continues to shrink as the population expands. . . . The Santa Monicas constitute the last surviving unpreserved open space close to the nation's second most populous urban area. To Los Angeles' millions, this geologically, biologically, and geographically diverse mountain range is a backyard Big Sur, an Everyman's Sierra Nevada. . . .

Ironically, the very attribute that makes this range especially valuable as open space—its proximity to a giant urban area—also makes it attractive to developers. And now, as never before, these mountains and the adjacent seashore are threatened by mindless development.

Joseph E. Brown, "The Mountains and the Megalopolis," Sierra Club *Bulletin*, February 1973, 5–7.

Brush Fires

RICHARD G. LILLARD

With interests spanning literature and earth sciences, Richard G. Lillard was an environmentalist long before that became fashionable. His commentary on the terrors of a running fire in the chaparral whipped by a Santa Ana is drawn from his book-length warning on the hazards created by man's meddling with the southern California environment.

Some California forest fires are natural, such as those caused in summer and fall by lightning from dry thunderstorms (the rain evaporating as it falls). But in an age of fire protection, fires are bigger and more intense than in primeval days, once they get started, because dead and fallen growth has accumulated for years. And in an era of big, uncontrollable population, there are more people along the roads to start fires—smokers, saboteurs, campers, perverts, children with matches, target shooters using tracer bullets, litterers who throw away bottles that can act as lenses, autoists who back their spark-throwing exhaust pipes into dry brush.

Most parts of the San Gabriel Mountains are burned over every forty years or so, and the stored energy of the sunshine goes off in heat and wind and smoke. One large fire, the Monrovia Peak fire of 1953, which burned over 14,000 acres, released as much energy as five atomic bombs of the Hiroshima type. Man-caused fires have reduced the overall area in which groves and forests can now survive, replacing their lower margins with brush. These blazes, partly the result of the dry "Santa Ana" desert winds and low humidity, are a pillar of cloud by day, and by night a pillar of fire, potentially a wrathy doom to standing timber, watersheds, wildlife, human life, and property. As suburbs and resorts have pushed into brushy hills and forested highlands, the danger has increased, and the annals of the past half century are filled with disasters. While some fires covered huge tracts, those that incinerated homes or burned men alive were more important.

A big fire in the San Gabriel Mountains in 1924 burned for three weeks, clear over to the desert, leaving charcoal and ash on 92,000 acres. In 1928 a fire north of Ojai burned more than 200,000 acres, mostly in Los Padres National Forest. In 1933 a small, sudden fire on a steep slope in Griffith Park, Los Angeles, trapped twenty-nine inexperienced fire fighters—men on relief—and burned them to death. In 1955 the Refugio fire between Santa Barbara and Ojai burned 77,000 acres, destroying mountain cabins and small homes. The next year a fire in Orange and San Diego counties burned more than 44,000 acres and killed eleven men, and a fire that started in Malibu Canyon killed one man, blackened 40,000 acres of grass and brush, and burned up seventy-two houses. In 1958 a December fire starting on the mountains above Lake Elsinore covered more than 68,000 acres of forest, destroyed fourteen summer cabins, and killed one fire fighter. Three years later the Laurel Canyon fire in the Hollywood Hills burned in a ravine whose inhabitants had refused to let a fire station be built there because its presence would lower property values. Intense flames burned 300 acres and obliterated forty-three homes.

City Limits or New Horizons

In a droughty March, 1964, during a Santa Ana that had raised temperatures to the 80's and lowered the humidity to 6 per cent, brush fires in Glendale and Burbank destroyed twenty-four new homes and scorched several hundred more, and some months later the big September blaze from Santa Barbara north burned eleven days, covered upwards of 80,000 acres, killed one person and injured forty-six, and destroyed around a hundred buildings, some of them elegant mansions and Montecito palaces. Robert Maynard Hutchins, who lost his home, expressed the opinion that mankind might well stay away from the moon until it had learned how to suppress disasters like these forest fires.

Especially famous for property losses and personal associations was a fire that began in mountainous Los Angeles on November 6, 1961, and roared through the Santa Monica Mountains from Beverly Glen westward through Bel-Air, flew across the freeway at Sepulveda Canyon, and raced on through the Brentwood hills and toward another fire in the Malibu country. Like the fires in Malibu, Burbank, Glendale, and Santa Barbara, this fire did not destroy the cabins of homesteaders or squatters or poor whites, the types who used to pioneer in dry brushy areas with thin, rocky soils. On the contrary, the homes were the pioneering mansions on winding, twisting lanes amid virgin brush, of wealthy people—motion-picture stars like Zsa Zsa Gabor, Burt Lancaster, or Joe E. Brown, industrialists, surgeons, inventors, collectors, and other capitalists with elaborate dwellings and "fabulous" furnishings. Close to 500 homes were burned; of these 437 were total losses. Twenty-five million dollars of the damages was covered by insurance. One Bel-Air homeowner claimed $700,000 in insurance. Whole blocks of fine new homes were completely burned, with only the chimneys, the plumbing, and the kitchen appliances, warped and blackened, left in sight. Next to scores of these sooty skeletons were swimming pools, full of water. A fancy private school and part of Mount St. Mary's College went up in flames.

Combustible shingle roofing, later declared illegal; large, unprotected window openings; insufficient clearance between homes and native bushes; failures of the water supply; narrow streets; and the sheer impossibility of promptly getting fire-fighting equipment face-to-face with a fire that was burning fifteen acres a minute—so fast it burned only a few inches of topsoil and killed few shrubs and jumped half a mile at a time as burning shingles flew through the air, blown by a Santa Ana, the humidity near zero—all of these helped the destruction along. But as newspapers pointed out with equal emphasis, no lives and no automobiles were lost. The Red Cross set up emergency housing at a school, but this was no common-man disaster. The stars and the financiers stayed at hotels, motels, and friends' ten-room homes. Their rescued pets—horses, ponies, cats, and dogs—were put in the charge of the rescue mission.

The city and the county fought this fire as they fight other brush fires, as the United States Forest Service fights brush and forest fires, as if engaged in battle, with battalions of trained men brought in by air to the front, with bombing planes that drop borate solutions to smother flames, with observation planes and helicopters, with intercoms, strategy meetings, convoys of equipment and water, columns of tanklike bulldozers smashing out firebreaks, with cordons of armed guards to keep out intruders. A fire line has the sounds of the firing lines in war—the explosions of clumps of dry brush, the massive thud of falling trees, the roar of flames through the bush and treetops, and whirling smoke, the blasts of wind, the yells of fire fighters, the sudden retreats of men as they rush from a new hot spot in order to regroup, and the zooming of bombers as they come in close.

Richard G. Lillard, *Eden in Jeopardy* (New York: Alfred A. Knopf, 1966), 108–111.

Black Mesa
WILLIAM BROWN

In the larger perspective a city may be assigned some responsibility all the way back to the sources of its material needs —how the grapes are picked, how the fuel oil is transported across Alaska. When this supply service is mounted by private enterprise the responsibility at most is indirect. But Los Angeles, having for sufficient and good reason ventured into

*the electric power business, is itself a party to energy procure-
ment and production as far away as the Four Corners. That
circumstance adds a degree of accountability for what is
happening to Black Mesa, the Navajo, and the Hopi.*

Dot Klish Canyon is a long way from Los Angeles. In fact, it's a long
way from any place, unless you think of Navajo trading posts like
Piñon and Shonto as places.

But Los Angeles and Las Vegas, Tucson and Phoenix, and even
Washington, D.C., have come to Dot Klish Canyon in a big way.
They have ripped across it to get to Black Mesa's coal fields. They will
strip mine the coal, then ship it to power plants being built at Page,
Arizona, and Mohave, Nevada.

A few days ago I stood in Dot Klish Canyon and looked at the
mess. The road to the coal plant smashes across the canyon twice. The
bulldozers hit a steep ridge the first time, so they just turned around
and rammed through another one. The double roadbed dams the
wash in the bottom of the canyon, destroying the natural drainage. A
Navajo garden downstream lies dry and abandoned in the sun. A
nearby hogan stands vacant. It is a scene of brutal devastation, com-
pounded by the most careless scalping kind of non-engineering. . . .

The far Southwest and Southern California keep booming.
Nobody asks if the growth is wise, if the earth can provide. These
things are assumed. Utility companies and government agencies
scramble to get power and water to fuel the growth.

All parties to this process reinforce each other. The Federal Power
Commission warns of brownouts in Los Angeles. Business, industry,
and local governments take heed and join the chorus that demands
more power. Tucson and Phoenix must have more water from the
Colorado River, because they have already mined groundwater far in
excess of natural recharge. The U.S. Bureau of Reclamation needs
more power to pump water from the river into the Central Arizona
Project. So it becomes the lead federal agency pushing coal-fired
power plants, which are trade-offs for the dams it couldn't build in
Grand Canyon. . . .

Conservationists and ecologists are concerned about the coal-fired power plants operating, being built, and proposed in the Southwest. One that is operating near Farmington, New Mexico, daily spews out hundreds of tons of fly ash and invisible poisonous gases. Aerial tracking of the visible air pollution shows that this single plant (not yet in full operation) soils air, water, land and people over an area of 100,000 square miles in the Four Corners region of New Mexico, Arizona, Colorado, and Utah.

What's going to happen when the Farmington plant is joined by its sister San Juan plant, by two more proposed in Utah, by two now under construction at Page and Mohave? Projecting the answer from the observed effects of the Farmington plant, Dr. Joseph H. Devaney of the Los Alamos Scientific Laboratory paints a noxious smear from Southern California to the Rocky Mountains. Long-term weather inversions typical of this region will concentrate the smog. . . .

But the effects of this huge power complex go far beyond esthetics. Thousands of tons of oxides of sulfur and nitrogen will poison the visible pall. These poisons have cumulative, and largely unknown, impacts on living things, including man.

Water from the Colorado River and its tributaries will be heated and consumed in vast quantities. This will concentrate the river's already high salinity, with serious effects on domestic, agricultural and industrial water uses in California, Arizona and Nevada, not to mention our good neighbor Mexico.

On and on the questions go—what about coal dust, pipelines, ash dumps, transmission lines, leaching of soil, road and railroad construction, runoff from chemical and industrial processes? What will be the direct and indirect environmental results of these insults? No wonder ecologists are worried.

A few statistics on one plant, the Navajo Generating Station at Page, hint at the magnitude of operations: 23,000 tons of coal consumed daily; stacks 700 to 800 feet high; 40,000 acre feet of water used annually (water flows through cooling towers at 270,000 gallons each minute); 800 miles of transmission lines to get power to delivery points; plant cost $328 million, transmission lines $172 million, railroad from Black Mesa coal plant more than $20 million.

All of this investment and consumption will give the Page plant a 2,310 megawatt capacity. The total system of plants will have close to a 14,000 megawatt capacity. To get the size of the octopus spreading across the Southwest, multiply the Page plant figures by six. . . .

Back, then to Black Mesa, Dot Klish Canyon, and the wrecked home of a Navajo family. . . . Black Mesa is a great highland in the Navajo and Hopi Reservations of northeast Arizona. It is hundreds of square miles of high valleys, dry washes, and aspen-laced piney canyons descending from a surrounding rim to a basin-like center. Navajo Indians live in the northern part—gardening and grazing sheep and cows. The southern end breaks away in a series of deep canyons interspersed by high peninsulas of the mesa. Here the Hopi Indians have their villages. These remarkable people have lived here nearly a thousand years—just about the way they live now. . . .

But then there is the coal. It is spread thin over the 64,000 acre mining lease in the Navajo Indian Reservation and the Navajo-Hopi joint use area. That means extensive stripping and wide-spread devastation. . . .

The people are traditional Navajos. Few of them speak English. Although they and their ancestors have lived here for hundreds of years, they will be displaced; "relocated" is the term. But to where? For traditional Navajos (not the urbanized, Anglicized progressives of Window Rock who signed the lease contracts), there simply aren't any places to go. All favorable areas of the largely barren Navajo Reservation are already occupied. Functionally illiterate and unemployable for industrial and urban life, deprived of their gardens and pastures, these people will be refugees.

William Brown, "The Rape of Black Mesa," *Sierra Club Bulletin*, August 1970, 14–15.

Smog for Export
WILLIAM GREENBURG

At a time when the garbage fill near Candlestick Park was about to top out, Lassen County and the Western Pacific tried

Smog for Export

*to interest San Francisco in a daily garbage train to a capacious
desert site east of the Sierra Nevada. Los Angeles, it develops,
has a comparable export. In the early fifties the center of affliction from eye-smarting smog was downtown. By the seventies, many antismog devices later, it appears that, while partly
cleaning its own nest, Los Angeles has allowed the effluvia to
flow eastward and southward and even over the mountain
passes to its desert neighbors. Scientists and technicians still
work on controls and, as Greenburg implies, they must sometimes be tempted to start by killing off all the politicians.*

"That pall we used to see hanging over downtown Los Angeles when
we used to ride the bus down from Hollywood in 1948 has now
spread over the entire basin," said Gladys Meade, the first citizen-
activist ever named to the state Air Resources Board. . . . The basin
she referred to is a vague geopolitical area bounded by the Pacific
Ocean on the West, hemmed in by the mountains on the other three
sides, and hermetically sealed much of the year by a chronic inversion
layer of warm air. Known as the Los Angeles Basin, this huge air trap
extends from the coast some 80 miles inland. Officially called the
South Coast Air Basin by the state, and the Los Angeles Air Quality
Control Region by the federal government, the basin is one of the
worst air-pollution zones in the world. All year round, but especially
during the summer, when an enormous high pressure system sits off
the Pacific Coast, smog is a constant and daily oppression to the residents of the region.

Today, smog is spilling beyond the brim of the basin, over the
mountain walls into the deserts beyond. The desert community of Indio is about 150 miles from downtown Los Angeles and some 75 miles
beyond the eastern fringe of the Los Angeles Basin, yet in 1974 by
September 30 Indio had registered 723 hours when the smog level exceeded the state standard, more hours than anywhere else in the state.
Palm Springs, Indio's wealthy neighbor to the west, did not do much
better, recording 702 hours when the state standard was exceeded.
This is a far cry from the old days, when A. J. Haagen-Smith, the
Caltech scientist who discovered the photochemical reaction that

459

produces smog, was threatened with a lawsuit for daring to suggest that Palm Springs had a smog problem. Today, neither lawsuits nor the manicured greens of the exclusive country clubs are able to guard the rich against smog.

Victorville, another desert community, is separated from the Los Angeles Basin by a 9,000 foot mountain range, but in 1974 by September 30 it had recorded 381 hours when the state smog standard was exceeded. During the same period, Riverside, a city on the eastern edge of the basin, exceeded the standard for 330 hours; San Bernardino, a few miles north, for 397 hours, the worst year on record for that city. On June 21 and 22, 1974, the San Bernardino Valley suffered its worst smog attack in 15 years. Readings peaked at .68 and .71 parts per million of ozone for hours at a time. These levels are enough to make people sick. They are above the "never-to-be-reached" third-stage alert levels. The year before, San Bernardino, for the first time, registered average maximum hourly smog readings greater even than those of Pasadena, which is located right in the heart of the Los Angeles Basin smog cauldron.

In other words, despite all protestations otherwise by the Los Angeles Air Pollution Control District, a public agency that ranks in American mythology right alongside the Tennessee Valley Authority, smog is getting worse in most of the Los Angeles region despite some 30 years of pondering the problem. Why? Roger Harlow, the mayor of Indio and former head of the Regional Anti-Pollution Authority, a onetime private organization that has now been incorporated into the Coachella Valley Association of Governments, provided a succinct answer when he described smog as "a scientific problem in a political context." In other words, contrary to the traditional wisdom of many agencies, smog cannot be eliminated by technological solutions alone. For of all the issues involving environmental, economic, and political considerations, air pollution—especially in Los Angeles—may be the most complicated. Four counties, dozens of cities, and numerous federal, state, and local agencies are engaged today in a jurisdictional dispute and debate over control strategies that have become so heated that it is almost impossible to tell where science leaves off and politics begins.

William Greenburg, "Smog and Politics in Los Angeles," *Sierra Club Bulletin*, February 1975, 22.

A New Force—the Blacks

JOHN & LA REE CAUGHEY

On the tenth anniversary of the Watts Riot, an on-the-scene stocktaking found the area as distressed and distressing as in 1965. There was one important improvement, the Martin Luther King Memorial Hospital. Built as a symbol of the new Watts, it was beautiful, expensive, well appointed, and, as J. K. Obatala has pointed out, staffed by a cadre of dedicated young black doctors, imbued with social and political consciousness. For the city, however, despite Judge Alfred Gitelson's 1970 order, school segregation had become more impacted than ever. Other accumulated deficits remained, in particular disproportionate unemployment of blacks. But in the community at large, blacks had achieved a much more effective role. This retrospective assessment explores how they became a force more nearly commensurate with their numbers.

The day when blacks resolved to become a force in Los Angeles can be pinpointed. On Sunday, May 26, 1963, Martin Luther King came to speak at a rally at Wrigley Field. He came by invitation of concerned leaders representing NAACP, CORE, ACLU, the Community Relations Conference of Southern California, the American Jewish Congress, and many churches. Fifty thousand people turned out. Reviewing the struggle for fair treatment and equal opportunity in the South, King pled eloquently for a like commitment in Los Angeles. Asked what could be done to help Birmingham, he answered, "The best thing you can do is make Los Angeles free."

From the very founding of the pueblo, blacks had been a presence. Late Spanish and Mexican censuses showed just a few and American censuses began with only a handful, but even a casual search through the local annals would yield the names of scores well known or mentioned in passing and some outstanding for their individual contributions.

Although many Los Angeles residents were from southern states,

461

an episode in 1856 revealed strong sentiment against slavery. Robert Smith, a Mormon from the San Bernardino colony, came to Los Angeles to outfit a three-wagon train, which would then move on to Texas. He was taking fourteen blacks with him, two sisters and their children ranging from infancy to teenage, all of whom, once in Texas, would become slaves. Warned on what was about to happen, the sheriff took these people under protective custody and brought Smith before Judge Benjamin Hayes. Finding that Smith, by persuading these blacks to let him take them to a slave state, had violated an anti-kidnapping provision in California law, Hayes ruled that he could not be permitted to carry them off into slavery. Therefore, he appointed the sheriffs of Los Angeles and San Bernardino as their guardians.

Biddy Mason, one of the beneficiaries of this decision, found work as a nurse and midwife and prospered. At her home the First African Methodist Church was organized in 1872. Investing wisely in real estate, she put her money to public-spirited use. At the time of a particularly damaging overflow of the Los Angeles River, she invited flood victims to use her charge account at a Third Street grocery.

As Los Angeles grew, its black element grew and at a slightly more rapid rate. Less than one percent in 1880, blacks were 2.71 percent in 1920. By that time there was a black neighborhood that has been called a "spatial ghetto." Consisting of single-family bungalows characteristic of Los Angeles, it did not remind of the slums of the typical eastern city. Most black pupils attended regular schools. Edwin L. Jefferson, later a judge of the Court of Appeals, was one of thirteen black pupils at Manual Arts High, and Ralph Bunche was similarly integrated at Jefferson High.

In the twenties and thirties the black percentage continued its gradual rise. Some individuals prospered in business or as property owners or made a mark in the professions, among them financiers Louis Blodgett and Norman O. Houston, Dr. H. Claude Hudson, publisher Leon Washington, Jr., editor Charlotta Bass, and editor and lawyer Loren Miller.

At the same time prejudice became more overt. Jefferson was startled to find, after passing the bar examination, that he was not eligible for the bar association. Covenants and hostility restricted escape from the ghetto. White parents urged the school board to "protect" existing schools by making other provision for blacks. Blacks suffered underemployment; many with college degrees had to settle for custodial work. Posting a sign "We reserve the right to refuse service," restaurants and other public accomodations turned them away. Barbers in Westwood insisted, "We don't know how to cut that kind of hair," and at the UCLA women's dormitory a black girl who had been accepted by mail was told when she appeared that there was no room for her. In relation to other cities Los Angeles no doubt was a better than average home for blacks, but it practiced many of the stereotyped discriminations.

In 1916 the Watts district sent the first black assemblyman to Sacramento, Frederick Roberts, who introduced an antidiscrimination bill aimed at restaurants and theaters. He was succeeded by Augustus Hawkins. In the twenties the newly formed Los Angeles Forum addressed itself to problems of discriminations and segregation. It bore down against the word "negress" and insisted on capitalization of "Negro." With the slogan, "Don't spend your money where you can't work," Leon Washington in the thirties aroused sentiment against exclusion from employment.

In the huge migration produced by war jobs in the early forties and the postwar prosperity that followed, blacks poured in. By midsixties Los Angeles had eight times as many as in 1940, almost matching the total population of San Francisco and constituting one fifth of the Los Angeles total.

During the war, with construction at a standstill, most of these newcomers had to squeeze in or double up in existing housing. Although restrictive covenants were struck down soon after the war, their consequences lingered on. The old ghetto expanded but became much more congested and its walls rose. Dispersal of industry to distant suburbs and the increasing inadequacy of public transportation handicapped central-city residents in the job market. Families able to find housing outside, provided it was not in a satellite ghetto such as Pacoima, Venice, or the Harbor area, could enroll their children in integrated schools, but, throughout the vast compacted central city, assignments were to a great phalanx of schools deeply segregated.

Wendell Green, editor of the *Sentinel*, saw that blacks could capitalize at the polls on their segregated housing. He promoted the Committee for Representative Government. Its efforts led to the election of Augustus Hawkins to Congress, Mervyn Dymally and Rev. F. Douglas Ferrell to the legislature, and Tom Bradley and Billy Mills to the city council, followed shortly by the appointment of Gilbert Lindsay.

Meanwhile, televised reporting and news pictures called attention to the struggle for equal rights in the South. Los Angeles had seen Bull Connor and his dogs, the cattle prods used against demonstrators, and the mob at Central High in Little Rock. It knew the heroism of protest by nonviolence—braving imprisonment, bombings, and murder. Just ahead was the March on Washington.

Juxtaposition of the dramatic events in the South, the persistent discriminations in Los Angeles, and the breakthrough into political office set the stage for the call to Martin Luther King. Responding immediately to the enthusiasm roused, more than seventy organizations coalesced as the United Civil Rights Council and demanded elimination of discriminations in housing, employment, education, and police practices.

Under black leadership, UCRC won attention but very few concrete gains. In 1964, although President Johnson pushed through the Civil Rights Act, the local climate worsened. On initiative by the state association of realtors, the voters wrote into the state constitution protection of racial discrimination in the sale of most residential property. Three years later the courts would void it as patently unconstitutional, but meanwhile the vote stood as a barometer of white opinion and to blacks as a slap in the face.

A summer later a police incident hardly more than routine ignited the Watts Riot, unexpected and unplanned but America's largest urban race outburst. Most residents in outer Los Angeles were taken completely by surprise. Life in the metropolis had become fragmented, and by freeway westsiders habitually drove over the ghetto and barrio without so much as noticing the people living there.

An immediate reaction was fear and revulsion, fear that the fire-setting and violence would spread to white areas and, on the part of many, a turning against blacks. Others felt remorse for having allowed ghetto conditions to come to such a pass. A blue ribbon committee was appointed by the governor to report on the riot and outline

464

remedies for the root causes. Meanwhile the city undertook an agonizing reappraisal which brought Watts a small amount of investment capital, a cultural center with attention to art and creative writing, temporary improvement of bus service and, eventually, a hospital. Perhaps more fundamental, the riot put the spotlight on Los Angeles blacks.

Only a small fraction of those in the riot area participated in the shooting, arson, or looting. Out of this tragedy, however, came an intensification of solidarity. "Black" replaced "Negro" as the in-group designation. "Brother" and "sister" rose above church-group usage, and "skin" replaced the handshake. Among blacks there were differences of opinion on how to proceed: by the Black Panther route, through a rival brotherhood called US, in the traditional approach of NAACP, through the now more militant program of CORE, in accord with the teachings of King or of Malcolm X, by separatism, or by changing the larger system. In fact, all these methods were tried.

From what seemed to be an all-time low in their prospects in the wake of the 6-day 46-square-mile riot, Los Angeles blacks have come a long way. Encouraged by black advances in other parts of the state and nation and by a legion of white friends, they fortified themselves with pride in being black. Insisting on the importance of black achievements and contributions, they helped bring reform in the content of study in the schools, not just for themselves but for all minorities. Insisting on affirmative action for equitable employment and professional school admissions, they helped gain equity for women as well as for other racial and ethnic groups.

Increased strength is most evident in the field of politics. Over the dozen years after the historic rally, blacks have consistently held three of the fifteen seats in the city council and have been ably represented in both houses of the legislature and in the House of Representatives. In 1965 James Jones won election citywide to a four-year term on the Board of Education and in 1975 Diane Watson duplicated that success. Moreover, Angelenos Mervyn Dymally and Wilson Riles have been elected lieutenant governor and state superintendent of instruction, respectively, and in 1973 Tom Bradley was elected mayor. Los Angeles blacks have emerged as a force to be reckoned with.

UCLA

NANCY NEWHALL

Higher education reached Los Angeles with the launching of St. Vincent's College (now Loyola) in 1865. Fourteen years later the University of Southern California opened its doors, to be followed within the next decade by Occidental, Pomona, Redlands, Whittier, and a Southern Branch of the State Normal School at San Jose. Later entrants include Throop Institute (Now California Institute of Technology), three California State Universities plus a fourth at Long Beach, and UCLA, a unit in the University of California system.

Like the great medieval universities on the Continent, UCLA is urban —not only surrounded by the city, but intimately and deeply related to it. In 1915, the University of California, recognizing the sudden rise in population and, consequently, in the need for higher education in Southern California, opened in Los Angeles a headquarters for University Extension. These programs were so enthusiastically attended that the University, two years later, established an annual summer session.

When in 1919, Governor William D. Stephens signed the legislation transferring the grounds, buildings and records of the old Los Angeles State Normal School to the University of California, it marked the culmination of years of effort by Regent Edward A. Dickson and other dedicated citizens to establish a "southern branch" of the University in Los Angeles.

Within a few years it became obvious that the old campus on Vermont Avenue was too small for the rapidly growing young institution, and the Regents finally selected 383 acres of rolling hills at the foot of the Santa Monica Mountains, from which one could look across Los Angeles to the Pacific. The owners of the land offered to sell the site for one million dollars, and the neighboring cities of Los Angeles, Beverly Hills, Santa Monica, and Venice raised nearly the whole amount through bond issues.

UCLA

The site suggested Italy—the rolling hills, the brilliant sunlight, and glimpses of the blue sea—and the first buildings, such as Royce Hall, named after the philosopher Josiah Royce, and the Library, were modeled after cathedrals and universities in Milan, Bologna, and

John Swope

Walking Man by Auguste Rodin in the UCLA Sculpture Garden

Verona. Built of red brick, with cast stone trim and tiled roofs, their domes and towers and arched portals flank the original Quadrangle, from which the brick stairway and terracotta balustrades of the Janss Steps lead down to the playing fields. From this central theme the campus has developed along courts and malls connected by stairs. The hilltops have been leveled, and an arroyo filled in; concern for the noble use of urban open spaces, which characterizes great cities and great civilizations, continues to be the dynamic principle of planning on this campus.

If Los Angeles is concerned with its University, UCLA in turn is profoundly concerned with Los Angeles—with its tremendous problems as a sudden megalopolis and its equally tremendous potentials. The cultural awakening which has swept over what Aldous Huxley once called "the city of dreadful joy" is due in no small part to UCLA's meteoric rise to distinction. . . .

Los Angeles believes urbanization is inevitable; UCLA's responsibility is to reach into every aspect of the onrushing twenty-first century, to face it without resentment or regret, and to solve its problems.

"Mankind in its current need and agony," Chancellor Franklin D. Murphy asserted in the sixties, is the University's chief concern, and its function is to provide "leadership for a world crying out for the solution to an ever-growing avalanche of real problems, needs, and expectations. . . .

"We must be in the library, but we must also be in Watts. We must be in the laboratory, but we must also be on the moon. We will be in the lecture rooms, but we will also be in the operating rooms. Without apology, indeed with undisturbed and I hope growing commitment, we will serve the world of pure scholarship and the world of man and his problems, and both with distinction.

"This we will do within the ancient University tradition of the free market place of ideas where all matters are open for discussion and analysis, without fear of retribution, and where dissent is as necessary as agreement for the vitality and integrity of the dialogue."

Ansel Adams and Nancy Newhall, *Fiat Lux: The University of California* (New York: McGraw-Hill, 1967) 30, 33.

Parthenon of the West

GREGOR PIATIGORSKY

In the Los Angeles Civic Center, amidst the power structures of City Hall, the Federal Building, the County Courthouse, the Hall of Supervisors, and the Water and Power headquarters, there is one cultural grace note—the Music Center. In that company Welton Beckett's contemporary expression of classical architecture in the Chandler Pavilion stands out. Its square, 3,250-seat concert hall and the multiple uses for which it was intended posed an acoustical challenge very well met by Vern O. Knudsen. In this advantageous setting, with an extraordinarily effective director in Zubin Mehta, and enthusiastic community support, the Philharmonic Orchestra is one of the nation's finest.

My intuitive belief in the immense cultural potentiality of Los Angeles came instantly with my first visit and appearance with the Los Angeles Philharmonic Orchestra in the old Philharmonic Auditorium during the 1929–30 season. There was something pulsating in the atmosphere in the hall. The eagerness and the need for music of the audience was different from most places in the world where so often the enthusiasm of the young seemed replaced by the tradition of the old.

The orchestra, I thought, was not inferior to a number of orchestras abroad; the hall was. But it left me unimpressed, for I knew how much easier it is to build a building than the spirit.

I saw and continue to see Los Angeles grow to one of the most important culture centers of the world. We have great educational institutions, in one of which I teach, and we have an orchestra and its leader which are second to none. And we have a concert hall, which, not unlike a fine Stradivari, would be silent unless there is a master to produce sound worthy of its maker. I am glad to live and work in a place where one can participate in something bigger than oneself, a privilege which makes an artist's life meaningful.

The Music Center Story, 1964–1974 (Los Angeles, 1974), 23.

"All in the Family"

HOWARD F. STEIN

In the 1960s television took over a major role in dispensing news and more emphatically replaced the movies as the foremost American entertainer. The TV news empire centered in New York but in the entertainment branch Los Angeles loomed large. Although serious programming entered at some of the fringes, what predominated was prime time pablum. All too often the entertainer who ventured political or social criticism was phased out.

Then in 1970 came an electrifying experiment, a situation comedy built around a two-generation family arguing the visceral issues of the times. Reaction was vociferous and the Bunkers became the nation's best-known family. Soon, in rapid succession, Norman Lear, indefatigable producer and concerned citizen, liberated Maude, then crossed the color line to "Sanford and Son," "The Jeffersons," "Good Times," and "That's My Mama." In all these shows there was a carryover of dramatic license to grapple with a whole galaxy of human problems and controversial issues. Cultural anthropologist Howard F. Stein measures the relation of the Bunker family to contemporary American culture.

All in the Family is the dramatization of the vanishing and constricting world of *the man*, the self-made, self-reliant, self-activating frontiersman, now become captive. Everything in the series is a staging of this archetypal situation. It is a portrait of a man losing and holding on for dear life. One difference between Archie and other current television series is that in it there is no clearly demarcated role allocation of good and evil. The very restraint exercised in articulating the polarities, rather than choosing sides, is the common denominator that engages to the conflict all parties among the viewing public. This style of characterization is what makes All in the Family extraor-

470

dinary: it presents sympathetically each person's participation in the on-going conflict. Archie becomes "lovable" not because he is a "bigot" (as many ethnic-Americans misperceive, for their own very good reasons), but because he is, in actor Carroll O'Connor's words, a "three dimensional man." This is the image and character that O'Connor wishes to project in Archie and that the program's originator, Norman Lear, has attempted to create. It is the ambivalence and contradictoriness in Archie that resonate with the viewing public, not simply his "bigotry."

One historical note on the program must be considered: that of its timing and timeliness. In 1967, ABC did two pilots, which they quickly dropped. In 1970, a new regime at CBS championed it for its freshness, its contemporaneity, and its "realism." A resounding success in the ratings, it is now [in 1974] in its fourth season. The nature and timing of that success must be accounted for. Surely this program, whose themes express cynicism, satire, protest, anger, doubt, bitterness, despair, and nostalgia (to name only a few), could not have succeeded at the apogee of the Kennedy New Frontier, the period of limitless hope, faith, optimism, vigor, and expectation. All in the Family is a product of the twilight of the New Frontier, the Great Society, and Imperial America. Like Archie, much of the nation refuses to acknowledge this reality and the part it has played in the creation of this reality, denying the "facts" and vowing to "go down fighting."

The sense of demoralization and rage that is at the core of the "white backlash" is what underlay the humorous "Archie Bunker for President" sloganeering and demonstrating in 1972. This was at a time when American commercial enterprise had already saturated the ready market with Archie Bunker buttons, posters, books, T-shirts, cups, ashtrays, and the like. The "Wit and Wisdom of Archie Bunker" became for a while the cynical American equivalent of the "Writings of Chairman Mao" in the People's Republic!

Archie is a lower middle-class, nominally Protestant, Caucasion male, recently turned fifty (though denying it, protesting it's only forty-nine); a petty boss at the loading docks with a couple of subordinates, moonlighting by driving a cab; married to Edith, a devoted, obedient, scatterbrained, and foolishly wise servant; with one daughter, Gloria, a girlish woman in her twenties, who lives with her husband, Mike Stivic, a perpetual student, in the Bunker home. Archie's home is a row house in Queens, in a neighborhood "integrated" a couple of years ago by one black family, the Jeffersons, whose son Lionel is a good friend of Mike and Gloria. Filling in the details, the Bunker family becomes the prototypical struggling, middle-class white American household. . . .

A moment's listening identifies Archie as trapped and outraged, afraid and embittered, confused and resolute. The world is no longer his world, and America, land of the free and home of the brave, is teeming with pinkos, fags, meatheads, and intellectuals. Everything he sees and hears reminds him of what he has lost or is in danger of losing. He denies his entrapment: America is still a free country, and with hard work a man can still make it. He insists that he is the man around the house, the provider, and the final authority, *pater potestas*, on all matters temporal and spiritual. He curses anyone who would threaten even remotely what it took him a lifetime to earn and mouths every American slogan he can muster to convince himself all is not lost. . . .

Although the series is overwhelmingly enjoyed—as the show remains high in the ratings, with some eighty million Americans fixed on it—consideration must be given to the "minority" who are utterly repelled by Archie and feel persecuted by his image and image-makers. Leaders of such organizations as the B'Nai Brith, the Kosciusko Foundation, the Polish-American Historical Society, the Urban League, and the International Teamsters Union have vehemently condemned the racism and stereotyping that they perceive as being the singular message of the series. . . .

Those who condemn the series have a common reaction: outrage, fright, disgust, righteous indignation, denial, assertive pride, and vicious counter-stereotyping. For them Archie is a narrow-minded boor who should be silenced, "stifled." He is an evil influence on our culture and on our children. He teaches our children bigotry. He makes bigotry respectable, cute, a joke, an "in thing." He threatens every social good we have sought to achieve; he incarnates every evil we combat. . . .

Those who identify with Archie and his generation hardly take

472

notice of Archie's attacks . . . ; they would be more likely to cheer Archie on when he inveighs against blacks, Puerto Ricans, welfare recipients, "pinko meatheads," and the like. They identify with his nightmarish vision of a world closing in and slipping away and share his fear that he is master of nothing save his frame house and jealously guarded chair. . . . In terms of over-all response, black respondents liked the show slightly better than white respondents—perhaps they had the dual pleasure of seeing "Mr. Bigot" repeatedly done in and witnessing an "Amos 'n Andy" in reverse staged for them. Finally, some viewers will not "take sides" but will empathize with the whole —its humor and pathos. . . .

Archie represents and in some respects speaks for the American Everyman. . . . O'Connor has commented: "Archie's dilemma is coping with a world that is changing in front of him. He doesn't know what to do except lose his temper, mouth his poisons, look elsewhere to fix the blame for his own discomfort. He isn't a totally evil man. He wouldn't burn a cross. He's shrewd. But he won't get to the root of his problem, because the root of his problem is himself, and he doesn't know it."

Howard F. Stein, "All in the Family" as Mirror of Contemporary American Culture," *Family Process*, 13 (1974), 279–315.

Slaves and Masters of the Freeways
REYNER BANHAM

A presumed truism has it that foreign visitors see the essence of a life style better than the local residents. Reyner Banham brings this sixth sense to apply in his analysis of the interrelationship of architecture and social ecology in modern Los

Angeles, that is, of private and public constructions with the
way of life.
    Only drivers of the Los Angeles freeways will appreciate to
the full his codification of the unwritten law of these roads, in-
cluding the imperative of forehanded lane choice and the in-
fallibility of the great sign poster in the sky.

The freeway is where the Angelenos live a large part of their lives. Such daily sacrifices on the altar of transportation are the common lot of all metropolitan citizens of course. Some, with luck, will spend less time on the average at these devotions, and many will spend them under far more squalid conditions (on the Southern Region of British Railways, or in the New York subway, for instance) but only Los Angeles has made a mystique of such proportions out of its com-

INTERLAND ©1975, LOS ANGELES TIMES

"I knew American ingenuity and Detroit
would come up with a compact car to
answer the energy shortage!"

muting technology that the whole world seems to know about it. . . .
Los Angeles is famous as the home of the Freeway.

There seem to be two major reasons for their dominance in the city
image of Los Angeles and both are aspects of their inescapability;
firstly, that they are so vast that you cannot help seeing them, and
secondly, that there appears no alternative means of movement and
you cannot help using them. There are other and useful streets, and
the major boulevards provide an excellent secondary network in
many parts of the city, but psychologically, all are felt to be tributary
to the freeways.

Furthermore, the actual experience of driving on the freeways
prints itself deeply on the conscious mind and unthinking reflexes. As
you acquire the special skills involved, the Los Angeles freeways
become a special way of being alive, which can be duplicated in part,
on other systems (England would be a much safer place if those skills
could be inculcated on our motorways) but not with this totality and
extremity. If motorway driving anywhere calls for a high level of at-
tentiveness, the extreme concentration required in Los Angeles seems
to bring on a state of heightened awareness that some locals find
mystical.

That concentration is required beyond doubt, for the freeways can
kill—hardly a week passed but I found myself driving slowly under
police control past the wreckage of at least one major crash. But on the
other hand the freeways are visibly safe—I never saw any of these incidents, or even minor ones, actually happening, even in weeks where
I found I had logged a thousand miles of rush-hour driving. So one
learns to proceed with a strange and exhilarating mixture of long-
range confidence and close-range wariness. . . . I cannot find it in me
to complain about the freeways in Los Angeles; they work uncom-
monly well. . . .

For most Angeleno freeway-pilots, their white-wall tyres are singing over the diamond-cut anti-skid grooves in the concrete road surface, the selector-levers of their automatic gearboxes are firmly in
Drive, and the radio is on. And more important than any of this, they
are acting out one of the most spectacular paradoxes in the great
debate between private freedom and public discipline that pervades
every affluent mechanized urban society.

City Limits or New Horizons

The private car and the public freeway together provide an ideal —not to say idealized—version of democratic urban transportation: door-to-door movement on demand at high average speeds over a very large area. The degree of freedom and convenience thus offered to all but a small (but now conspicuous) segment of the population is such that no Angeleno will be in a hurry to sacrifice it for the higher efficiency but drastically lowered convenience and freedom of choice of any high-density public rapid-transit system. Yet what seems to be hardly noticed or commented on is that the price of rapid door-to-door transport on demand is the almost total surrender of personal freedom for most of the journey.

The watchful tolerance and almost impeccable lane discipline of Angeleno drivers on the freeways is often noted, but not the fact that both are symptoms of something deeper—willing acquiescence in an incredibly demanding man/machine system. The fact that no single ordinance, specification or instruction manual describes the system in its totality does not make it any less complete or all-embracing—or any less demanding. It demands, first of all, an open but decisive attitude to the placing of the car on the road-surface, a constant stream of decisions that it would be fashionable to describe as "existential" or even "situational," but would be better to regard simply as a higher form of pragmatism. The carriage-way is not divided by the kind of kindergarten rule of the road that obtains on British motorways, with their fast, slow, and overtaking lanes (where there are three lanes to use!). The three, four, or five lanes of an Angeleno freeway are virtually equal, the driver is required to select or change lanes according to his speed, surrounding circumstances and future intentions. If everybody does this with the approved mixture of enlightened self-interest and public spirit, it is possible to keep a very large flow of traffic moving quite surprisingly fast.

But at certain points, notably intersections, the lanes are not all equal—some may be pre-empted for a particular exit or change-over ramp as much as a mile before the actual junction. As far as possible the driver must get set up for these pre-empted lanes well in advance, to be sure he is in them in good time because the topology of the intersections is unforgiving. Of course there are occasional clods and strangers who do not sense the urgency of the obligation to set up the lane required good and early, but fortunately they are only occasional (you soon get the message!), otherwise the whole system would snarl up irretrievably. But if these preparations are only an unwritten moral obligation, your actual presence in the correct lane at the intersection is mandatory—the huge signs straddling the freeway to indicate the correct lanes must be obeyed because they are infallible.

At first, these signs can be the most psychologically unsettling of all aspects of the freeway—it seems incredibly bizarre when a sign directs one into the far left lane for an objective clearly visible on the right of the carriageway, but the sign must be believed. No human eye at windscreen level can unravel the complexities of even a relatively simple intersection (none of those in Los Angeles is a symmetrical cloverleaf) fast enough for a normal human brain moving forward at up to sixty mph to make the right decision in time, and there is no alternative to complete surrender of will to the instructions on the signs.

But no permanent system of fixed signs can give warning of transient situations requiring decisions, such as accidents, landslips or other blockages. It is in the nature of a freeway accident that it involves a large number of vehicles, and blocks the carriageway so completely that even emergency vehicles have difficulty in getting to the seat of the trouble and remedial action such as warnings and diversions may have to be phased back miles before the accident, and are likely to affect traffic moving in the opposite direction in the other carriageway as well. So, inevitably the driver has to rely on other sources of rapid information, and keeps his car radio turned on for warnings of delays and recommended diversions.

Now, the source of these radio messages is not a publicly-operated traffic-control radio transmitter; they are a public service performed by the normal entertainment stations, who derive the information from the police, the Highway Patrol, and their own "Sigalert" helicopter patrols. Although the channels of information are not provided as a designed component of the freeway system, but arise as an accidental by-product of commercial competition, they are no less essential to the system's proper operation, especially at rush hours. Thus a variety of commanding authorities—moral, governmental, commercial, and mechanical (since most drivers have surrendered control of the transmission to an automatic gearbox—direct the

477

freeway driver through a situation so closely controlled that, as has been judiciously observed on a number of occasions, he will hardly notice any difference when the freeways are finally fitted with computerized automatic control systems that will take charge of the car at the on-ramp and direct it at properly regulated speeds and correctly selected routes to a pre-programmed choice of off-ramp.

But it seems possible that, given a body of drivers already so well trained, disciplined, and conditioned, realistic cost-benefit analysis might show that the marginal gains in efficiency through automation might be offset by the psychological deprivations caused by destroying the residual illusions of free decision and driving skill surviving in the present situation. However inefficiently organized, the million or so human minds at large on the freeway system at any time comprise a far greater computing capacity than could be built into any machine currently conceivable—why not put that capacity to work by fostering the illusion that it is in charge of the situation?

If illusion plays as large a part in the working of the freeways as it does in other parts of the Angeleno ecology, it is not to be deprecated. The system works as well as it does because the Angelenos believe in it as much as they do; they may squeal when the illusion is temporarily shattered or frustrated; they may share the distrust of the Division of Highways that many liberal souls currently (and understandably) seem to feel; but on leaving the house they still turn the nose of the car towards the nearest freeway ramp because they still believe the freeways are the way to get there. They subscribe, if only covertly, to a deep-seated mystique of freeway driving, and I often suspect that the scarifying stories of the horrors of the freeways are deliberately put about to warn off strangers.

Partly this would be to keep inexperienced and therefore dangerous hayseeds off the carriageways, but it would also be to prevent the profanation of their most sacred ritual by the uninitiated. For the Freeway, quite as much as the Beach, is where the Angeleno is most himself, most integrally identified with his great city.

Reyner Banham, *Los Angeles: The Architecture of Four Ecologies* (New York: Harper & Row, 1971), 214–221.

Serendipity at 55 m.p.h.
PHIL KERBY

In the winter of 1973–74 the energy crunch brought about by the Arab oil embargo struck at the heart of Los Angeles' value system and code of behavior. Queuing up for gas and odd/ even rationing were part of the travail, but not to compare with the inhuman restraint of a 55 m.p.h. speed limit. Phil Kerby's essay is of early-shortage vintage.

The other day, as the sun sank in the west, I made the sweeping curve off Broadway, circled back under the Broadway overpass, up the Hollywood Freeway onramp and prepared to maneuver my compact (which goes putt-putt-putt, not oom-oom-oom) into the traffic flow.

It is always a close decision. On one occasion in the not so distant past, I didn't make it across to the Hollywood. No driver would yield, and I careened off to the right and went snarling north on the Pasadena Freeway.

This time was different. As always at the evening rush hour, the Hollywood was a continuous line of flowing steel. I edged cautiously toward the outside lane, the compact's left rear blinker dutifully signaling my intention.

One of those beautiful monsters, long and black and humming with surplus power, pulled up alongside me. I glanced at the driver. He was a handsome fellow, trim mustache, fiftyish, and looking so comfortable and confident I knew his father must have been one of the elect who had bought a lot on Wilshire long ago at the right time and right place.

He was not a man to take second place in anything. I knew absolutely. I'm good at that sort of instant analysis. Then the unthinkable happened: he motioned me to move into the lane ahead of him. Ahead of him? Me and my little compact?

479

Now safely into the lane courtesy of the confident man, I headed into the twilight in a mellow mood. The traffic moved along briskly until we struggled past the Vermont bottleneck, then picked up speed and slowed again past Melrose, Santa Monica and Sunset. The usual pattern. By the time the Highland Avenue turnoff sign loomed ahead, all lanes were moving at a satisfactory clip.

It was then that this young fellow, tooling along in an orange Mustang with a vicious black body stripe, tried to sneak in front of me. Impudent kid. Arrogant. Long hair, too. I started to step on the gas, but didn't. An unnatural emotion came over me. I waved him somewhat grandly into the lane. He grinned and waved back. "Nice kid," I thought.

I eased onto the offramp and came to a smooth stop at the Highland Avenue traffic signal. My pulse was steady, my breathing regular, my conscience clear, for I had flung no vain oaths at other drivers and had done nothing to earn their curses in return.

I reached home contented and relaxed. My wife thought something wonderful must have happened at the office. But I said no, it was just the spirit of accommodation and courtesy at 55 m.p.h.

Whatever you may think of the energy crisis, it's taken the keen, angry edge out of freeway commuting. Thanks, Sheik Yamani, or whoever you are.

Los Angeles *Times*, December 1973.

Three Prongs in the Fountain
JACK SMITH

At the Civic Center, the palace of the Department of Water and Power was deliberately planned to set an example of conspicuous consumption of the department's two commodities.

480

Three Prongs in the Fountain

The glass building is heated by its lights which never go off and the wide reflecting pool is enlivened by splashing fountains. Or rather, so it was until the energy crunch when the lights were dimmed and the water turned off. Volunteer artists came to the rescue, relying merely on battery power. The effect, as all admit, was pleasing, but by bureaucratic knee-jerk reaction the art form was promptly erased. No wonder this episode calls to mind the Pink Lady of Malibu Canyon Road, another work of art summarily blotted out by bureaucratic fiat, all for lack of an art appreciation requirement in the civil service eligibility standards.

I am disconsolate that I didn't get to see the irreverent sculpture that stood for a few hours last Friday morning in the reflecting pools of the Department of Water and Power building in the Civic Center.

The first I knew of its brief life was when I brought the paper in on Saturday morning and saw the picture on the front page. It showed three men in hip boots pulling down the sculpture in front of a gallery of Civic Center workers whose mood could only be guessed at.

The story said the work of art had sprouted overnight in the pool, describing it as "a three-pronged, serpentine, green-bronze, hollow beanstalk topped by orange and yellow translucent lotuses which alternately lighted up and spouted water."

In the picture the "sprouts" looked about three times as tall as the men in hip boots. They were thicker at the bottom, growing thinner, like elephant trunks thrusting up out of the water and balancing the lotus blossoms, as big as washtubs, at the top. They reminded me of that remarkable creation of the Baja desert, the boojum tree, which also resembles an elephant's trunk with a flower at the top.

I am disconsolate, as I say, that I was not there Friday morning when these insouciant intruders were discovered, alternately lighting up and spouting water, by DWP employees showing up for another day's work.

As the story in the paper said, some of them welcomed the spouting lotuses as "the most exciting thing to happen around here since the energy shortage," and they must have been disappointed when,

481

long before the sun was overhead, the maintenance crew waded into the pool and stolidly began their nihilistic task.

It was inevitable. The sculpture after all was contraband. It was installed by its creator and his helpers in dark of night, and its presence was not only an affront to the dignity of the DWP but a break of the standard committee procedures by which works of art are procured in a proper bureaucracy.

The picture of the workmen executing their cheerless assignment, while the crowd hung back, too prudent to protest, reminded me sharply of the Pink Lady affair of a few years ago.

The Pink Lady, you may remember, was a nude woman, 60 feet high, who appeared at dawn one morning, very much like the sprouting lotuses, on a sheer rock cliff above a tunnel on Malibu Canyon Road.

She was exuberant and free. One hand clutched a sprig of wildflowers and her long dark tresses flowed backwards as she gamboled across the rock, nude and pink as a rose.

To a populace worn ragged by bad news and worse politics, the Pink Lady was a refreshment; a symbol of uninhibited joy. In 24 hours she was a cause celèbre. Cars gorged the roadside for a half-mile back from the tunnel. Crowds gawked, wondering at the nerve and skill of the anonymous artist. They took movies and snapshots and argued about art and morality. The Pink Lady's message, said the editorial page of The Times, was "toujours gai."

But of course, she was contraband; a witch. She had to go. They set the fire department on her first, but the Pink Lady was not to be easily exorcised. High-power hoses failed to dissolve her. Paint remover only turned her pinker. The first day's assault ended in darkness and humiliation.

They were back the next morning, trampling on leaflets describing them as "brutal, sadistic, prudish, inartistic and Victorian." In the end, they had to paint the lady out with spray guns. Like insects they stood on her ears, her lips, her knees, inch by inch despoiling her flesh until at last she was only a pink shadow of herself.

Like the Pink Lady, the Civic Center lotus sculpture was an irresistible outcropping of joy in a joyless time. The godfathers of the DWP, seeking to set an example for a simpleminded public in the energy crisis, had turned off their own lights and fountains and taken to public acts of asceticism like Hindu fakirs.

Is it any wonder that now and then the frustrated cockroach in us cries out "toujours gai, mehitabel, toujours gai!"?

Los Angeles *Times*, June 19, 1974.

Planning for the Future
ALLAN TEMKO AND HARVEY S. PERLOFF

Architects of the future of Los Angeles seek to combine the best of both possible worlds—revival of the pristine ambiance and garden setting and, along with that, regeneration of the economy, including a "reasonable" resumption of population growth.

Writing in 1966, Allan Temko expressed confidence that the burgeoning art of urban planning would rise to the challenge.

A decade later, at a time when the growth rate and the appetite for growth had fallen markedly, Harvey S. Perloff assessed the resources and outlined the parameters for strengthening the central business district and improving housing and employment for the ghetto and barrio. Thereby substantial benefits would flow to the outer city and suburbs.

TEMKO: The future of Southern California is potentially magnificent; and by many standards it is already one of the most civilized places on earth, where Aldous Huxley, who had such sane misgivings about the future, did not disdain to live and where Igor Stravinsky and Charles Eames live today. In virtually all of the creative arts, particularly movies, TV, electronic music, and other nonofficial art forms that have sprung out of our own technological age, Los Angeles more than holds its own.

However, Southern California represents a deeply disturbing phase in urban history. Never before has so far-flung a pattern of random, low-density settlement erupted so swiftly, ruthlessly and senselessly. Few civilizations have had the opportunity to build in a setting of such sweeping grandeur, blessed with a climate which until recently was one of the most benign on earth. Precisely because of its beauty, this land demanded the most exquisite sensibility on the part of developers, for it wounds easily.

Moreover, individual man has found his basic need for urbane social intercourse thwarted by excessive diffusion of cultural resources. Over hundreds of square miles, there are few places to walk, few occasions for the civilized surprise, the beautiful chance meetings, almost birthrights for citizens of richly venerable cities such as London and Rome. The only discernible urban structure, on the scale that the Super-City requires, is the freeway network. To make this a truly great city, rather than simply a mammoth one, all sorts of new structures must be interwoven logically in a strengthened urban tissue.

Considered as a population magnet alone, this is clearly one of the most attractive places on earth. Very likely 20 million—and possibly 3 or 4 million more—will dwell in Super-City by the turn of the century, with no end of growth yet in sight.

There is room enough in the Super-City . . . if only we have the wisdom to conserve the resources which remain unspoiled, and to renew the resources which have been wantonly damaged. We must decide where we should build, and where the wisest course would be to leave land undeveloped, according to the full scope of future needs.

Not only people but machines are proliferating, and they must also be taken into account if any realistic attempt is made to create a biotechnic civic order where all now appears to be disorder.

All this would require political and social maturity such as Americans have yet to prove they possess, as well as efficient management such as we have never achieved in spite of pretensions of "Yankee know-how." For obviously there is much, at this still primitive stage of human development, that we do not know, that we cannot do. The only way to learn is to accept the reality of the new scale of urban civilization, to rejoice in its challenge, and above all to realize that we possess the wealth and strength to make it the good thing it can easily and swifly become.

Adapted from Allan Temko, "Reshaping Super-City: The Problem of Los Angeles," *Cry California* (Spring, 1966), 4–10.

PERLOFF: Urban renewal and "model cities" have usually emphasized problem areas and situations often seen in limited and isolated perspective—rundown neighborhoods, declining central business districts, the most extreme poverty areas, and the like. Whether concentrating on slum clearance and substitution of better housing or on razing business blocks and erecting more imposing structures, the result too often has been creation of small islands of improvement in a sea of decline.

Although numerous factors such as heavy dependence upon the automobile, an extensive freeway system, and considerable readily available land have combined to make Los Angeles' economic activities more dispersed than is the case in most other American cities, contrary to popular belief this does not imply that the city lacks a clearly defined center. Los Angeles has retained a "downtown" focus, with a major governmental, commercial and banking center at the main freeway crossroads in the heart of the urbanized area. While there are significant competing centers, most of these are close to or oriented towards the central sections of the city.

In terms of office and commercial activity, the central business district is by far the largest single center of the county. The largest single employment center is downtown. Major shopping centers are more dispersed, but even these tend to be most strongly represented at or near the city core. The center of the city has a natural geographic advantage and great overall accessibility. Located near the "middle," it is obviously closer to more areas of the city than any of the more outlying subcenters. Such factors illustrate the importance of central Los Angeles to the well-being of the city as a whole.

The central business district is clearly the single largest economic and social asset. Logically, the core sector of a comprehensive development program would focus upon the central business district. It acts as a magnet for numerous service industries. Private investment

485

in urban renewal (Bunker Hill) may ultimately exceed $1 billion. Efforts already well advanced to produce a "Downtown Plan" could become the foundation for a broader revitalization strategy. Thus, downtown Los Angeles would anchor a citywide development program.

The Wilshire Corridor, running about 25 miles west from the central business district to the Pacific, is a most striking feature in the economic geography of the region. It is virtually a linear downtown of office buildings, commercial services, industrial headquarters, cultural and recreational facilities, and both high and low density residential land. In office space, stores, apartments, and employment this attenuation of downtown matches the Central Business District.

Los Angeles International Airport is the most rapidly growing major acitivity node in the Los Angeles region, an emerging city within the city. The airport is the largest single-place employer in Southern California with primary and secondary employment reaching 101,688 in 1970 and projected to reach 172,000 in 1980.

Perhaps uniquely in Southern California, the efforts of the "industrial cities" to attract and retain major employers show what can be achieved when the idea of "public-private partnership for economic development" is stretched to its logical conclusion. It may be true, as some allege, that these cities are successful because of their ability to internalize benefits and externalize costs to the rest of the region.

The City of Industry was incorporated in 1957, primarily for warehousing, distribution and manufacturing. Local residents number only about 700, while total employees of the 335 firms located there now number over 35,000. The city is 18 miles long and varies in width from 2 miles to 200 feet. It includes within its boundaries main east-west trackage for both Southern Pacific and Union Pacific Railroads.

Growth was rapid during the 1960s; 1470 acres were developed and 25,000 employees were added. It is estimated that an additional 1150 acres within the city will be developed during the 1970s. Few of the tax dollars generated by the economic activity taking place redound to the benefit of the City of Los Angeles and other adjacent cities which house the employees of the City of Industry.

This city, along with the City of Commerce, Vernon, Huntington Park, South Gate, and some others, make up what is known as the Industrial Corridor extending southward some fifteen miles just to the east of South Central Los Angeles. The corridor represents an employment base of over 250,000 primarily labor intensive jobs, but because of discriminatory practices it has actually employed relatively few blacks from south Los Angeles.

When low income, high unemployment, poor housing, segregated schools, and other indicators of impacted poverty are mapped, pockets show in the Pacoima, Venice, and Harbor areas, but the concentration is chiefly in central Los Angeles. An area south of the central business district, with an arm reaching to the harbor and another westward toward Venice coincides with the main concentration of black population. Another area reaching east of the central business district and extending beyond the city limits has predominantly Spanish-speaking residents. Taken together, these areas represent what may be the most geographically extensive zone of urban poverty in any American city.

Not surprisingly, the oldest housing is found near the center of the urbanized area. Other structures and the associated streets, utilities, and other facilities are correspondingly old. Thus, although Los Angeles may be a somewhat younger city than most urban centers of the east, much of the housing and infrastructure at its center is near or past the limits of expected usefulness.

Several areas can be singled out as "ripe" in need for developmental assistance. Perhaps the most noteworthy is Watts, which could in fact qualify as the prototype for such an area. Long the focus of numerous public and private programs, Watts possesses an increasingly effective array of community organizations and an aware, concerned resident population which might become strongly involved in a developmental effort. Watts might form the logical southern extension of the first phase of a "new town intown" core development sector.

Further north the residential communities around the University of Southern California and Exposition Park also stand out as a likely "primary impact area." Already the focus of several major public efforts (Hoover Urban Renewal Project, Normandie Neighborhood

Development Project, Pico-Union NDP), this area also benefits from its ready accessibility to the surrounding public and private institutions and facilities.

East Los Angeles/Boyle Heights, immediately adjacent to the central business district, will benefit from whatever revitalization successes are scored downtown in terms of increased opportunities for employment, services, etc. While East Los Angeles' organizational matrix is still in the formative stages, the growing Chicano consciousness could prove a valuable strength. Its unique character and resources suggest many residents would benefit significantly through the expansion of opportunities resulting from a successful "new town intown" program.

Although enhancing opportunity for the less advantaged would be an important objective, little would be accomplished if redevelopment efforts were restricted to areas where the less advantaged are concentrated. Such isolated approaches have almost invariably failed in the past.

Adapted from Harvey S. Perloff, *Modernizing the Central City: New Towns Intown—and Beyond* (Cambridge, Mass.: Ballinger Publishing Company, 1975).

Prospects of New Horizons
*

At the three-quarter mark in the twentieth century Los Angeles found itself caught in a serious recession, a fall-off in business and production, construction at a standstill, and unemployment distressingly high. Bewilderingly, prices and taxes were still going up, as was real estate. School enrollments had dropped and more people were moving away than moving in.

The Chamber of Commerce, the realtors, the banks, the press, City Hall, the county supervisors, and most residents remained optimistic. Accustomed to thinking of theirs as preeminently a growth city, they were not about to sell Los Angeles short. In varying degree they had awareness of the prodigious growth it had achieved over the past several generations and they counted on another such surge in the next couple of decades.

A more searching look at the growth pattern would have noted that the great advances in the economy owed much to new additives such as the movies, automobiles, and gushing oil wells in the twenties, and the freeways, computers, weapons contracts, and moon race in the next great prosperity.

Economists agreed that resumption of a 4 to 5 percent per annum growth rate was prerequisite to prosperity. They saw few lines of current production that promised that rate of increase. Nor was a grand new elixir for the metropolitan economy identifiable.

By the seventies the economists, and the environmentalists even more vociferously, warned of impending disaster. There had been signals. The brown pelicans forewarned that "better living through chemistry" could mean extinction. The Los Angeles River, perhaps because it carried water only when there was storm runoff, did not

489

make the list of most polluted streams, but the harbor at its mouth became another Lake Erie. Air pollution along with urban sprawl put a great crimp in the once flourishing agriculture of the Los Angeles area. Although the basin was yet to have a killer smog, smog worsened in frequency and in extent. A hint on what was happening came when the coroner, seeking to identify a girl murdered on Mulholland, certified that she must have arrived very recently because her lungs were clean, a conclusion subsequently confirmed.

Citing evidence that the local ecology was already at the breaking point, environmentalists warned that it cannot be expected to hold up if we add another 10 million residents or even half that many. More persons can be shoehorned in; there are slopes that can be bulldozed into building pads and there are single-family homes that could be replaced by multiple housing. But a two-for-one increase in housing, automobiles, streets and parking places, shopping centers, schools and public facilities, ballparks, tennis courts, air conditioners, and wastes to dispose of would threaten not just a despoiling but the ruination of the natural setting, so central a component of life in Los Angeles.

There was a time when Los Angeles cringed at a specter of no growth; now growth itself had become the specter.

Short of Butler's *Erehwon* or Huxley's *Brave New World*, are there new and better horizons for Los Angeles? Those who say yes throw in a few provisos: with concentration on clean business and industry, with substitution of clean energy, with increased self-sufficiency for each of a couple of hundred neighborhoods, by trading in the internal combustion engine for combustion outside the basin, and by curbing technology and housebreaking science. The implications include genuinely metropolitan planning, redirection of science and technology from war games to the life sciences and social sciences, a widespread restraint that will permit a regreening of Los Angeles, and, above all, recognition that there is an ecological imperative.

Pessimists and optimists agree that if life in Los Angeles is not made better, it will become worse.

Acknowledgments

For permission to reprint selections indicated we thank these copyright holders:

Southwest Museum: "People of the Chaparral" and "Vagrant Rivers," Bernice Eastman Johnson, *California's Gabrielino Indians,* © 1962.

Glen Dawson: "Channel Island Artifacts," Arthur Woodward, *The Sea Diary of Fr. Juan Vizcaino,* © 1959.

University of California Press: "Talking to Grizzlies," Tracy Storer and Lloyd P. Tevis, Jr., *California Grizzly,* © 1955; "First Travelers through the Land," H. E. Bolton, *Fray Juan Crespi,* © 1927; "Three Tortillas a Day" and "The Mission Flourishes," Bolton, *Anza's California Expeditions,* © 1930; "License To Marry," Susanna Bryant Dakin, *A Scotch Paisano,* © 1939; "Crime and Punishment," Leonard Pitt, *The Decline of the Californias,* © 1966; "The Captivity of Olive Oatman," William B. Rice, *The Los Angeles Star,* © 1947; "A Most Lovely Locality," W. H. Brewer, *Up and Down California,* © 1930; "Pacific Electric" and "Abbot Kinney's Venice," Franklin Walker, *A Literary History of Southern California,* © 1950; "The Crime of the Century," Grace Heilman Stimson, *Rise of the Labor Movement in Los Angeles,* © 1955; "UCLA," Ansel Adams and Nancy Newhall, *Fiat Lux,* © 1967.

California Historical Society: "First Glimpse of the Coast," H. R. Wagner, *Juan Rodriguez Cabrillo,* © 1941; "Along the Coast in 1602," Wagner, *Spanish Voyages to the Northwest Coast,* © 1929; "The Pueblo of Los Angeles Is Founded," E. A. Beilharz, *Felipe de Neve,* © 1971; "A Rascally Set," Doyce B. Nunis, Jr., *The California Diary of Faxon Dean Atherton,* © 1964.

Arthur H. Clark Co.: "A Mission at Climax," H. C. Dale, *The Ashley-Smith Explorations,* © 1918; "The Failure of San Francisquito Dam," Charles Outland, *Man-Made Disaster,* © 1963.

Henry E. Huntington Library and Art Gallery: "Life on the Ranchos and "The Passing of the Cow Counties," R. G. Cleland, *The Cattle on a Thousand Hills,* © 1941; "Madame Modjeska's Utopian Dream," R. V. Hine, *California's Utopian Colonies,* © 1953; "A Health Rush Begins," John E. Baur, *The Health-Seekers of Southern California,* © 1959; "A Carefully Measured Conclusion," G. S. Dumke, *The Boom of the Eighties,* © 1944; "Smog Settles over Los Angeles," John Anson Ford, *Thirty Explosive Years,* © 1961.

Robert C. Post: "Steel Ropes into the Howling Wilderness," *Street Railways in Los Angeles,* © 1967.

Josephine Kingsbury Jacobs: "Sunkist Advertising—the Iowa Campaign," *Sunkist Advertising,* © 1966.

491

Acknowledgments

Maxim Lieber: "The Rape of Owens Valley" and "Millionaires' Retreat," Morrow Mayo, *Los Angeles*, © 1933.

Remi Nadeau: "There It is—Take It," *The Water Seekers*, © 1950; "Enter the Moviemakers" and "Supersubdivider," *Los Angeles from Mission to Modern City*, © 1960.

John O. Pohlmann: "The Missions Romanticized," *California's Mission Myth*, © 1974.

Southern California Quarterly: "The Real Estate Boom of the Twenties," W. W. Robinson, © 1942.

Westernlore Press: "The Miracle of the Boysenberry," Roger Holmes and Paul Bailey, *Fabulous Farmer*, © 1941.

University of Oklahoma Press: "Simon Rodia," Andrew F. Rolle, *The Immigrant Upraised*, © 1968.

Olivier, Maney & Co. "Introducing the Cut-Rate Drug Store," David E. Albert, *Dear Grandson*, © 1950.

Rinehart & Co.: "Building Boulder Dam," Frank Waters, *The Colorado*, © 1946.

University of North Carolina Press: "Raymond Chandler's Los Angeles," Philip Durham, *Down These Mean Streets*, © 1963.

Ad Schulberg: "What Makes Sammy Run?" Budd Schulberg, *What Makes Sammy Run?* © 1941.

H. Marshall Goodwin, "The First Freeway," © 1969.

Carey McWilliams: "When I Return from a Trip to the East," *Southern California Country*, © 1946; "The Garment Industry," *California the Great Exception*, © 1949.

Dalton Trumbo: "Johnny Got His Gun," © 1939, 1959.

Los Angeles *Times:* "The Great Los Angeles Air Raid" and "Three Prongs in the Fountain," Jack Smith, © 1975, 1974; "H₂O'Malley, or, Let 'em Drink Beer," Jim Murray, © 1962; "Serendipity at 55 mph," Phil Kerby, © 1973.

Roger Daniels: "Why It Happened Here," *Racism in California*, © 1972

John D. Weaver: "War on the Zoot-Suiters," *L.A.: El Pueblo Grande*, © 1973.

Earl Pomeroy: "From War Profits to Peace Profits," *The Pacific Slope*, © 1965.

Abraham Polonsky: "The Sign-Up," *A Season of Fear*, © 1956.

Harper & Row and Mrs. Laura Huxley: "Hyperion to a Satyr," Aldous Huxley, *Tomorrow and Tomorrow and Tomorrow*, © 1956.

Lawrence Lipton: "A Revolution under the Ribs," *The Holy Barbarians*, © 1959.

Elizabeth Poe: "Nobody Was Listening," *Frontier*, © 1965.

California Tomorrow: "Home Is a Freeway," William Bronson, and "Planning for the Future," Allan Temko, *Cry California*, © 1966.

Prentice-Hall: "Overview," Neil Morgan, *The California Syndrome*, © 1969.

Sierra Club Bulletin: "The Mountains and the Megalopolis," Joseph E.

Acknowledgments

Brown, © 1973; "Black Mesa," William Brown, © 1970; "Smog for Export," William Greenburg, © 1975.

Alfred A. Knopf: "Brush Fires," Richard G. Lillard, *Eden in Jeopardy*, © 1966.

Gregor Piatigorsky: "Parthenon of the West," © 1974.

Howard F. Stein: "All in the Family," *Family Process*, © 1974.

Harper and Row: "Slaves and Masters of the Freeways," Reyner Banham, *Los Angeles, The Architecture of Four Ecologies*, © 1971.

Harvey S. Perloff: "Planning for the Future," *Modernizing the Central City*, © 1975.

Selected Readings

General

Lynn Bowman. *Los Angeles: Epic of a City* (1974).
John Caughey. *California: A Remarkable State's Life History* (1970).
John & LaRee Caughey. *California Heritage* (1971).
Laurance L. Hill. *La Reina: Los Angeles in Three Centuries* (1929).
Remi Nadeau. *Los Angeles from Mission to Modern City* (1960).
Earl Pomeroy. *The Pacific Slope* (1965).
Lawrence Clark Powell. *California Classics* (1971).
W. W. Robinson. *Land in California* (1948).
_____. *Lawyers of Los Angeles* (1959).
_____. *Los Angeles, a Profile* (1968).
_____. *Panorama: A Picture History of Southern California* (1953).
_____. *What They Say About the Angels* (1942).
Andrew F. Rolle. *California, a History* (1963).
John D. Weaver. *L.A.: El Pueblo Grande* (1973).
Max Yavno and Lee Shippey. *The Los Angeles Book* (1950).

The Gabrielino and Their Home

Gerónimo Boscana. "Chinigchinich," in Alfred Robinson, *Life in California* (1846), and reprinted separately (1933).
John Caughey, ed. *The Indians of Southern California in 1852: The B. D. Wilson Report* (1952).
S. F. Cook. *The Conflict between the California Indian and White Civilization* (1943).
Bernice Eastman Johnston. *California's Gabrielino Indians* (1962).
Hugo Reid. "The Indians of Los Angeles County," Los Angeles *Star*, 1851; reprinted (1926).

The Spaniards Steal the Scene

Edwin A. Beilharz. *Felipe de Neve* (1971).
Herbert E. Bolton. *Anza's California Expeditions*, 5 volumes (1930).
_____. *Fray Juan Crespi, Missionary Explorer* (1927).
John Caughey. *The Pueblo Water Right of Los Angeles, Historically Considered* (1969).

Selected Readings

Miguel Costansó. *Diary*, edited by F. J. Teggart (1911).
Zephyrin Engelhardt. *San Gabriel Mission* (1927).
Historical Society of Southern California. *Annual Publication* (1931).
Adele Ogden. *The California Sea Otter Trade* (1941).
William Shaler. *Journal of a Voyage*, edited by Lindley Bynum (1935).
Theodore E. Treutlein. "Los Angeles California, the Question of the City's Original Spanish Name," *SCQ* 55 (1973), 1–9.
_____. "The Portolá Expedition," *CHQ* 47 (1968), 271–314.
Henry R. Wagner. *Juan Rodriguez Cabrillo: Discoverer of the Coast of California* (1941).
_____. *Spanish Voyages to the Northwest Coast* (1929).

Pastoral Interlude

Hubert Howe Bancroft. *California Pastoral* (1888).
Robert G. Cleland. *The Cattle on a Thousand Hills* (1941).
Susanna B. Dakin. *Scotch Paisano* [Hugo Reid] (1939).
Richard Henry Dana. *Two Years Before the Mast* (1840).
Augusta Fink. *Time and the Terraced Land* [Palos Verdes] (1966).
Robert Gillingham. *Rancho San Pedro* (1961).
C. Alan Hutchinson. *Frontier Settlement in Mexican California* (1969).
James Ohio Pattie. *Personal Narrative* (1831).
Alfred Robinson. *Life in California* (1846).
W. W. Robinson. *Ranchos Become Cities* (1939).
W. W. Robinson and Lawrence Clark Powell. *The Malibu* (1958).
Nellie Van de Grift Sánchez. *Spanish Arcadia* (1929).

American Takeover

George W. Ames, Jr., ed. *A Doctor Comes to California* (1943).
Horace Bell. *On the Old West Coast* (1930).
_____. *Reminiscences of a Ranger* (1881).
Edwin Bryant. *What I Saw in California* (1848).
John Caughey. "Don Benito Wilson," *HLQ* II (1939), 285–300.
Benjamin Hayes. *Pioneer Notes*, ed. by Marjorie Tisdale Wolcott (1929).
Werner Marti. *Messenger of Destiny: Archibald Gillespie* (1960).
Harris Newmark. *Sixty Years in Southern California* (1916; 1930).
Leonard Pitt. *The Decline of the Californios* (1966).
William B. Rice. *The Los Angeles Star* (1947).
W. W. Robinson. *People versus Lugo* (1962).

An American City Emerges

Mary Austin. *The Flock* (1906).
_____. *The Land of Little Rain* (1903).

Selected Readings

John E. Baur. *The Health Seekers of Southern California* (1959).
Earle Crowe. *Men of El Tejon* (1957).
Glenn S. Dumke. *The Boom of the Eighties* (1944).
Robert M. Fogelson. *The Fragmented Metropolis* (1967).
Helen S. Giffen and Arthur Woodward. *Story of El Tejon* (1942).
Helen Hunt Jackson. *A Century of Dishonor* (1885).
Walter Lindley and J. P. Widney. *California of the South* (1888).
Remi Nadeau. *City-Makers* (1948).
Charles Nordhoff. *California: For Health, Pleasure, and Residence* (1872).
Ludwig L. Salvator. *Los Angeles in the Sunny Seventies*, translated by
    Marguerite Eyer Wilbur (1929).
Ben C. Truman. *Tiburcio Vásquez* (1874; 1941).
T. S. Van Dyke. *Millionaires of a Day* (1890).
J. J. Warner, Benjamin Hayes, and J. P. Widney. *Historical Sketch of Los
    Angeles* (1876; 1936).
J. Albert Wilson. *History of Los Angeles County* (1880).

Specter of No Growth

Mary Austin. *The Ford* (1917).
Edwin R. Bingham. *Charles F. Lummis, Editor* (1955).
Spencer Crump. *Ride the Big Red Cars* (1962).
Donald Duke. *Pacific Electric Railway* (1958).
Dudley Gordon. *Charles F. Lummis, Crusader in Corduroy* (1972).
J. A. Graves. *My Seventy Years in California* (1927).
Morrow Mayo. *Los Angeles* (1933).
Remi Nadeau. *The Water Seekers* (1950).
Vincent Ostrom. *Water and Politics* (1953).
Charles C. Teague. *Fifty Years a Rancher* (1944).
Franklin Walker. *Literary History of Southern California* (1950).

Autos and Movies and Oil

Ralph D. Connell. *Conspicuous California Plants* (1938).
Guy W. Finney. *The Great Los Angeles Bubble* (1929).
Francis M. Fultz. *The Elfin Forest of California* (1923).
David Gebhard and Robert Winter. *A Guide to Architecture in Southern
    California* (1965).
Phil Townsend Hanna. *The Wheel and the Bell* (1950).
Robinson Jeffers. *The Californians* (1916).
Esther McCoy. *Five California Architects* (1960).
Carey McWilliams. *Southern California Country* (1946).
Nancy Barr Mavity. *Sister Aimee* (1931).
Wallace Stegner. *The Preacher and the Slave* (1950).
Grace Heilman Stimson. *Rise of the Labor Movement in Los Angeles* (1955).

Selected Readings

Anton Wagner. *Los Angeles: Werden, Leben und Gestalt der Zweimillionenstadt in Südkalifornien* (1935).

A Time of Catastrophe

David E. Albert. *Dear Grandson* (1950).
James M. Cain. *Three of a Kind* (1944).
Philip Durham. *Down These Mean Streets a Man Must Go: Raymond Chandler's Knight* (1963).
F. Scott Fitzgerald. *The Last Tycoon* (1941).
David Gebhard and Harriette Von Breton. *L.A. in the Thirties* (1975).
Gladwin Hill. *Dancing Bear: An Inside Look at California Politics* (1968).
Roger Holmes and Paul Bailey. *Fabulous Farmer: The Story of Walter Knott and His Berry Farm* (1941).
Aldous Huxley. *After Many a Summer* (1946).
Esther McCoy. *Richard Neutra* (1960).
Charles F. Outland. *Man-Made Disaster* (1963).
J. B. Priestley. *Midnight on the Desert* (1937).
Budd Schulberg. *What Makes Sammy Run?* (1941).
Upton Sinclair. *I, Governor of California, and How I Ended Poverty* (1933).
_____. *I, Candidate for Governor, and How I Got Licked* (1934).
Nathanael West. *The Day of the Locust* (1939).
Luther Whiteman and Samuel L. Lewis. *Glory Roads: The Psychological State of California* (1936).

Adjusting to War and to Peace

Libbie Block. *The Hills of Beverly* (1957).
Allan R. Bosworth. *America's Concentration Camps* (1967).
Roger Daniels. *Concentration Camps USA* (1971).
_____. *The Decision To Relocate the Japanese* (1975).
Roger Daniels and Spencer C. Olin, Jr., *Racism in California* (1972).
John Anson Ford. *Thirty Explosive Years in Los Angeles* (1961).
Beatrice Griffith. *American Me* (1948).
Morton Grodzins. *Americans Betrayed* (1949).
Carey McWilliams. *California the Great Exception* (1949).
Lillian Ross. *Picture* (1952).
Dalton Trumbo. *Johnny Got His Gun* (1939).
Evelyn Waugh. *The Loved One* (1948).
Matt Weinstock. *My L.A.* (1947).

Megalopolis

John & LaRee Caughey. *School Segregation on Our Doorstep* (1966).
John Caughey. *The Shame of Los Angeles* (1971).

Selected Readings

John Cogley. *Report on Blacklisting*, 2 volumes (1956).
Winston W. Crouch and Beatrice Dinerman. *Southern California Metropolis* (1964).
Jack Jones. *The Voice from Watts* (1967).
Seymour Kern. *The Golden Scalpel* (1960).
Gavin Lambert. *The Slide Area* (1959).
Cynthia Lindsay. *The Natives Are Restless* (1960).
Lawrence Lipton. *The Holy Barbarians* (1959).
McCone Commission. *Violence in the City* (1965).
Abraham Polonsky. *A Season of Fear* (1956).
Christopher Rand. *The Ultimate City* (1967).

City Limits or New Horizons

Ansel Adams and Nancy Newhall. *Fiat Lux: The University of California* (1967).
Reyner Banham. *Los Angeles, The Architecture of Four Ecologies* (1971).
John Caughey. *To Kill a Child's Spirit* (1974).
George H. Knoles, ed. *Essays and Assays: California History Reappraised* (1973).
Richard G. Lillard. *Eden in Jeopardy* (1966).
Carey McWilliams, ed. *The California Revolution* (1968).
Neil Morgan. *The California Syndrome* (1969).
Harvey S. Perloff and others. *Modernizing the Central City: New Towns Intown—and Beyond* (1975).
Art Seidenbaum. *This Is California: Please Keep Out!* (1975).
Jack Smith. *The Big Orange: Jack Smith's Los Angeles* (1976).

Index

Index

Braude, Marvin, 450

Brewer, William H., "A Most Lovely Locality," 152–155

Bronson, William, "Home Is a Freeway," 433–438

Brookins, H. H., 429

Brothers, The, success story, 320–325

Brown, Edmund G. (Pat), 387; "A Plea for Abolition of the Death Penalty," 417–422

Brown, Joseph E., "The Mountains and the Megalopolis," 450–452

Brown, William, "Black Mesa," 455–458

Buffum, E. Gould: quoted, 111; "The Most Favourable Portion," 117–119

Bunche, Ralph, 462; "Across the Generation Gap," 282–287

Bungalow, California, 247

Bunker, Archie, bigot and Everyman, 470–473

Bunker Hill, 326

Burns, William, 263–265

Cable cars, Los Angeles' first, 192–198

Cabrillo, Juan Rodríguez, "First Glimpses of the Coast," 43–45

California Fruit Growers Exchange, 215–218

Californians, described, 93–97

California Sportswear, 392–393

California Supreme Court: on pueblo water right, 73–74; on death penalty, 418; on loyalty oath, 438–444

Carretas, 134–135

Carrillo, José Antonio: "apology" of, 108–111; hosts ball, 129–130

Carter, Jesse, dissent, 441

"Casey Jones—the Union Scab," 265–266

Catalina Island, visits to, 44–48

Caughey, John: "The Country Town of the Angels," 73–78; "Farewell to California's 'Loyalty' Oath," 438–444; "A New Force—the Blacks," 461–465

Caughey, LaRee: "The Long Beach Earthquake," 301–304; "A New Force—the Blacks," 461–465

Censuses, 75–78

Centennial Parade, 163–166

Chaffey, George, 188–192

Chamber of Commerce, 209–215, 231, 291, 489

Chandler, Dorothy, 401

Chandler, Raymond, Los Angeles described by, 332–336

Chaparral, 268–272; fires in, 271–272

Chavez Ravine, 422–426; picture, 423

Chessman Caryl, 417–418

Chicanos, 431–433, 488

Chinese, exclusion opposed, 250

Chinese Massacre, 161

Chisera, at Tejón, 182

Civic Center, lotus sculpture, 482–483

Cleland, Robert G.: "Life on the Ranchos," 104–106; "The Passing of the Cow Counties," 155–158

Cold War, 401

Colleges and Universities, 466–468

Community Relations Conference of Southern California, 461

Conrad, Paul, cartoon, 382

Construction industry, 399–400

County Hospital, first unit, 172

Cow Counties, passing of, 155–158

Crespi, Juan, "First Travelers through the Land," 49–54

Crime and Punishment, 87–90, 140–145

Croix, Teodoro de, "Instruction for the Recruitment," 66–68

Cucamonga Rancho, 123

Cultural enrichment, 400–401

Cut-Rate Drug Store, 319–325

502

Index

Index

504

Index

Index

507

Index

Index

Traffic congestion, 1925, picture, 277
Transportation revolution, 400
Trumbo, Dalton: blacklisted, 360–361; "Johnny Got His Gun," 360–363

UCLA, 466–468
United Civil Rights Council, 429–430, 464
U.S. Reclamation Service, 226–231
University of Southern California, 466, 487
Urban planning, challenge to, 483–488
Urban renewal, 485–488
Urban sprawl, in tract housing, 401–404

Vancouver, George, quoted, 39, 74–75
Van Dyke, T. S., "The Great Southern California Boom," 201–204; quoted, 206
Vásquez, Tiburcio, capture of, 161
Venice: creation of, 235–239; home of the beats, 413–417; picture, 238
Ventura County *Star*, quoted, 300
Victorville, reached by smog, 460
Vigilantes: of 1836, 89–92; in 1850s, 140–144; invoked against Japanese Americans, 367–368
Vizcaíno, Juan, diary, 15–20
Vizcaíno, Sebastián, 45–49
Vogel, Robert, 443
Von Breton, Harriette, quoted, 291

Wagner, Henry Raup, translations by, 43–49
Walker, Franklin: "Pacific Electric," 218–222; "Abbot Kinney's Venice," 235–239
Warner, J. J., "The Centennial Parade," 163–167
Warren, Earl, prompts Levering Oath, 441
Washington's Birthday Ball, 128–131
Water Rights, tied to the land, 188–192
Waters, Frank, "Building Boulder Dam," 325–332
Water transfer from Owens Valley, 222–235
Watson, Diane, 465
Watts: becomes a ghetto, 426–431; riot, 426, 430–431, 464–465; resources of, 487; picture, 428
Watts Towers: construction of, 317–319; picture, 292
Weaver, John D., "War on the Zoot-Suiters," 378–381
Weinstock, Matt, "The White Wing as Artist," 337–339
Widney, J. P.: quoted, 157, 220; "The Centennial Parade," 163–167
Williams, C. Scott, translation by, 54–57
Wilshire Boulevard, 333
Wilshire Corridor, 486
Wilson, Benjamin D.: "Laborers and Servants," 26–28; described, 126–129; ranch home, 154–155
Wirin, A. L., 442
Witmer, Henry Clay, 194–197
Wolfskill, William: vineyard of, 119–120; orange grove of, picture, 160
Women warworkers, picture, 375
Woodward, Arthur, "Channel Island Artifacts," 15–20
Wright, Frank Lloyd, 354

Zanjas, 137–138
Zoot-Suit Riots, 378–381

509